The Correspondence of Severus and Sergius

Texts from Christian Late Antiquity

11

Series Editor
George Anton Kiraz

TeCLA (Texts from Christian Late Antiquity) is a new series presenting ancient Christian texts both in their original languages and with accompanying contemporary English translations.

The Correspondence of Severus and Sergius

Translation and Introduction by
Iain Torrance

gorgias press
2011

Gorgias Press LLC, 954 River Road, Piscataway, NJ, 08854, USA

www.gorgiaspress.com

2011 ܒ

ISBN 978-1-59333-971-5 **ISSN 1935-6846**

Library of Congress Cataloging-in-Publication Data

Torrance, Iain R.

The correspondence of Severus and Sergius / by Iain Torrance.

p. cm. -- (Texts from Christian late antiquity ; v. 11)

Includes bibliographical references (p.).

1. Severus, of Antioch, ca. 465-538--Correspondence. 2. Sergius, the Grammarian, fl. 515-517--Correspondence. 3. Jesus Christ--History of doctrines--Early church, ca. 30-600. I. Severus, of Antioch, ca. 465-538. Correspondence. English & Syriac. Selections. II. Sergius, the Grammarian, fl. 515-517. Correspondence. English & Syriac. Selections. III. Torrance, Iain R. Christology after Chalcedon. IV. Title.

BT198.T63 2011

232'.8--dc22

2011002147

Printed in the United States of America

For our much loved son and daughter
of whom we are very proud
Hew David Thomas Torrance
Robyn Alison Meta Torrance
20 November 2010
(Cassiopea's 16th birthday)

TABLE OF CONTENTS

ACKNOWLEDGMENTS

I am most grateful to my old friend, George Kiraz of Gorgias Press, whom I so greatly admire, for suggesting that we bring this translation back into print, setting the Syriac side by side with the English translation. I am grateful to Katie Stott for her efficiency and speed with the typesetting and help with fonts.

As I looked through it, I was conscious yet again of how much I learned from Sebastian Brock, how much he helped me, and what an example of generous scholarship he is to all his students.

And, as always, I acknowledge the help of my dear wife Morag, without whom anything I do would be so much diminished.

Iain R. Torrance
Princeton Theological Seminary
64 Mercer Street, Princeton, NJ 08540
20 November 2010

INTRODUCTION

A. SEVERUS, ANTONINUS AND SERGIUS

The correspondence between Sergius and Severus comprises three letters from Sergius, three replies by Severus and an apology from Sergius. The first letter from Sergius was addressed originally not to Severus, but to Antoninus, the Bishop of Aleppo, who seems to have asked Severus to reply.

The outline of Severus' life is relatively well known.[1] Apart from his own very numerous letters, and hints which he gives in his theological writings, there are three ancient 'Lives of Severus'.[2] Though we may doubt their historical value, these lives even attempt to give something of a description of Severus. Thus, Athanasius says that Severus was a man 'delicate in body and fine in person'.[3] When he did the work of his brethren in the monastery, the blood used to run from his hands. Athanasius again stresses

---

[1] A number of modern histories of doctrine give the basic facts: cf. e.g. J. Lebon, (1951) 'La christologie du monophysisme syrien', in A. Grillmeier and H. Bacht (eds), *Das Konzil von Chalkedon. Geschichte und Gegenwart*, vol. 2, Würzburg: Echter Verlag, [subsequently abbreviated as *Chalkedon*], p. 426, n. 4; W. H. C. Frend, *The Rise of the Monophysite Movement* (Cambridge 1972), esp. pp. 201-8; W. A. Wigram, *The Separation of the Monophysites* (London 1923), esp. pp. 57-60; R. C. Chesnut, *Three Monophysite Christologies* (Oxford 1976), pp. 4-5.

[2] By Athanasius of Antioch, John of Beth Aphthonia and Zacharias Rhetor. A fourth ancient life was discovered by A. Vööbus: cf. 'Découverte d'un memra de Giwargi évêque des arabes, sur Sévère d'Antioche', *Le Muséon* 84 (1971), pp. 433-436, and 'Discovery of New Important memre of Giwargi, the Bishop of the Arabs', *JSS* 18 (1973), pp. 235-237. Vööbus noted that Giwargi made use of the biographies of Severus by John of Beth Aphthonia and Zacharias Rhetor, as well as some other sources of unknown provenance. See Kathleen E. McVey (ed. and tr.) *George, Bishop of the Arabs : a homily on Blessed Mar Severus, Patriarch of Antioch*, Louvain: E. Peeters, 1993.

[3] Athanasius of Antioch, *The Conflict of Severus*, *PO* 4, p. 602.

that Severus was a compassionate man[4] and this is an important quality in understanding him. All the early biographers emphasise Severus' asceticism, and Severus himself, writing to Justinian, says that his life was habitually frugal.[5]

Severus was born in Sozopolis in Pisidia about 465. His family was well-to-do, and as a young man, not yet baptised, he was sent to Alexandria to study γραμματική and ῥητορική. From Alexandria he went to Beirut to study Roman law. At Beirut Severus came under the influence of a group of Christian students and began to study Basil and Gregory Nazianzen. At this stage he was baptised at the shrine of Leontius at Tripoli.[6]

We are told that after his baptism Severus became increasingly ascetic, spending much of his time in church. He qualified as an advocate, and visited Jerusalem where he decided to follow the monastic life. From Jerusalem, looking for a still more ascetic life, he went into the desert of Eleutheropolis. Here he eventually became ill and was persuaded to enter the convent of Romanus. At this time he shared out with his brothers the property he inherited from his parents and, after giving most of his share to the poor, bought a convent near Maiuma.

Severus was already actively involved in opposing the Council of Chalcedon. Maiuma had been the episcopal seat of Peter the Iberian, one of the (probably) two bishops who consecrated Timothy Aelurus,[7] and Severus was to follow in this tradition. He already belonged to the more

---

4 *Ibid.*, p. 613.

5 *The Syriac Chronicle*, Bk. 9, ch. 16, p. 257.

6 Athanasius, John of Beth Aphthonia and Zacharias Rhetor concur in telling us that Severus received baptism at the shrine of Leontius. What is more interesting is that there is evidence in Coptic, though not in Syriac, that until the time of his studies in Beirut, Severus was a pagan and came from a pagan family. This evidence is presented by G. Garitte, from a Coptic homily which has parallels to the Syriac Homily 27. The Coptic homily (ch. 4, sections 2-6), contains a passage in which Severus, at the shrine of Leontius, prayed that he might be saved from pagan worship and the customs of his family. Garitte argues that the Coptic represents the original Greek of Severus' sermon, and that this detail has been suppressed in the Syriac version. See G. Garitte, 'Textes hagiographiques orientaux relatifs à saint Léonce de Tripoli. II: L'Homélie copte de Sévère d'Antioche', *Le Muséon* 79 (1966), pp. 335-386.

7 On Peter the Iberian, cf. John of Beth Aphthonia, *Vie de Sévère*, *PO* 2, pp. 219-223; D. M. Lang, 'Peter the Iberian and his biographers', *JEH* 2 (1951), pp. 158-168. In his letters, Severus acknowledges the influence of Peter on him (cf. *Select Letters*, Section 5, Letter 11).

extreme Miaphysite party, which rejected the Henoticon of Zeno. Liberatus, the archdeacon of Carthage, wrote of Severus that 'dum sederet prius in monasterio Iberi, non suscipiebat Zenonis edictum, nec Petrum Mongon ... exinde missus est permanere Constantinopolim . . .'[8] As Liberatus noted, Severus was indeed sent to Constantinople. A Chalcedonian monk, Nephalius, stirred up the bishops in Palestine against the anti-Chalcedonian monks, who began to be harassed. John of Beth Aphthonia tells us that Nephalius even wrote an *Apologia* for Chalcedon, which Severus destroyed as if it had been a cobweb, with his two *Orationes*.[9] This was the first important anti-Chalcedonian work of Severus that we have, and it was written around 508.[10] Cobweb or not, Evagrius tells us that Severus was expelled from his own monastery by Nephalius and his party, and thence proceeded to Constantinople, to plead the case of himself and those expelled with him.[11]

Severus spent the years 508-11 in Constantinople. He seems quite quickly to have gained the sympathy of Anastasius, who was already not over fond of the Patriarch Macedonius, who had definite leanings towards Chalcedon. The Chalcedonians in the capital made a collection of edited excerpts from Cyril, in an attempt to show that Cyril himself supported the Chalcedonian account of the two natures. This work was apparently given to Macedonius, who gave it to the emperor. Severus, in turn, wrote his *Philalethes*, giving the true context of the quotations from Cyril.[12] Relations between Severus and Macedonius steadily deteriorated. Macedonius' position was not strong. He had already undermined his support from the extreme Chalcedonians by promising to uphold the Henoticon.[13] In addition, Anastasius had a personal grudge against him. Euphemius, the previous Patriarch, had withheld his approval from the elevation of Anastasius, unless he wrote an agreement to maintain the faith of Chalcedon inviolate. This document had passed into the hands of

[8] *Breviarium causae Nestorianorum et Eutychianorum*, XVIIII, in *Acta Conciliorum Oecumenicorum*, ed. E. Schwartz [subsequently *ACO*] 2.5. p. 133.13-16. For Severus' own condemnation of Peter Mongus, cf. *Select Letters*, Section 4, Letter 2.

[9] cf. John of Beth Aphthonia, *op. cit.*, p. 232.

[10] For the dating, cf. Lebon, *Le Monophysisme*, pp. 120-121.

[11] cf. Evagrius, *The Ecclesiastical History*, ed. J. Bidez and L. Parmentier (London 1898), Bk. 3, ch. 33.

[12] Between 509-511. cf. J. Lebon, *Le Monophysisme sévérien*, Louvain: J. Van Linthout (1909), pp. 124-125 [subsequently abbreviated as Lebon, *Le Monophysisme*].

[13] cf. Zacharias Rhetor. *Vie de Sévère*, *PO* 2, p. 113.

Macedonius and, according to Evagrius, Anastasius' objection to this document was largely the cause of Macedonius' expulsion.[14] In 511 he was replaced by Timothy.

The removal of Macedonius was only part of a concerted effort by the Miaphysites. While Severus had been in the capital, Philoxenus had been busy in Palestine, undermining the position of Flavian of Antioch. At Anastasius' order, a Synod was assembled at Sidon in 512. Flavian was presented with a list of seventy-seven anathemas as well as the request openly to anathematise Chalcedon. Flavian refused, being unwilling to 'arouse the sleeping dragon, and corrupt many with his poison'.[15] This was not to satisfy Philoxenus: his monks informed Anastasius that Flavian was a heretic, and they received an order for his ejection. In November 512, Severus was consecrated Patriarch of Antioch in his place.

In his enthronement address,[16] Severus affirmed Nicea, Constantinople and Ephesus. He affirmed the Henoticon of Zeno as 'an orthodox confession of the faith', but explicitly anathematised Chalcedon and the Tome of Leo, as well as Nestorius and Eutyches, and Diodore and Theodore, 'the masters of Nestorius'. Added to the list are Ibas of Edessa, Barsumas of Nisibis and Cyrus and John of Aigai.[17] In a Synod held at Tyre around 514,[18] the assembled bishops openly anathematised Chalcedon and the Tome, and Severus joined with Philoxenus in expounding the Henoticon as annulling Chalcedon.[19] Evagrius also tells us that Severus ceased not daily to anathematise Chalcedon.[20]

---

[14] Evagrius, *op. cit.*, Bk. 3, ch. 32.

[15] *The Syriac Chronicle*, Bk. 7, ch. 10, p. 179 (Hamilton and Brooks' translation).

[16] *PO* 2, pp. 322-325.

[17] It is interesting to note that in his *Letter of Apology*, Sergius also condemns 'Persia' (presumably Barsumas of Nisibis) and Cyrus and John (*Severi Antiocheni orationes ad Nephalium, eiusdem ac Sergii Grammatici epistulae mutuae*, ed. and tr. J. Lebon, *CSCO* 119 (text) and 120 (trans.), Louvain: *CSCO*, 1949, p. 186.24. [This is subsequently abbreviated as EM, followed by the page of the Syriac text and the line.]

[18] See Honigmann, *Évêques et Évêchés Monophysites* (*CSCO* 127, Sub. 2, Louvain, 1951), pp. 16-17, for the difficulties in dating the Synod.

[19] *The Syriac Chronicle*, Bk. 7. ch. 10. For Severus' attitude to the Henoticon, see his *Collected Letters* (ed. Brooks), *PO* 12, Letters 46 (p. 320) and 49 (p. 324). He held that though it contained an orthodox confession of faith, by itself (without an explicit anathema on Chalcedon) it was unable to bring the healing that was needed.

[20] Evagrius, *op. cit.*, Bk. 4, ch. 4.

In Antioch he must have made his presence felt. John of Beth Aphthonia tells us that, on becoming bishop, he sent away the cooks from the episcopal palace, and demolished the baths he found there.[21] In his Cathedral Homilies, he warned his people against resorting to the races[22] and the theatre,[23] and his letters show his energy and the trouble he had in financial matters. But his time as Patriarch was not to be long.

Anastasius died in July 518, and Evagrius tells us that, many contentions having arisen in the church, Justin, in the first year of his reign, ordered Severus to be arrested and punished.[24] Severus, with a number of the Miaphysite bishops, managed to escape to Egypt. Philoxenus was sent into exile at Gangra. In Egypt, Severus lived a harried existence,[25] but wrote some of his most important works. He completed his correspondence with Sergius from his exile. Lebon dates his great anti-Chalcedonian work, the *Liber contra impium Grammaticum,* to around 519.[26] Sadly, the exiled Miaphysites began to quarrel amongst each other, and Severus' works against Julian of Halicarnassus also belong to this period.[27]

Around 530 Justinian relaxed persecution of the Miaphysites, and in 532 he summoned the leading Miaphysites to a *collatio* with the Chalcedonians in Constantinople. Though invited, and promised immunity by Justinian, Severus did not attend this conference.[28] He came instead, again at the summons of Justinian, in the winter of 534/5. At about the same time Anthimus of Trebizond, whom Zacharias tells us would not receive the Synod of Chalcedon into the faith,[29] succeeded Epiphanius as

---

[21] John of Beth Aphthonia, *op. cit.*, p. 243.

[22] Homily 26.

[23] Homily 54.

[24] Evagrius, *op. cit.*, Bk. 4, ch. 4.

[25] He mentions this twice in his *Third Letter to Sergius*: EM p. 158.6-7; p. 176.14-17.

[26] cf. Lebon, *Le Monophysisme*, p. 153.

[27] Lebon dates them to between 518 and 528: cf. *Le Monophysisme*, p. 174. *The Syriac Chronicle*, Bk. 9, chs. 9-13, shows the reluctant way in which Severus entered this quarrel. On Julian, see R. Draguet, *Julian d'Halicarnasse et sa controverse avec Sévère d'Antioche sur l'incorruptibilité du corps du Christ* (Louvain, 1924), and the useful review of Draguet's work by R. P. Casey, 'Julian of Halicarnassus', *HTR* 19 (1926), pp. 206-213.

[28] *The Syriac Chronicle*, Bk. 9, ch. 16, gives Severus' letter to Justinian, refusing to come to the royal city.

[29] *Ibid.* Bk. 9. ch. 19.

Patriarch of Constantinople, and Theodosius, a friend of Severus, became bishop of Alexandria.

This unity in the Miaphysite camp so alarmed the orthodox Ephraim of Antioch that he sent a special envoy to Agapetus in Rome.[30] Justinian was then engaged in an operation to regain Rome, and the Goths sent Agapetus to Constantinople to treat with Justinian on their behalf. Agapetus arrived in Constantinople in 536. Zacharias tells us that he perverted the love of the king to Severus and Anthimus. Justinian's interest clearly lay in the West, and Anthimus was replaced by Menas as Patriarch of Constantinople. Though Agapetus died in April 536, the political advantage of Severus and the Miaphysites was lost.

Severus and his friends were condemned[31] at a σύνοδος ἐνδημοῦσα in Constantinople lasting from May to June 536. The synod was confirmed by an edict of Justinian on the 6th of August 536. According to the edict, Severus was guilty of both Nestorianism and Eutychianism,[32] his books were to be banned,[33] and he was to be banished.[34]

According to Athanasius, Severus left Constantinople with the help of the Empress Theodora.[35] He returned to Egypt, and there, about 538, 'the Lord visited him with a light disorder, and ... he fell asleep'.[36]

Antoninus was Bishop of Aleppo. His predecessor was Peter, one of the bishops who assisted at the consecration of Severus in 512.[37] While he was Patriarch, Severus wrote to him several times.[38] Antoninus was expelled in 519, taking refuge in Alexandria. The Chronicle to the year 846 records

---

30 *Ibid.* Bk. 9, ch. 19.

31 Among other things, Severus was accused of being an 'Akephalist' (*ACO* 3, p. 137.8-10); a Eutychian and Manichaean (*ACO* 3, p. 147.35-36); of conducting uncanonical baptism (*ACO* 3, p. 112.35-36); and of holding illegal meetings (*ACO* 3, p. 113.14-16). The old slur about his pagan background was also brought up (*ACO* 3, p. 40.16-24).

32 cf., *ACO* 3, p. 121.5-9.

33 *Ibid.*, lines 22-27.

34 *Ibid.*, lines 30-34.

35 Athanasius, *op. cit.*, pp. 709-710.

36 *Ibid.*, p. 716.

37 cf. *Chronicon anonymum ad AD 846 pertinens*, ed. E. W. Brooks (*CSCO* 3, Syr. 3, 1904), p. 221, line 12.

38 cf. *Select Letters*, Section 1, Letters 14, 15 and 16 (pp. 63-70 in Brooks' text). Also *Collected Letters*, Letter 29, *PO* 12, p. 260.

that, having suffered persecution in various places, Antoninus died in Constantinople.[39]

Of Sergius, Lebon notes, 'nous ne connaissons ni sa patrie, ni les événements de son histoire, en dehors de la polémique dont nous avons parlé'.[40] We can see from his letters that he was a Miaphysite of an exaggerated sort. He seems to have remained in the East,[41] after Justin became emperor, so it is not unreasonable to assume that, though he had a certain prominence, he was not a bishop.

We do not know the background to the origin of the correspondence between Sergius and Severus, but we can surmise some of it. In the unnamed town where Sergius was living, a severe attitude was taken to converted Dyophysites. Sergius had a brief statement or κεφάλαιον, which seems to have been used as a doctrinal test[42] for the converted Dyophysites. This was, 'We do not speak of two natures or (two) proprieties after the inexpressible union'.[43] Sergius' κεφάλαιον had been submitted to an assembly, of which Antoninus of Aleppo was a member. The opinion of the assembly corrected Sergius, stating, 'We do not speak of divided proprieties'.[44] Sergius claimed to find this judgment difficult to understand, and it is a question of prime importance for the commentator to ask if 'propriety' was understood in the same way, in both Sergius' κεφάλαιον and in the answer of the assembly. Sergius characterised the judgment as a concession,[45] rehearsed several of his objections to it, and begged the assembled Fathers to help him. The request was passed to Severus and the correspondence began.

The question of the exact date of the correspondence is not easy. Sergius was clearly addressing an assembly of bishops when he wrote, 'Good Fathers ....'[46] Lebon asks, 'Etait-ce un synode?'[47] We cannot say. Was Antoninus at its head? Possibly, as Sergius writes to him, but Severus him-

---

[39] *Chron. a. 846*, *op. cit.* p. 226, lines 7-11. Also cf. Honigmann, *op. cit.*, pp. 25-26.

[40] *Le Monophysisme*, p. 170.

[41] EM p. 156.4-7.

[42] At EM p. 95.22, Severus, answering Sergius' *First Letter*, urges him instead to make the Nicene Creed his test.

[43] EM p. 71.1-3.

[44] EM p. 71.4-5.

[45] EM p. 70.23.

[46] EM p. 72.27.

[47] *Le Monophysisme*, p. 166,

self was not available at the time, being, as he says, 'Far off'.[48] If it was a synod, can we deduce more about it? Lebon suggests it was the Synod of Tyre in 514,[49] which would allow a date of perhaps 515[50] for Sergius' *First Letter.*

There is easier internal evidence for dating the end of the correspondence, for both Sergius' and Severus' *Third Letters* point to a date after 518. To take these points in turn: in Sergius' *Third Letter,* he speaks of the spark of his feeble tongue being used, 'because of the remoteness of bishops in the east',[51] which very probably refers to the expulsion of the Miaphysites after the death of Anastasius in 518. Later in the same letter,[52] Sergius, having prayed that Severus be given long life, says he looks forward to when he will say to the Lord God, 'Thou hast turned away the captivity of Jacob ...'.[53]

Severus, in his *Third Letter,* clearly demonstrates a post-518 date, when he challenges Sergius, 'Therefore show (me) when, in the six years I spoke in the Church of the Antiochenes, and wrote many letters, at any time I once said Emmanuel is one ousia, and of one signification and of one particularity'.[54] Later in the same letter, Severus describes himself as put to flight by enemies in his tracks,[55] and at the end of the letter, Severus refers to Dioscorus II of Alexandria, who died on 14th October, 517[56] as if he were already dead.

B. EARLIER STUDIES OF SEVERUS

Beyond question, the foundational work on the Miaphysites is that by Lebon: *Le Monophysisme sévérien.* This was published in Louvain in 1909, and Lebon brought it up-to-date[57] with his long article, 'La Christologie du monophysisme syrien', which was published in 1951. Much of the material of the earlier book is covered by this superb 160 page article, and it is to this that I will mainly refer.

---

48 EM p. 158.22.

49 *Le Monophysisme*, p. 168.

50 Lebon is followed by Honigmann, *op. cit.*, p. 26 n. 6, on this date.

51 EM p. 156.6.

52 *Ibid.*, p. 157.6-7.

53 Ps. LXXXIV 2. All OT references are to LXX.

54 EM p. 172.19-23.

55 *Ibid.*, p. 176.14-15.

56 Honigmann, op. cit., p. 144. (Cf. Schwartz, *ACO* 2.5, p. 134 note 7).

57 Lebon, *Chalcedon*, p. 453.

Lebon intended to provide an over-all view of Miaphysite theology, and so considered Timothy Aelurus and Philoxenus as well as Severus. His study fell into two parts: the first, entitled 'La doctrine monophysite de l'incarnation' was short and descriptive;[58] the second, entitled 'La dogmatique monophysite de l'incarnation'[59] was far longer and more analytical.

In his first section, Lebon sketched where the Miaphysites may be placed in terms of the widely accepted distinction between Alexandrian and Antiochene tendencies in Christology. He immediately introduced the Christology of Cyril of Alexandria, showing that this became central to the Miaphysites.[60] He then gave an outline description of Miaphysite doctrine, picking out particular key concepts. Thus, he stressed the Miaphysite exclusion of any type of change from the incarnation.[61] God the Word was made flesh, but remained who God was. Similarly, the Miaphysites went to great pains to deny that the union to one nature involved any mixture or confusion.[62] He showed the Miaphysite use of the union of body and soul as a model, with the insistence that this union did not produce an identity of *ousia*, of such a kind as would be destructive of the difference of the things which had been united.[63]

Commenting on this, Lebon wrote that, however frequently the Miaphysites denied it, they were always suspected of introducing a mixture or confusion into the union. He, however, saw them as *terminological* traditionalists,[64] who borrowed the vocabulary of the Cappadocians and Cyril, who used 'mixture' words to express a very intimate union, but without ever wanting to imply any idea of confusion of the elements coming together in union.

Lebon's methodology is disclosed in this. As an historian, he notes the Miaphysite denials of confusion in the union, and the *terminological* parallels with earlier writers.

Lebon began his second section by taking two questions around which the Miaphysite quarrel raged:

---

58 *Ibid.*, pp. 425-450.

59 *Ibid.*, pp. 451-580.

60 *Ibid.*, p. 431.

61 *Ibid.*, p. 440.

62 *Ibid.*, p. 442 ff.

63 *Ibid.*, pp. 447-449.

64 *Ibid.*, p. 444 and cf. pp. 578-579.

1. The question of whether there are one or two natures in Christ. This is the question raised by the Chalcedonian ἐν δύο φύσεσιν.
2. The question of whether the ἰδιότης of each nature in the union is preserved or not. This is the question raised by the Chalcedonian σωζομένης δὲ μᾶλλον τῆς ἰδιότητος ἑκατέρας φύσεως.

He divided the section into two parts: one to examine each question. To answer question (1), he led his readers through a careful and detailed study of the vocabulary of the Miaphysites, to show how their terms and usages differed from those of the Chalcedonians.

This section of his study fell into three sub-sections. In the first, 'Les éléments de l'incarnation',[65] Lebon showed that the Miaphysites used φύσις, ὑπόστασις and πρόσωπον as being perfectly synonymous.[66] Thus φύσις, like ὑπόστασις and πρόσωπον, referred to what is concrete and individual. According to Lebon, then, the Miaphysites ultimately read Nestorianism into the Chalcedonian perspective, thereby reducing all Dyophysitism to the confession of two really distinct beings.

In the second sub-section, 'L'acte de l'incarnation', Lebon stressed that, to the Miaphysites, the incarnation was an *act,* a ἕνωσις. The Miaphysites never formally defined the term, and Lebon tried to illustrate it by considering the conditions required for 'un groupement de choses' to merit the name 'ἕνωσις'.[67] Ἕνωσις, for example, had no more radical enemy than number: if the constituent elements in a ἕνωσις could be numbered, it would follow, within the Miaphysite presuppositions, that they were independently existing and not united entities. Similarly, to illustrate the concept of ἕνωσις, Lebon contrasted it with συνάφεια and παράθεσις,[68] and showed that to note *the act* of the incarnation the Miaphysites used other terms: συνδρομή, σύνοδος, σύμβασις, and in Severus, σύνθεσις.[69]

In the third sub-section, 'Le terme de l'incarnation', Lebon turned to the major formula of the Miaphysites, μία φύσις τοῦ Θεοῦ Λόγου σεσαρκωμένη. He explained that the nature of which the formula affirms the singularity is that belonging to God the Word, who is the subject in the incarnation. The formula is thus distinctively Cyrillian and anti-Nestorian.[70]

---

65 *Ibid.*, p. 454 ff.
66 *Ibid.*, p. 461 ff.; pp. 464-465.
67 *Ibid.*, p. 467.
68 *Ibid.*, p. 468.
69 *Ibid.*, p. 472.
70 *Ibid.*, p. 483.

Illustrating his main point, as before, through comparisons, he briefly discussed the phrases μία φύσις σύνθετος and μία φύσις διττή,[71] and then turned to consider apparently Dyophysite expressions permitted by the Miaphysites. The Miaphysite condemnation of Chalcedon and Nestorianism is well known, as well as their understanding that ἐν δύο φύσεσιν implied two natures in independent existence. Lebon now showed that to defend himself against the accusation of teaching a confusion, Severus allowed that one could speak of δύο φύσεις, but only ἐν θεωρίᾳ.[72] Similarly to defend himself against the charge of confusion, Severus taught that the Word incarnate is (μία φύσις) ἐκ δύο.[73] For both these expressions, Lebon showed Severus' dependence on Cyril.[74]

In the second part to his second section, Lebon turned to the second question he outlined at the beginning: the 'conservation ou destruction de la propriété des natures après l'union'.[75] He first showed the problem. On the one hand Severus was presented with the Tome teaching, 'Agit enim utraque forma cum alterius communione *quod proprium est*', and Chalcedon stating that 'σωζομένης δὲ μᾶλλον τῆς ἰδιότητος ἑκατέρας φύσεως', which appeared to argue for the preservation of the ἰδιότης of the natures which came together into union, but in such a way that the independent *existence* of each nature seemed also to be implied. On the other hand, Severus was presented with the extreme miaphysitism of a writer like Sergius, who wanted to exaggerate the nature of the unity to such an extent that he preached unification of ἰδιότης as well as of φύσις in the union.

In an excellent terminological examination, Lebon showed that in the face of this dilemma Severus hammered out his own understanding of ἰδιότης. Qualifying ἰδιότης as 'φυσική'; 'ἡ κατὰ φύσιν'; 'ὡς ἐν ποιότητι φυσικῇ'[76] he consciously followed Cyril, saying that ποιότης φυσική expresses ὁ λόγος τοῦ πῶς εἶναι of a thing.[77] According to Lebon, ποιότης φυσική expresses 'l'essence spécifique',[78] and in this indicates the continuing difference between the natures that Severus insists on. This understanding enabled Severus to steer between the apparent Nestorianism of recognising

---

[71] *Ibid.*, pp. 486-490.
[72] *Ibid.*, pp. 489-504.
[73] *Ibid.*, pp. 510-516.
[74] *Ibid.*, p. 505 and p. 514f.
[75] *Ibid.*, pp. 534-576.
[76] *Ibid.*, pp. 537-538.
[77] *Ibid.*, cf. pp. 538-539.
[78] *Ibid.*, p. 539.

two independent natures in the union, and the apparent Eutychianism of allowing that one or both of the natures in the union lost its integrity of identity.

But here again, Lebon made what was largely a terminological point. The *theological* point was that Severus, in making this distinction, was doing something totally different from either Nestorianism or Eutychianism, quite apart from steering a terminological path between the two extremes.

Lebon's paper is described at some length, because he has produced a quarry of detailed references, terminology and historical background from which all who study the Miaphysites must borrow. However, as has been suggested, though his contribution was enormous, his work was essentially map-making over new and difficult terrain.

Working within the map-making Lebon gave us, there is room for supplementary study. The ἕνωσις of which Severus tells us, and which Lebon described so well, was not simply a terminological singularity, but a uniting, *an act* of God the Word, *for a purpose.* I would suggest that *this purpose*, far from being exterior to the union, *is part of what makes the union what it is.* To see the goal of the union as a determinative part of the nature of the union is to inject a new dimension into the study of Severus. This soteriological dimension does not appear when one is map-making. Instead, it is to see the terms in a dynamic as well as a static or descriptive way. Even with the short but very dense text of the letters between Severus and Sergius, it is possible to ask new and fruitful questions.

As has been noted, Lebon's paper was published in 1951. Since then there has been a growing interest in the Miaphysites. An example is that of Roberta Chesnut.[79] Chesnut's interest is to study the relationship between Christ and our knowledge of God in the three very different theological systems of Severus, Philoxenus and Jacob of Serug. Chesnut gave a detailed description of some of Severus' major terms and concepts, but was concerned neither with soteriology, nor with Severus' relation to Cyril, and so her work was able to contribute relatively little illumination to the exchange with Sergius. Another modern work, though of necessity a very general one, is that by John Meyendorff. In his *Christ in Eastern Christian Thought*,[80] he provided a perceptive account of the debates after Chalcedon, showing Severus' important role in the formation of the theology of the separating Miaphysite churches.

---

[79] *Three Monophysite Christologies* (Oxford, 1976).

[80] Washington and Cleveland, 1969.

It is within the Miaphysite churches that some of the most stimulating modern work on Severus has been done. Since 1964 there have been unofficial theological conferences between theologians of the Eastern and Oriental Orthodox Churches.[81] The Panorthodox Conference at Chambésy in 1968 decided that a theological dialogue should start between the Eastern and Oriental Orthodox Churches. Consequently, the Orthodox Churches set up a Commission for the Theological Dialogue with the Ancient Oriental Churches.[82] This Commission first met in Addis Ababa in 1971, and then with the Non-Chalcedonian Commission in Athens in 1973 and in Addis Ababa in 1975.

Significant contributors to the ecumenical discussion included V. C. Samuel of the Syrian Orthodox Church, and N. A. Zambolotsky of the Russian Orthodox Church. Samuel set out his aim very clearly. It was to question the view that because Severus criticised Chalcedon and the Tome, he could not have taught the faith of the Church in its purity.[83] The question was whether the rejection of Chalcedon by Severus was the result of a Christology which explained away the human reality of Christ.[84] To show that Severus did not dissolve the human nature of Christ, Samuel pointed to the heresies he rejected: Manichaeism, Apollinarianism and Eutychianism.[85] He also considered the accusations made against Severus in 536.[86] On the basis both of this, and of Severus' positive teachings, Samuel argued 'that Severus was not a Monophysite'.[87] This was a provocative line to take, but Samuel justified it in a very interesting statement: 'Severus never objected to the dynamic continuance of the two natures in the one Christ, and the ascription of the term "monophysite" to his theological position is

---

81 At Aarhus in 1964: Bristol in 1967; Geneva in 1970 and Addis Ababa in 1971. The papers from these conferences may be seen in *The Greek Orthodox Theological Review*, 10 pt. 2 (1964-5) (Aarhus); 13 pt. 2 (1968) (Bristol); 16 pts. 1 and 2 (1971) (Geneva and Addis Ababa).

82 cf. Methodios Fouyas, *The Person of Jesus Christ in the Decisions of the Ecumenical Councils* (Addis Ababa, 1976), p. 223ff.

83 'The Christology of Severus of Antioch', *Abba Salama* (Athens), 4 (1973), p. 126.

84 cf. 'Further Studies in the Christology of Severus of Antioch', *Ekklesiastikos Pharos* (Athens), 58 pts. 3-4 (1976), p. 284.

85 *Ibid.*, pp. 286-296 and cf. *Abba Salama*, pp. 145-151.

86 *Ibid.*, pp. 283-286.

87 *Abba Salama*, p. 145 and cf. pp. 160-161.

nothing but the legacy of the polemics of a bygone age'.[88] As a consequence of this, Samuel argued that in the dispute between Severus and John the Grammarian, the issue was not whether or not the manhood of Christ was real, but *how the manhood was to be understood and interpreted.*[89] Throughout all of this argument, Samuel showed beyond doubt the Cyrillian foundation on which Severus stood.

If Severus was not a Monophysite, what was he? Samuel explained that Severus did not object to the *dynamic continuance* of the two natures. The exchange of letters between Severus and Sergius provides ample opportunity to study in detail the status and role of the human nature in the incarnation, and what implications this had for our understanding of the union.

From the Chalcedonian side, Zambolotsky showed himself to be in considerable agreement with Samuel.[90] He approached Severus through Lebon, and saw him as rooted in the theology of Cyril. Zambolotsky took up Samuel's contention, that as regards the Miaphysite formula μία φύσις τοῦ Θεοῦ Λόγου σεσαρκωμένη, 'Severus' position cannot agree with such interpretation of μία as simply "one"'.[91] The point was that Severus was not a Monophysite in any bad sense, which would involve dissolving the reality of the human nature in the union. Zambolotsky examined this contention carefully,[92] and concluded that the reality of Christ's humanity was indeed strongly confirmed by Severus. It is appropriate to ask then how it was confirmed, what was its status and what was the nature of the union. Zambolotsky hinted at an answer to this. It was shown above that Samuel spoke of the 'dynamic continuance' of the two natures in Severus' Christology. Zambolotsky suggested that 'Severus' human nature is not "hypostatic" but like the human nature of Leontius of Byzantium and John of Damascus "hypostatized", received into the unity of the hypostasis of the Logos'.[93] This perceptive comment may hold the key for future study of Severus' Christology. Iain R. Torrance took this trajectory further in his

---

[88] *Ibid.*, pp. 161-162.

[89] cf. *Ekklesiastikos Pharos*, p. 277, and *Abba Salama*, p. 173.

[90] 'The Christology of Severus of Antioch', *Ekklesiastikos Pharos*, 58 pts. 3-4 (1976), pp. 357-386.

[91] Zambolotsky, *ibid.*, p. 367; cf. Samuel, *Abba Salama*, pp. 145 and 160-161 and 'One Incarnate Nature of God the Word', *Greek Orthodox Theological Review*, 10 pt. 2 (1964), p. 48.

[92] Zambolotsky, *ibid.*, pp. 367-373.

[93] *Ibid.*, p. 377.

Christology after Chalcedon: Severus of Antioch and Sergius the Monophysite[94] and a subsequent paper examining Severus' use of Gregory of Nazianzus.[95] This line of interpretation of Severus was largely followed by Aloys Grillmeier and Theresia Hainthaler in *Christ in Christian Tradition*, volume 2, part 2, *The Church of Constantinople in the Sixth Century.*[96]

C. MANUSCRIPT AND TRANSLATION

The letters between Severus and Sergius were, of course, written in Greek. In the preface to his edition of the Syriac text, Lebon refers to A. Baumstark, who judged that the Syriac translation was made by Paul of Kallinike.[97] M. Brière agrees with this.[98] Paul was banished from his see around 519. He later went to Edessa, where he translated many of Severus' works. He died in exile.[99]

The manuscript translated is that edited by Lebon in 1949.[100] It is BL Add MS 17154. Wright described the manuscript as being of vellum, about 7 7/8 inches by 6 5/8, and consisting of 52 leaves, some of which are slightly stained, especially at the beginning. Each page is divided into two columns, of from 31-42 lines, and he told us that the volume is written in a good, regular Estrangela hand of the 7th century.[101] Lebon told us that Wright forgot to note that there is a gap in the manuscript between the present folios 6 and 7. Photography seems to reveal that 3 folios have been cut out.[102]

Lebon believed Add 17154 to be the only manuscript of the letters.[103] In an article published in 1975 Sebastian Brock has shown that fragments of the letters survive in an 8th or 9th century manuscript, Harvard

---

94 Cambridge: Canterbury Press, 1988 and Eugene, Oregon: Wipf and Stock, 1998.

95 'Paradigm change in sixth century Christology' in *Greek Orthodox Theological Review*, volume 36, part 3-4, 1992, pp 277-285.

96 London: Mowbray (ET 1995). The discussion of the exchange between Severus and Sergius is on pp. 111-128.

97 EM p. v.

98 'Introduction Générale à toutes les Homélies', *PO* 29, p. 17.

99 Honigmann, *op. cit.*, p. 54.

100 *CSCO* 119 (Syr. 64).

101 W. Wright, *Catalogue of the Syriac Manuscripts in the British Museum* (London, 1872), pt. 2, pp. 557-558.

102 Lebon, *Le Monophysisme*, p. 163, n. 2.

103 cf. EM p. iv.

(Houghton Library) syr. 22.[104] In a report, Brock described the manuscript as containing 80 folios, the vast majority of which are loose, and many of which are badly damaged.[105] The folios are out of order and many have been lost. Keeping to the order of the modern foliation Sebastian Brock was kind enough to give me a list of what fragments of the letters the manuscript preserves. This goes slightly beyond the list he gave in his report.[106] The reference is to the pagination of Lebon's edition of the Syriac text.

H. syr. 22
f.12^{b} = Lebon p. 70.3-25
<7 ff lost>
50 = 90.29- 94.16
39 = 94.16- 98.11
37 = 98.12-101.25
23 = 101.25-105.10
47 = 105.10-108.19
59 = 108.19-112.1
<1 f lost>
45 = 115.15-118.20
<3 ff lost)
26 = 129.23-133.17
25 = 133.17-136.26
36 = 136.26-140.6
33 = 140.6 -143.16
24 = 143.16-146.25
<4 ff lost>
44 = 160.24-[164.3]
72 = 164.3-167.18
<1 f lost>
34 = 171.1 -174.18

104 'Some New Letters of the Patriarch Severus', *Studia Patristica* 12 (*Texte und Untersuchungen zur Geschichte der altchristlichen Literatur*, Band 115), Berlin 1975, pp. 17-24.

105 *Ibid.*, p. 18.

106 *Ibid.*, pp. 19-20.

35 = 174.18-177.28
62 = 177.28-181.12
<end lost>

Brock tells us that the Harvard manuscript provides the same translation as that found in Add 17154.[107] In the translation of Lebon's edition I refer in several instances to the Harvard reading, which Sebastian Brock most generously made available to me.

The translation is fairly literal. As the letters were written in Greek, it is a version, not an original that is translated here, and inevitably certain obscurities and difficulties remain.

Words supplied for the sense, but absent in the Syriac, are placed in round brackets ( ). The page references to Lebon's edition of the Syriac text are given in *italics* within round brackets. Where a suggested emendation, or a variant in Harvard syr. 22, is translated instead of Add 17154, the word or phrase is placed in square brackets [ ]. Diamond brackets < > are used to show a lacuna in the manuscript.

107 *Ibid.*, p. 19.

TEXT AND TRANSLATION

Letter I of Sergius

The Letters to each other of Sergius the Grammarian and of Severus, Patriarch of Antioch (*Lebon p. 70*).[1]

The First Letter of Sergius the Grammarian to the venerable Severus, Patriarch of Antioch, in which he asks how those who think Christ is from[2] two natures are to be reconciled, who have used the name of Antoninus, Bishop of Aleppo. The letter is as follows.

To my Lord who is holy in all things, and venerable spiritual Father, Bishop Antoninus: Sergius a humble Grammarian: Greetings in our Lord.

When just now I looked out upon these divine matters, my faculty of sight cringed back, as if I (were) looking directly into the rays of the sun. And the promises of the ship[3] are awaited by me anxiously, because I have no clear opinion, but rather I look to "The depths of the navigation[3] of the wisdom and of the knowledge of God".[4] And as I was thrust out from this with diverse reasonings, I read the law of the one who sings, which says "Ask your Fathers, and they will inform you".[5] Now is the time of uncertainty: I shall speak now with the (rest of the) city.[6]

I made a request from your holy gathering: for we are asking for the eradication of the confession from those who fell and returned to themselves, while you make enormous concessions. I stammered as much as I was able about matters of the rule of the faith, (and) I wrote as much as I understood.[6] (*Lebon p. 71*)

But the summing up of it all was: "We do not speak of two natures or proprieties after the inexpressible union". But this, which did not seem to be expressed in accordance with reason, was corrected as follows by you: "We do not speak of divided proprieties". And my mind is shaken by this, and though I turned my reasoning up and down, even now I am unable to ascend to comprehension of the proposition.

What then? Shall we speak of two proprieties, so that we may remove the foolishness of the metousiasts, flesh being understood as flesh, and divinity not descending to confusion? But this is to keep (two) ousiai, and by no means just proprieties. For God and flesh are ousiai, but it is the [propriety][7] of God to be eternally, but of flesh to

(70) ܐܓܪ̈ܬܐ ܕܟܬ̈ܝܒܐ ܕܣܪܓܝܣ ܓܪܡܛܝܩܘܣ ܘܕܣܘܝܪܐ ܦܛܪܝܪܟܐ ܕܐܢܛܝܘܟܝܐ.

ܐܓܪ̈ܬܐ ܩܕܡܝܬܐ ܕܣܪܓܝܣ ܓܪܡܛܝܩܘܣ ܠܘܬ ܚܣܝܐ ܣܘܝܪܐ ܦܛܪܝܪܟܐ ܕܐܢܛܝܘܟܝܐ. ܕܒܗ̇ ܫܐܠ ܕܐܝܟ ܙܕܩ ܕܢܬܐܡܪܘܢ ܗܠܝܢ ܕܡܢ ܬܪ̈ܝܢ ܟܝ̈ܢܝܢ ܡܫܡܗܝܢ ܘܐܝܬܝܗܘܢ ܡܫܝܚܐ: ܟܕ ܐܬܚܕܘ ܒܚܕܐ ܘܐܠܗܝܐ ܐܦܝܣܩܘܦܐ ܕܝܠܟ. ܘܡܠܚ ܗܟܢܐ⁘

ܠܡܪܐ ܕܟܠ ܡܕܡ ܒܟܘܠ: ܘܚܣܝܐ ܐܒܐ ܪܘܚܢܐ: ܐܠܗܝܐ ܐܦܝܣܩܘܦܐ ܣܪܓܝܣ ܟܪܝܐ ܓܪܡܛܝܩܘܣ: ܒܡܪܢ ܚܕܝ.

ܟܕ ܗܘܐ ܟܠܗ ܗܠܝܢ ܠܟܬ̈ܒܬܐ ܐܪܝܟܬܐ: ܘܐܝܟ ܡܐ ܕܪ̈ܚܡܬܐ ܡܦܫܩܐ ܡܣܘܛܠܝܢ ܚܙܐ ܐܢܐ: ܡܬܩܦܣܝܢ ܗܠܝܢ ܕܚܙܬ: ܘܟܠܗ̇ ܦܘܫܩܐ ܚܣܝܪ ܠܟ ܒܝܘܕܥܐ ܘܫܘܐܠܐ: ܕܝܢ ܕܐܘܚܕܢܐ ܚܬܝܬܐ ܟܬܒ ܠܟ. ܚܙܐ ܐܢܐ ܕܝܢ ܒܘܚܢܐ ܕܦܘܫܩܐ. ܗܘ ܕܫܟܝܚܬܐ ܘܡܕܥܐ ܕܐܠܗܐ. ܘܟܕ ܡܢ ܗܘܐ ܒܩܢܘܡܬܐ ܦܪ̈ܨܘܦܐ ܡܬܝܕܥ ܐܢܐ: ܢܣܘܒܐ ܦܪܝܫ ܕܗܘ ܕܦܘܫܩ: ܕܐܡܪ ܕܥܠܝܗ ܠܐܟܠܗܘܢ ܘܡܣܘܟܢ ܠܟ. ܙܟܝܐ ܗܘ ܗܟܝܠ ܕܦܘܫܩܐ. ܐܬܐ ܗܘܐ ܠܟܝ ܡܕܝܢܬܐ:

ܡܢ ܒܣܘܡܐ ܕܠܟܘܢ ܒܘܚܢܐ ܦܪܝܫܐ: ܕܠܘܬܟܘܢ ܕܗܟܢ ܘܠܘܬܗܘܢ ܗܠܝܢ: ܬܠܝܢ ܚܕ ܒܣܪܐ ܕܐܬܝܕܥܬ ܕܡܢ ܗܠܝܢ. ܟܕ ܐܝܬܘܗܝ ܬܪ̈ܬܝܢ ܡܫܡܗܝܢ ܐܝܬܘܗܝ. ܘܒܣܪܐ ܕܚܝܐ ܠܟܕ ܡܬܬܦܝܠܐ ܗܘܐ ܬܝܠܝܢ ܕܦܘܫܩܐ ܕܐܝܬܝܗ̇ ܕܐܝܬܘܬܐ ܟܣܝܐ ܕܡܬܝܕܥ ܗܘܐ ܬܝܠܝܢ ܠܡܪܢ ܗܘܐ. (71) ܬܠܬܝܗܘܢ ܕܝܢ ܕܠܒܘܗܝ ܐܝܬܘܗܝ ܗܘܐ ܕܠܗ ܬܪ̈ܝܢ ܟܝ̈ܢܝܢ ܐܡܪܝܢ ܚܕ ܒܬܪ ܚܝܘܬܐ ܠܐ ܡܬܐܡܪܢܝܬܐ. ܘܠܐ ܕܟܝܢܝܬܐ. ܐܠܐ ܗܘܐ ܘܐܡܬܟܪܐ ܕܠܗ ܒܩܢܘܡܬܐ ܐܬܚܒܪܬ: ܬܬܐܪܙ ܗܘܬ ܡܫܝܚܐ. ܐܝܟ ܗܝ ܕܠܗ ܕܟܝܢܝܬܐ ܦܪ̈ܨܘܦܐ ܐܡܪܝܢ. ܘܡܢ ܗܘܐ ܡܦܠܓܝܢ ܠܟ ܗܠܝܢ ܕܝܫܘܥ. ܘܟܕ ܠܟܠܠ ܘܠܐܝܟ ܡܣܘܦ ܬܘܒ ܗܘܝܐ: ܠܐ ܒܪܟܠ ܗܟܐ ܡܫܝܚ ܐܢܐ ܕܐܦܣ ܠܘܬ ܚܕܬܐ ܕܚܕܝܘܬܐ ܣܓܝܐܐ.

ܣܓܝ ܓܝܪ. ܬܪ̈ܝܢ ܕܟܝܢܝܬܐ ܐܡܪܝܢ ܚܕ: ܐܝܟܢܐ ܕܠܒܘܪܬܐ ܕܦܪ̈ܨܘܦܐ ܐܘܣܝܐ ܢܐܡܪ: ܟܕ ܒܣܪܐ ܡܫܬܠܡܠ ܒܣܪܐ ܘܠܐܠܗܘܬܐ ܠܐ ܚܝܬܐ ܒܟܝܢܘܬܐ. ܐܠܐ ܗܘܐ ܕܢܬܪ ܐܘܣܝܣ ܐܠܗܝܐ ܘܠܗ ܣܝܡ ܕܟܝܢܝܬܐ. ܠܟܠܗ ܓܝܪ ܘܒܣܪܐ ܐܘܣܝܣ ܐܠܗܘܬܗ. ܕܟܝܢܝܬܐ ܕܝܢ ܠܠܟܠܗ: ܗܘ ܕܡܬܘܡܝܬ ܐܠܗܘܬܗ. ܕܒܣܪܐ ܕܝܢ ܗܘ ܕܗܘܐ ܘܡܬܐܢܫܠ. ܐܦ ܕܝܢ ܬܐܡܪ ܕܦܪܨܘܦ ܕܟܝܢܝܬܐ. ܐܝܟܢܐ ܟܕ ܟܠܗ ܣܘܟ̈ܠܐ ܚܕܝܢ ܡܣܬܟܠܝܢ ܗܠܝܢ. ܠܟܠܗ ܓܝܪ ܡܢ ܡܬܦܪܫ ܕܡܢܗ: ܗܘ ܕܠܐ ܡܬܚܙܐ ܘܠܐ

become and to be corrupted. But if we should say that the proprieties persist how will we find them, when we enquire about the facts in question? For the propriety of God, to be sure, is that he is not seen or touched:—yet God came visibly, and "was seen on earth, and had dealings with men",[8] and "we saw him, and his appearance was not honourable, and was despised by men",[9] .... "that which was from the beginning, which we have heard and seen, and our hands have touched, concerning the Word of Life...".[10] But it is the propriety of flesh that it is brought forth from two parents, and when once it is brought forth, that it should also be corrupted. But where are these things in the case of the flesh of Life? For no man was father of Christ, for without the bush being burned,[11] and the door being still sealed,[12] the Lord went forth endowed with a body. Hence because he was not born in accordance with the propriety of the flesh, neither did his flesh see corruption. But every propriety belongs to an underlying nature, and if we speak of two proprieties, (*Lebon p. 72*) we are obliged also to speak of two natures. But if we suppose that the proprieties are undivided, neither do those (Dyophysites) divide the natures, but everywhere proclaim to us (natures) which are undivided. And this is the summing up of the sickness of Chalcedon and the madness of Leo, which, while it divides the activities with the natures, says (each form does what is proper) undividedly "in partnership with the other".[13] Therefore how shall we escape from such frenzy, we who teach one nature of the Word incarnate after the union, unless, just as we believe Christ is one from two natures, so also we accept one propriety from two of God incarnate, of him who out of kindness undertakes to be seen, but transcended the human propriety by means of the supreme union: thus he walked on the waters without being dragged by the burden of the flesh into the depth of the sea. And when they sealed the sepulchre, he was not held in, and closed doors were unable to prevent his entrance.

And so henceforward, neither is any propriety of God to be recognised in [his][14] Logos, nor is any (propriety) of flesh to be seen (in him either), but the entire manner of the economy points towards one propriety, that which is with God incarnate. For just as laughter is the propriety to "man", and none of the other animals is like him *in this*, so also there is one propriety of Christ, in which no-one from those who are invisible or visible shares. For only God who was incarnate is born from the Virgin, and performed everything and suffered on our behalf, and from where he descended, there again he ascended, endowed with the flesh.

ܡܬܓܫܡ. ܐܠܐ ܠܟܠܗ ܡܬܡܫܚܢܘܬܗ ܐܝܟ ܘܡܬܬܪܒܐ ܐܬܚܙܝ ܘܥܡ ܒܢ̈ܝܢܫܐ ܐܬܗܦܟ. ܘܢܝܣܝܢܘܗܝ ܘܡܘܬܗ ܠܐ ܡܫܟܚ ܕܚܙܝܢ ܡܢ ܩܠܝܠ ܐܢܫ. ܗܘ ܕܐܝܬܘܗܝ ܡܢ ܒܪܝܫܝܬ. ܗܘ ܕܡܫܟܚ ܘܚܝܠ. ܘܐܬܝܗ ܙ̈ܒܢܐ ܡܫܬܠܛ ܡܚܝܠܘܬܐ ܕܚ̈ܝܐ. ܐܠܐ ܘܡܚܝܠܘܬܐ ܕܒܣܪܐ: ܕܡܢ ܛܥܝܢ ܐܝܠܝܢ ܕܐܘܠܕܗ ܢܠܡܕ. ܘܟܕ ܚܕܐ ܙܒܢ ܐܬܡܠܟ ܐܦ ܠܡܬܒܥܠ. ܐܝܟܢܐ ܕܝܢ ܗܢܘܢ ܠܒܣܪܐ ܕܚ̈ܝܐ. ܐܝܟ ܓܒܪ ܕܡܫܝܚܐ ܘܠܐ ܚܕ ܒܪܢܫܐ. ܟܕ ܠܐ ܓܒܪ ܡܢ ܚܝܠܐ ܘܡܛܠܬܗ ܛܘܒܐ ܡܫܝܚܘܬܐ ܢܦܩ ܡܢܗ. ܡܢ ܗܘܒܐ. ܡܫܬܠܛ ܕܒܗ ܐܝܟ ܗܘ ܕܡܚܝܠܘܬܐ ܕܒܣܪܐ ܐܬܡܠܟ: ܘܠܐ ܒܣܪܗ ܚܕܐ ܚܝܠܐ. ܟܠ ܕܝܢ ܕܡܚܝܠܘܬܐ ܕܚܝܠܐ ܕܗܘܝܢ ܐܝܬܘܗܝ. ܘܐܦ ܛܥܢܝܢ ܐܡܪܝܢ ܚܢܢ ܕܡܚܝܠܐ: ܛܥܢ (72) ܘܚ̈ܫܐ ܡܬܐܠܨܝܢ ܕܢܐܡܪ. ܐܦ ܕܝܢ ܕܠܐ ܬܬܦܠܓܝܢ ܕܬܚܝܠܐ ܡܫܬܥܒܕܝܢ: ܐܦܠܐ ܗܢܘܢ ܠܚ̈ܝܠܐ ܡܬܦܠܓܝܢ. ܐܠܐ ܠܐ ܬܬܦܠܓ ܠܟܠ ܘܡܬܚܫܚ ܡܕܒܫܢ ܠܝ. ܘܗܢܘ ܡܠܠܗܝ ܕܒܘܪܗܢܐ ܘܡܫܘܕܥܢܐ ܘܡܫܘܚܬܐ ܕܠܐܗܝ. ܘܟܕ ܡܬܦܠܓܐ ܠܡܫܟܚܢܘܬܐ ܥܡ ܚ̈ܝܠܐ: ܥܡ ܡܬܦܫܬܐ ܕܗܘ ܐܝܬܝܐ: ܠܐ ܡܬܦܠܓܢܐ ܐܡܪܐ. ܐܝܟܢܐ ܗܘܝܐ ܡܢ ܦܪܘܫܘܬܐ ܕܐܝܟ ܕܚܝܠܐ ܒܪܘܚܐ: ܐܝܟܢ ܕܚܕ ܚܝܠܐ ܕܡܚܝܠܘܬܐ ܕܒܣܪܐ ܡܬܦܠܓܝܢ ܒܠܗ ܚܝܘܬܐ. ܐܦ ܕܗܘ ܕܠܐ ܐܝܟ ܗܘܐ ܕܡܢ ܛܥܢ ܚ̈ܝܠܐ ܚܕ ܠܒܣܪܐ ܡܚܝܢ: ܗܘܝܐ ܘܚܕܐ ܕܡܚܝܠܘܬܐ ܡܢ ܛܥܢܝܢ ܕܠܟܠܗ ܕܒܣܪܐ ܢܓܠܠ. ܕܗܘ ܕܠܐܚܪܐ ܦܢܝ ܡܬܠܠ ܡܫܬܠܛ ܒܡܫܘܚܬܐ. ܒܟܪ ܕܝܢ ܠܕܡܚܝܠܘܬܐ ܐܝܟܢܐ ܟܕ ܚܝܘܬܐ ܙܢܝܐ. ܡܬܡܫܚ ܗܘܐ ܗܘܐ ܠܟܠ ܦܢܝܢ. ܟܕ ܠܐ ܡܬܦܠܓ ܗܘܐ ܡܢ ܣܘܦܐ ܕܒܣܪܐ ܠܚܝܘܬܐ ܕܡܢܐ. ܘܟܕ ܛܥܝܢ ܗܘܘ ܡܢܪܐ. ܠܐ ܡܬܚܠܦ ܗܘܐ. ܘܛܥܢܐ ܕܐܣܝܪ ܕܢܦܫܗ ܡܚܝܠܘܬܐ ܠܒܗ ܗܘܐ ܠܒܗܘܢ.

ܠܐ ܗܘܝܐ ܡܫܬܠܛ ܘܠܐ ܕܠܟܠܗ ܕܡܚܝܠܘܬܐ ܡܕܡ ܒܡܫܟܠܬܐ ܕܠܗ ܡܬܡܥܒܕܐ: ܘܠܐ ܕܒܣܪܐ ܡܬܚܝܠܐ. ܒܠܗ ܕܝܢ ܙܠܐ ܕܡܢܕܥܢܘܬܐ ܒܟܠ ܚܕܐ ܕܡܚܝܠܘܬܐ ܡܢܐܙ. ܗܘ ܕܒܟܠܗ ܕܠܟܠܗ ܡܫܟܚܐ ܐܝܬܘܗܝ. ܐܝܟ ܡܢ ܓܒܪ ܕܒܪܢܫܐ ܕܡܚܝܠܘܬܐ ܠܓܘܫܡܘܬܐ: ܘܠܐ ܡܕܡ ܡܢ ܗܠܝܢ ܚܘܬܐ ܐܝܬܝܘܬܐ ܒܓܘܐ ܕܦܐ ܠܗ: ܗܘܝܐ ܘܡܚܝܠܘܬܐ ܚܕܐ ܘܡܫܟܚܐ. ܕܒܗ ܐܦ ܠܐ ܐܝܟ ܡܢ ܠܐ ܬܬܚܝܠܐ ܘܬܬܚܫܚܐ ܡܫܡܠܝܐ. ܒܟܠܗܘܢ ܓܒܪ ܕܠܟܠܗ ܘܐܬܡܫܚ ܡܢ ܒܟܠܗܘܢ ܡܫܟܚܐ ܡܠܟ. ܘܡܠܟܝܢ ܒܟܠ ܘܒܗ ܚܠܦܝܢ. ܘܡܢ ܐܝܟܢܐ ܕܢܒܥܐ: ܛܘܒ ܡܫܒܚ ܒܪܢܫܐ.

ܡܢ ܗܢܐ ܦܘܠܓܐ ܡܫܟܠ. ܕܐܦܘܡ ܐܚܪ̈ܢܐ ܛܥܝܢ ܗܘܐ ܠܟܘܢ ܡܫܬܐܠܢܐ. ܘܡܫܟܚܘܢ ܘܠܟܘܢ ܡܫܬܡܥܝܢ ܬܫܡܫܬܐ ܒܒܗ: ܘܠܟܠܗ ܗܘܝܢ ܕܒܟܠܗܘܢ ܛܥܢܘ ܐܦܫܘ. ܘܠܐ ܛܥܡܘܢ ܕܒܪܘܚܐ ܘܡܬܪܘܢܐ. ܟܕ ܡܬܛܝܒܝܢ ܐܠܗܝ ܒܡܫܟܚܐ ܙܢܐ ܬܫܘܬܐ: ܗܘ

Good Fathers, let it be your concern that I should emerge from this grievous doubt. And enquire by yourselves into my contemptible thoughts, and correct and raise them to your own, and do not reject my smallness and youth, being like Christ, the chief of shepherds, who (*Lebon p. 73*) did not reject the children when they came near. But as you are high priests of his, you plan by all means to offer pure sacrifices; now this is the sacrifice of him who was inhominated on our behalf: a pure mind fulfilled in the knowledge of the Spirit.

The First Letter of Sergius the Grammarian to the holy Patriarch Severus has ended.

Notes

1. "*Lebon p. 70*" refers to the pagination of Lebon's edition of the *Letters*, CSCO 119 (Syr. p. 64).
2. ܕܬܪܝܢ ܬܐܘܡܝܢ Lebon notes that the text should probably be emended to read ܕܒܬܐܘܡܝܢ ("in two natures"), i.e. the Chalcedonian formula ἐν δύο φύσεσιν.
3. Lebon notes that the Syriac translator seems to have taken the word πλούτου to be the genitive of πλοῦς.
4. cf. Rom. xi. 33.
5. cf. Deut. xxxii. 7. All OT references are to LXX.
6. The text of these two paragraphs is particularly obscure.
7. Reading ܕܡܠܬܐ for ܕܡ̈ܠܬܐ (cf. lines 17 and 22, below).
8. Baruch iii. 38.
9. Is. liii. 2–3.
10. 1 Jn. i.1.
11. cf. Ex. iii.2–3.
12. cf. Ezek. xliv.1–2.
13. PL 54.767B. *Ep. XXVIII, ad Flavianum* ("*The Tome*").
14. Reading ܕܡܠܗ for ܕܡܠܗ̇. ܡܠܬܐ is translated by "Logos". An easier meaning might be given if it is translated by "condition": "in [his] condition . . .".

ܕܟܬܒ̈ܐ ܟܕ (73) ܡܬܦܪܢܣܝܢ ܠܐ ܕܡܟ ܗܘܐ. ܟܕ ܕܝܢ ܩܪ̈ܝܒܢ ܟܬ̈ܒܐ ܕܗܘܐ ܐܬܟܬܒܘ.
ܡܢ ܟܠ ܦܪܘܫ ܘܬܘܪܓܡܗܘܢ، ܕܚ̈ܝܐ ܕܟܬ̈ܒܐ ܡܬܬܪܓܡܝܢ ܐܬܘܢ. ܗܢܐ ܕܝܢ ܐܬܬܘܗܝ
ܕܚܝܐ ܕܗ̇ܘ ܕܡܬܬܠܐ ܐܬܟܪܝܟ: ܢܦܫܐ ܕܟܝܢܐ ܕܟܢܘܫܬܐ ܡܬܡܬܚܢܐ.
❖ ܫܠܡܬ ܐܓܪ̈ܬܐ ܩܕܝܫܬܐ ܕܣܪܓܝܣ ܓܪܡܡܛܝܩܘܣ. ܠܘܬ ܩܕܝܫܐ ܣܘܝܪܐ
ܦܛܪܝܪܟܐ❖

Letter I of Severus

A copy of the Letter of holy and blessed Severus, Archbishop and Patriarch of Antioch, to chaste Sergius the Grammarian, who was asking about particularities and activities and about the sufferings which bring salvation.

I praise your Chastity, who wanted to explain the problem expressed in the letter logically and at the same time in the fear of God. For there is, furthermore, the prophetic saying which permits that we should make enquiry, along with the fact that enquiry should be restrained by an anchor of the fear of God, saying as follows, "If you enquire, enquire, but dwell with me",[1] and (The Book of) Proverbs introduces this instructively, when it defines, "Unchastened education goes astray".[2] [And I admired][3] your coming to me in humility, which bears witness to your wisdom. For the same (Book of) Proverbs may be heard, which says: "Wisdom is meditated upon in the mouth of the humble".[4] And the writings of the law order priests to resolve what is uncertain, and to expound those things which would otherwise be anywhere unclear, and to distinguish what is good from what is not good, when it says to them as follows: "The law is for ever for your generations, that you should distinguish between what is holy and what is profane, and between what is pure (*Lebon p. 74*) and what is not pure, and that you should teach the children of Israel all the laws which the Lord has spoken to them".[5]

It is recognised through these things that you have asked well, and that we ought to (give an answer) to the question. But since questions of doctrine are considered hard to comprehend and hard to express, I shall write as regards the question so far as I can grasp (the matter), looking towards him who gives a word of knowledge and a word of wisdom. For the word of the Proverbs says again: "The desire of the heart belongs to man, but the answer of the tongue comes from the Lord".[6]

Know, therefore, that professing the natural particularity of the natures from which there is the one Christ is not just recently determined by us. Far from it—for we remember that holy Cyril wrote as follows in the Second Letter to Succensus: (CYRIL): "For even if

܀ܦܘܫܩܐ ܕܐܓܪ̈ܬܐ ܕܩܕܝܫܐ ܘܛܘܒܬܢܐ ܣܐܘܝܪܐ ܪܒܐ ܕܐܦܝܣܩܘܦܐ ܘܦܛܪܝܪܟܐ ܕܐܢܛܝܘܟܝܐ: ܟܬܒܐ ܫܬܝܬܝܐ ܡܢ ܓܒܝܬܐ ܒܐܦܣܛܘܠܣ: ܕܒܬܪ ܡܛܠ ܕܬܟܬܒܬܐ ܘܡܬܟܬܒܢܘܬܐ ܘܡܛܠ ܫܢܝ ܦܘܪ̈ܣܐ܀

ܡܫܝܚܐ ܠܐܦܝܣܩܘܦܐ ܕܪܘܡܐ ܘܐܢܘܢ ܐܘܪܚܐ ܕܐܬܐܡܝܢܘܬܐ ܠܐܓܪ̈ܬܐ ܡܛܠܬܗ ܐܝܟ ܚܕܐ ܘܒܝܫܘܬܗ ܠܠܗܐ. ܡܛܠ ܕܐܦ ܡܠܬܐ ܢܣܝܬܐ: ܗܝ ܕܢܒܥܐ ܡܦܩܐ: ܟܡ ܗܝ ܕܐܬܗܘܬ ܐܦܣܪܐ ܒܡܠܬܐ ܠܐܘܡܢܐ ܕܪܘܚܐ ܠܠܗܐ. ܟܕ ܐܡܪܐ ܗܘܢܐ. ܕܐܢ ܚܒܠ ܐܢܬ ܟܕ ܘܟܠܗ ܚܟܡ. ܘܩܛܠܐ ܕܝܢ ܟܠܗ ܗܘܐ ܡܫܠܡܢܘܬܐ: ܟܕ ܡܛܠܗ ܘܐܡܪ. ܡܪܕܘܬܐ ܕܝܢ ܕܠܐ ܡܬܚܫܚܐ ܛܒܐ. ܘܐܬܒܥܪ ܟܕ ܐܬܐ ܠܟܝ: ܒܡܫܡܫܢܘܬܐ ܗܝ ܕܡܫܘܕܐ ܠܟ ܡܫܝܚܐ. ܐܝܟ ܓܒܪ ܠܫܡܫܢ ܠܗ ܟܕ ܠܗ ܠܒܢ̈ܝܐ ܕܐܡܪ: ܒܦܘܡܐ ܕܝܢ ܕܩܕܝܫܐ ܡܬܗܓܝܐ ܡܫܝܚܐ. ܘܠܒܢ̈ܝܐ ܕܝܢ ܕܢܦܪܘܗܝ ܦܘܩܕܐ: ܘܢܦܪܘܗܝ ܐܡܝܢ ܕܐܣܪ̈ܝܢܐ ܟܕܘܡ ܠܐ ܠܒܢ̈ܝܐ. ܘܕܢܦܪܘܗܝ ܗܝ ܕܛܒܐ ܡܢ ܗܝ ܘܠܐ ܛܒܐ: ܡܠܬܐ ܢܡܘܣܝܐ ܦܩܕ ܟܕ ܐܡܪ ܠܒܢܘܗܝ ܗܟܢܐ. ܢܡܘܣܐ ܕܒܠܒܗܘܢ ܠܡܬܒܠܥܘܢ. ܕܐܦܪܘܗܝ ܟܡܐ ܡܬܝܐ ܠܛܒ̈ܬܐ: ܘܟܡܐ ܗܠܝܢ ܕܕܝܢ (74) ܠܟܡܐ ܗܠܝܢ ܕܠܐ ܕܝܢ. ܘܐܠܦܘܗܝ ܠܒܢ̈ܝ ܐܝܣܪܐܝܠ ܡܠܘܗܝ ܢܡܘܣܐ: ܐܡܝܢ ܕܡܛܠ ܡܪܝܐ ܠܐܒܗ̈ܝܗܘܢ.

ܕܐܦ ܐܢܐ ܗܟܢܐ ܡܦܪܫ ܛܠܝܐ: ܘܕܝܢܘܗ ܕܐܦ ܚܕ ܟܠܐ ܡܘܬܐ ܟܕ ܗܠܝܢ ܐܬܝܕܥ. ܡܛܠ ܕܝܢ ܕܚܩܩܘ ܠܐܘܪܚܐ ܘܚܩܩܘ ܠܡܬܡܠܠܘ ܡܫܬܠܒܢ ܦܩ̈ܘܕܐ ܕܕܘܓܡܛܐ: ܟܕ ܚܙܐ ܐܢܐ ܟܠܐ ܗܘ ܕܝܗܒ ܡܠܬܐ ܕܚܝܠܬܐ ܘܡܠܬܐ ܕܫܒܝܠܐ. ܐܝܟܘܬ ܟܠܐ ܦܘܠܐ ܗܘ ܡܚܝܡ ܕܐܬܐ ܟܠܐ ܡܕܪܟܢܘܬܐ ܕܡܟܢ. ܬܘܒ ܓܒܪ ܡܠܬܐ ܕܩܛܠܐ ܐܡܪܐ: ܠܒܪܢܫܐ ܙܟܝܐ ܕܟܠܐ: ܘܡܢ ܡܪܝܐ ܦܘܫ ܦܠܓܘܬܐ ܕܟܝܢܐ.

ܕܝܢ ܗܟܢܐ ܕܗܝ ܕܕܡܠܬܐ ܚܝܠܬܐ ܕܒܢ̈ܝܐ ܕܡܢܗܘܢ ܚܕ ܡܫܝܚܐ ܢܘܚܐ. ܠܗ ܡܢ ܚܕܐܝܬ ܡܬܦܫܩܐ. ܠܐ ܬܗܘܐ. ܒܬܘܟܝܢ ܓܒܪ ܠܩܕܝܫܐ ܦܘܪܫܢܗ ܘܠܒܟ ܠܐܓܪ̈ܬܐ ܕܐܬܩܪܝ ܕܟܠܐ ܦܘܩܕܢܗ ܗܟܝܠ. ܦܘܪܫܢܗ܀ ܐܦ ܓܒܪ ܘܚܕ ܡܬܐܡܪ ܡܢ ܚܝܠܐ ܒܪܗ ܕܐܠܗܐ ܕܡܠܟܐ ܘܡܠܟܬܐ. ܠܐ ܫܒܩ ܡܛܠ ܗܘܐ: ܐܝܟ ܕܡܫܬܠܒܢܐ ܠܦܢܝܢ. ܘܠܐ ܚܙܐ ܠܚܝܠܐ ܕܟܦܢܐ ܗܘ ܕܡܠܬܐ. ܐܠܐ ܘܠܐ ܗܘ ܕܟܦܢܐ ܠܦܘ ܕܡܠܗ. ܐܠܐ ܟܕ ܕܡܠܬܐ ܗܝ ܕܚܝܠܐ ܟܠܗ ܚܕ ܡܢܗܘܢ ܡܬܠܐܢ ܐܚܝܕܐ ܘܡܬܠܒܟܐ: ܐܝܟ ܡܠܬܐ ܕܐܬܝܠܕ ܡܢ ܗܘܐ. ܚܕܝܘܬܐ ܠܐ ܡܬܡܫܚܠܦܢܘܬܐ ܘܠܐ ܡܬܐܡܪܢܝܬܐ: ܚܕ

the Only-Begotten Son of God, incarnate and inhominate, is said by us to be one, he is not confused[7] because of this, as he seems to those people; nor has the nature of the Word passed into the nature of the flesh, nor indeed has the nature of the flesh (passed into) that which is his, but while each one of them continues together in the particularity that belongs to the nature, and is thought of in accordance with the account which has just been given by us, the inexpressible and ineffable union shows us one nature of the Son, but as I have said, incarnate".[8] Observe, therefore that when the Doctor has confessed one nature of God the Word, who is incarnate, he says that each one of them continues together and is understood in the particularity that belongs to the nature.

But the same (Cyril) elucidates what the particularity that belongs to the nature is, by writing again as follows in the Treatise against Diodore: (CYRIL): "Therefore let us recognise that even if the body which was born (*Lebon p. 75*) at Bethlehem is not the same, that is, as far as natural quality is concerned, as the Word which is from God and the Father, yet nevertheless it became his, and did not belong to another man beside the Son. But the Word incarnate is to be considered one Son and Christ and Lord".[9]

And after other points, as he sets out this very matter, he adds these as well: (CYRIL): "Because we say too that, with respect to particularity, flesh is completely of another nature from the Word which sprang from God and the Father: nevertheless it became his, in an inseverable union, with the result that the Word who shone forth from the ousia of God and the Father, is also named "seed of Abraham" in the flesh; when the economy calls him this, it in no way detracts from his being what he is. For although he is God by nature, he became in truth Son of man as well, and he is also Son of God and the Father, not in a spurious way nor with a false name, but he is he who ineffably and inexplicably is born from him, even though he is not thought of without the flesh after the union".[10]

It is therefore already made known for your Chastity from these things that particularity (implies) the otherness of natures of those things which have come together to union, and the difference (lies) in natural quality. For the one is uncreated, but the other created. And the one is not seen, but the other is seen, and the one is not touched, but the other is subject to touch. Nevertheless, while this difference, and the particularity of the natures, from which (comes) the one Christ, still remains without confusion, it is said that the Word of Life was both seen and touched, and the Gospel says that those theologian Disciples were spectators and ministers of the Word[11];

ܟܝܢܐ ܚܘܝܬ ܠܟ ܕܒܪܐ. ܒܪܡ ܐܝܟ ܕܐܡܪܢܐ ܕܡܣܟܢ܀ ܐܬܟܢܐ ܗܟܝܠ ܕܟܕ ܚܕ ܟܝܢܐ
ܐܘܕܝ ܡܫܝܚܐ ܕܡܠܬܐ ܐܠܗܐ ܕܡܣܟܢ: ܐܡܪ ܕܗܟܝܠ ܚܕ ܡܢܗܘܢ ܒܝܠܕܬܐ ܗܘ
ܕܒܚܝܠ ܡܛܠܬܢ ܐܢܫܐ ܘܡܫܬܡܠܐ.
ܡܢܐ ܕܝܢ ܐܠܗܘܬܗ ܕܡܠܬܐ ܗܝ ܕܟܝܢܐ: ܗܘ ܟܕ ܗܘ ܠܘܬ ܒܬܐܡܪܐ ܕܟܠܐ
ܕܚܘܝܘܗ ܡܫܢܝܐ ܟܕ ܥܠܬ ܗܟܝܠ. ܀ܩܘܪܝܠܘܣ܀ ܚܕ ܗܟܝܠ ܕܦܓܪܐ ܕܐܬܠܒܫ
(75) ܥܡܗ ܠܒܫܗ: ܐܦ ܠܗ ܗܘܝܘ ܟܕ ܗܘ ܒܡܫܘܚܬܐ ܐܡܪ ܐܢܐ ܟܝܢܝܬܐ ܠܘܬ
ܡܠܬܐ ܕܡܢ ܐܠܗܐ ܐܒܐ: ܐܠܐ ܒܪܡ ܕܝܠܗ ܗܘܐ. ܘܠܐ ܕܐܝܟ ܐܚܪܢ ܫܩܠܗ ܡܢ ܕܒܪܐ.
ܚܕ ܕܝܢ ܒܪܐ ܘܡܫܝܚܐ ܘܡܪܢܐ ܢܫܬܟܚ ܡܠܬܐ ܕܐܬܒܣܪ܀ ܘܟܠܗ ܐܢܫܘܬܐ ܕܝܢ
ܟܕ ܗܝ ܗܘܐ ܢܦܫ ܡܘܡܫ ܘܗܘܠܝܢ. ܀ܩܘܪܝܠܘܣ܀ ܡܛܠ ܕܐܦ ܚܢܢ ܐܡܪܝܢ:
ܕܐܝܟ ܡܠܬܐ ܕܕܝܠܝܘܬܐ: ܐܚܪܢܝ ܟܝܢܐ ܐܠܗܘܬܗ ܡܢ ܡܠܦܢܘܬ ܟܬܒܐ: ܠܘܬ ܡܠܬܐ
ܕܗܘܝ ܡܢ ܐܠܗܐ ܐܒܐ. ܒܪܡ ܕܝܠܗ ܗܘܐ ܟܝܢܝܘܬܐ ܘܠܐ ܡܫܬܠܝܘܬܐ. ܐܝܟܢܐ ܕܐܦ
ܡܠܬܐ ܕܕܝܠܗ ܡܢ ܐܘܣܝܐ ܕܐܠܗܐ ܐܒܐ: ܕܢܚܐ ܕܐܟܪܙܘ ܫܠܝܚܘ ܒܟܬܒܐ. ܟܕ ܗܢܐ
ܠܗ ܠܗܘܐ ܡܒܪܢܫܘܬܐ. ܘܡܫܬܟܚܐ ܘܠܐ ܡܒܝܢ ܠܟܘܢ ܕܗܘܐ ܐܠܗܘܬܗ ܗܘ ܡܠ
ܕܐܠܗܘܬܗ. ܟܕ ܐܠܗܐ ܓܒܪ ܐܠܗܘܬܗ ܟܝܢܐ: ܗܘܐ ܒܡܙܪܐ ܐܦ ܒܪܗ ܕܐܢܫܐ.
ܘܐܠܗܘܬܗ ܒܪܐ ܕܐܠܗܐ ܐܒܐ: ܠܐ ܕܐܦܫܐ ܘܠܐ ܕܫܒܩ ܗܘܐ. ܐܠܐ ܗܘ ܗܘ ܘܠܐ
ܡܬܡܠܠܢܝܬ ܘܠܐ ܡܬܦܫܛܢܝܬ ܡܟܝܠ ܡܢܗ: ܐܦ ܗܘ ܕܠܗ ܘܠܐ ܒܣܪܐ ܡܬܪܢܐ
ܠܗܘ ܚܕܝܘܬܐ܀
ܦܪܫܬ ܗܟܝܠ ܐܝܬ ܡܢ ܗܟܢ ܠܩܘܒܠܐ: ܘܐܚܪܢܝܬܐ ܩܢܝܐ ܕܗܟܢ ܘܐܬܐ
ܐܚܝܕܐ ܠܝܠܕܘܬܐ: ܕܡܠܬܐ ܐܠܗܝܐ: ܘܡܫܟܚܐ ܗܘ ܕܐܝܟ ܕܒܡܫܘܚܬܐ ܟܝܢܝܬܐ.
ܗܘܐ ܓܒܪ ܐܠܗܘܬܗ ܠܐ ܒܚܒܠܐ: ܗܘܐ ܕܝܢ ܒܚܒܠܐ. ܘܗܘܐ ܦܓܪ ܠܐ ܡܬܚܫܢܐ ܗܘܐ ܕܝܢ
ܡܬܚܫܢܐ. ܘܗܘܐ ܦܓܪ ܘܠܐ ܒܚܒܠܐ: ܗܘܐ ܕܝܢ ܢܦܠ ܒܚܒܠܐ. ܒܪܡ ܟܕ ܗܘܐ
ܡܫܝܚܐ ܘܡܠܬܐ ܕܒܪܐ ܕܡܢܗܘܢ ܚܕ ܡܫܝܚܐ: ܘܠܐ ܒܫܘܚܠܦ ܡܫܘܐ: ܡܠܬܐ ܕܚܝܐ
ܡܬܐܡܪ ܘܐܬܐܚܕ ܘܐܬܚܒܠ. ܘܕܝܠܗ ܠܐܚܘܒܐ ܡܫܬܡܫܢ ܠܟܠܗܝܢ ܕܝܠܗ ܗܘܘ ܚܝܠܐ
ܘܡܫܡܫܢܐ ܕܡܠܬܐ: ܐܡܪ ܡܠܟܐ ܐܘܪܚܐ. ܠܗ ܕܦܫ ܡܢ ܟܝܢܐ ܠܐ ܡܬܚܫܢܐ
ܘܠܐ ܒܚܒܠܐ. ܐܠܐ ܕܐܬܚܝܕ ܠܗܘ ܕܡܬܚܫܢܐ: ܘܚܫܘܫܐ ܚܫܐ ܘܠܐ ܦܓܪ ܒܚܒܠܐ.
(76) ܠܐ ܗܟܝܠ ܚܠܦ ܗܘܐ ܠܚܘܕܝܬܐ ܚܕܝܬܐ ܘܡܫܝܚܘܬܐ: ܡܫܝܚܘܬܐ ܕܣܩܘܢܩܢܝܬܐ
ܠܦܘܠܘܣ. ܠܗ ܓܒܪ ܐܝܟ ܠܐ ܗܘܐ ܕܦܫ: ܐܦ ܚܕ ܐܝܟܢܐ ܠܐ ܬܟܠܐ ܦܘܠܝ:
ܘܒܟܝܢܬܐ ܠܟܝܢܬܐ ܡܬܐܡܪ ܚܕ: ܘܒܟܝܢܐ ܠܒܟܝܢܐ ܕܢܦܫܝ: ܗܘ ܕܡܬܐܡܪܐ.

not that he[12] changed from his invisible nature, devoid of flesh, but he was united to a visible and solid body, not denying touch. (*Lebon p. 76*)

Therefore do not ascribe the folly of the Synousiasts to this exact profession of the faith. For we are not ignorant in accordance with their madness, and cure evil with evil, and, as the saying is, thrust out a nail with a nail. But know quite clearly that precision and an accuracy for the truth demand this. For we say as well that a man like us is a living being, rational, mortal, capable of reason and knowledge, (and) because there is one nature and hypostasis from two, the whole living being is said to be mortal, and the whole is called rational, and we do not say that we do not know what (part) is living, and what (part) is rational; No, the fact that we know this does not divide the composition from which the one living being is constituted. For holy Cyril too, while making a defence against Andrew who found fault (with him) viciously in the Third Chapter, says as follows about the study of Emmanuel: (CYRIL): "There is no share in any blame that one should recognise, for example, that the flesh is one thing[13] in its own nature, apart from the Word which sprang from God and the Father, and that the Only-Begotten is another again, with respect to his own nature. Nevertheless, to recognise these things is not to divide the natures after the union."[14]

And your Chastity will recognise that it is of necessity that rational nature all has a difference with regard to everything apprehended by sense, and not a difference only, but also a distinction: for these things are also removed from each other in quality of nature and in that they stand apart (*Lebon p. 77*) in place. And they are removed distinctly from each other, and with the difference is yoked entire distinctness and remoteness. But when a single hypostasis is completed by a coming together in natural union from a rational nature and from a sensible one, we see that the difference of those things which have come together to be one, (the difference that is) which lies in natural quality, has not been suppressed, because there is no confusion of the union; but the division has been removed, because those things which were different in natural quality do not exist independently, but complete one hypostasis from two.

Well then, let us transfer this to the study of Emmanuel, and let us make an enquiry of the divinity and the humanity. They are not only different in everything but they are removed from each other and distinct as well. But when union is professed from the two of them, the difference, again, in the quality of the natures from which there is the one Christ is not suppressed, but in conjunction by hypostasis

ܐܠܐ ܒܠܚܘܕܝܬ ܕܝܘܡܬ ܢܦܩ ܐܢܬ: ܕܗܘܐ ܒܟܠ ܫܠܡܘܬܐ ܘܒܣܝܒܪܘܬܐ ܕܫܪܪܐ. ܡܛܠ ܘܐܦ ܒܪܢܫܐ ܘܐܒܗ̈ܝ ܐܡܪܝܢ ܕܐܢܬܘܢ: ܚܕܘܬܐ ܡܫܠܡܬܐ ܡܗܝܡܢܘܬܐ. ܡܫܡܫܢܝܬܐ ܕܗܘܝܐ ܘܡܕܒܪܢܬܐ. ܡܛܠ ܕܡܢ ܩܕܡ ܚܕ ܗܘ ܟܝܢܐ ܘܦܘܡܐ. ܒܟܠܗ ܚܕܘܬܐ ܡܬܐܡܪܐ ܡܗܝܡܢܘܬܐ ܘܒܟܠܗ ܡܫܬܡܗܐ ܡܫܠܡܬܐ: ܘܠܐ ܐܡܪܝܢ ܘܠܐ ܦܪܫܝܢ ܚܕ ܡܢܐ ܦܘ ܡܗܘܬܐ: ܡܢܐ ܕܝܢ ܡܫܠܠ. ܐܠܐ ܠܗ ܗܘ ܕܗܘܐ ܢܦܩ: ܡܦܠܓܐ ܠܪܘܚܐ ܕܡܢܗ ܡܬܡܫܚܐ ܚܕܐ ܚܘܬܐ. ܗܟܢܐ ܓܝܪ ܐܡܪ ܩܕܝܫܐ ܦܘܠܘܣ: ܐܦ ܟܠ ܠܐܘܪܚܐ ܘܒܡܫܘܐܠܠ : ܒܝ ܢܦܩ ܒܪܘܚܐ ܟܠܐ ܐܝܪ̈ܘܬܗ ܘܠܐܒܐ ܚܠܝܡܬ ܒܡܫܠܡܘܬܗ ܘܠܟܠܐ. ❖ܦܪܘܫܘܬܗ❖ ܘܠܐ ܡܫܢܝܐ ܗܘ ܕܝܢ ܕܒܟܠ ܡܦܘܡܐ: ܗܘ ܕܢܦܩ ܐܘ ܠܐܒܪܐ ܘܐܡܪܝܢ ܗܘ ܒܟܝܢܐ ܕܡܢܗ ܒܫܪܪܐ: ܠܒܪ ܡܢ ܡܫܠܡܐ ܗܘ ܕܡܢ ܐܠܗܐ ܘܐܒܐ ܡܦܩ: ܐܡܪܝܢ ܕܝܢ ܠܘܬ ܡܫܝܚܐ ܐܝܟ ܡܫܠܡܐ ܕܒܪܗ. ܐܠܐ ܠܗ ܗܘ ܕܢܦܩ ܗܟܝܠ: ܕܢܦܠܓ ܟܢ̈ܫܐ ܒܟܠ ܚܕܘܬܐ ܐܝܬܘܗ❖

ܘܗܘ ܕܝܢ ܠܘܬ ܢܦܩܐܝܬ: ܡܢ ܗܟܢ ܕܐܠܗ̈ܝ ܐܝܬܘܗ: ܕܟܝܢܐ ܡܫܠܠ: ܗܘܝܢܐ ܐܝܬ ܒܗ ܒܟܠ ܟܠܗ ܟܘܠ ܡܬܕܒܪܢܐ. ܘܠܗ ܗܘܝܢܐ ܒܟܝܢܗ: ܐܠܐ ܘܦܘܪܫܢܐ. ܢܦܩܝܢ ܓܝܪ ܗܟܢ ܡܢ ܬܪ̈ܝܢ ܐܦ ܒܡܫܘܕܥܘܬܐ ܕܟܝܢܐ. ܘܒܗ ܒܗ ܕܡܫܡܫܝܢ ܒܪܘܚܐ (77) ܒܝܘܡ. ܘܡܦܪܫܐܝܬ ܒܪܘܚܐ ܡܢ ܬܪ̈ܝܢ ܢܦܩܝܢ ܘܒܗܘܢ ܗܘܝܢܐ ܒܝܕ ܐܦ ܦܘܪܫܐ ܕܒܟܠ ܘܢܦܩܘܬܐ. ܐܡܠܟ ܕܝܢ ܕܡܢ ܟܝܢܐ ܡܫܠܠ ܘܡܢ ܗܘ ܡܬܢܓܕܢܐ: ܚܕ ܦܘܡܐ ܡܕܝܢ ܡܫܬܡܫܠܠ: ܒܬܠܬܐ ܕܐܝܟ ܚܕܐ ܕܒܚܕܝܘܬܐ ܟܝܢܬܐ. ܗܘܝܢܐ ܦܘ ܕܗܟܢ ܕܐܒܕܐ ܬܠܬ ܠܒܝ: ܗܘ ܕܐܝܟ ܕܡܫܘܕܥܘܬܐ ܟܝܢܬܐ: ܡܛܠ ܠܐ ܒܘܟܠܐ ܕܚܕܝܘܬܐ: ܢܦܩܝܢ ܘܠܐ ܕܒܝ. ܐܬܬܪܡ ܕܝܢ ܦܘܠܓܐ: ܡܛܠ ܕܠܗ ܡܢܗܘܢ ܘܠܗܘܢ ܘܒܦܪܘܬܐ ܡܫܡܫܝܢ: ܗܟܢ ܕܒܡܫܘܕܥܘܬܐ ܟܝܢܬܐ ܡܡܫܠܚܝܢ. ܚܕ ܕܝܢ ܦܘܡܐ ܡܢ ܠܘܬ ܡܡܫܠܚܝܢ.

ܡܕܝܢ ܢܒܥ ܗܘܐ. ܘܟܠܐ ܠܐܘܪܚܐ ܕܡܫܘܐܠܠ : ܘܫܠܒܐ ܕܠܗܘܬܐ ܘܐܢܫܘܬܐ: ܠܗ ܒܟܝܢܗ ܒܟܠ ܡܡܫܠܚܐ: ܐܠܐ ܘܦܪܫܝܢ ܗܟܢ ܡܢ ܬܪ̈ܝܢ ܘܡܦܪܫܝܢ. ܒܝ ܕܝܢ ܢܦܩܘܬܐ ܕܡܢ ܠܐܬܝܗܘܢ ܡܬܐܘܪܐ: ܠܘܬ ܗܘܝܢܐ ܕܡܫܘܕܥܘܬܐ ܕܟܢ̈ܫܐ ܕܡܢܗܘܢ ܚܕ ܡܫܝܚܐ: ܠܐ ܕܟܝܢ: ܒܝܬܘܬܐ ܕܝܢ ܗܘ ܕܒܝܬܘܬܐ ܠܗܢܐ ܦܘܠܓܐ. ܘܚܕ ܠܗ ܕܗܘܐ ܢܦܩܐܝܬ ܦܠܓ ܚܝܡܐ ܡܦܪܫܘܬܗ: ܠܡܫܡܫܐ ܕܠܘܬ ܕܠܡܫܡܠ ܠܦܘܪܫܐ ܕܡܫܪܫܘܗܝ. ❖ܡܦܪܫܘܬܗ❖ ܘܐܝܬܘܬܐ ܓܝܪ ܘܕܠܗܘܬܐ ܡܢܐ ܐܝܬ ܐܘ ܐܝܬ: ܕܗܘܝܢܐ ܡܫܬܐ ܐܢܬܘܢ ܐܘ ܦܘܪܫܐ. ܐܡܪܝܢܬܐ ܓܝܪ ܩ̈ܢܘܡܝܢ ܗܟܢ

division is driven out. And look how wise Cyril clearly teaches this, in the Second Volume against the blasphemies of Nestorius. (CYRIL): "For I too allow that there is a great difference or distinction between humanity and divinity. For these things which were named are seen to be other, according to the mode of how they are, and they are not like each other in anything. But when the mystery which is in Christ has come for us into the middle, the principle of union does not ignore the difference but it removes the division; not because it confuses with each other or mixes the natures, but because the Word of God has shared in flesh and blood, thus again the Son too is understood and named as one."[15] But if someone should wrongfully divide Emmanuel with a duality (*Lebon p. 78*) of natures after the union, there also occurs a division at the same time, along with the difference of the natures, and the properties are divided in every respect to suit the (two) natures. And wise Cyril again learnedly explained this in the same volume, when he said as follows after other things: (CYRIL): "God is not touchable, but the Word became subject to touch by means of his own flesh; he is invisible by nature, but he became visible by means of the body. But you again, in making distinctions in every way, play craftily with the truth, in that on the one hand you keep distinct the natures, but on the other hand you unite, so you say, the worship. But if you keep distinct the natures, the properties of each one of them naturally go with them as well. Then the principle of difference occurs in everything, (and) thus two are confessed."[16]

It is clearly established, therefore, from these things which have been quoted, that natural quality is the principle of how (a thing) is, for the Doctor said: with respect to how they are, these things which are named are seen to be different and are unlike each other in anything. And so we confess the difference and the particularity and the otherness of the natures from which Christ is, for we do not quarrel about names, but (we confess) the particularity which (lies) in natural quality and not that which will be set in parts,[17] each one existing independently. For holy Cyril writes as follows too, in the Treatise of question and answer *That Christ is One*: (CYRIL): "Therefore, as I have said, it is not right that we should make a division into an independent diversity, so that they should become separate and apart from each other; rather we ought to bring (them) together to [undivided][18] union. For the Word became flesh, according to the word(s) of John."[19] (*Lebon p. 79*)

For we do not refuse to confess the difference, God forbid, but we flee from this, that we should divide the one Christ in a duality of

ܘܐܬܡܠܟܘ: ܐܝܟ ܡܫܝܚܐ ܗܘ ܘܐܝܟ ܐܬܐܢܫ. ܘܐܦܠܐ ܒܟܝܢܗ ܕܩܢܘܡ ܠܟܝܢܘܬܐ. ܟܕ
ܐܬܐ ܠܗ ܕܝܢ ܠܡܕܒܪܢܘܬܐ ܙܪܐ ܕܟܝܢܝܐ: ܡܫܝܚܐ ܘܝܚܝܕܝܐ ܠܐ ܓܒܠܐ ܗܝ ܠܡܫܘܚܬܐ.
ܡܫܚܐ ܕܝܢ ܠܡܦܠܓܬܐ. ܠܗ ܟܕ ܚܕܐ ܚܕ ܢܝܫܐ ܐܘ ܡܫܡܠܝܐ ܟܝܢܐ. ܐܠܐ ܟܕ
ܠܒܣܪܐ ܘܢܦܫܐ ܐܬܚܘܝ ܡܫܝܚܐ ܕܐܠܗܐ: ܚܕ ܬܘܒ ܐܘ ܗܟܢܐ ܒܪܐ ܡܫܬܚܠܦ
ܘܡܫܬܡܠܝܘ܀ ܐܢ ܕܝܢ ܢܦܠܝ ܐܝܟ ܠܡܫܬܘܐܠܘ ܚܘܠܐܝܬ ܒܛܘܝܒܘܬܐ (78) ܕܟܝܢܐ
ܠܗܘ ܚܝܘܬܐ: ܟܕ ܡܫܘܚܬܐ ܕܟܝܢܐ ܡܢ ܠܡܦܪܫܘ ܕܗܘ ܐܚܝܕܐ ܐܘ ܦܘܠܓܐ.
ܘܟܠܗ ܡܕܡ ܩܛܠܦܢ ܕܬܠܝܐ ܠܡܫܬܠܡܘ ܟܝܢܐ. ܘܗܕܐ ܬܘܒ ܒܗ
ܠܦܘܫܩܐ ܢܦܫ ܡܬܚܠܒܢܘܬ ܡܫܡܫܢܐ ܡܘܫܠܚܘܣ: ܘܟܠܗ ܐܢܬܝܬܐ ܐܦܢ ܐܘ
ܘܠܗܝ. ܀ܡܘܫܠܚܘܣ܀ ܗܘܐ ܐܠܗܐ ܘܠܐ ܓܒܠܐ ܐܬܚܙܝ. ܐܠܐ ܘܡܬܓܫܡܢܐ ܗܘܐ
ܡܫܝܚܐ ܐܝܟ ܕܟܢ ܒܟܢܫܐ. ܠܐ ܡܬܚܙܝܢܐ ܒܟܝܢܐ. ܐܠܐ ܐܬܚܙܝ ܗܘܐ ܘܡܬܚܙܝܢܐ ܒܟܢ
ܦܓܪܐ. ܐܝܟ ܕܝܢ ܬܘܒ ܟܕ ܦܦܪܘܣ ܐܝܟ ܠܝ ܒܟܘܠܗ ܥܠܐ: ܡܬܓܫܡ ܐܝܟ ܠܒܪܐ.
ܕܟܝܢܐ ܦܝ ܦܦܪܘܣ ܐܝܟ: ܡܫܝܚ ܐܝܟ ܕܝܢ ܐܝܟ ܘܐܡܪ ܐܝܟ ܡܬܝܠܕܐ. ܐܠܐ ܐܢ
ܦܦܪܘܣ ܐܝܟ ܠܟܝܢܐ: ܐܢܬ ܒܟܘܢ ܐܘ ܕܬܠܝܐ ܘܟܠܗ ܚܕ ܡܫܝܚܐ ܟܝܢܐ.
ܦܓܪܐ ܕܝܢ ܡܫܝܚܐ ܘܡܫܘܚܬܐ ܟܠܗ. ܬܘܒ ܗܟܢܐ ܡܬܬܘܕܝܢ.
ܡܢ ܗܟܝܠ ܗܟܢܐ ܘܐܬܐܡܝܢ ܐܬܩܢܝ ܒܝܬܗ: ܘܡܫܡܠܝܘܬܐ ܟܝܢܝܐ ܐܬܝܠܕ
ܡܫܝܚܐ ܘܐܝܟ ܐܬܐܢܫ. ܐܡܪ ܓܝܪ ܡܫܡܫܢܐ: ܘܐܝܟ ܡܫܝܚܐ ܗܘ ܘܐܝܟ ܐܬܐܢܫ:
ܐܢܬܝܬܐ ܩܛܝܢܝܢ ܗܟܢ ܘܐܬܡܠܟܘ. ܘܠܐ ܕܩܢܘܡ ܠܟܝܢܐ ܒܟܝܢܗ. ܡܫܘܝܢ ܗܟܢܐ
ܘܡܫܘܚܬܐ ܘܡܬܚܙܝܢܐ ܘܐܬܚܙܝܬܐ ܕܟܝܢܐ ܘܡܫܘܚܢ ܡܫܝܚܐ. ܡܛܠ ܓܝܪ ܡܫܡܫܢܐ
ܠܐ ܡܬܚܙܝܢ. ܘܡܫܝܚܐ ܕܝܢ ܗܘ ܘܐܝܟ ܕܒܡܫܡܫܢܘܬܐ ܟܝܢܝܐ: ܘܠܗ ܗܘ ܘܒܟܝܢܘܬܐ
ܐܬܩܢܝ: ܘܡܢܗ ܘܠܗ ܟܠ ܚܕܐ ܡܫܘܚܢ ܬܘܒ ܐܠܗܐ. ܠܗܘ ܓܝܪ ܡܫܡܠܝܐ
ܡܫܘܚܬܗ ܒܬܚܘܡܐ ܘܡܫܘܠܐ ܘܡܫܘܚ ܦܘܠܓܐ: ܒܗܘ ܕܝܢ ܗܘ ܡܫܝܚܐ ܐܘ
ܗܟܝܢ. ܀ܡܘܫܠܚܘܣ܀ ܠܐ ܓܝܪ ܗܘܐ ܘܢܦܠܝ ܐܝܟ ܘܐܡܪܝܢ: ܠܐܬܝܬܘܬܐ ܘܡܫܘܚܬܐ
ܘܗܘ ܕܗܘܐ ܙܢܝܢ ܡܢ ܚܕ ܢܝܫܐ ܘܡܫܝܚܐ. ܦܠܐ ܕܝܢ ܕܝܠܐ ܠܡܬܚܙܝܢܐ ܐܚܝܕܐ
ܒܚܝܘܬܐ ܘܠܐ ܡܬܦܫܛܐ. ܗܘܐ ܓܝܪ ܡܫܝܚܐ ܒܟܝܢܐ: ܐܝܟ ܒܪܐ ܡܠܟܐ ܘܡܘܠܕ܀
(79) ܠܐ ܒܦܪܝܫ ܓܝܪ ܕܗܘܐ ܡܫܘܚܬܐ. ܠܐ ܡܬܩܒܠ ܬܘܒ ܗܘܐ. ܡܢ ܗܘ ܕܝܢ ܕܢܦܠܝ
ܠܛܘܝܒܘܬܐ ܕܟܝܢܐ ܠܟܠ ܡܫܚܐ ܠܗܘ ܚܝܘܬܐ ܒܪܫܝܬ. ܐܚܕܘ ܓܝܪ ܕܡܬܦܠܓܝܢ:
ܐܚܝܕܐ ܩܛܠܦܢ ܒܗܘ ܐܘ ܕܬܠܝܐ ܘܠܟܕ ܡܢ ܟܝܢܐ. ܘܡܫܚܐ ܠܟܠܟܕ ܡܫܘܚܢ
ܗܘ ܘܠܗ. ܟܕ ܕܝܢ ܚܝܘܬܐ ܡܫܘܡܠܝܐ ܡܬܬܘܕܝܐ: ܘܐܬܐܡܝܢ ܡܫܡܠܝܐ ܗܘ ܘܡܢ

natures after the union. For if he is divided, the properties of each one of the natures are divided at the same time with him, and what is its own will cling to each one of them. But when a hypostatic union is professed, of which the fulfilment is that from two there is one Christ without confusion, one person, one hypostasis, one nature belonging to the Word incarnate, the Word is known by means of the properties of the flesh, and the properties of the humanity will become the properties of the divinity of the Word; and again the properties of the Word will be acknowledged as the properties of the flesh, and the same one will be seen by means of both (sets of properties), both touchable and not touchable, and visible and not visible, and belonging to time and from before time, and we shall not attribute the properties of each nature, dividing them up.

And the clear and astute words of wise Cyril will again teach and instruct us clearly (in) these things, for he writes as follows in the Third Volume against the blasphemies of Nestorius: (CYRIL): "Does he then lie, when he said that the Son of Man, who is himself, descended from heaven? Far from it! For he is himself the truth. Therefore how may 'the Son of Man from above' be understood rightly? Because although he is God the Word and from the ousia which is above every (ousia), it is said that he descended and took the form of a servant, and then speaks with us, not, from then on, as the naked Word, but as a man like us, and as one who is understood already as one with flesh united to him. (*Lebon p. 80*)

Just as, for the sake of that which is proper to the emptying, he takes for his own all those things which are of the body, even though he is incorporeal by nature, so too, he, being from above and from heaven, attributes (the words) 'he came from above' to himself, while he was man, even though he was in the flesh with us from woman. Therefore the properties of the Word became properties of manhood, and those of manhood, properties of the Word. For thus one Christ and Son and Lord is understood."[20]

Therefore when we anathematise those who say Emmanuel has two natures after the union, and (speak of the) activities and properties of these, we are not saying this as subjecting to anathema the fact of speaking of, or naming, natures, or activities or properties, but speaking of two natures after the union, and because consequently (those natures) attract their own activities and properties which are divided along with the natures completely and in everything, whether we say (this) or not. For if this were not so, it would be right for us not to profess Emmanuel even to be "from two natures", if the word "natures" were to be shunned. But now, when we say

ܐܝܟ ܠܐ ܡܬܦܠܓܢܐܝܬ ܐܝܬܘܗܝ ܚܕ ܡܫܝܚܐ. ܚܕ ܦܪܨܘܦܐ: ܚܕ ܩܢܘܡܐ: ܚܕ ܒܪܐ ܗܘ ܕܝܠܗ ܕܡܠܬܐ ܘܕܒܣܪ. ܟܕ ܕܟܝܢܬܐ ܕܒܣܪܐ ܡܠܬܐ ܡܠܒܫܐ. ܘܕܟܝܢܬܐ ܕܐܢܫܘܬܐ ܕܟܝܢܬܐ ܢܩܘܡ ܕܐܠܗܘܬܐ ܕܡܠܬܐ. ܘܕܟܝܢܬܐ ܠܘܬ ܕܡܠܬܐ ܘܕܟܝܢܬܐ ܕܒܣܪܐ ܢܬܐܩܦ: ܘܗܘ ܟܕ ܗܘ ܢܗܘܐ: ܕܟܕ ܗܠܝܢ ܘܗܠܝܢ ܡܬܚܝܕܐ. ܘܡܬܦܪܫܢܐ ܘܠܐ ܡܬܦܪܫܢܐ. ܘܡܬܚܝܕܐ ܘܠܐ ܡܬܚܝܕܐ. ܘܕܟܝܢܐ ܗܘܐ ܘܕܡܐ ܥܕܡ ܪܩܝܐ. ܘܠܗ ܕܟܝܢܬܐ ܕܟܠ ܚܕܐ ܡܫܬܟܚܐ ܒܠܘܕ.

ܘܗܠܝܢ ܐܠܦܝܢ ܠܘܬ ܘܐܘܕܝܢ ܢܣܛܘܪܝܣ ܒܪܐ ܗܠܐ ܘܢܘܟܪܝܬܐ ܘܡܫܒܚܐ ܡܦܪܫܝܢ. ܠܘܬ ܓܒܪ ܒܦܘܣܩܐ ܕܐܠܗܐ ܕܟܘܡܟܠ ܚܩܘܦܐ ܕܡܬܦܪܫܝܢ ܗܟܝܠ. ܀ܡܦܪܫܝܢ܀ ܦܪܨܘܦܐ ܗܟܡܐ ܟܢܘܫܝܐ: ܘܐܡܪ ܕܢܣܒܗ ܡܢ ܡܪܝܐ ܒܪܗ ܘܐܢܫܐ: ܗܢܘ ܕܝܢ ܗܘ. ܠܐ ܬܗܘܐ. ܗܘ ܓܝܪ ܐܝܬܘܗܝ ܚܙܘܐ. ܐܟܢܐ ܗܟܝܠ ܡܢ ܠܟܠ ܒܪܗ ܘܐܢܫܐ ܢܣܒܗ ܢܫܬܟܚ ܙܕܩܐܝܬ. ܕܟܕ ܐܝܬܘܗܝ ܐܠܗܐ ܡܠܬܐ ܘܡܢ ܐܘܣܝܐ ܕܠܟܠ ܡܢ ܩܕܡ: ܡܬܐܡܪ ܕܢܣܒܗ ܘܩܒܠ ܕܡܘܬܐ ܕܥܒܕܐ. ܘܡܬܐܡܪ ܡܫܬܠܡ ܠܘܬܢ: ܠܗ ܐܝܟ ܡܠܬܐ ܒܪܝܬܐ ܡܫܬܒܚܐ ܐܝܟ ܒܪ ܐܢܫܐ ܘܐܒܘܢ. ܘܐܝܟ ܦܝ ܕܚܕ ܡܢ ܟܕܘ ܡܬܐܡܪ: ܒܗ ܒܒܣܪܐ ܘܐܬܚܙܝ ܠܗ. ܐܝܟ (80) ܡܐ ܕܝܢ ܕܡܫܬܠܡ ܗܘ ܕܐܬܐ ܠܡܦܪܩܘ: ܕܝܠܗ ܕܟܕ ܡܠܘܗܝ ܗܠܝܢ ܕܦܪܘܩܐ: ܟܕ ܝܗܒ ܒܪܐ ܘܠܐ ܓܝܪ ܐܝܬܘܗܝ: ܗܟܢܐ ܘܟܕ ܡܢ ܟܠܗܝܢ ܐܝܬܘܗܝ ܗܘ ܘܡܢ ܡܫܝܚܐ: ܗܘ ܕܡܢ ܠܟܠܗܘܢ: ܠܗ ܠܘܬ ܡܢܗ ܘܟܕ ܗܘܐ ܒܪ ܐܢܫܐ. ܐܦ ܗܘܐ ܒܒܣܪ ܒܟܢ ܡܢ ܐܠܗܐ. ܗܘ ܗܟܝܠ ܕܟܝܢܬܐ ܦܝ ܕܡܠܬܐ: ܗܠܝܢ ܕܐܢܫܘܬܐ. ܕܟܝܢܬܐ ܕܝܢ ܠܘܬ ܕܐܢܫܘܬܐ: ܗܠܝܢ ܕܠܗ ܕܡܠܬܐ. ܚܕ ܓܝܪ ܗܟܝܠ ܡܫܬܟܚܐ ܡܫܝܚܐ ܒܪܐ ܘܡܪܝܐ܀

ܐܟܢܐ ܗܟܝܠ ܕܡܣܬܪܩܝܢ ܠܟܝܢܗܝ ܘܐܡܪܝܢ ܠܡܦܫܛܘܬܐ ܐܝܟ ܟܝܢܝܢ ܠܟܠܘܬ ܣܘܥܪܢܐ: ܘܡܫܬܘܕܥܢܘܬܐ ܕܗܠܝܢ ܘܕܟܝܢܬܐ: ܠܗ ܟܕ ܠܟܘ ܠܗܘܐ ܘܢܐܡܪ ܐܘ ܢܣܒܘ ܟܝܢܐ ܐܘ ܡܫܬܘܕܥܢܘܬܐ ܐܘ ܕܟܝܢܬܐ: ܡܫܡܫܝܢ ܠܐܝܟ ܚܕܐ: ܐܡܪܝܢ ܗܘܐ. ܐܠܐ ܠܟܘܢ ܘܢܐܡܪ ܠܗܘ ܣܘܥܪܢܐ ܐܝܟ ܟܝܢܝܢ: ܘܡܫܬܐܠܝܢ ܕܝܢ ܗܠܝܢ ܡܫܬܘܕܥܢܘܬܐ ܕܡܠܘܗܝ ܘܕܟܝܢܬܐ: ܐܠܝܢ ܕܟܠܗ ܘܡܢ ܡܠܦܢܘܬ ܟܢ ܟܝܢܐ ܩܛܠܝܢ. ܘܟܕ ܢܐܡܪ ܚܕ ܘܟܕ ܠܐ ܢܐܡܪ. ܠܗܘ ܓܝܪ ܗܘܐ ܠܐ ܐܝܬܝܗ ܗܘܬ: ܙܘܓ ܗܘܐ ܕܐܦ ܠܐ ܡܢ ܐܝܟ ܟܝܢܝܢ ܢܗܘܐ ܠܡܬܘܐܡܠ: ܐܝܟܘ ܕܠܘܬܐ ܗܘ ܚܕܐ ܕܟܝܢܐ. ܗܟܐ ܕܝܢ ܟܕ ܐܡܪܝܢ ܡܢ ܐܝܟ ܟܝܢܝܢ: ܘܚܕ ܡܚܝܢ ܠܠܒܘܬ ܗܘ ܘܐܬܟܣܪ ܘܐܬܒܪܝܢ ܠܐ ܡܬܡܚܫܠܢܐܝܬ: ܘܡܫܬܘܕܥܢܘܬܐ ܠܐ ܡܬܟܠܟܠܐ ܡܬܘܡܫܝܢ ܕܗܘܐ: ܡܚܝܢ ܠܠܒܘܬ: ܘܕܟܝܢܬܐ ܕܟܝܢܐ ܕܡܫܝܚܝܢ

"from two natures", and acknowledge one God who was immutably incarnate and inhominate, and believe that there was an unconfused union, we are obliged to acknowledge as well the particularities of the natures from which Emmanuel is. And we call this a particularity and name it: (that is,) that which (lies) in difference of natural quality, which (definition) I will not cease repeating many times, and not that (which lies) in (independent) parts,[21] and natures in independent existence are implied, (*Lebon p. 81*) for to say this belongs to those who mutilate (Christ) with a duality after the inexpressible union, and not to us, who profess him to be one from two.

And then about activities: we find a distinct opinion when we have recourse to the quotations of the God-clad Fathers. For Basil, great and wise in divine matters, wrote, in the Treatise of refutations against Eunomius, that he who acts is one thing, and activity is another, and another that which was enacted, and these things are quite removed from each other. For he who acts is he who is impelled towards doing something, but the activity (is) like an active movement and impetus of the will which is directed on and indicates doing something, and is set in motion at once. In the case of activity, that which wills (it) remains complete and momentarily impelled to action, but (activity) is not a hypostasis, but the things which are enacted, which are brought to completion as a result of this and exist, (are hypostases). For when evil Eunomius had said that the Son was made, and was not an off-spring of the Father, holy Basil says to him ensnared in intellectual nets by perverted opinions and human arguments: If, according to your word, the Son is an effect, what do you understand an effect to be? That which is completed from activity. Then he is third from the Father and not second, if the Father is understood as he who acts, and activity is an active movement, and that which is enacted is what is completed by movement. But he says as follows—for we ought to quote the words of the Doctor verbally: BASIL: "If the Son (*Lebon p. 82*) is an activity, and not an off-spring, he is neither the agent, nor the product, for an activity is something other than these. But he is also without hypostasis, for no activity is hypostatic. But if he is that which is enacted, he is third from the Father, and not without an intermediary. For he who acted is first, and then activity, and then that which was enacted."[22]

Therefore what has thus been clarified and made known is that he who acted is one thing, and activity is another, and another (still) that which was acted upon, or effected. And activity is something in the middle, that is, an active movement, between him who acted and

ܠܡܫܘܐܠܐ: ܘܗܘܐ ܐܡܪܝܢ ܕܡܠܬܐ ܘܡܫܡܫܢܝܢ. ܗܢܝ ܕܐܝܟ ܕܒܡܫܝܚܘܬܐ ܘܡܫܠܡܢܘܬܐ ܒܫܡܝܐ. ܕܗܘ ܓܝܪ ܟܕ ܗܘ ܐܡܪ ܕܟܠܗܝܢ ܡܫܡ̈ܫܝܢ ܠܐ ܦܠܛ ܐܢܐ. ܘܠܗ ܗܢܝ ܕܒܟܗܢܘܬܐ ܘܒܡܫܡܫܢܘܬܐ ܕܡܢܗ (81) ܘܠܗ ܡܫܡܫܝܢ ܟܗ̈ܢܐ. ܗܘܐ ܓܝܪ ܕܗܢܘܢ ܘܦܫܛܝܢ ܠܗ ܠܡܬܪܥܝܘܬܐ ܠܡܬܪ ܚܕܝܘܬܐ ܠܐ ܡܬܐܡܪܢܝܬܐ ܐܠܗܝܐ ܕܢܐܡܪܘܢ: ܘܠܗ ܕܠܟ. ܐܠܝܢ ܕܚܕ ܡܢ ܬܠܬܐ ܩܢܘܡܝܢ ܠܗ.

ܘܡܛܠ ܡܥܡܘܕܝܬܐ ܬܘܒ: ܟܕ ܟܠܐ ܟܢܫ ܩܠܐ ܘܐܒܗ̈ܬܐ ܠܟܢܫܐ ܠܐܠܗܐ ܕܗܘܝܢ: ܡܡܚܣܝܢ ܘܡܦܪܢܣܐ ܡܠܬܐ. ܗܘ ܓܝܪ ܪܒܐ ܘܡܫܡܫܢܐ ܒܗܠܝܢ ܠܐܠܗ̈ܘܬܐ ܒܫܡܠܘܬܗ: ܒܥܐܡܪܐ ܕܗܘܦܟ ܚܩ̈ܠܬܐ ܕܠܡܫܠܡܢܘܬܗ ܟܠܗ: ܕܐܝܢܐ ܗܘ ܗܘ ܕܟܕ ܘܐܝܢܐ ܡܥܡܘܕܝܬܐ: ܘܐܝܢܐ ܗܘ ܕܐܬܥܒܕ. ܘܗܠܝܢ ܡܫܚܐ ܕܢܚܬܝܢ ܡܢ ܫܡܝܐ. ܗܘ ܓܝܪ ܕܟܕ ܐܠܗܘܗܝ: ܗܘ ܕܟܠܐ ܗܢܝ ܕܢܚܬ ܡܢܗ ܡܬܐܡܪܐ. ܡܥܡܘܕܝܬܐ ܕܝܢ ܗܢܝ ܕܐܝܟ ܡܠܐ ܕܪܘܚܐ ܡܥܡܘܕܝܬܐ: ܘܗܝ ܕܐܦܠܐ ܐܝܟ ܐܢܫ ܕܢܐܡܪ ܕܪܘܚܢܐ: ܗܘ ܕܟܠܐ ܗܢܝ ܕܢܚܬ ܡܢܗ ܡܬܡܠܐ ܘܡܠܐ. ܘܡܫܚܐ ܡܬܐܡܪܐ. ܡܥܡܘܕܝܬܐ ܕܝܢ ܕܪܚܐ ܦܠܛ ܘܡܫܡܠܝܐ. ܘܡܫܬܠܡܢ ܐܬܐܡܪܬ ܘܡܢܘܡ: ܘܠܐ ܩܢܘܡ ܗܘ. ܗܠܝܢ ܕܝܢ ܘܡܬܚܙܝܢ: ܗܠܝܢ ܕܡܢ ܗܢܐ ܡܬܩ̈ܠܡܢܝܢ ܘܩܢܘܡ. ܟܕ ܓܝܪ ܙܘܠܐ ܐܘܟܝܬ ܐܡܪ ܗܘܐ: ܕܗܘ ܗܢ ܕܡܬܚܙܐ: ܘܠܗ ܡܟܒܐ ܕܐܝܬ ܐܠܗܘܗܝ ܒܪܐ: ܡܫܚܐ ܒܫܡܠܘܬܗ ܟܕ ܡܢܗ ܕܦܘܠܚܢܗ ܡܬܩܠܐ ܘܩܢܝܐ ܐܢܫܐ ܒܡܥܢܝܬܐ ܩܠܝܠܐ ܡܫܡܠܐ ܠܗ ܐܡܪ. ܐܝܟܢ ܕܡܬܚܙܐ ܐܠܗܘܗܝ ܒܪܐ ܐܝܟ ܡܫܡܠܝܐ: ܡܢܐ ܡܫܬܡܠܝܢ ܗܘ ܘܡܬܚܙܐ. ܐܦܐ ܗܘ ܕܡܢ ܡܥܡܘܕܝܬܐ ܡܫܡܠܝܐ: ܡܢܝܢ ܕܐܠܗܐ ܡܢ ܐܒܐ ܐܠܗܘܗܝ ܘܠܗ ܕܐܬܝܗ. ܐܘ ܗܘ ܕܐܬܚܙܝ ܟܕ ܐܒܐ ܡܫܡܠܝܐ. ܡܥܡܘܕܝܬܐ ܕܝܢ ܙܘܓܐ ܡܥܡܘܕܝܢܐ. ܗܘ ܕܡܬܚܙܐ ܕܝܢ ܫܘܡܠܝܐ ܗܘ ܕܡܢ ܙܘܓܐ. ܐܡܪ ܕܝܢ ܗܟܝܠ. ܙܕܩ ܓܝܪ ܕܒܗ ܒܡܠܬܐ ܢܫܡܥ ܠܡܠܐ ܘܡܫܝܚܐ ܀ܒܫܡܠܘܬܗ܀ ܐܘ ܒܪܐ (82) ܡܥܡܘܕܝܬܐ ܗܘ ܘܠܗ ܡܠܝܐ: ܘܠܐ ܗܘ ܕܐܬܚܙܝ ܘܠܐ ܗܘ ܟܕ ܕܐܬܚܙܝ ܐܠܗܘܗܝ ܗܘ: ܡܥܡܘܕܝܬܐ ܓܝܪ ܡܢܝܢ ܐܢܫܝܢ ܠܒܪ ܡܢ ܗܠܝܢ. ܐܠܐ ܘܠܐ ܩܢܘܡ. ܘܠܐ ܚܕܐ ܓܝܪ ܡܥܡܘܕܝܬܐ ܩܢܘܡܝܬܐ. ܐܘ ܕܝܢ ܗܘ ܕܐܬܚܙܝ: ܕܐܠܗܐ ܗܘ ܡܢ ܐܒܐ: ܘܠܗ ܕܠܐ ܡܬܚܙܝܐ. ܗܘ ܕܟܕ ܓܝܪ ܡܫܚܐ. ܘܠܡܪܢ ܡܥܡܘܕܝܬܐ: ܘܗܘܢ ܗܘ ܕܐܬܚܙܝ܀

ܟܕ ܗܘܐ ܗܟܝܠ ܗܟܢܐ ܐܬܦܪܫܬ ܘܐܬܚܙܝܬ ܡܫܡܠ: ܕܐܝܢܐ ܗܘ ܕܟܕ: ܘܐܝܢܐ ܡܥܡܘܕܝܬܐ: ܘܐܝܢܐ ܗܘ ܕܐܬܚܙܝ: ܐܘ ܟܠܗ ܕܐܬܐܬܚܙܝ: ܘܡܬܚܝܕܬܐ ܡܢܝܢ ܐܠܗܘܗܝ ܡܥܡܘܕܝܬܐ: ܗܘܝܘ ܕܝܢ ܙܘܓܐ ܗܘ ܡܥܡܘܕܝܬܐ: ܕܗܘ ܕܟܕ ܘܗܘ ܕܐܬܚܙܝ: ܐܦ ܘܠܗܘܢ

that which was acted upon, even if in the case of God, his wishing is the accomplishment of an action, and it is not easy to find that which is in the middle, when everything exists in a moment, and as in the blink of an eye, as Paul says.[23] We will apply (this) reasoning to what was set down earlier.

And first, let us test this on the example of a man like us. Thus, some of the things which are done by a man like us are intellectual, and some are sensible and bodily. For example, to reckon up and think about something that should be done, and to fulfil and plan in thought, and to fix and determine intention, is a thing which is done intellectually, such as arranging how it is fitting to prepare a city or a house or a ship. But to build a house or to construct a ship, is sensible and bodily. And the man who acts (in both cases) is one, consisting of soul and body, and the activity is one, for the active movement is one, which is the impetus of volition, but the things which are done are diverse, for one is intellectual but the other is sensible and bodily. One can see the same in the case of Emmanuel. (*Lebon p. 83*) For there is one who acts, that is the Word of God incarnate; and there is one active movement which is activity, but the things which are done are diverse, that is (the things) accomplished by activity. For example, bodily to walk on the earth and to make a journey is something human, but to raise up and order to run those who are lame in the feet, and unable to use their soles, but who are prostrate and crawl like reptiles, is most proper to God. But there is one Word which was incarnate, and one activity of his, which is an active movement, which performed the one and the other. And it is not the case that, because these things which were done were of different kinds, we say that consequently there were two natures which were effecting those things, for as we have said, a single God the Word incarnate performed both of them. And just as no-one divides the Word from the flesh, so also it is impossible to divide or separate these activities. For we also recognise a variety of utterances: for some are proper to God, while others are human, but one Word incarnate spoke both the former and the latter. For there are utterances which make known at the same time the divine character of Emmanuel and the humanity as well, as "One Lord Jesus Christ, through whom are all things",[24] and "From whom is Christ, in the flesh, who is God blessed for ever, above all things".[25] And no-one, unless he is mad, dares to divide or distinguish into two these statements, which establish the same (Christ) as indivisible, being both from Israel in the flesh, and God blessed for ever. And again the same one is anointed because he was incarnate, for the act of being

ܠܐܠܗܐ ܘܐܦ ܗܘ̇ ܕܐܝܟܐ ܡܫܡܫܢܘܬܐ ܐܠܗܝܬܐ ܕܚܒܪܐ: ܘܥܠ ܕܥܠܠܐ ܕܗܘ ܡܪܟܒܬܐ ܢܦܫ: ܒܗܘ ܕܡܬܥܒܪ ܒܙܒܢܐ ܩܠܝܠ: ܘܐܝܟ ܕܒܪܦܦ ܥܝܢܐ ܐܝܟ ܕܐܡܪ ܦܘܠܘܣ: ܟܠܗ ܗܘ̇ ܕܡܫܝܚܐ ܫܡܫܐ ܢܗܝܪܐ ܠܥܠܡܐ.

ܘܡܬܩܪܝܢ ܥܠ ܐܣܘܬܐ ܕܒܪܢܫܐ ܕܐܝܬܘܗܝ: ܗܘܐ ܢܦܫ. ܕܒܪܢܫܐ ܗܘܢܐ ܕܐܝܬܘܗܝ ܗܠܝܢ ܕܩܕ̈ܡܝܢ: ܗܠܝܢ ܡܢ ܐܝܬܝܗܝܢ ܡܬܒܪ̈ܝܢܝܬܐ: ܗܠܝܢ ܕܝܢ ܡܬܦܪ̈ܫܢܝܬܐ ܘܦܪ̈ܝܫܬܐ. ܐܟܘܬ ܕܗܘ̇ ܕܐܝܬܘܗܝ ܘܐܝܩܢܐ ܡܛܠ ܡܕܡ ܙܘܓ ܕܐܬܚܒܪ: ܘܢܦܫܐ ܘܪܘܚܐ ܒܪܘܚܢܐ: ܘܢܦܫ ܘܠܝܬ ܚܘܫܒܐ: ܗܘ ܕܡܬܐܡܪܝܢ ܐܝܬܘܗܝ ܡܬܒܪܝܢܐ. ܐܝܟ ܡܐ ܕܢܦܫ ܘܐܝܟܢܐ ܗܠܐ ܕܡܬܒܪܝܢܐ ܢܗܘܐ: ܐܘ ܒܗܝܐ ܐܘ ܠܐܠܗܐ: ܗܘ̇ ܕܝܢ ܕܐܝܟܢܐ ܒܗܝܐ: ܐܘ ܢܦܫܗ ܠܐܠܗܐ: ܡܬܦܪ̈ܫܢܝܬܐ ܘܡܫܡܫܢܝܬܐ: ܘܚܕ ܡܢ ܒܪܢܫܐ ܗܘ ܕܡܬܒܪܝ: ܗܘ ܕܡܢ ܢܦܫܐ ܘܦܓܪܐ: ܘܚܕܐ ܡܬܒܪܝܢܘܬܐ. ܚܕ ܓܝܪ ܙܘܓܐ ܗܘ ܡܬܒܪܝܐ: ܗܘ ܕܐܝܬܘܗܝ ܚܝܘܬܐ ܡܠܝܠܬܐ ܕܗܘ ܒܪܢܫܐ. ܗܠܝܢ ܕܝܢ ܩܕ̈ܡܝܬܐ ܡܬܦܠܓܢܝܬܐ ܗܘܝ ܡܢ ܓܝܪ ܡܬܒܪܝܢܝܬܐ. ܗܝ ܕܝܢ ܡܬܦܪ̈ܫܢܝܬܐ ܘܡܫܡܫܢܝܬܐ. ܗܟܝܠ ܐܦ ܥܠ ܡܫܡܫܢܘܬܐ (83) ܠܥܠܡܐ. ܕܚܕ ܗܘ ܡܢ ܗܘ̇ ܕܩܕܡܝ: ܗܢܘ ܕܝܢ ܗܘ ܡܠܬܐ ܕܐܠܗܐ ܕܡܬܒܪ. ܘܚܕ ܙܘܓܐ ܘܡܬܒܪܝܐ ܗܘ̇ ܕܐܝܬܘܗܝ ܡܬܒܪܝܢܘܬܐ. ܡܫܡܫܝܢ ܕܝܢ ܗܠܝܢ ܕܩ̈ܕܡܝܢ. ܗܢܘ ܕܝܢ ܡܫܡܫܢܐ ܕܡܢ ܡܬܒܪܝܢܘܬܐ. ܕܐܝܟ ܐܡܪ. ܗ̇ܘ ܕܦܪ̈ܝܫܬܐ ܠܥܠܡܐ ܢܗܘܐ ܘܢܚܘܐ: ܐܝܟܢܐ ܗܘ. ܗܘ̇ ܕܝܢ ܕܠܗܘܢ ܘܡܬܦܪܫ ܒܡ̈ܠܐ: ܘܡܫ̈ܡܫܢܘܬܐ ܠܐ ܡܫܡܫܝܢ ܠܐܠܗܘܬܗ: ܡܬܦܪܫܝܢ ܕܝܢ ܕܢܦܫ ܐܝܟ ܕܢܝܐ: ܢܦܫ ܘܦܓܪܗ ܕܢܗܘܐ: ܠܐܬܪ ܡܢ ܟܠ ܦܓܪܐ ܠܐܠܗܐ. ܐܠܐ ܚܕ ܗܘ ܡܠܬܐ ܕܐܬܒܪ: ܘܚܕܐ ܡܬܒܪܝܢܘܬܗ: ܗܘ̇ ܕܐܝܬܘܗܝ ܙܘܓܐ ܡܬܒܪܝܐ: ܕܗܘܐ ܘܗܘ ܐܡܪ. ܘܥܠ ܡܛܠ ܕܡܫܡܫ ܗܠܝܢ ܕܐܡܪ: ܡܛܠ ܗܘܐ ܠܐܬܪ ܒܬܪܝܢ ܠܗܠܝܢ ܕܡܫܡܫܝܢ ܐܡܪܝܢ. ܚܕ ܓܝܪ ܐܡܪܝܢ ܘܐܡܪܝܢ ܡܠܬܐ ܠܐܠܗܐ ܕܐܬܒܪܝܢ ܡܢ ܠܬܪܝܗܝܢ. ܘܐܡܪܝܢ ܘܠܐ ܐܝܟ ܦܠܓܝܢ ܡܠܬܐ ܡܢ ܒܬܪ: ܗܟܝܠ ܘܠܐ ܗܠܝܢ ܡܬܒܪ̈ܝܢܘܬܐ ܦܠܓܝ ܐܘ ܦܪܫ ܡܫܡܫܐ. ܡܛܠ ܕܐܦ ܕܒܗ ܩ̈ܠܐ ܡܦܪܫ ܩܘܠܦܐ. ܗܢܘ ܓܝܪ ܐܝܬܘܗܝ ܦܠܓܗ ܠܐܠܗܐ. ܗܠܝܢ ܕܝܢ ܐܢܫܝܬܐ. ܚܕ ܕܝܢ ܡܠܬܐ ܗܘ ܕܐܬܒܪ. ܘܐܦ ܗܢܝܢ ܘܗܠܝܢ ܡܫܡܠܠ. ܐܠܐ ܓܝܪ ܦܠܓܗ ܩܠܐ: ܕܒܗ ܒܗ ܒܗ ܡܫܡܫܝܢ ܦܠܓܐ ܠܐܠܗܘܬܐ ܐܝܟ ܚܕܐ ܕܡܫܡܫܢܘܬܐ ܘܐܢܫܘܬܐ. ܐܝܟ ܗܘ ܕܚܕ ܡܢܢ ܢܦܫ ܡܫܝܚܐ: ܕܒܬܪܗܘܢ ܥܠ ܡܕܡ: ܘܡܢܗܘܢ ܡܫܝܚܐ ܕܒܟܠܗ̇. ܗܘ ܕܐܝܬܘܗܝ ܠܐܠܗܐ ܕܥܠ ܟܠ ܡܬܪܒܐ ܠܟܠܗܘܢ. ܘܠܗܘܢ ܘܠܐ ܐܦ ܚܝܠ ܐܝܟ ܡܡܠܠ ܕܦܠܓܝ

anointed belongs to the incarnation, and through the same (one) everything came into existence. (*Lebon p. 84*)

But what our Saviour said about the death of Lazarus is like those utterances as well, in that it shows at the same time the divine character and humanity: "Lazarus our friend is asleep, but I go that I may arouse him".[26] For it belongs to God that he should say that he would rouse him as if he were asleep, him who for four days had been reckoned among the dead, and had wasted away, and had putrified in the body, and in truth to change death into sleep, because of the hope of the resurrection; but it was human to say "I go and shall awake him". For he was able as God, even while he was far off, to do that. But he mingled the two, establishing that he is indivisibly one and the same Son and Word, who on our behalf unchangeably became man, speaking as befits God and humanly. Thus too it is often possible to see in his actions what belongs to the character of God and (what is) human mingled together. For how will anyone divide walking upon the water? For to run upon the sea is foreign to the human nature, but it is not proper to the divine nature to use bodily feet. Therefore that action is of the incarnate Word, to whom belongs at the same time divine character and humanity indivisibly.

It is possible to see that those things which are contained in the Tome of Leo go clearly against these things, and I quote them: LEO: "For each one of the forms does what belongs to it; the Word doing what belongs to the Word, and the body fulfilling those things which belong to the body, and the one of them is radiant with wonders, but the other falls under insults".[27] For if each form or nature does those things which are its own, those (*Lebon p. 85*) things are of a bastard partnership and of a relationship of friendship, such as a master's taking on himself the things which are performed by a servant, or vice versa, a servant's being glorified with the outstanding possessions of a master, while those things which are not properties of human nature are ascribed to him out of a loving friendship. For he is a man clad with God, who in this way makes use of a power which is not his own, and is impelled by one who acts, like an inanimate instrument, perhaps a saw or an axe, which is used by a craftsman.

But Jesus is not like that, away with you! For he is seen using his own power as God inhominate, and he confirms this with utterances worthy of God. And to the sea he says, "Be quiet, be restrained"[28], and to Peter when he called out "Order me to come to you on the water", he orders "Come",[29] and to the leper "I am willing: be

ܠܡܬܩܡ ܐܘ ܢܦܩܗ. ܕܠܗ ܕܝܢ ܠܗ ܡܫܡܫ ܠܐ ܡܬܦܠܓܐܝܬ: ܕܐܝܬܘܗܝ ܘܡܢ ܐܫܬܪܝܠܗ ܒܥܫܢ. ܘܠܐܠܗܐ ܒܟܠܗܘܢ ܡܒܪܟܐ. ܘܐܦ ܠܗ ܕܝܢ ܠܗ ܡܫܡܫܐ ܡܛܠ ܕܐܬܒܥܝ. ܠܡܬܒܥܝܢܘܬܐ ܓܝܪ ܠܚܢܢ ܫܘܒܪܐ ܕܡܫܡܫܘܬܐ. ܘܠܗ ܕܝܢ ܠܗ ܕܠܐܪ̈ܥܘܗܝ ܡܫܡܫܝܢ ܐܝܟ ܠܗܐ ܗܘܐ. (84) ܕܡܢܐ ܕܝܢ ܠܗܠܝܢ ܫ̈ܒܩ ܩܠܐ: ܐܦ ܗܘ ܕܠܗ ܕܝܢ ܠܗ ܦܠܚܘܬܐ ܠܐܠܗܐ ܡܫܡܫܐ ܘܐܝܬܘܬܐ: ܗܘ ܕܦܪܘܩܢ ܐܡܪ ܠܟܠ ܡܘܬܐ ܕܠܒܪ. ܠܒܪ ܢܫܡܫ ܕܟܝܢ. ܐܠܐ ܐܪܓܝܓܐ ܕܐܒܪܗܘܢ. ܦܠܚ ܗܘ ܓܝܪ ܠܐܠܗܐ: ܠܗܘ ܕܐܪܟܐ ܢܦܫܗ ܡܫܡܫܢܐ ܗܘܐ ܒܥܒ̈ܕܐ ܘܕܟܪ ܘܫܢܝ ܠܫܘܒܚܐ: ܢܐܡܪ ܕܡܫܡܫ ܐܝܟ ܗܘ ܕܡܫܡܫ. ܘܡܫܡܫ ܒܥܒ̈ܕܐ ܡܘܬܐ ܠܥܡܠܐ: ܡܛܠ ܫܒܪܐ ܘܡܫܡܠܐ. ܐܝܟܢܐ ܕܝܢ ܗܘ ܕܢܐܡܪ ܕܐܪܓܝܓܐ ܘܡܫܡܫ ܐܢܐ ܠܗ. ܡܫܡܫ ܗܘܐ ܓܝܪ ܐܝܟ ܠܐܠܗܐ ܕܐܦ ܕܝܢ ܕܢܫܡܫ ܢܥܒܕ ܗܘܐ. ܐܠܐ ܚܒܠ ܠܐܪ̈ܥܘܗܝ. ܕܝܢ ܡܫܡܫ ܘܠܐ ܡܬܦܠܓܐ ܐܝܬܘܗܝ. ܗܘ ܚܕ ܘܗܘ ܕܝܢ ܗܘ ܒܪܐ ܘܡܫܡܠܐ. ܗܘ ܕܡܫܡܠܢ ܠܐ ܡܫܬܠܫܠܐܝܬ ܗܘܐ ܒܪܢܫܐ. ܗܘ ܕܦܠܚܘܬܐ ܠܐܠܗܐ ܘܐܝܬܝܗ ܡܫܡܠܝܐ. ܗܘܝܐ ܘܒܗܠܝܢ ܕܐܬܒܥܝ ܐܝܟ ܕܡܫܡܠܝܘܬܐ ܚܝܐ ܕܡܫܝܚܘܬܐ: ܗܘ ܕܦܠܚܘܬܐ ܠܐܠܗܐ ܐܚܝܕܐ ܘܐܝܬܝܗ. ܗܘ ܓܝܪ ܕܟܠ ܕܡܫܡܠܝܐ ܢܗܘܐ ܐܚܝܕܐ ܐܝܟ ܢܦܫܗ. ܕܚܝܐ ܓܝܪ ܐܝܬܝܗ ܡܬܕܒܪܢܘܬܐ ܗܝ ܗܝ ܕܢܦܘܩ ܟܠ ܡܕܡ. ܠܐ ܒܡܫܡܠܝܘܬܐ ܕܝܢ ܒܚܝܐ ܠܐܠܗܐ ܗܝ ܕܒ̈ܝܬܐ ܦܪ̈ܝܫܝܬܐ ܢܡܫܡܫ. ܡܢܝܢ ܐܦ ܕܡܫܡܠܝܐ ܗܘ ܕܐܬܒܥܝ ܐܝܬܝܗ ܗܘܐ ܡܫܬܡܠܝܢܝܬܐ. ܘܐܝܟ ܠܗ ܦܠܚܘܬܐ ܠܐܠܗܐ ܐܝܟ ܚܝܐ ܘܐܝܬܝܗ ܠܐ ܡܬܦܫܫܢܬܐ.

ܘܠܥܡܠܐ ܕܗܠܝܢ ܐܝܟ ܠܥܡܪܐ ܕܐܬܐ ܓܝܪ ܠܡܬܠܐ: ܗܢܘܢ ܕܫܡܥܝܢ ܠܡܫܡܥܬܐ ܕܠܘܬܝ. ܘܐܢܬܘܢ ܐܡܪ ܐܢܐ. *ܠܠܗܘܢ ܡܫܡܥܬܐ ܓܝܪ ܡܠܝܠ ܡܢ ܕܩܢܘܬܐ ܗܘ ܡܕܡ ܕܐܝܬܘܗܝ ܕܠܗ. ܕܝܢ ܡܫܡܠܐ ܡܢ ܡܬܡܠܐ ܗܘ ܕܐܬܝܗ ܕܡܫܡܠܐ: ܦܓܪܐ ܕܝܢ ܡܫܡܠܠܐ ܗܘܠܝܢ ܕܐܝܬܝܗܘܢ ܕܦܓܪܐ. ܘܗܘܐ ܡܢ ܡܫܡܥܝܢ ܡܡܠܠܝܢ ܠܡܫܡܥܬܐ: ܗܘܐ ܕܝܢ ܒܪ̈ܢܫܐ ܢܦܠܐ * ܐܝܟ ܓܝܪ ܡܠܝܠܐ ܡܢ ܕܩܢܘܬܐ ܐܘ ܩ̈ܢܝܢܐ: ܗܘ ܕܠܗ ܡܫܡܠܐ: ܗܘܝܘ (85) ܘܡܫܬܡܠܝܢ ܠܡܫܡܠܐ ܘܒܡܫܡܠܝܘܬܐ ܕܢܫܡܫܘܬܐ ܐܝܬܝܗܝܢ: ܐܝܟ ܡܢ ܕܢܫܡܠ ܒܠܗܘܢ ܡܪܐ ܗܠܝܢ ܕܡܢ ܒܥܒܕܐ ܡܬܡܠܝܢ: ܐܘ ܒܡܫܡܠܐ ܒܥܒܕܐ ܒܩܢܝܢܐ ܡܫܡܠܝܢܐ ܕܡܪܐ ܢܡܠܟ: ܕܝܢ ܡܫܡܠܢ ܒܠܗܘܢ ܡܛܠ ܕܢܫܡܫܘܬܐ ܡܫܡܠܝܢܐ: ܗܠܝܢ ܕܠܐ ܐܝܬܝܗܝܢ ܕܬܡܠܐ ܕܢܦܫܐ ܐܝܬܝܐ. ܐܝܟ ܓܝܪ ܒܪܢܫܐ ܒܫܡܝܐ ܠܐܠܗܐ ܗܘܐ ܕܐܝܟ ܗܘܢܐ ܒܫܠܡܐ ܢܒܪܢܐ ܡܬܡܫܡܫ. ܘܡܢ ܗܘ ܕܡܫܡܫ ܡܬܡܛܝܢ ܐܝܟ ܐܘܪܫܠܡ ܘܠܐ ܢܦܩܐ: ܡܫܡܪܐ ܐܘ ܒܡܠܐ ܐܘ ܠܓܒܗ: ܕܡܬܡܫܡܫ ܒܗ ܐܝܟ ܡܢ ܐܪܥܝܐ.

clean".[30] And he lays down the law with the authority of God and says "But I say to you, do not be angry",[31] and nowhere does he say "The Lord says this", "In the name of the Lord I do such and such things". These things (are so) even though, because it was suitable to the economy, and because of the contentiousness and the difficulty of the coming of the Jews towards God, and (because of) the imperfection otherwise of those who were hearing, in many places he says that he has received a commandment from the Father,[32] and that he speaks those things which he heard from him.[33] But yet, showing (his) royal and unenslaved condition and equality of honour towards the Father, he said that the Father too works likewise,[34] and that the Father is in him, and he is in the Father,[35] because .... ⟨3 folios missing⟩

⟨Therefore he who divides Emmanuel, and defines him in two natures (*Lebon* p. 86) after the inexpressible union, along with the natures divides the activities and properties as well⟩[36] and establishes two natures which act and without diminishment undergo those things which are their own. But he who confesses one nature incarnate of God the Word, and teaches an unconfused union, does not deny awareness of the difference and particularity which lies in natural quality of the natures from which there is the one Christ. But it is foolish and uninstructed to say that Emmanuel was composed from two properties[37] or two activities. For because "to think" is a property of a rational mind, but "blackness" or "whiteness" for example (is a property) of a body, do we say because of this that a man is composed from "thinking" and from "whiteness" or from "blackness"? But no reasonable person says this: but he says that man exists from the natures of body and soul, to which (natures) those (properties) which were mentioned adhere and (from which) they are seen not to exist in isolation. But apart from this, how is it not absurd to speak of two properties or two activities? For there are many properties and not just two, of each nature. For example, of his humanity there is perceptibility, and visibility, and mortality, and being subject to hunger and to thirst and to other things like it. And there are many properties of the divine nature: invisibility, intangibility, being before the ages, (*Lebon p. 87*) being unlimited. The things which are done are similarly many and various, and all these are as many as the human and divine actions that a man can recount.

Thus he who divides Emmanuel in a duality of natures after the inexpressible union, divides with him, as we have said many times, the activities and properties as well. For it is customary often to call the things which are done "activity" and sometimes to call even him

ܐܠܐ ܡܛܘܠ ܠܐ ܕܐܝܟ ܗܘܝܐ. ܚܝܠܐ ܠܟܘܠ. ܡܬܚܙܐ ܓܝܪ ܕܒܚܝܠܐ ܕܢܦܫܗ ܡܬܚܫܒ
ܐܝܟ ܐܠܗܐ ܕܐܬܒܪܢܫ. ܘܟܕ ܚܙܝܢ ܩ̈ܠܐ ܦܐܝܬ ܠܐܠܗܐ ܗܘܐ ܡܫܪܙ. ܘܠܫܒܚܐ ܦܡ
ܐܡܪ: ܗܢܘ ܓܝܪ ܐܠܗ. ܠܦܠܓܘܬܗ ܕܝܢ ܕܐܘܪܚܐ ܕܦܢܘܝ ܠܗ ܕܐܬܐ ܙܪܝܙܐܝܬ ܠܘܩܒܠ
ܩܢܝܐ: ܦܦܝ ܕܝܐ. ܘܡܬܓܪܓܝܢܐ: ܙܟܐ ܐܢܐ ܐܬܝܬܐ. ܘܗܝܡܢ ܢܦܫܗ ܒܡܠܟܘܬܐ ܕܐܠܗܐ
ܘܐܡܪ. ܐܢܐ ܕܝܢ ܐܡܪ ܐܢܐ ܠܟܘܢ ܕܠܐ ܬܬܙܝܥܘܢ. ܘܠܐ ܒܝܘܡ ܐܚܪ ܕܗܘܐ ܐܡܪ ܡܪܝܐ:
ܡܫܡܫܘ ܘܡܢܝܐ ܙܒܠ ܚܕܢ ܐܢܐ: ܘܗܘܠܝܢ ܒܝ ܠܗܒ ܡܛܠ ܗܢܐ ܕܦܬܐ ܠܡܕܒܪܢܘܬܐ.
ܘܡܛܠ ܠܬܘܕܝܬܐ ܘܡܫܡܫܘܬܐ ܡܠܐܟܐ ܕܫܘܪܝܐ ܕܟܘܠܐ ܕܐܠܗܐ: ܘܐܫܬܘܕܝܬ ܠܐ
ܡܫܡܫܢܘܬܐ ܕܗܘܠܝܢ ܕܡܫܡܫܝܢ: ܐܡܪ ܒܪܘܚܢܝܬܐ ܡܫܬܐܠܬܐ ܕܦܘܩܕܢܐ ܚܦܝܛ ܡܢ
ܐܒܐ: ܘܕܗܘܠܝܢ ܕܫܒܩܘ ܡܢܗ ܡܫܡܠܠ. ܘܒܙܒܢ ܒܗ ܡܢܗܘ ܗܘ ܡܫܠܡܢܘܬܐ ܘܠܐ
ܗܘܒܒܐ: ܘܡܫܡܫܢܐ ܐܡܪܐ ܕܟܘܠܐ ܐܒܐ: ܐܡܪ ܕܐܦ ܗܘ ܐܒܐ ܒܗ ܒܡܫܘܬܐ ܒܢ̈ܝ ܒܢ̈ܝܐ.
ܘܕܐܬܠܘܗ ܐܒܐ ܒܗ ܘܗܘ ܦܐܒܐ: ܡܛܠ ......
ܡܢ ܗܘ ܕܡܦܠܓ ܠܗ ܠܥܢܘܝܘܬܐ: ܘܠܐܬܪ ܚܬܝܢ (86) ܡܬܚܙܐ ܠܗ ܒܠܬ
ܚܝܘܬܐ ܠܐ ܡܬܡܠܠܝܢܬܐ: ܡܦܠܓ ܓܝܪ ܚܬܝܐ ܘܡܫܬܒܪܢܘܬܐ ܘܕܬܠܬܐ ܘܐܬܪ ܚܬܝܢ
ܗܠܝܢ ܕܡܫܒܚܝܢ: ܘܠܐ ܒܪܘܚܬܐ ܚܠܦ ܗܠܝܢ ܕܡܠܟܘܢ. ܗܘ ܕܝܢ ܕܚܕ ܚܝܠܐ ܕܡܫܬܐܪ
ܕܐܠܗܐ ܡܬܠܬܐ ܡܫܬܐ: ܘܚܝܘܬܐ ܠܐ ܒܬܠܬܐ ܦܠܓ ܠܐ ܦܦܪ ܒܗܘ ܕܒܚܕ ܗܘܫܟܐ
ܘܕܠܝܘܬܐ: ܗܘ ܕܐܝܟ ܕܒܡܫܘܕܥܘܬܐ ܚܝܠܬܐ ܕܚܬܝܐ ܕܡܢܗܘܢ ܚܕ ܡܫܚܠܐ. ܗܘ ܕܝܢ
ܕܐܡܪ ܕܡܢ ܬܐܪ ܕܬܠܬܐ ܐܘ ܬܐܪ ܡܫܬܒܪܢܘܬܐ ܐܬܦܠܓ ܒܥܢܘܝܘܬܐ: ܫܦܠܬܐ ܗܘ
ܘܠܐ ܦܪܝܫܬܐ. ܐܦܐ ܓܝܪ ܡܛܠ ܕܗܘ ܕܐܬܚܙܝ ܕܡܠܬܐ ܗܘ ܕܢܦܫܐ ܡܬܠܬܬܐ:
ܕܓܫܡܐ ܕܝܢ ܐܘܫܡܘܬܐ ܐܘ ܚܘܪܘܬܐ ܐܝ ܬܓܒܗ: ܡܛܠ ܗܘܐ ܐܡܪܝܢ ܠܒܪܢܫܐ:
ܕܡܢ ܗܘ ܕܐܬܚܙܝ ܘܡܢ ܚܘܪܘܬܐ ܡܪܟܒ: ܐܘ ܡܢ ܐܘܫܡܘܬܐ: ܐܠܐ ܘܠܐ ܐܝܟ ܕܐܝܬ
ܠܗ ܗܘܝܐ ܐܡܪ ܗܘܐ. ܐܠܐ ܡܢܗܘܢ ܕܒܢ̈ܝܐ ܡܢ ܓܫܡܐ ܘܢܦܫܐ ܐܡܪ ܕܡܬܦܫܩ ܒܪܢܫܐ.
ܠܐܠܝܢ ܕܗܠܝܢ ܕܐܡܬܝ ܢܦܩ ܘܦܠܓܝܢ: ܘܐܚܕܐ ܠܐ ܡܦܪܫܬܐ ܡܢܗܝܢ. ܐܫܬܘܕܝܬ
ܕܝܢ. ܐܡܬܝ ܠܐ ܓܫܡܐ ܗܘ ܕܐܡܪ ܬܐܪ ܕܬܠܬܐ ܐܘ ܬܐܪ ܡܫܬܒܪܢܘܬܐ. ܚܝܘܬܐ
ܓܝܪ ܐܬܚܙܝ ܕܬܠܬܐ ܕܟܠ ܚܝܐ: ܘܠܗ ܬܐܪ ܒܢܦܫܗ. ܕܐܝܟ ܐܡܪ. ܕܐܝܬܘܗܝ
ܡܬܓܫܡܢܘܬܐ: ܘܡܬܚܝܢܘܬܐ ܘܡܫܘܕܥܢܘܬܐ. ܘܗܘ ܕܐܬܐ ܡܫܡܫܐ ܠܢܦܫܐ ܘܠܓܘܫܡܐ
ܘܠܗܠܝܢ ܐܬܚܝܠܬܐ ܒܗ ܒܪܝܘܬܐ. ܘܒܚܝܠܐ ܕܝܢ ܕܐܠܗܐ ܚܝܘܬܐ ܕܬܠܬܐ: ܠܐ
ܡܬܚܝܢܘܬܐ: ܠܐ ܡܬܓܫܡܢܘܬܐ: ܗܘ ܕܡܢ ܩܕܡ (87) ܒܟܠܗܝܢ: ܠܐ ܡܫܬܘܕܥܢܘܬܐ. ܒܗ

who acts "activity" because activity is, properly speaking, as we have shown in the things said above, itself an active movement. Hence Julius the Theologian too, who was Bishop of Rome, in the Treatise designated "Against those who contend against the divine incarnation of the Word on the pretext of the ὁμοούσιον",[38, 39] says this: (JULIUS): "But there is one nature, one hypostasis, one activity, one person, entirely God, entirely man, the same".[40] For because there is one who acts, both his activity and the active motion are one. But as we have said, the things which are done are many and diverse, but we who recognise one nature of God the Word incarnate say that these belong to one and the same, even if some are proper to God and some more human, just as we also believe the utterances proper to God and human were said by one and the same (person). (*Lebon p. 88*)

But those who divide (Emmanuel) by speaking of two natures after the union, divide with them also those things which, as properties, each one of the natures naturally attracts.

But let it not escape your notice that holy Julius, when he confesses one nature incarnate of God the Word, confesses that he also recognises the properties of the natures from which the one Christ is, and the difference between them, while rejecting division. For he wrote this in the same Treatise: (JULIUS): "For the body, and God whose is the body, are one and the same, without the flesh having been changed to what is not bodily, but possessing both what is its own, which is from us by the birth from the Virgin, and that which is above us, by the mixture or union of God the Word".[41] And again, in the Treatise designated "About the union of the body with the divinity of God the Word", he says as follows: (JULIUS): "But it is confessed that in him the created (being) is in union with the uncreated, and the uncreated in combination[42] with the created, while one nature is established from the two parts".[43] AND AFTER OTHER THINGS, "Hence necessarily, it is called both corporeal in everything and divine in everything. And he who is unable in these diverse things which are united to recognise what belongs to each of them, falls away into contradictions which do not agree, but he who both recognises the properties and preserves the union, neither defrauds the natures,[44] nor is forgetful of the union."[45] You see how he said he acknowledges the properties of the natures, and preserves the union, one nature existing from the two parts.

But regarding that thing which your Chastity said, that because (*Lebon p. 89*) the way of our Saviour's birth in the flesh was different from ours—for (he was born) from the Virgin and the Holy Spirit—

ܒܝܘܡܬܐ ܘܗܠܝܢ ܕܩܕܡܝܢ: ܡܫܝ̈ܚܝܬܐ ܘܡܫܝܚܝܘܬܐ. ܘܟܠܗܘܢ ܗܠܝܢ: ܟܠܗ ܕܐܡܪ ܐܢܐ ܕܐܝܬ ܡܫܘܕܥܢܘܬܐ ܐܢܫܝܬܐ ܘܐܠܗܝܬܐ.

ܗܘ ܗܟܝܠ ܕܦܠܓܝܢ ܠܡܫܘܐܠܐ ܠܐܘܪܚܐ ܟܝ̈ܢܐ ܥܠܡ ܚܝܘܬܐ ܠܐ ܡܬܦܪܫܢܝܬܐ: ܦܠܓܝ ܠܗܘܢ ܐܝܟ ܡܐ ܕܐܟ̈ܝܢ ܡܫܝ̈ܚܐ ܐܡܪܝܢ: ܘܡܬܚ̈ܝܕܘܬܐ ܘܟܝ̈ܢܝܬܐ. ܚܕܐ ܗܘ ܓܝܪ ܕܗܠܝܢ ܕܩܕܡܝܢ، ܐܘ ܡܬܚܝܕܘܬܐ ܢܦܫܐ ܕܟ̈ܝܢܐ ܡܫܝ̈ܚܐ. ܐܝܟ ܕܝܢ ܐܡܪܢ ܕܐܦ ܠܗ ܠܒܪܗ ܕܡܬܚܕ ܢܦܫܐ ܡܬܚܝܕܘܬܐ. ܡܛܠ ܕܡܬܚܝܕܘܬܐ ܡܦܪܫܐ ܐܝܬܝܗ: ܐܝܟܢܐ ܕܒܗܠܝܢ ܕܩܕܡ ܐܬܐܡܪ ܡܘܕܝܢ: ܗܘ ܕܝܢ ܡܬܚܕܢܐ. ܡܢ ܗܕܐ ܘܡܘܠܡܘܣ ܡܫܡܠܝܐ ܠܐܠܗܘܬܐ: ܗܘ ܕܗܘܐ ܐܦܣܩܦܐ ܕܪܗܘܡܐ: ܒܡܐܡܪܐ ܕܪܫܝܡ ܠܘܬ ܦܠܘ، ܘܡܠܬܠܬܝܢ ܠܘܩܒܠ ܡܬܚܒܪܢܘܬܐ ܠܐܠܗܘܬܐ ܘܡܠܬܐ: ܒܝܕ ܡܠܬܐ ܕܒܪ ܟܝܢܐ: ܗܘܐ ܐܡܪ. ܘܡܛܠܗܕܐ܀ ܐܠܐ ܐܬܠܘܗܝ ܚܕ ܟܝܢܐ. ܚܕ ܩܢܘܡܐ. ܚܕܐ ܡܬܚܝܕܘܬܐ. ܚܕ ܦܪܨܘܦܐ. ܡܠܗ ܠܐܠܗܐ. ܡܠܗ ܒܪܢܫܐ. ܗܘ ܟܕ ܗܘܐ܀ ܡܛܠ ܓܝܪ ܕܚܕ ܗܘ ܗܘ ܕܡܬܒܪ. ܚܕܐ ܐܝܬܝܗ ܐܦ ܡܬܚܝܕܘܬܗ. ܘܗܕܐ ܡܬܚܝܕܐ. ܗܠܝܢ ܕܝܢ ܕܩܕܡܝܢ ܐܝܟ ܡܐ ܕܐܡܪܢ: ܡܫܝ̈ܚܝܬܐ ܘܡܫܝܚܝܘܬܐ. ܠܗܠܝܢ ܕܝܢ: ܐܠܝܢ ܕܚܕܝܢ ܚܕ ܟܝܢܐ ܕܐܠܗܐ ܡܠܬܐ ܕܡܬܒܪ. ܘܚܕ ܩܢܘܡܗ ܟܕ ܕܡܠܗ ܐܡܪܝܢ ܕܐܬܐܡܪ. ܐܦ ܗܠܝܢ ܦܝ ܐܬܐܡܪ ܦܐܝܬ ܠܐܠܗܐ. ܗܠܝܢ ܕܝܢ ܐܢܫܝܬܐ: ܐܝܟ ܡܐ ܘܐܦ ܟܝ̈ܢܐ ܩܠܐ ܦܐܝܬ ܠܐܠܗܐ ܘܐܢܫܝܬܐ: ܘܡܢ ܚܕ ܘܗܘ ܟܕ (88) ܗܘ ܐܬܐܡܪ ܡܬܚܫܒܝܢ. ܗܠܝܢ ܕܝܢ ܕܡܫܠܡܝܢ: ܠܗܘ ܕܐܡܪܝܢ ܬܪܝܢ ܟܝ̈ܢܝܢ ܥܠܡ ܚܝܘܬܐ: ܡܫܠܡܝܢ ܒܗܘܢ، ܘܗܝ: ܐܠܝܢ ܕܐܝܟ ܕܟܝ̈ܢܝܬܐ ܚܝܠܗ ܡܠܝܢ ܡܢ ܟܝ̈ܢܐ ܬܪ̈ܝܢ: ܠܐ ܕܝܢ ܠܡܐܡܪ ܕܗܘ ܚܕ ܩܢܘܡܐ ܡܛܠܗܕܐ ܟܕ ܚܕ ܟܝܢܐ ܡܬܒܪܐ ܘܡܠܬܐ ܠܐܠܗܐ ܡܬܒܪܐ: ܡܬܒܪܐ ܕܒܝܕ ܐܦ ܕܟܝ̈ܢܝܬܐ ܕܟܝ̈ܢܐ ܕܩܢܘܡܗ، ܚܕ ܩܢܘܡܐ: ܘܡܫܘܚܠܦܐ ܕܗܠܝܢ: ܟܕ ܘܢܦܫ ܦܠܓܘܬܐ. ܐܝܟ ܓܝܪ ܠܗ ܟܕ ܠܗ ܒܡܐܡܪܐ ܗܠܝܢ. ܘܡܛܠܗܕܐ܀ ܚܕ ܓܝܪ ܘܗܘ ܟܕ ܗܘ ܦܠܓܐ ܘܐܠܗܐ ܘܕܡܠܗ ܦܠܓܐ. ܠܗ ܐܝܟ ܡܐ ܕܐܬܘܕܥ ܒܡܐܡܪܐ ܠܠܐ ܦܠܓܘܬܐ. ܐܠܐ ܟܕ ܐܝܬ ܠܗ ܘܡܠܬܐ ܗܘ ܕܡܢ: ܐܝܟ ܡܠܒܘܫܬܐ ܘܡܢ ܠܒܘܫܬܐ: ܗܘ ܕܠܟܠ ܡܢ: ܐܝܟ ܡܕܘܪܐ ܕܡܠܬܐ ܠܐܠܗܐ ܐܘ ܚܝܘܬܐ܀ ܘܐܦ ܒܡܐܡܪܐ ܕܪܫܝܡ: ܡܛܠ ܚܝܘܬܐ ܕܦܓܪܐ ܠܘܬ ܠܐܠܗܘܬܐ ܕܐܠܗܐ ܡܠܬܐ. ܗܠܝܢ ܐܡܪ. ܘܡܛܠܗܕܐ܀ ܡܬܐܡܪܐ ܠܗ ܕܝܢ: ܕܗܘܐ ܦܝ ܐܬܠܘܗܝ ܒܪܢܫܐ: ܒܚܝܘܬܐ ܕܠܐ ܒܪܢܫܐ. ܗܘܐ ܕܝܢ ܠܐ ܒܪܢܫܐ: ܒܚܫܝܫܘܬܐ ܕܐܢܫܐ ܕܒܪܢܫܐ. ܟܕ ܚܕ ܟܝܢܐ ܡܢ ܬܪ̈ܬܝܗܘܢ ܩ̈ܢܘܡܐ ܡܬܦܠܓܝܢ܀ ܘܟܠܡ ܐܢܫܝܬܐ܀ ܡܢ ܗܕܐ ܡܢ ܐܢܫܐ: ܗܘ ܠܡܫܝܚܐ

it was right that not even the properties of humanity should be seen as regards him, it is advantageous that we should introduce for you the words of wise Basil, which are written in the Treatise which we have mentioned, against Eunomius. For when that man had said that because the Father does not exist by birth, but the Son by birth, and the Spirit by procession, the ousia should also be divided, along with the difference of being of each hypostasis, that man learned in the Spirit and wise, in disposing of the objection says as follows: (BASIL): "If those things, which have the existence of what they are in different ways, have different ousia as well, not even men are alike[46] in ousia. For Adam, who was fashioned from the earth, had one existence, but Eve another, from his side, and Abel another, from copulation, and another had he who was from Mary, for he was only from a virgin."[47] Therefore, if they have the same ousia, both he who was fashioned from the earth, and she who was cut out from the rib, and he who came forth from the conjunction of a man and a woman, and he who was born in the flesh from a virgin, how does it not follow to think the properties of the ousia also appear in the same way on each one of them? But in this instance, because the Word of God had been hypostatically united to flesh which was rationally ensouled, from Mary who bore God, the Word was not allotting to his (own) flesh to suffer everything which belonged to it. But we say they "belonged to it" not so that we may distinguish the Word, for those things which we say the flesh suffers, (*Lebon p. 90*) are the sufferings of the incarnate Word, while his divinity does not lose impassibility. For to whom we say the flesh belongs, to this same (person) we reckon the sufferings of the flesh belong completely. For he does not, because the conception and birth from the Virgin is a wonder, therefore renounce in everything the human laws of nature. For Gregory the Theologian also says this in the Letter to Cledonius: (GREGORY): "If a man says that (Christ) flowed in the Virgin as through a pipe, but not that in her he was formed at the same time in a human and a divine way—in a divine way (because) without a man, and in a human way because in the law of conception—he is like an atheist".[48] And holy Cyril, in the Treatise of question and answer *That Christ is One* says: (CYRIL): "Nor would he have been a curse, when he suffered the cross on our behalf, unless he had become flesh, that is, he became flesh and was inhominate, and underwent a birth like us for our sake, humanly, that (birth) I say, which (took place) through the holy Virgin".[49]

Therefore when you hear that the conception of Emmanuel took place in a divine way and at the same time in a human way, how do

ܟܠ ܟܠܗ. ܘܗܘ ܠܐܠܗܘܬܐ ܟܠ ܟܠܗ ܠܐܬܐܡܪ. ܘܗܘ ܕܠܐ ܡܬܡܫܚ ܒܡܫܘܚܬܐ ܗܠܝܢ ܕܡܫܚܝܢ ܒܪܘܚ ܕܡܠܝܘܬܐ ܘܡܫܚܝܢ ܡܢܗܘܢ: ܒܡܫܘܚܬܐ ܘܠܐ ܩܠܝܠ ܢܦܠ. ܗܘ ܕܝܢ ܕܐܦ ܕܡܠܝܘܬܐ ܚܕܐ: ܘܡܫܘܚܬܐ ܢܛܪ: ܘܠܐ ܠܒ̈ܢܝܐ ܡܢܝ: ܘܠܐ ܠܡܫܘܚܬܐ ܠܗܠܝܢ܀ ܡܢܐ ܐܝܟ ܐܡܝܢܐ ܐܡܪ ܕܕܡܫܘܚܬܐ ܕܒܢ̈ܝܐ ܢܗܪ: ܘܡܫܘܚܬܐ ܢܛܪ: ܟܕ ܚܝܠܐ ܚܕ ܗܘ ܐܬܘܬܗܘܢ ܩܢܘ̈ܡܐ ܡܬܡܫܚܝܢ.

ܟܠܗ ܗܘ ܕܝܢ ܕܐܡܪܢܐ ܒܡܫܘܚܬܐ: ܕܡܛܠ ܕܡܫܘܚܬܐ (89) ܐܠܗܘܬܗ ܗܘܐ ܐܝܟ ܘܟܠܝ ܙܠܐ ܘܡܫܘܚܬܐ ܕܒܫܪ ܘܦܪܨܘܦ: ܡܢ ܟܠܗܘܢܐ ܟܡܢ ܘܫܘܝܐ ܡܫܘܚܬܐ. ܡܛܠܗܕܐ ܓܝܪ ܗܘܐ ܕܐܦ ܠܐ ܕܬܚܘܡܐ ܘܐܝܬܘܬܐ ܢܡܬܚܝܢ ܒܟܠܗ. ܡܫܘܚܬܐ ܕܡܠܝܐ ܟܠ ܠܡܦܠܓܬܐ: ܒܟܠ ܩܠܐ ܕܡܫܘܚܬܐ ܒܡܫܘܚܬܗܘܢ. ܕܠܐܬܝܢ ܒܡܐܡܪܐ ܗܘ ܕܐܬܐܡܪܘ ܘܟܠܐ ܐܘܢܝܬܗ. ܟܕ ܓܝܪ ܗܘ ܐܡܪ ܗܘܐ: ܕܡܛܠ ܕܐܦܠܐ ܡܬܚܙܝܐ ܐܠܗܘܬܗ: ܘܒܪܐ ܡܬܚܙܝܐ: ܘܫܘܝܐ ܢܦܩܐܝܬ: ܙܘܥ ܕܒܗ ܡܫܘܚܬܐ ܕܐܝܬܐ ܘܕܟܠ ܣܘܦܐ: ܠܐܦܢܝ ܐܦ ܐܘܣܝܐ. ܟܕ ܗܢܐ ܠܡܫܘܚܬܐ ܗܘ ܡܬܚܠܦܐ ܕܙܘܥ ܘܡܫܘܚܬܐ ܗܘܝܐ ܐܡܪ. ܀ܒܡܫܘܚܬܗ܀ ܐܢ ܗܘܝ ܕܡܫܘܚܬܐܝܬ ܐܝܬ ܠܗܘܢ ܡܠܐ ܕܗܘ ܕܐܠܗܘܬܗܘܢ: ܡܫܘܚܬܐ ܐܦ ܐܘܣܝܐ ܐܝܬ ܠܗܘܢ. ܐܦܠܐ ܒܟܝܢܐ ܕܩܢܘܡ ܐܘܣܝܐ ܐܠܗܘܬܗܘܢ. ܐܡܪܬܐ ܗܝ ܓܝܪ ܡܠܬܐ ܕܐܡܪ ܕܡܢ ܐܘܟܠ ܐܬܚܫܒܬ: ܐܡܪܬܐ ܕܝܢ ܚܕܐ ܕܡܢ ܟܠܟܠ ܙܘܥܐ: ܐܡܪܬܐ ܕܝܢ ܕܡܫܘܚܬܐ. ܡܢ ܙܘܥܐ ܓܝܪ: ܐܡܪܬܐ ܕܝܢ ܕܗܘ ܕܡܢ ܡܢܝܢ. ܡܢ ܟܠܗܘܢܐ ܓܝܪ ܟܠܡܕܡ܀ ܡܢܝܢ ܗܘܟܢܐ ܗܘ ܕܗܘ ܟܕ ܗܘ ܐܘܣܝܐ ܐܝܬ ܠܗ: ܘܠܗܘ ܕܐܬܦܠܓ ܡܢ ܐܘܟܠ: ܘܠܗܘ ܕܐܬܦܫܛ ܡܢ ܟܠܟܠ: ܘܠܗܘ ܕܡܢ ܢܦܫܬܐ ܕܐܦܠܐ ܕܐܝܬܬܐ ܘܙܘܥܐ ܢܦܫ: ܘܗܘ ܕܡܢ ܟܠܗܘܢܐ ܒܗܘܢ ܐܬܡܫܚ: ܐܡܝܢܐ ܠܐ ܢܦܩܐ ܕܠܡܫܘܚܬܐ: ܕܐܦ ܕܬܚܘܡܐ ܘܐܘܣܝܐ: ܟܠ ܟܠ ܚܕ ܡܢܗܘܢ ܒܗ ܒܢܝܐ ܡܫܘܚܬܢܝܐ. ܒܪܡ ܕܝܢ ܗܘܝܐ. ܡܛܠ ܕܡܫܘܚܬܐ ܘܐܠܗܐ ܡܫܝܚ ܗܘܐ ܡܬܡܫܚܢܐ ܠܒܣܪܐ ܗܘ ܕܡܢ ܡܟܝܠ ܐܠܗܐ ܡܢܝܢ: ܕܡܬܡܫܚܢܘܬܗ ܡܬܚܫܚ ܗܘܐ: ܠܗ ܡܠܘܢ ܢܗܘܐ ܗܘܐ ܡܫܝܚܐ ܠܒܣܪܗ: ܕܚܣܢ ܗܠܝܢ ܕܡܠܗ. ܘܡܠܗ ܕܝܢ ܐܡܪܝܢ: ܠܗ ܡܛܠ ܕܡܫܝܚܐ ܢܦܩܐ: ܗܠܝܢ ܓܝܪ ܕܐܡܪܝܢ ܕܡܫܚܐ ܒܣܪܐ. ܗܠܝܢ (90) ܚܝܠܐ ܕܡܫܝܚܐ ܘܐܬܒܣܪ ܐܠܗܘܬܗ: ܟܕ ܠܐܠܗܘܬܗ ܠܐ ܡܫܚܐ ܟܠܠ ܡܫܘܚܬܐ. ܘܗܘ ܓܝܪ ܕܒܣܪܐ ܘܡܠܗ ܐܡܪܝܢ: ܘܡܠܗ ܕܗܘܐ ܡܢ ܡܠܦܢܘܬܗ ܘܚܝܠܐ ܕܒܣܪܐ ܡܫܚܝܢ. ܠܗ ܓܝܪ ܡܛܠ ܕܐܘܣܝܘܬܐ ܗܘ ܒܚܝܠܐ ܘܡܠܝܐ ܗܘ ܕܡܢ ܟܠܗܘܢܐ: ܡܛܠ ܗܘܐ ܒܟܠܡܕܡ ܒܢܩܘܫܐ ܐܢܫܐ ܕܡܠܐ ܦܘܪ. ܗܘܐ ܓܝܪ ܘܦܪܨܘܦܘܗܝ ܡܫܘܚܬܐ ܠܐܠܗܘܬܐ

you completely remove him from human properties, which the incarnate Word receives willingly? For unless we say the flesh was capable of receiving the things which belonged to it, with the exception of sin—for this is not a part of the ousia, but a sickness which, as I have said, occurs as a result of inattention—he was able neither to suffer the cross on our behalf nor to endure death. But it is well known that he was undergoing these things in that of which it was the nature to suffer. And he who was incarnate is also he who suffered (*Lebon p. 91*) in the flesh, while he remained, in that he is God, impassible. And if we separate him from our statement that he suffered, we separate him as well, at an earlier point, from the flesh in which he willingly underwent suffering. For because of this the ark was prepared from wood which would not rot, and outside and inside it was smeared over with gold, because gold as a type represented (the) divinity, and the wood (the humanity), so that we see one Christ prefigured from the two of them.[50] And in the same way as the wood does not rot, neither does it sustain corruption from worm or maybe from moth, but it allows the cutting of iron and the burning of fire; so too the humanity which the Word of God united hypostatically to himself did not endure the corruption from sin, which corrupts like (the corruption) from moth and worm. For it was not able to be downtrodden as far as sinning is concerned, but it was capable of receiving the cutting of iron and other torments, since the incarnate Word allowed that it should suffer this when he wished. In this it is said that he was scourged, and pierced by the nails, and died in the flesh, and underwent burial, even though by the resurrection he was seen to be above these things, and he was not left in Sheol, nor did his flesh see corruption.

But that the teachings of the God-clad Fathers agree with these things, hear again the quotation, which is inspired by God, of Cyril, who says as follows in the Treatise of Address to the God-fearing emperor Theodosius: "Is it not then already known—for it is not unknown to anyone at all—that the Only-Begotten became like us, that is, fully man, in order that he might set free our earthly body from intrusive corruption, imparting his own life to it, in the economy through the union. (*Lebon p. 92*)

But he made the human soul his own that he might show it superior to sin, and he imparted to it the firmness and unchangeableness of his own nature, as dye in a fleece. For I think words about these things which far surpass what is not to be seen require examples; for we see with difficulty the divine and mind-transcending mysteries in a mirror and in riddles.[51] But as I think, the matter was not 'not to

ܠܓܒܪܐ ܕܟܠܐ ܦܠܛܘܢܝܩܘܣ ܐܡܪ. ܓܪܝܓܘܪܝܘܣ܀ ܐܘ ܐܝܟ ܐܝܟ ܕܝܢ ܫܡܠܝܘܬܐ ܐܡܪ ܕܢܘܬܝܢ ܒܡܠܘܟܠܐ: ܐܠܐ ܠܗ ܘܡܢܗ ܐܬܓܠܝ ܠܐܠܗܐ ܐܚܪ̈ܢܐ ܘܐܢܫܝܢ: ܠܐܠܗܐ ܕܝܢ ܕܫܦܝܪ ܡܢ ܓܒܪܐ: ܐܢܫܐ ܕܝܢ ܕܒܢܝܢܫܐ ܘܟܠܗ: ܒܗ ܒܢܦܫܗ ܘܠܐ ܠܟܠܗ ܐܠܗܘܬܗ܀ ܘܦܪܝܫܐ ܕܝܢ ܦܘܪܝܠܘܣ: ܒܥܡܪܐ ܕܗܘܬܐ ܘܦܘܣ ܦܠܓܘܬܐ ܘܚܕ ܗܘ ܡܫܝܚܐ ܐܡܪ. ܦܘܪܝܠܘܣ܀ ܐܦܠܐ ܗ̇ܘܐ ܗܘܐ ܠܗܠܝܢ ܒܟܝܢܐ ܚܕ: ܗ̇ܘ ܕܡܫܝܚܐ. ܠܗ ܠܐ ܕܗܘܐ ܒܣܪܐ. ܗܘ ܕܝܢ ܕܐܬܒܣܪ ܘܐܬܒܪܢܫ: ܘܡܬܝܕܥܐ ܘܐܚܪܢܐ ܡܫܝܚܐ ܦܘܠܐ ܐܢܫܐ ܫܒܩ: ܗ̇ܘ ܕܟܕ ܒܠܚܘܕܘܬܐ ܦܪܝܫܬܐ ܐܡܪ ܐܢܐ܀

ܒܝ ܡܫܟܚ ܐܝܟ ܗܒܠ ܘܠܐܠܗܐ ܐܚܪܢܐ ܘܐܢܫܐ ܕܗܘܐ ܟܠܗ ܕܒܫܘܬܦܘܬܐ. ܐܝܟܢܐ ܦܫܝܩ ܐܝܟ ܠܗ ܒܡܫܟܚܢܘܬ ܡܢ ܘܕܝܠܝܬܐ ܐܢܫܝܬܐ: ܗܠܝܢ ܕܒܝ ܟܠܐ ܕܗܘ ܡܫܝܚܐ ܗܘ ܘܐܬܒܣܪ ܡܠܬܐ. ܐܠܐ ܓܝܪ ܢܐܡܪ ܕܡܫܝܚܐ ܗܘ ܒܣܪܐ ܕܗܠܝܢ ܕܡܠܗ ܫܦܝܪ ܡܢ ܣܘܟܠܐ: ܗܘܐ ܓܝܪ ܠܗ ܡܫܝܚܐ ܗܘ ܘܐܠܗܐ: ܐܠܐ ܗ̇ܘ ܕܐܡܪܝܢ ܒܦܘܪܫܐ ܕܟܝܢܐ ܡܢ ܠܐ ܚܠܘܬܐ: ܐܦܠܐ ܕܚܕ ܟܝܢܐ ܕܚܠܦ ܡܢܗܘܢ ܗܘܐ. ܘܠܐ ܕܢܗܘܐ ܢܫܬܘܬܦ. ܐܠܐ ܫܦܝܪ ܚܠܦܐ: ܕܟܠܗ ܕܡܢ ܠܚܘܕ ܡܫܟܚ ܗܘܐ ܗܟܢ. ܘܗܘ ܕܐܬܒܣܪ ܗܘ ܐܠܗܘܬܗ ܗܘ ܕܐܦ ܚܕ (91) ܒܒܣܪ ܟܕ ܗܘܝ ܒܗ̇ ܘܐܠܗܘܬܗ ܠܟܠܗ ܠܐ ܚܫܘܫܐ. ܘܐܦ ܗܘ ܕܡܢ ܗܘ ܕܢܐܡܪ ܕܚܕ ܒܒܪܢܫܘܬܗ: ܦܪܝܫܝܢ ܚܕ ܡܬܒܪܝܢ ܠܗ ܘܡܢ ܒܣܪܐ ܘܒܗ ܒܝ ܟܠܐ ܡܟܠܠ ܚܫܐ. ܡܛܠ ܗܘܐ ܓܝܪ ܘܡܘܬܐ ܡܢ ܡܝ̈ܬܐ ܠܐ ܡܬܟܠܝܐ ܡܬܚܙܝܐ ܗܘܐ. ܘܡܢ ܠܒܪ ܘܡܢ ܓܘ ܡܫܝܚܐ ܗܘܐ ܒܪܘܚܐ. ܘܗܘܝܐ ܕܝܢ ܠܦܘܫܠܗ ܕܚܕ ܗܘܐ ܠܐܠܗܘܬܐ. ܩ̈ܢܘܡܐ ܕܝܢ ܐܢܫܝܐ. ܐܝܟܢܐ ܕܡܢ ܠܐܕܪ̈ܐܘܗܝ ܕܝܢ ܡܫܝܚܐ ܦܪܝܫ ܡܬܚܙܐ ܗܘܐ. ܘܐܝܟܢܐ ܘܐܚܪܢܐ ܕܒܣܪܐ ܠܐ ܡܬܟܠܝܐ: ܡܛܠ ܓܝܪ ܕܡܢ ܠܘܬܐ ܘܡܢ ܫܦܝܪ ܐܘ ܠܐܓܝܪ ܠܐ ܫܟܠ: ܠܫܦܝܪܐ ܕܝܢ ܗܘ ܕܡܢ ܦܪ̈ܝܫܐ ܦܫܩ: ܘܡܬܒܣܪܐ ܕܡܢ ܢܘܪܐ: ܗܟܢܐ ܘܐܝܬܘܗܝ ܗܘ ܕܝܢ ܠܗ ܡܬܦܫܩܢܐ ܡܬܚܙܐ ܕܠܐܠܗܐ: ܠܚܫܐ ܓܝܪ ܕܡܢ ܡܬܚܙܝܢܐ ܘܐܝܟ ܕܡܢ ܫܦܝܪ ܘܐܝܟܢܐ ܡܫܬܟܚ ܠܐ ܡܬܦܠܓ. ܐܝܟܢܐ ܗܘܐ ܓܝܪ ܠܐ ܡܬܦܪܫܢܘܬܐ ܠܟܠܗ ܘܐܝܟܢܐ. ܘܦܫܝܩܐ ܕܝܢ ܕܡܢ ܦܢܝܬܐ ܘܡܢ ܚܕܬܐ ܐܢܫܝܐ ܡܫܬܟܚܢܘܬܐ ܐܝܟܢܐ ܗܘܐ. ܟܕ ܡܠܬܐ ܕܐܬܒܣܪ ܗܘܐ ܘܐܢܫ ܚܕܝܢ ܗܘܐ ܐܝܟܢܐ ܕܒܪܐ ܗܘܐ. ܒܗܘܐ ܘܐܬܓܠܝ ܡܬܐܡܪ ܘܐܬܚܙܝ ܒܬܪ̈ܐ: ܘܡܫܝܚܐ ܒܒܣܪ: ܘܐܬܓܠܝ ܠܗ ܡܫܘܕܥܐ. ܐܦ ܗܘ ܕܡܫܝܚ ܘܗܠܝܢ ܐܠܗܝܐ ܘܡܟܝܠ ܟܕ ܡܫܝܚܐ: ܘܠܐ ܐܬܚܠܦ ܒܝܫܘܬܐ ܘܠܐ ܒܫܪܪܗ ܚܕ ܡܛܠ.

be seen', for it supplies in it a consideration which is probable, or rather, valid. For just as (the flesh), because it became the flesh of the Word who gives life to all, was above the grasp of death and corruption, in the same way, I think, (the soul) because it became the soul of him who knew not how to sin, possessed an established and unchanging position in all good things, and became incomparably more powerful than the sin which once opposed us. For Christ (was) the first man on earth who 'did no sin, nor was deceit found in his mouth'."[52,53] AND AGAIN AFTER A LITTLE, "But it is marvellous and there is no-one at all to whom it is not stupifying, that a body, which is corruptible by nature, should revive; for it belonged to the incorruptible Word. And again the soul, having obtained a combination like this [with him][54] and union, descended into Sheol using the power and authority appropriate to God, and appeared to the spirits there."[55] And again he seals up the things said in the Treatise by adding this: AND AGAIN: "(There is) one Lord Jesus Christ, and through him the Father created everything. Therefore he is both Creator as God, and Life-giver as life, and he is composed so as to become one in the middle from human properties and from those which are above man.[56] For he is mediator between God and men, according to the scriptures: for he is God by nature (*Lebon p. 93*) and not without flesh; while truly man, and not mere (man) like us, but he is he whom he was, even though he became flesh. For it is written 'Jesus Christ, yesterday and today, the same for ever'."[57] And that (which is written) in the prophet Isaiah, "And we saw him, that he had neither form nor beauty, but his appearance was not honourable but inferior to men"[58] makes known the greatness of the contempt and insult which came upon him when he was tested. And he was beaten upon his cheeks blows which were utterly shameful, and he did not turn away his face from the disgrace of spitting, but he endured the cross and disregarded the shame, as the Apostle said. For he brought no rejection of the flesh or change or transformation of the human ousia: for it belonged to Christ in this too that he should overcome more than men. And he did not open his mouth, but he came to slaughter without an utterance like a lamb. And he endured everything humbly and with supreme long-suffering:— all this while he was God by nature and knowing no sin, even if he was, the same, man in truth. Greatest of all, (the fact) that his glory also effects the size of the disgrace, means that no man from among men who suffered shall ever be compared to him.

Your Chastity therefore being aware of these things and guided by the teachings of these former teachers of the mysteries in the Church,

ܕܩܠܝܠ ܕܝܢ ܠܗܠܝܢ: ܐܦ ܡ̈ܫܡܫܢܘܬܐ ܘܐܚ̈ܘܬܐ ܠܒܢ̈ܝܫ ܠܐܠܗܐ. ܡܫܝܚ ܓܝܪ ܠܒܪܢܫܐ
ܡܠܐ ܢܦܫܗ ܡܢ ܐܠܗܐ ܕܡܬܘܕܥܘܗܝ. ܘܒܡܐܡܪܐ ܦܪܘܣܦܘܢܝܘܢ ܗܘ ܕܠܘܬ ܕܝܠܟ
ܠܐܠܗܐ ܦܠܚܐ ܠܐܘܪܫܠܡ ܐܡܪ ܗܟܢܐ܀ ܐܢܐ ܗܟܝܠ ܠܐ ܦܪܫܬ ܐܬܦܪܫܬ: ܘܠܐ ܐܬܠܝܗ
ܠܐܝܟ ܡܢ ܗܠܝܢ ܕܐܬܝܗܘܢ ܠܐ ܡܬܕܢܝܢ: ܘܐܟܘܬܗܘܢ ܗܘܐ ܐܣܝܪܐ: ܗܘ ܕܝܢ
ܡܡܠܠܐܝܬ ܒܪܢܫܐ: ܐܡܪܐ ܕܡܢ ܚܛܐ ܦܢܐ ܠܒܘܬܐ: ܢܗܘܐ ܠܓܘܡܪܐ ܐܘܚܢܐ
ܠܡܫܪܝܘܬܐ ܕܚܕܝܘܬܐ: ܟܕ ܡܠܐ ܕܠܗ ܡܪܐ (92) ܒܗ: ܒܥܠܡܐ ܕܝܢ ܗܢܐ ܐܡܪܬܐ
ܘܠܗ ܚܕܝ: ܕܚܘܒܗ ܕܡܫܟܚܐ ܡܢ ܚܛܝܬܐ: ܘܗܘ ܡܫܪܝܘܬܐ ܘܠܐ ܡܬܚܫܒܢܘܬܐ
ܕܢܦܫܗ: ܐܝܟ ܙܒܢܐ ܒܥܡܪܐ ܛܒ ܒܗ. ܦܩܘܕ ܓܝܪ ܦܐܪ ܐܢܐ ܩܠܐ ܕܡܛܠ
ܗܠܝܢ: ܟܠ ܐܢܫܘܬܐ ܕܡܫܬܢܐ ܒܒܢ̈ܝ ܠܗܘܢ ܘܠܐ ܡܬܚܫܒܐ. ܠܡܫܟܚ ܓܝܪ ܚܘܝ
ܚܕ ܒܡܫܬܐ ܕܒܝܬܐ: ܘܐܢܐ ܠܐܠܗܐ ܘܒܟܠܗ ܡܢ ܗܘܐ. ܗܘܐ ܕܝܢ ܗܘ ܡܫܒܪܢܐ:
ܠܗ ܠܐ ܡܬܚܫܒܐ ܐܝܟ ܕܦܐܪ ܐܢܐ. ܡܛܠ ܕܗ ܓܝܪ ܡܫܟܚܬܐ ܕܕܡܝܐ. ܡܬܒܪܐܝܬ
ܕܝܢ ܡܫܪܝܘܬܐ. ܐܚܝܕ ܓܝܪ ܕܡܛܠ ܕܗܘܐ ܒܡܪܐ ܕܡܠܬܐ ܡܫܐ ܟܠܗ: ܡܟܝܠ ܡܢ
ܐܘܚܕܢܐ ܕܡܘܬܐ ܘܚܛܝܬܐ: ܒܗ ܒܝܬ ܦܐܪ ܐܢܐ: ܕܡܛܠ ܕܗܘܐ ܢܦܫܐ ܕܗܘ ܕܠܐ ܚܙܝ
ܕܚܛܐ: ܡܘܬܐ ܡܬܚܒܠ ܡܫܬܠܛ ܕܒܟܠܗܘܢ ܢܦ̈ܫܬܐ ܠܐ ܡܬܡܚܠܦ ܐܝܟ ܒܗ.
ܘܡܢ ܚܛܝܬܐ ܗܝ ܕܒܗܝܢ ܡܬܕܢܐ ܒܠܝܢ: ܘܠܐ ܦܫܝܛܐ ܠܡܐܪ ܚܛܝܬܐ. ܒܪܢܫܐ ܓܝܪ
ܡܬܡܠܐ ܒܫܘܪܝܐ ܗܘ ܘܠܐ ܒܥܒܕ ܚܛܝܬܐ: ܘܠܐ ܐܬܚܙܝ ܢܦܠܐ ܒܦܘܡܗ ܡܫܝܚܐ܀ .
܀ܘܒܠܚܘܕ ܒܦܘܪܥܢܐ ܬܘܒ܀ ܡܫܝܚܐ ܕܝܢ ܘܠܐ ܠܐܝܟ ܡܢ ܗܠܝܢ ܕܐܬܝܗܘܢ ܐܬܝܗ ܠܐ
ܬܡܝܗܐ: ܕܦܓܪܐ ܦܢ ܚܝܐ ܗܘ ܕܒܚܝܐ ܡܬܚܫܒܢܐ ܗܘ. ܐܬܝܗܘܢ ܗܘܐ ܓܝܪ
ܘܠܗ ܕܡܛܠ ܠܐ ܡܬܚܫܒܢܐ. ܢܦܫܐ ܕܝܢ ܬܘܒ ܕܡܛܠܗ ܡܬܬܐ ܕܐܝܟ ܗܘܐ ܕܠܘܬܗ
ܘܚܝܘܬܐ: ܚܝܠܐ ܦܢ ܠܡܘܬܐ. ܟܕ ܚܝܠܐ ܕܝܢ ܘܒܡܘܬܐ ܦܐ ܠܐܠܗܐ
ܡܬܚܫܒܐ: ܐܦ ܠܒܘܝܬܐ ܕܐܡܢ ܡܬܒܪܝܐ ܗܘܬ܀ ܡܢܠܬܢ ܕܝܢ ܬܘܒ ܗܠܝܢ
ܕܐܡ̈ܪܝ ܒܗ ܒܡܐܡܪܐ ܟܕ ܐܘܡܦ ܗܠܝܢ. ܀ܘܬܘܒ܀ ܚܕ ܡܪܝܐ ܝܫܘܥ ܡܫܝܚܐ
ܘܒܐܪ̈ܙܘܗܝ ܟܠ ܡܕܡ ܒܪܐ ܐܒܐ. ܟܕ ܕܝܢ ܘܐܬܝܗܘܢ ܘܒܪܘܚܐ ܠܐܠܗܘܬܐ. ܘܡܛܠ
ܚܝܐ ܐܝܟ ܚܝܐ. ܘܒܪ̈ܝܬܐ ܐܢܫܬܐ ܘܒܗܠܝܢ ܕܒܠܠ ܡܢ ܒܪܢܫܐ: ܠܚܕ ܡܕܡ
ܘܒܡܕܒܪܬܐ ܡܪܒܒ. ܡܕܒܪܐ ܓܝܪ ܐܬܝܗܘܢ ܕܐܠܗܐ ܘܒܪ̈ܝܬܐ ܐܝܟ ܡܠܟܐ. ܕܒܚܝܐ
ܦܢ ܐܬܝܗܘܢ ܐܠܗܐ (93) ܘܠܗ ܫܛܪ ܡܢ ܒܫܪܐ. ܒܪܢܫܐ ܕܝܢ ܒܡܪܘܐ: ܘܠܗ
ܡܫܡܫܐ ܐܟܘܬܝ. ܐܠܐ ܐܬܝܗܘܢ ܗܘ ܦܢ ܕܐܬܝܗܘܢ ܗܘܐ: ܐܦ ܗܘܐ ܒܫܪܐ. ܡܛܠ
ܓܝܪ ܕܝܫܘܥ ܡܫܝܚܐ ܐܬܡܠܟ ܘܝܘܡܢ ܗܘ ܟܕ ܗܘ ܘܠܥܠܡ܀ ܗܘܝ ܕܝܢ ܕܐܬܡܢܐ

you should not limp or be dim sighted, but should confess Emmanuel from two natures, divinity and humanity, and not deny difference and particularity with respect to natural quality of the natures from which the one (Christ) is brought together to an indivisible union. And you should think it iniquitous to divide Christ into a duality (*Lebon p. 94*) of natures after the union, and consequently their activities and properties. For in a duality everything is cut at the same time, and reduced to a diversity which is divided and cut in everything, whether you speak of activities or properties. For when we denounce the division (resulting from) a duality of natures after the union, we do not, as you have thought, instead introduce, as evil men advocate, the phrase "two united natures". But we say what is indisputably the case, namely that duality is cutting and division. For "If the union is true, they are not two in any way, but one Christ is understood from two",[59] as holy Cyril said when he was writing in reply to evil Theodoret's complaints against the Chapters. And he sent the same thing to Succensus, thus: (CYRIL): "So that the two should henceforth be no longer two, but through the two one living thing has been completed".[60]

But let no-one ignorantly think that natural quality is ascribed only to the body, as for example the quality of being solid, or of taste, or of density, or of weight, or of thickness or transparency. For, because of the poverty of human intellects, we are obliged to make use of words having a corporeal signification about divine things as well, and they cannot be spoken of otherwise. Holy Cyril acknowledged this, in the first book of the Commentary on John's Gospel, when he says as follows: (CYRIL): "Therefore as far as approaches subtlety of mind (*Lebon p. 95*) and the acuteness of movement in it, let us look at the varied beauty of the divine nature, but expressing these things about it rather in a human way and in our vocabulary, for the tongue is incapable of extending to the measure of truth".[61] Because of this, the same man in the second book of the same Commentary, interpreting the non-corporeal divinity of the Father and the Son, says as follows: (CYRIL): "The offspring are thought of as being a certain natural quality so to speak, of their begetters, showing what the begetter is in ousia, and displaying the natural quality[62] of their source".[63]

We have, therefore, sent these things as we have understood them. And we rejoice with you at (your) growth and increase towards divine knowledge. Because of this we aptly say to you the word of the Apostle: "Meditate on these things, remain in these things, that your growth may be obvious to everyone".[64] But avoid writing doc-

ܢܦܫܐ: ܘܡܚܝܡܘܗܝ ܕܟܠܗ ܗܘܐ ܠܗ ܚܝܘܐ ܘܠܐ ܡܘܦܩܪܐ. ܐܠܐ ܚܝܘܗ ܠܐ ܡܫܟܚ ܕܦܪܝܢ ܡܢ ܒܢܝ̈ܢܫܐ. ܠܪܒܘܬܐ ܕܫܡܝܘܬܐ ܘܕܪܒܢܐ ܗܘ ܕܟܠ ܠܗ ܟܕ ܡܬܚܫܒܐ ܡܘܕܥܐ. ܘܟܠܗ ܟܠ ܦܬܓܡܘܗܝ ܡܫܩܠܬܐ ܕܠܐ ܡܢ ܟܠ ܚܠܝܡ: ܘܠܐ ܐܗܦܟ ܐܦ̈ܘܗܝ ܡܢ ܟܘܠܬܐ ܕܙܘܥܐ. ܘܡܩܒܠ ܢܦܫܐ: ܘܟܠ ܟܘܠܬܐ ܐܚܝܗ. ܗܘ ܕܐܡܪ ܚܟܝܡܐ. ܠܗ ܓܒܪ ܡܘܙܢܐ ܕܡܫܪܐ ܡܩܒܠ: ܘܡܣܟܠܐ ܘܡܣܓܝܢܐ ܕܐܘܨܦܐ ܐܢܫܝܬܐ. ܐܝܟ ܠܗ ܓܒܪ ܘܕܡܘܬܐ ܠܚܟܝܡܐ ܗܘ ܕܝܕܥ: ܕܠܐ ܡܢ ܒܢܝ̈ܢܫܐ. ܘܠܐ ܦܬܝܚ ܦܘܡܗ. ܐܠܐ ܠܟܠ ܢܦܫܗ: ܘܠܐ ܒܪܐ ܡܠܐ ܐܬܐ ܐܝܟ ܐܡܪܐ. ܘܡܬܟܝܢ ܡܫܬܠܡ ܘܡܠܘܠܠ ܡܢ ܡܠܬܗ ܡܫܪܪܐ ܙܘܥܐ ܡܫܒܪ. ܘܗܟܝܢ ܟܕ ܐܠܗܘܗܝ ܠܗܘܐ ܒܚܝܐ: ܘܠܐ ܢܦܩ ܡܬܚܫܒܬܐ: ܐܦ ܐܝܟ ܕܒܥܪܒܐ ܒܪ ܐܢܫܐ ܐܠܗܘܗܝ ܗܘܐ ܗܘ ܟܕ ܗܘ. ܗܘ ܓܒܪ ܕܙܟܐ ܕܐܬܟܘܫܠܗ ܒܟܒܪ ܐܦ ܙܟܘܬܐ ܕܪܒܪܐ. ܐܝܟܢܐ ܕܐܦ ܠܐ ܐܢܫ ܡܢ ܒܢܝ̈ܢܫܐ ܕܚܫ ܡܢ ܡܠܘܗܝ ܢܟܝܢܐ ܠܗ܀

ܟܕ ܗܟܝܢ ܗܘܟܠ ܚܕܐ ܢܦܫܗ: ܘܡܩܠܚܐ ܠܗܘܢ ܡܠܘܗܝ ܕܗܟܝܢ ܩ̈ܠܝܠܢ ܩ̈ܪܐ ܕܒܪܝܟ ܕܟܪܐ. ܕܘܟ ܘܠܐ ܠܐܣܝܪ ܘܠܐ ܠܐܪܘܙ ܡܫܘܚܠܦ. ܠܐܘܝܘܗܝ ܕܝܢ ܠܡܫܘܐܠܟ ܡܢ ܠܘܬ ܒܢ̈ܝܢ ܠܟܘܠܬܐ ܦܢ ܘܐܢܫܘܬܐ. ܘܠܐ ܠܐܚܘܪ ܒܡܘܣܟܠܐ ܘܡܟܘܬܐ: ܗܘ ܕܐܝܟ ܕܒܡܫܘܕܥܘܬܐ ܚܝܡܬܐ ܕܒܢ̈ܝܐ ܕܡܝܗܘܢ ܗܘ ܚܝ ܡܒܝܢ ܒܟܠ ܚܝܘܬܐ ܠܐ ܡܬܦܠܓܝܢܬܐ. ܘܒܠܐ ܠܐܣܘܒ ܠܗܘ ܕܐܦܫܡܘܗܝ ܠܡܫܝܚܐ ܠܡܠܘܝܬܐ (94) ܕܒܢ̈ܝܐ ܗܘ ܕܟܠܪ ܚܝܘܬܐ: ܘܢܦܠܬܐ ܠܡܣܬܒܪܘܬܐ ܘܬܟܝܬܐ ܘܗܟܝܢ. ܟܠܡܘܬܐ ܓܒܪ ܡܠܟܝܢ ܐܚܪܢܐ ܡܬܦܫܩ: ܘܦܬܚ ܠܐܣܪ̈ܝܢܘܬܐ ܡܦܠܓܬܐ ܘܦܫܝܛܬܐ ܒܟܠܟܝܢ. ܘܐܦ ܡܣܬܒܪܘܬܐ ܠܐܡܪ: ܘܐܦ ܕܬܟܝܬܐ. ܟܕ ܦܘܠܓܐ ܓܒܪ ܡܦܠܓܢܝܢ ܕܠܐܣܝܘܬܐ ܕܒܢ̈ܝܐ ܟܠܪ ܚܝܘܬܐ: ܠܐ ܡܬܟܠܝܢ ܡܫܘܚܠܦ ܐܝܟ ܕܐܫܟܚܬܐ: ܐܝܟ ܡܦܫܩܢܘܬܐ ܡܟܝܢܬܐ ܕܒܩܠܠܐ: ܗܘ ܕܠܐܘܝܢ ܒܢ̈ܝܐ ܡܬܢܝܚܐ ܢܘܪܐ. ܐܠܐ ܟܕ ܗܘ ܕܐܝܟܢܐ ܐܦܪܢܝܢ ܘܠܐ ܚܙܝܢ. ܕܠܐܘܝܬܐ ܦܫܝܛܐ ܘܦܘܠܓܐ ܐܝܟܢܐ. ܐܦ ܓܒܪ ܡܪܢܐ ܚܝܘܬܐ. ܠܗ ܠܐܘܝܢ ܒܕܘܪ ܡܢ ܟܠ ܦܪܘܫ ܐܝܟܢܘܗܝ. ܐܠܐ ܚܕ ܡܢ ܠܐܘܝܢ ܡܫܬܟܠܠ ܡܚܝܠܐ: ܐܝܟ ܡܐ ܕܐܡܪ ܚܕܝܐ ܡܘܢܟܘܣ: ܟܕ ܟܠܗ ܠܟܠ ܒܩܘܠܐ ܕܠܐܘܪܚܐ ܒܟܠܐ: ܗܘܝ ܕܠܡܫܟܠ ܩ̈ܠܠܐ: ܘܗܝ ܟܕ ܗܝ ܠܟܠ ܡܫܘܚܠܦܘܬ ܡܓܝܣ ܗܟܝܠ. ܘܡܘܢܟܘܣ܀ ܐܝܟܢܐ ܕܠܐܘܝܢ ܠܐ ܡܫܬܟܠ ܦܢ ܢܗܘܘܢ ܐܝܟܢܘܗܝ ܠܐܘܝܢ. ܟܕ ܠܐܘܝܢ ܕܝܢ ܚܕܐ ܚܝܘܬܐ ܐܝܬܝܟܝܬܐ܀

trinal teachings and do not easily approach this, for such things belong, as you know, to those who are much instructed and have meditated diligently on the Scripture inspired by God, and have grown rich on the toils of the things of the same Spirit, the tested former teachers of mysteries in the holy Church, and not to those recently instructed in the knowledge of the divine teachings. But if somewhere you are compelled to make a pronouncement—as men frequently (affirm that) they will repent, and pursue the orthodox faith, and make profession—do you only lay down the creed of the 318 Fathers, and anathema on those who oppose (it), both on individuals and on teachings, just as previously in our vicinity too those who have repented have done. (*Lebon p. 96*) For it is proper and prudent that we follow them in these words, and proceed in everything in the footsteps of those who journeyed before, and be fearful and stand in awe, lest even unwillingly we put a foot anywhere and in anything untrod and difficult. For the (words), spoken in counsel in the Book of Proverbs, "We should carry knowledge[65] on our lips",[66] as I think, lead in this direction.

But our Lord Jesus Christ, God and Saviour, with whom are treasuries of wisdom and knowledge, as the Apostle has said,[67] grant that you may abound in every word and in all knowledge, and that you may gain the reward of a man zealous in faith and works, both in the present age and in that to come.

The First Letter of the Patriarch Lord Severus to Sergius the Grammarian has ended.

Notes

1. Is. xxi.12.
2. Prov. x.17.
3. Reading ܘܐܬܕܪܫܬܘܢ for ܘܐܬܕܪܫܘܢ.
4. Prov. xi.2.
5. Lev. x.10–11.
6. Prov. xvi.1 (Hexaplaric ms. only).
7. The root here is ܚܠܛ. Please see Appendix C on "mixture words".
8. PG 77.241B (=ACO I, 1, 6a, p. 159.18–160.2).
9. Cyril, Pusey edn. Vol. 5, p. 499.17–500.4. Syriac only.
10. *Ibid.*, p. 500.6–501.4. Syriac only.
11. cf. I Jn. i.1–3.
12. That is, the Logos.
13. The contrast in Cyril is ἑτέρα μὲν . . . . ἕτερος δὲ.
14. PG 76.329D (=Pusey edn. Vol. 6, p. 286.3–8). *Apol. pro XII Cap. contra Orient.*
15. PG 76.85A–B (=Pusey edn. Vol. 6, p. 113.7–16).
16. PG 76.105A–B (=Pusey edn. Vol. 6, p. 128.25–129.2).

ܡܫܘܕܥܘܬܐ ܕܝܢ ܒܚܝܠܬܐ ܠܐ ܐܝܟ ܠܐ ܦܘܠܛܝܬܐ ܢܣܒܪ ܕܟܠ ܓܘܫܡܐ ܒܟܝܢܗ̇ ܡܬܐܡܪܐ: ܐܝܟ ܡܐ ܕܡܫܘܕܥܘܬܐ ܕܓܘܫܡܐ: ܐܘ ܒܛܒܥܬܐ: ܐܘ ܒܟܝܢܘܬܐ: ܐܘ ܒܡܫܪܘܬܐ: ܐܘ ܒܡܫܡܫܘܬܐ: ܐܘ ܚܫܚܘܬܐ. ܒܟܠܠ ܓܝܪ ܕܐܝܬ ܠܗܘܢ ܡܫܘܕܥܐ ܓܘܫܡܢܐ ܡܛܠ ܡܫܡܫܢܘܬܐ ܕܚܫ̈ܚܬܐ ܐܢܫܐ: ܡܬܐܡܪܝܢ ܚܕ ܘܟܠ ܗܠܝܢ ܠܐܠܗܐ ܐܚܝܕܐ ܒܢܝܢܫܐ: ܘܐܣܬܪܝܗ̇ ܕܐܬܐܡܪ ܠܐ ܡܫܡܫܢ. ܗܘ ܕܡܫܘܐ ܗܘ ܦܪܝܫܐ ܡܬܦܠܓܘܢ: ܒܟܠܗܘܢ ܦܪ̈ܝܫܐ ܕܦܘܫܐ ܘܐܦܝ̈ܠܝܗܘܢ ܕܗܝܡܢ: ܟܕ ܐܡܪ ܗܟܢܐ. ܀ܡܦܘܪܟܘܗ܀ ܡܕܝܢ ܐܝܟ ܡܐ ܕܐܬܐܬܐ ܒܛܒܥܘܬܐ ܕܗܘܝܐ (95) ܘܒܝܢܬܐܘܬܐ ܕܙܘܓܐ ܕܒܗ: ܗܘܦܟܐ ܡܦܠܓܐ ܕܚܝܠܐ ܠܐܠܗܐ ܢܦܫܐ: ܡܬܩܠܩܠܝܢ ܕܝܢ ܗܠܝܢ ܕܡܬܦܠܓܢܘ ܠܡܢ ܐܝܬܝܗ. ܘܒܡܠܠܬܐ ܗܘ ܕܝܢ. ܟܕ ܟܠܗ ܠܗ ܠܠܡܫܐ ܕܠܡܫܡܫ ܟܠܐ ܡܫܘܚܬܐ ܕܦܪܘܫ܀ ܡܛܠ ܗܘܐ ܗܘ ܟܕ ܗܘ ܒܟܠܟܠ ܕܐܬܩܢ ܕܠܗ ܟܕ ܕܠܗ ܘܦܘܫܐ: ܟܕ ܡܬܦܠܓܐ ܘܒܪܐ ܦܠܓܐ: ܘܠܐܠܗܘܬܐ ܘܠܐ ܓܘܫܡ ܗܘܝܐ ܐܡܪ. ܀ܡܦܘܪܟܘܗ܀ ܕܡܫܘܕܥܘܬܐ ܡܕܡ ܒܢܝܫܬܐ ܐܚܝܕܐ ܕܗܘܝܐ ܐܡܪ. ܕܗܘܝܢ ܕܡܕܝܢ ܡܬܐܡܪ ܗܠܝܢ ܕܡܬܐܡܪܝܢ ܕܗܝܠ ܐܬܐܠܗܐ ܒܐܘܣܝܐ ܗܘ ܕܐܝܟ ܡܫܡܫܝܢ: ܘܡܫܘܕܥ ܠܡܫܘܕܥܘܬܐ ܕܒܚܝܠܐ ܕܡܫܘܡܝܐ ܕܠܗܘܢ܀

ܗܠܝܢ ܘܒܠܐܟ ܐܝܟ ܕܐܘܪܒܝܢ ܡܠܝܢ. ܢܡܝܢ ܕܝܢ ܒܫܡ: ܒܣܘܟܠܐ ܘܒܠܡܪܒܝܬܐ ܕܒܗ ܡܕܒܪܬܐ ܠܐܠܗܐ. ܡܛܠ ܗܘܐ ܘܡܫܡܫܢܘܬܗ ܡܫܠܡܐ ܗܘ ܕܡܫܡܫܢܐ ܐܡܪܝܢ ܠܗ. ܗܠܝܢ ܐܬܝܠܕ. ܒܗܠܝܢ ܕܝܢ. ܐܡܪܝܢ ܕܡܫܘܡܫܝܢ ܓܒܝܐ ܗܘܘ ܠܟܠܗܘܢ. ܒܪܡ ܒܪܘܟ ܡܢ ܗܘ ܕܐܬܡܘܟ ܡܕܡ ܕܪܘܓܫܬܐ. ܘܠܐ ܦܫܝܛܐ ܠܡܗܘܐ ܠܗܘܢ ܐܬ̈ܐ ܐܬܐ. ܕܗܠܝܢ ܓܝܪ ܕܫܘܚܠܦ ܡܫܡܫܝܢ: ܘܐܬܪܓܫܘ ܒܪܘܚܐ ܒܡܠܐ ܒܟܠܟܠ ܢܦܫ ܡܢ ܠܐܠܗܐ: ܘܒܟܘܟܒܐ ܕܗܠܝܢ ܕܝܢ ܟܕ ܗܘ ܡܘܪܐ ܒܠܡܪܘ: ܦ̈ܠܓܐ ܕܪ̈ܐܐ ܒܚܝ̈ܐ ܕܟܠܝܢ ܕܒܝܬܐ ܦܪܝܫܬܐ: ܐܠܗܝܢ ܐܝܟܢ ܕܐܡܪ ܗܟܢܐ: ܐܚܝܕܐ ܕܢܒܝܐ ܐܡܪ: ܘܟܠܗ ܕܗܠܝܢ ܕܗܘܐ ܐܬܝܗܒ ܒܡܕܝܢܬܐ ܕܢ̈ܦܫܬܐ ܠܐܠܗܐ. ܐܢ ܕܝܢ ܒܢܘܗܪ ܐܦ ܠܐܬܐܬܐ ܕܐܬܝܗܒ: ܟܕ ܐܝܟ ܪ̈ܘܚܐ ܦ̈ܠܓܐ ܕܠܗܘܢ ܘܢܬܚܙܘܢ ܒܗܘܢ ܡܫܡܫܢܘܬܐ ܠܐܘܪܚܐ ܡܫܘܚܐ: ܘܐܘܪܚܬܐ ܢܡܫܘܢ: ܗܡܫܡܫܢܘܬܐ ܒܟܠܗܘܢ ܘܐܠܗܘܬܐ ܘܐܫܬܠܡܬ ܐܒܗ̈ܬܐ ܕܗܘܝܐ ܗܐܡ ܐܡܪ: ܘܚܪܒܐ ܕܗܘܝܢ ܕܒܡܘܬܐ. ܘܒܦ̈ܪܘܫܐ ܘܒܢ̈ܘܗܪܐ. ܐܚܝܕܐ ܕܐܦ ܒܡܪ̈ܟܒܬܐ ܡܢ ܦܪܝܫ: ܗܠܝܢ ܕܐܬܘ (96) ܒܟܝܢܘ. ܗܟܢܐ ܓܝܪ ܘܐܘܪܚܐ ܕܒܗܘܢ ܦ̈ܠܓܐ ܠܗܠܝܢ ܢܦܫ: ܘܒܝܘܬܪܢܐ ܕܗܠܝܢ ܕܦܪܝܫܘ ܚܕܘ ܒܡܠܟܝܢ ܢܗܘܐ. ܘܗܘܐ ܦܢܝܬܝܢ ܘܕܚܠܝܢ ܚܕ: ܕܟܠܐ ܒܝܘܡ ܘܒܡܒܝܢ ܠܐ ܡܕܪܫܐ ܘܦܫܝܛ: ܘܟܕ ܠܐ ܪܫܝܡ ܢܦܫܐ ܠܒܪܢܫܐ:

17. On p. 118.3 the Syriac ܒܡܢܬܐ translates the Greek ἀνὰ μέρος. It is possible that ܒܡ̈ܢܘܬܐ is also intended to represent that Greek phrase, and could be translated "apart". Without this conjecture, we may make better sense by translating, "in (separate) parts".

18. Reading ܠܚܕܝܘܬܐ for ܠܚܕܘܬܐ. (= εἰς ἕνωσιν ἀδιάτμητον).

19. PG 75.1289C (= Pusey edn. Vol. 7, p. 364.2–5).

20. PG 76.137B–C (= Pusey edn. Vol. 6, p. 153.18–154.3).

21. cf. p. 118.3. Internal cross-references are to page and line of Lebon's edition of the Syriac text of the *Letters*.

22. PG 29.689C. *Adv. Eun. Lib. IV*.

23. cf. 1 Cor. xv.52.

24. 1 Cor. viii.6.

25. Rom. ix.5.

26. Jn. xi.11.

27. PL 54.767A–B.

28. Mk. iv.39.

29. Mt. xiv.28–29.

30. Mk. i.41; Lk. v.13.

31. cf. Mt. v.22.

32. Jn. x.18.

33. cf. Jn. viii.26.

34. cf. Jn. v.19.

35. Jn. xiv.10.

36. This section is quoted at *Lebon p. 184*, below, from which the words included here in diamond brackets are taken.

37. cf. above, EM p. 72.10.

38. ܕܒܪ ܟܝܢܐ = τοῦ ὁμοουσίου.

39. Lietzmann, H.: *Apollinaris von Laodicea*, (Tübingen, 1904), p. 194. Note on line 15: Title—ἰουλίου ἀρχιεπισκόπου ῥώμης πρὸς τοὺς κατὰ τῆς θείας τοῦ Λόγου σαρκώσεως ἀγωνιζομένους προφάσει τοῦ ὁμοουσίου.

40. *Ibid.*, p. 199.16–17.

41. *Ibid.*, p. 199.23–27.

42. Syriac ܒܡܘܙܓܘܬܐ ܕܐܣܟܡܐ. Greek ἐν συγκράσει.

43. Lietzmann, *op. cit.*, p. 187, lines 5–8.

44. Greek τὴν φύσιν.

45. Lietzmann, *op. cit.*, pp. 192–3, lines 14–17 and 1–2.

46. As Lebon notes, the Syriac translator here seems to have read ὁμοιούσιοι with Ps. Basil, while Severus, as is clear from what follows, wrote ὁμοούσιοι.

47. PG 29.681A–B. *Adv. Eun. Lib. IV*.

48. PG 37.177C.

49. PG 75.1264B (= Pusey edn. Vol. 7, p. 342.6–10).

50. Severus undoubtedly borrows this parallel from Cyril (cf. *Scholia*, Pusey edn. Vol. 6, Ch. 11, pp. 518–521). That the ark was overlaid with gold outside indicates that the Word was united to the holy flesh. That the ark was overlaid with gold inside indicates that the Word also made his own the reasonable soul that was within the body.

51. cf. 1 Cor. xiii.12.

52. Is. 1.9.

53. PG 76.1161C–D (= Pusey edn. Vol. 7, p. 61.14–62.14).

54. Reading ܕܠܘܬܗ (= H. syr. 22) for ܕܠܘܬܗ̇, and translating ܡܪܟܒܬܐ as "combination".

55. PG 76.1165A. (= Pusey edn. Vol. 7, p. 68.2–8).

56. This passage, quoted here first by Severus, is especially difficult for Sergius. cf. below, p. 102.8; p. 121.2 ff; p. 161.6 ff.

57. PG 76.1193B–C (= Pusey edn. Vol. 7, p. 134.10–18). *De Recta Fide ad Theod.*

58. cf. Is. liii.2–3.

ܐ ܒܪܬܐ ܕܡܪܝ ܒܗܢܡ ܒܪܣܛܘܡܘܣ ܘܕܣܘܣܐܪܐ ܕܐܬܠܒܫܐ

ܟܕ ܗܘܐ ܒܪ ܫܒܥܐ ܡܫܠܡܐ ܐܝܟ ܕܡܦܪܫ ܐܢܐ: ܗܘ ܕܗܠܐ ܕܒܣܦܩܘܬܐ ܗܘܐ ܠܛܒܝܒ ܡܫܠܡܘܬܐ ܕܡܢ ܟܠܗ ܡܠܟܐ ܐܚܪܢܐ ܕܒܥܠܡܐ.

ܡܢ ܕܝܢ ܡܥܠܝ ܡܫܝܚܐ ܠܟܠܗ ܘܦܪܘܩܢ: ܕܟܠܗ ܫܡܥܬܐ ܕܫܒܚܬܐ ܘܕܘܒܪܬܐ: ܗܘ ܕܐܡܪ ܡܫܝܚܐ: ܢܡܠܠ ܠܟ ܕܐܬܠܡܕ ܒܟܠ ܡܠܬܐ ܘܒܟܠ ܚܕܬܐ. ܒܗ ܗܘ ܕܐܦ ܠܡܛܘܦ ܐܡܪܐ ܕܛܝܒܐ ܕܗܝܡܢܘܬܐ ܘܕܒܩܠܐ ܘܥܗܘܠ ܒܥܠܡܐ ܘܥܒܕܘ ܕܒܠܚܘܕ.

܀ܡܫܡܫ ܠܒܪܐ ܚܕܝܡܐ ܕܦܛܪܝܪܟܐ ܡܢ ܫܠܘܕܐ ܕܟܠܗ ܣܢܚܪܝܒ ܒܪܣܛܘܡܘܣ܀

59. PG 76.445B (= Pusey edn. Vol. 6., p. 484.1–2).

60. PG 77.245B *ὥστε τὰς δύο, μηκέτι μὲν εἶναι δύο, δι᾽ ἀμφοῖν δὲ τὸ ἓν ἀποτελεῖσθαι ζῶον*. (= ACO I, I, 6a, p. 162.8–9). *Ep. XLVI. Ad Succ. Ep. II.*

61. PG 73.132B (= Pusey edn. Vol. 3, p. 114.23–27).

62. Syriac: ܡܥܒܕܢܘܬܐ. Notwithstanding the marginal note on p. 109 below, the Greek is *τὴν κατὰ φύσιν ἐνέργειαν*.

63. PG 73.281B, lines 25–9. (= Pusey edn. Vol. 3, p. 255.15–18).

64. 1 Tim. iv.15.

65. Note in margin: Knowledge of (the one who) knows himself.

66. Prov. xvi.23.

67. Col. ii.3.

Letter II of Sergius

The Second Letter of Sergius the Grammarian to the Patriarch Lord Severus.

Sergius, humble Grammarian, to our holy and blessed Lord, to the Father of Fathers and ecumenical Doctor, to the Patriarch.

"Who am I, your servant, that you have looked on a dead dog like me?"[1] For (these) words are more fitting to me than to Mephibosheth. For though the estates of his father's house and a servant for labour were permitted for the mark of honour of that man, (David) did not heal his lameness with this. But more than he, I was enriched, who have escaped from all this poverty of ignorance and my own lameness has been made straight, and these things at a time which is poor as regards the things of *(Lebon p. 97)* God, when the word of the Lord is rare, and when vision is not distinct.[2] And how shall I express what happened to me in the midst of reading in front of a porch? In front of the holy writings I saw the writings of the wise Bishop Antoninus and my name was inscribed. And when I lifted up the seals with calmness, I opened the chapters of the letter and at once I was happily confident, for I feasted well on the sight. And afterwards as I advanced little by little, I cast (my) eyes on chapters of the other writings, and saw something great and divine. When little by little I had altered what I was seeing, I retraced my tracks, and I believed that I was hearing cither music, (which played) "This is the door of the Lord by which the just enter in".[3] And I said many times, "It is not my writing and the letter is not to me". And again I departed outside. And why should I require many words? Youth loves to be rash from ignorance of the beautiful.[4] But being rash again, I compelled (my) eyes to go with me on this road, and I have knocked again, and little by little have entered inside. And who did I become after these things? I need tranquillity[5] that I can speak: but I shall tell this which I have remembered with difficulty; because I had ceased to think of such divine matters; and I was leaping about somewhere out of (my) mind, in the frequent visions which the Fathers were putting out along with most divine words, even though I again thought of the smallness of (my) reasoning.

And when along with these things I meditated also on the visions

❊ܐܬܪܐ ܕܐܬܘܪ ܕܡܢܝܟܘܣ ܒܪܣܛܘܡܘܣ ܟܠܗ ܘܦܛܪܝܪܟܐ ܡܪܝ ܫܠܘܙܐ❊
ܠܡܪܐ ܕܡܢ ܩܕܝܫܐ ܘܬܘܠܒܬܐ: ܠܐܒܐ ܕܐܒܗ̈ܬܐ ܘܡܠܟܘܬܐ ܕܐܡܝܢ: ܠܦܛܪܝܪܟܘܬ:
ܡܪܟܘܣ ܒܪܝܐ ܒܪܣܛܘܡܘܣ.

ܡܢܗ ܐܠܗ ܐܢܐ ܒܟܝܢ: ܕܝܢܐ ܟܠܗ ܡܠܟܐ ܡܠܟܬܐ ܒܗܘ ܙܒܢܐ ܠܗ. ܠܥܒܕܝܢ ܠܗ ܠܝܢ ܩܛܠܐ ܡܠܟ ܡܢ ܡܥܒܕܢܘܬܗ: ܐܦ ܠܝܢ ܠܐܡܪܐ ܕܝܢ: ܐܠܗܘܬܐ ܕܥܡܗ ܐܒܘܢܐ ܘܒܪ ܒܠܬܐ ܠܦܘܠܚܢܐ ܡܠܦܩܝܢ ܗܘܐ: ܐܠܐ ܠܗ ܒܗܘܐ ܠܡܫܝܚܘܬܐ ܕܦܓܠܐ ܡܬܬܣܐ ܗܘܐ. ܟܠܙܐ ܕܝܢ ܐܢܐ ܡܠܟ ܡܢ ܗܢܐ: ܕܡܢ ܡܠܟܗ ܗܘܐ ܡܫܡܫܢܘܬܐ ܕܠܐ ܡܟܠܬܐ ܒܪܦܠܗ ܘܡܫܝܚܘܬܐ ܕܝܫܘܥ ܐܬܬܐܙܝܐ. ܘܗܠܝܢ ܒܗ ܙܒܢܐ ܡܫܡܫܝܢ ܠܗܘܢ ܗܠܝܢ (97) ܠܟ̈ܗܢܐ: ܐܡܠܗ ܕܡܠܟܬܐ ܕܡܢܐ ܡܫܒܐ: ܘܐܡܠܗ ܕܝܗܘܐ ܠܥܡܗ ܕܡܦܪܩܗ. ܘܐܡܥܢܐ ܐܦܢ ܗܠܝܢ ܕܦܠܓܗ ܒܗ ܒܡܥܒܕܬܐ ܕܡܢܐ ܡܢܝܢ ܫܦܠ ܡܢܝܢ: ܕܡܢܝܢ ܡܠܟ̈ܬܐ ܩ̈ܝܡܬܐ ܐܠܗ ܗܘܐ: ܡܠܟ̈ܬܐ ܕܐܬܛܘܝܒܐ ܙܒܢܐ ܣܡܝܟܐ ܢܣܒܗ. ܘܒܗܘܝܐ ܕܡܠܟ ܕܠܟܦ. ܘܒܪ ܒܡܠܟܘܬܐ ܠܦܠܓܐ ܐܘܦܣܗ: ܠܐܬܪܐ ܕܐܠܗܪܐ ܦܠܡܢܗ. ܘܒܫܠܬܐ ܦܢ ܠܐܦܠ ܗܘܝܘ ܗܘܠܝܢ: ܕܝܠܐ ܙܒܢܐ ܗܘܝܘ ܒܡܦܪܐ. ܘܒܠܙܘܡ ܒܗ ܡܠܟܠ ܡܠܟ ܡܫܟܚ ܗܘܝܘ: ܒܬܪܐ ܒܠܙܘܒܐ ܘܡܠܟ̈ܬܐ ܐܣܬܢܝܢܬܐ ܐܘܦܣܗ: ܘܡܫܒܪܢܐ ܡܢܝܢ ܙܒܢܐ ܘܠܟܘܡܐ ܢܣܒܗ: ܒܗ ܡܠܟܠ ܡܠܟܠ ܗܠܝܢ ܕܝܗܘܐ ܡܫܟܚ ܗܘܝܘ: ܗܦܟ ܗܘܝܘ ܠܥܡܐ. ܘܡܠܙܐ ܡܫܡܫܢܐ ܦܬܪ ܗܘܝܘ ܕܦܣܩ ܐܢܐ. ܗܘܘ ܠܙܒܢܐ ܕܡܢܐ ܕܙܘܓܐ ܚܠܝܢ ܒܗ. ܘܙܩܝܡ ܫܠܝܚܐ ܐܦܪܐ: ܕܠܗ ܕܡܟ ܡܠܟܬܐ: ܘܠܐ ܟܠܗ ܐܠܗܪܐ. ܘܐܘܦ ܠܟܪ ܚܣܠܗ: ܘܡܢܐ ܩ̈ܠܟܝܢ ܠܗ ܩܛܠܐ ܫܠܝܚܐܬܐ. ܙܡܢܐ ܠܢܘܬܐ ܕܐܡܪܚ. ܡܢ ܠܐ ܡܫܡܫܢܐ ܠܢܘܬܐ. ܘܐܘܦ ܐܢܐ ܡܪܢܐ ܠܐܟܪ ܗܘܝܘ ܠܟܬܒܐ: ܕܐܬܐܬܐ ܒܥܡܗ ܟܠܗ ܕܡܠܟܗ ܕܐܘܪܚܐ ܘܐܘܦ ܢܦܫܗ. ܘܒܥܠܡܠܟ ܡܠܟܠ ܠܝܗ ܚܠܟܗ. ܘܡܢܗ ܗܘܝܘ ܟܠܙ ܗܠܝܢ: ܡܫܡܫܢܘܬܐ ܡܠܟܝܢܐ ܕܐܡܝܢ ܠܥܠܡܝܢ. ܗܘܐ ܕܝܢ ܕܠܡܫܡܫܢ ܐܠܒܘܙܐ: ܐܦܢ ܐܢܐ: ܕܐܝܟ ܗܠܝܢ ܠܟ̈ܗܢܐ ܦܠܝܚܗ ܗܘ ܕܐܠܙܒܐ. ܘܠܒܪ ܡܢ ܠܙܘܒܠܬܐ ܒܗܘܢ ܙܦܫ ܗܘܝܘ: ܒܢܝܘܐ ܡܫܡܫܐ ܕܐܒ̈ܗܬܐ ܡܕܡܝܢ ܗܘܘ: ܒܡ ܩܕܡܗ ܩܠܐ ܕܡܠܟ ܠܟ̈ܗܢܬܐ. ܒܗ ܠܒ ܕܝܢ ܗܘ ܙܒܘܪܐ ܕܡܫܡܫܢܬܐ ܦܢܐ ܗܘܝܘ ܡܠܙܒܐ ܗܘܝܘ.

ܘܒܗ ܒܡ ܗܠܝܢ ܡܠܗܘܟܐ ܗܘܝܘ ܐܢܐ ܐܦ ܒܢܝܘܐ ܕܕܝܠܝܠܟ: ܡܢܐ ܡܫܡܫܢ ܗܘܝܘ ܕܚܙܐ ܐܢܐ ܕܐܡܠܗ ܠܗܘ ܒܬܪܐ: ܘܦܘܫܐ ܕܬܘܙܘܒܬܐ ܡܫܡܠܟ ܗܘܐ. ܐܠܐ ܒܡܠܟܠ ܡܠܟܠ ܡܠܟܢ ܗܘܝܘ ܠܡܕܝܢܬܐ. ܘܒܗ ܙܩܝܡ ܫܠܝܚܐ ܐܝܟ ܕܠܡܐܡܪ ܡܢ ܡܦܠܓܗ ܫܡܠܬܐ

of Daniel, I believed that I saw the horn which had eyes and a mouth, which spoke great things.[6] But gradually I became used to marvellous things, and when many times, so to speak, I was called from the midst of the sleep of negligence, (*Lebon p. 98*) I persuaded my tongue to say "Speak Lord, for your servant had heard".[7] And at once he removed ignorance from me, and I was taught rightly to know the wisdom of the Father, the cause of all, and to understand mystical words, and the dark word and symbols.[8] And when I went up to the darkness of these divine things, I heard the trumpet with all ears and I saw henceforward "the true light which enlightens every man who comes into the world".[9] And when I was fully initiated in these great matters, I went out from the letter, which my right hand had introduced into my mind, not like the judge Ehud who killed Eglon.[10] And after these things for those encamped on this side and on that I suddenly became a mighty armed man. But how double war was kindled against us, wait upon the word, Father of Fathers: I shall tell (it).

Some of those who were infected with the lack of knowledge with which I was infected before, many times made crass accusations as they summoned some holy writing of yours to judgement and urged forward many things against proprieties. Some others were coming from Chalcedon somewhere, and were making excerpts from passages of your (writings), and were attempting to cast us out here, while they were publishing these proprieties. And you instruct me to proceed in the middle, and to interrupt the onset of the two of them with words, and were saying that I should call witnesses. And when I received your writing, I read the laws to them. And quite speechless, as they were overcome by the exactness of these divine (doctrines), these (points) of dispute went home to them at once, unless they were perverse in argument.

But I, who pass from war after war, and with difficulty have (*Lebon p. 99*) sacrificed peaceful things to God, and was acquainted with the war-trumpet, suffered a human passion: we observe that those who have been freed from a constant sickness of the eyes have an insatiableness for light, and this has frequently led back to sickness. For the rich diet of your words, Father, made the earlier sickness to wither, but caused a second (illness) of ignorance to spring forth in me. For when I diligently read the dazzling light of wise Cyril in your holy writings, I was obliged to close my eyes, and the salt tear of ignorance flowed.

At all events, you say, O Theologian, that (Cyril) made this contradictory statement: "Not confusing with each other and mixing

ܕܡܗܝܡܢܘܬܐ (98) ܡܬܦܪܐ ܗܘܬ. ܐܦܝܣܬ ܠܠܡܝܐ ܕܢܐܡܪ: ܡܛܠ ܡܪܝܐ ܡܛܠ ܕܥܒܕ ܚܒܝܒ. ܘܡܚܝܐ ܠܗ ܗܠܝܢ ܕܠܐ ܢܫܬܐ ܐܘܪܚ. ܘܕܐܘܒ ܡܚܡܬܐ ܕܐܬܐ ܚܒܬܐ ܕܚܠ: ܡܬܡܠܟ ܗܘܬ ܠܘܩܒܠܗ. ܘܐܦܬܟܠ ܩܠ̈ܐ ܩܕܝܫܬܐ ܘܡܠܬܐ ܣܥܘܕܬܐ ܘܩܕܡܐ. ܘܟܕ ܠܗܐ ܣܥܘܕܐ ܕܗܠܝܢ ܠܠܩܕܝܫܬܐ ܚܠܦܗ: ܒܥܠܘܡܝܢ ܐܘܪܐ ܡܦܩܕ ܗܘܬ ܠܡܫܘܪܐ: ܘܟܠܗܘܪܐ ܡܢܪܐ ܗܘ ܕܡܥܘܪ ܠܟܠܠ ܒܪܢܫܐ ܘܐܬܐ ܠܚܠܡܐ. ܡܢ ܗܘܪܐ ܢܗܝܪܐ: ܘܟܕ ܒܗܠܝܢ ܙܘܥܬܐ ܐܬܡܥܠܬ ܢܦܩܬ ܡܢ ܠܒܪܐ ܕܐܬܐ ܡܥܝܢܐ ܒܢܦܫܐ. ܠܗ ܗܘܬܐ ܐܝܟ ܐܗܘܪ ܕܢܝܐ: ܗܘ ܕܠܒܝܫܬܗ ܡܬܠ: ܘܟܠܘܪܝ ܠܗܠܝܢ ܕܡܬܐ ܘܡܬܐ ܓܪܝܢ ܗܘܘ. ܡܢ ܗܟܝܠ ܡܪܝܐ ܡܫܬܐܠ ܗܘܐ ܗܘܬ ܐܢܐ. ܐܝܟ ܕܝܢ ܡܬܡܠܟܘܢ ܗܘܐ ܒܠܝܢ ܡܪܬܐ ܒܥܡܐ: ܡܥܒܪ ܐܬܐ ܘܐܒܗ̈ܬܐ ܠܥܡܠܬܐ. ܐܢܐ ܕܝܢ ܐܬܝܬ.

ܐܝܟ ܡܢ ܗܘܢ ܕܒܪܝܟܝܢ ܗܘܘ ܠܐ ܢܫܬܐ ܗܘ ܕܒܪܝܟ ܗܘܬ ܐܢܐ ܡܒܥܝܐ: ܬܒܥܬܐ ܕܚܝܘܬܐ ܪܡܝܢ ܡܫܬܠܝ ܡܡܢܘ: ܟܕ ܡܬܡܟܢܘܬܝ ܡܕܡ ܡܒܥܝܬܐ ܦܪܝܢ ܗܘܘ ܠܚܝܠ ܕܒܝܬ: ܘܡܫܬܠܬܐ ܠܗܡܟܠ ܕܬܚܡܬܐ ܡܢܘܬܗܝܢ ܗܘܘ. ܐܝܟܢ ܐܡܪܝܢ ܡܢ ܡܬܡܒܘܥܐ ܡܢ ܕܡܢ ܐܬܝܢ ܗܘܘ. ܘܡܢ ܕܒܥܬܐ ܕܡܠܬܗ ܡܫܬܡܥܝܢ. ܘܕܢܚܘܢ ܠܢ ܗܘܪܐ ܡܢܝܢ ܗܘܘ: ܟܕ ܕܬܚܡܬܐ ܗܠܝܢ ܡܬܚܒܢܝܢ ܗܘܘ. ܘܕܡܥܒܕܬܐ ܐܦܠܘ ܙܪܐ ܐܝܬ ܠܗ: ܘܡܠܐܟܐ ܠܘܩܒܠܗ ܐܦܝܣܘ ܚܩܠܐ. ܘܕܐܦܪܐ ܐܢܐ ܡܬܘܕܐ ܐܦܢ ܗܘܬ. ܘܟܕ ܬܠܐ ܕܡܢ ܡܦܩܬ: ܡܪܝܐ ܠܗܘܢ ܢܦܫܬܐ. ܘܟܕ ܡܬܡܝܢ ܦܬܓܡ ܟܕ ܡܕܘܟܝܢ ܗܘܘ ܡܢ ܣܬܡܘܬܐ ܕܗܠܝܢ ܠܠܩܘܡܬܐ: ܠܗܠܝܢ ܦܝ ܒܪܟܬܐ ܡܣܝܐ: ܐܦ ܒܩܝܡܝܢ ܡܕܘܬܐ ܠܡܬܡܗܘܢ: ܗܠܝܢ ܕܡܕܘܬܐ ܐܦܬܟܠ.

ܐܢܐ ܕܝܢ ܟܕ ܡܪܐ ܡܢ ܡܪܬܐ ܚܪܢ ܐܢܐ: ܘܠܡܫܝܚ (99) ܗܠܝܢ ܕܡܠܟܬܐ ܕܒܪܢܫܐ ܠܠܚܘܐ: ܘܐܘܪܚܬܐ ܐܢܐ ܒܡܫܘܪܐ ܕܡܕܝܢ: ܡܦܩܬ ܡܢܐ ܐܝܡܐ: ܠܐܝܠܝܢ ܕܐܪܚܘܗ ܡܢ ܟܐܒܐ ܐܡܝܢܐ ܕܚܢܢܐ: ܠܐ ܡܫܬܠܚܢܘܬܐ ܕܗܘܪܐ ܢܗܝܪ ܕܐܬܐ ܠܗܘܢ. ܗܘܝܐ ܪܡܝܢ ܡܫܬܠܝ ܠܚܘܪܗܐ ܐܦܝܣܬ. ܡܚܒܠ ܓܒܪ ܕܩܢܐ ܩܬܡܝ ܐܘ ܐܒܐ: ܒܡܘܪܗܐ ܦܝ ܡܕܡܐ ܐܡܥܢ. ܠܐ ܢܫܬܐ ܕܝܢ ܕܠܐܩܘܡ ܐܚܕ ܒܗ. ܟܕ ܪܚܡܐ ܓܒܪ ܕܡܣܬܟܠ ܣܝܡܐ ܒܬܡܟܬܐ ܡܒܥܝܬܐ ܕܡܠܟܘܢ ܣܬܡܠܬܗ ܡܪܝܐ: ܐܬܐܠܝܐ ܕܐܒܝܢ ܚܪܝܢ: ܘܕܡܟܬܐ ܕܠܐ ܢܫܬܐ ܡܬܚܣܢܬܐ ܕܟܠܗ.

ܘܡܢ ܡܬܦܪܘܫ ܐܦܢ ܐܝܬ ܐܘ ܡܫܬܠܠ ܠܠܩܘܡܬܐ: ܕܐܦܢ ܡܬܟܠܬܐ ܗܘ ܡܬܐܡܪܚܢܬܐ. ܠܗ ܟܕ ܡܬܚܬܟܠܠܬܐ ܒܡ ܢܒܝܐ ܘܡܥܡܪ ܐܬܐ ܩܢܝܐ. ܐܠܐ ܢܒܥ ܐܬܐ

the natures".[11] Now, I acknowledge that once the divine union is mentioned, confusion is set aside, (but here) the union is not thought of in a faulty way when the natures are unmixed in a divine and inexpressible mingling and in a hypostasis.[12] How (then) shall I proclaim one nature incarnate of the Word, and accuse of folly those who acknowledge two natures for Christ? And how shall I find fault with that Theological Wisdom[13] which states that the natures are mixed in a composition which is beyond description, which it calls συμφυΐα[14] through which I learn that the natures are not (merely) placed beside each other, but are utterly mingled to (become) one image and one hypostasis, so that the composition being thus accurately understood, the ousia of the divine Trinity, which is only concerned with three persons, is not increased? And we shall keep the definition of the Fathers safe, teaching one nature of God the Word incarnate, and not expounding this royal doctrine wrongly like the opposition. For they say they speak of one nature of the Word, but in the word "incarnate" there is seen a mark of the other (nature): (*Lebon p. 100*) not that the Word has joined this to itself hypostatically, and thus there is naturally one from two, but that, so they babble, an accidental union[15] has taken place, (the word) "incarnate" being a token of a nature standing in its own right. The righteous word which truly acknowledges one nature incarnate of the Word refutes these things.

But it is time to return to what was set down earlier. For I am aware of someone who objects and says: "Listen carefully to the consequences: the Son is understood as one in this way as well". But I remember that Nestorius also says this. Thus, I learn that the combination of two or more simples into one belongs to the principle[16] of composition, in which what is complete is also a (constituent) part, and (yet) afterwards the (constituent) parts are not from then on adjudged according to the principle of duality, since once and for all one ousia and quality has come into being.[17] Therefore unless the natures, from which Christ is, were mixed inconfusedly, how shall I say that those things which thus remained unmixed with each other were hypostatically united? How shall I retain the principle of composition, when the natures are retained just as they were? For it is impossible for me to conceive of a union of things mutually unmixed, as they say, and necessarily thereby Christ would have to be thought of (lit. we should have to think of) as two natures.

It seems right, therefore, that I should repeat the discussion about properties which I learned from your holy lines: "For although the Word is something and keeps that thing, he also became something

ܦܢ: ܕܟܕ ܚܕܘܬܐ ܠܐܠܗܘܬܐ ܡܫܠܡܘܬܐ: ܡܪܢܫܝܢ ܗܠܝܢ ܕܒܘܟܠܐ. ܟܕ ܠܐ ܡܬܡܪܟܢ ܒܢ̈ܝܐ: ܒܫܘܠܛܢܐ ܠܐܠܗܐ ܘܠܐ ܡܬܐܡܪܢܐ ܘܒܝܫܘܬܐ: ܠܗ ܕܡܬܠܬ ܡܬܘܕܝܐ ܚܕܘܬܐ. ܘܐܡܟܝܠ ܐܝܟ ܚܕ ܟܕ ܦܢ ܡܟܬܒܪܐ ܕܡܠܟܘܬܐ ܐܪܥܐ. ܠܗܠܝܢ ܕܝܢ ܕܝܠܗܝܢ ܠܗ. ܠܡܫܡܫܐ ܬܘܒ ܒܢ̈ܝܢ ܐܪܥܐ ܡܫܥܒܕܐ ܗܘܬ. ܐܡܟܝܠ ܕܝܢ ܘܠܗܘܢ ܣܓܝܐܬܐ ܡܫܠܛܢ ܠܐܠܗܘܬܐ ܐܚܪܢܝܬܐ ܘܐܡܪܐ: ܗܢܘ ܕܒܫܥܒܕܘܬܐ ܕܒܝܫܬܐ ܡܢ ܡܠܟܐ ܡܬܡܪܟܢ ܒܢ̈ܝܐ: ܘܡܫܡܫܢܐ ܚܘܫܒܬܐ ܕܐܢܫܐ. ܕܡܬܒܪܝܢ ܒܢ̈ܝܐ ܠܗ ܕܫܡܫܝܢ ܠܗܘܢ ܚܝܕܐ ܢܦܫ ܐܢܐ: ܐܠܐ ܕܚܠܝܠܝܢ ܗܦܟܝܢ ܡܬܬܠܬ ܠܗܘܢ ܚܕ ܡܘܬܐ ܘܚܕ ܡܘܬܐ. ܐܡܟܝܠ ܕܟܕ ܗܘܝܐ ܡܬܬܠܬ ܡܬܘܕܝܐ ܡܫܥܒܕܘܬܐ: ܐܘܣܝܐ ܕܐܠܗܘܬܐ ܠܐܠܗܘܬܐ ܠܐ ܐܬܬܠܬ: ܕܠܗܘܢ ܐܠܗܐ ܦܪ̈ܘܨܐ ܒܠܚܘܕ ܚܕܐ. ܘܐܣܘܟܐ ܐܚܘܬܐ ܚܕ ܢܘܗܪ ܟܕ ܡܦܠܚ ܚܕ: ܚܕ ܟܝܢܐ ܕܡܠܟܐ ܠܐܠܗܐ ܕܡܟܬܒܪ. ܘܕܠܗ ܐܝܟ ܗܢܘܢ ܕܒܘܟܠܐ: ܒܫܘܠܛܢܐ ܗܘܐ ܡܠܟܐ ܒܢ̈ܝܬܐ ܡܫܡܫܝܢ. ܐܡܪܝܢ ܓܝܪ ܐܡܪܝܢ ܚܕ ܟܝܢܐ ܕܡܠܟܐ. ܒܗܢܘ ܕܝܢ ܕܡܟܬܒܪ: ܫܘܪܝܐ ܕܗܘ ܐܡܪܢܐ (100) ܡܬܐܡܪܐ. ܠܗ ܕܗܘܐ ܐܦܠ ܠܗ ܡܠܟܐ ܒܫܘܠܛܢܐ. ܘܗܘܝܐ ܡܢܗ ܚܕ ܡܢ ܬܘܒ. ܐܠܐ ܕܚܕܘܬܐ ܕܠܗܘܢ ܫܡܫܐ ܐܝܟ ܕܡܫܡܫܝܢ ܗܘܐ. ܟܕ ܗܢܘ ܕܡܟܬܒܪ: ܡܫܘܕܥܢܘܬܐ ܕܟܝܢܐ ܕܡܢܗ ܘܠܗ ܫܡܫ ܐܠܗܐ. ܗܠܝܢ ܕܗܘܦܟܐ ܡܠܟܐ ܕܒܪܝܬܐ: ܕܚܕ ܟܝܢܐ ܡܟܬܒܪܐ ܕܡܠܟܐ ܡܪܢܝܬܐ ܚܕܐ.

ܐܠܐ ܕܟܝܢܐ ܗܘ ܕܠܗܘܢ ܗܢܘ ܕܚܕܝܬܐ ܫܡܫܐ ܢܘܗܪܐ. ܡܪܢܐ ܐܝܟ ܓܝܪ ܒܐܝܕ ܕܒܐ ܘܐܡܪ: ܕܗܠܝܢ ܕܡܪܢܐ ܒܪܢܫܐ ܒܒܠܐ ܡܫܒܚ. ܘܐܝܟ ܚܕ ܒܪܐ ܘܗܘܝܐ ܡܫܬܡܠܐ. ܗܘܐ ܕܝܢ ܘܦܝܠܣܘܦܘܣ ܒܗܘܢ ܐܢܐ ܘܐܡܪ: ܗܘܝܐ ܢܦܩ ܐܢܐ ܘܐܝܬ ܠܗ ܠܡܠܟܐ ܕܡܬܒܪܘܬܐ. ܗܢܘ ܕܡܢ ܬܘܒ ܐܘ ܡܣܟܢܐ. ܡܫܒܚܐ ܠܗܘܢ ܒܫܘܠܛܢܐ ܐܝܬ. ܕܠܗ ܘܡܫܡܫܢܐ ܡܫܠܛܐ ܐܝܬܘܗܝ. ܘܠܡܪܗ ܠܐ ܡܫܟܚ ܦܫܘܛܐ ܐܝܟ ܡܠܟܐ ܕܬܪܝܨܘܬܐ ܡܬܕܝܢ. ܟܕ ܚܝܐ ܕܝܢ ܚܝܐ ܐܘܫܛܐ ܗܘܝܐ ܐܦ ܡܫܘܕܥܢܘܬܐ. ܐܘ ܗܘܝܐ ܒܢ̈ܝܐ ܕܡܢܗܘܢ ܡܫܡܫܐ ܠܐ ܡܫܬܟܠܠܐ ܠܐ ܐܬܡܪܟܢ ܐܚܝܕܐ: ܐܡܟܝܠ ܗܠܝܢ ܕܗܘܝܢ ܗܘܘ ܠܐ ܡܫܬܡܪܟܢ ܒܢܝܕܐ: ܘܐܬܚܝܕܘ ܡܫܡܫܝܬܐ ܐܡܪ: ܐܡܟܝܠ ܕܝܢ ܡܠܟܐ ܕܪܘܫܡܐ ܐܠܗܐ: ܟܕ ܡܬܬܠܬܝܢ ܒܢ̈ܝܐ ܐܝܟ ܕܐܝܬ ܗܘܐ ܠܗܘܢ. ܕܗܠܝܢ ܓܝܪ ܕܠܐ ܡܡܪܟܢ ܠܗܘܢ ܒܢܝܕܐ ܐܝܟ ܕܗܢܘܢ ܐܡܪܝܢ: ܚܕܘܬܐ ܕܐܬܝܠܕ ܠܗ. ܐܝܟܢܐ ܘܒܗܘܐ ܬܘܒ ܒܢ̈ܝܢ ܙܘܥ ܕܒܝܫܘܬܗ ܠܚܕ ܡܫܡܫܐ.

else, obviously not involving a lessening of divinity, but through the supreme union of inhomination he had at the same time these properties and those which he (already) had, and he shows that he was become one incarnate nature".[18] But holy Father, how I am to understand that the natures are not mixed is a great (obstacle) to me. (*Lebon p. 101*) For after this I am unable to go up to centurions or chiliarchs, but to you Moses, who was worthy to speak these more divine things face to face, and who explains the greater things. For my mind is wearied by labour and is unable to ascend to such a height and all the more when learned men from Chalcedon were stirring up battle from common notions on the one side, and on the other side were excommunicating these Fathers and telling us on all sides (of) the two natures. But when divine grace descends upon my humble tongue, it often drives out the first kind (of difficulty).

But how shall I pass over to this second (type of difficulty), since the laws of the Fathers are read to me and I do not know at (any) one time how to keep silent, lest "the natures" of those who are pursuing should take me? But when I add thought upon thought and make my mind to pass to desire for the fear of God, I seem like one who slips and like those athletes who are exhausted. How not to fall in everything, but to overcome, I shall learn from you, Doctor and Witness of right belief.[19] And with this I shall avoid the second ignorance also for it is time that I say this too.

I remember that in my lines there is (the formula that Christ) is "from two natures", and all the propriety of the inhomination of the Word is a mystery. But I also received the point gladly and approved the fatherly correction that it was thought foolish to say "a gathering of properties",[20] just as no-one will rashly say that a man is constituted from "being rational" and "blackness", although the two words are not being thought equal in every respect. For "being rational" completes an ousia that it should be one: thus (a man is) a rational mortal living thing, and if someone should remove (*Lebon p. 102*) that "being rational", he destroys the subject in every respect. But blackness (is) not in the hypostasis but is a sign of that which is laid down (and) when it fades to whiteness it leaves the ousia (just) as it is naturally.

Therefore as I keep silent wise Cyril again urges on (my) thoughts, who speaks best by means of your priestly tongue, but is not yet understood by me, who am of small account. But I read the law to you as well: "He is composed so as to become one in the middle, of human properties, and those which are above man".[21] The Father seems to say that the incarnate Word was one in every respect, I

ܡܣܪܐ ܗܘܠܐ ܘܡܬܠܐ ܘܡܫܠܐ ܕܬܠܡܝܕܐ: ܡܢ ܣܘܦܣܛܝܩܘܣ ܒܢܘܝܐ ܢܦܫܗ ܐܝܬܝ. ܟܕ ܐܬܠܘܗܝ ܓܒܪ ܡܫܠܡܐ ܡܢܗ ܘܢܦܫ ܗܘܐ: ܗܘܐ ܘܡܢܗ ܐܣܝܪ. ܘܡܝܬܐ ܘܠܗ ܐܝܟ ܦܘ ܘܐܬܦܪܣܐ ܠܟܘܠܐ. ܩܘܡ ܠܗ ܕܝܢ ܟܕ ܗܘܐ ܟܝܢܝܘܬܐ ܘܣܡܝܬܐ ܘܡܬܒܢܝܢܘܬܐ ܕܬܠܡܝܕܐ ܗܠܝܢ. ܘܦܢܝ ܘܐܝܬ ܗܘܐ ܠܗ. ܘܡܫܢܝܐ ܕܗܘܐ ܡܢ ܟܝܬܐ ܘܡܟܢܫ܆ ܐܠܐ ܐܡܝܢܐ ܐܫܬܥܠܝܘ ܐܦܠܐ ܡܝܬܐ: ܘܠܐ ܡܫܬܠܝܢ ܟܝܬܐ ܐܚܪܝܐ: ܙܟܐ ܗܘ ܠܗ. (101) ܟܠܢ ܗܘܐ ܓܝܪ ܘܦܐܫ ܠܟܐ ܕܢܦܫ ܡܢܘܬܐ ܐܘ ܕܢܦܫ ܠܟܠܗ ܠܐ ܡܫܟܚ ܐܝܬ. ܐܠܐ ܠܟܠܗ ܡܫܡܥ: ܗܘ ܕܐܦܝ ܠܟܠ ܐܦܝ ܗܠܝܢ ܕܡܢܝܢ ܠܟܘܠܗܝܢ ܐܝܬܘܗܝ ܕܡܫܠܛ: ܘܡܬܕܒܪܐ ܦܩܘܕܐ. ܠܐܦܝ ܟܠ ܓܝܪ ܗܠܝܢ ܕܢܦܫܐ: ܘܠܐ ܣܦܩܐ ܕܟܠ ܡܠܘ ܗܘܝ ܙܘܥܐ ܢܦܫ. ܘܡܬܕܐܡ ܐܝܬܘܗܝ ܕܡܕܒܪܐ ܘܡܬܡܨܝܐ: ܟܕ ܗܘܐ ܦܝ ܡܢ ܬܫܡܫܬܐ ܕܓܘܐ ܡܫܬܡܫܝܢ ܦܪܓܐ: ܟܕ ܗܘܐ ܕܝܢ ܠܐܝܟܢܐ ܗܠܝܢ ܡܫܬܡܫܝܢ: ܘܟܠܗ ܘܡܬܡܚܐ ܢܩܝܦ ܟܬܝܒ ܡܬܡܚܝܢ ܠܝ. ܐܠܐ ܐܦܠܐ ܦܝ ܗܘ ܡܕܡܐ ܟܕ ܟܠܐ ܠܚܝܘ ܡܬܡܠܝܐ ܠܡܦܠܐ ܠܟܘܠܐ ܚܝܠܐ: ܪܒܝܢ ܣܓܝܐܐ ܕܢܦܫܐ.

ܡܛܠ ܕܝܢ ܕܟܠܐ ܗܘ ܠܐܘܪܚܐ ܐܚܪܝ: ܟܕ ܢܦܫܗ ܐܚܪܢܐ ܡܬܡܪܝܢ ܠܗ: ܘܐܬܠܘܗܝ ܦܝ ܟܝܪܐ ܙܟܝ ܠܐ ܢܦܩ ܐܝܬ. ܘܠܐ ܟܝܬܐ ܕܦܢܝ ܕܙܘܥܢ ܢܫܬܘܚܢ. ܟܕ ܕܝܢ ܡܪܢܝܬܐ ܟܡܐ ܡܪܢܝܬܐ ܦܩܝܩ ܐܝܬ: ܘܟܠܐ ܙܟܝܐ ܕܢܚܬܗ ܠܟܘܠܐ ܡܫܒܪ ܐܝܬ ܠܐܘܪܚܬܐ: ܡܫܬܡܫܢ ܐܝܬ ܐܝܟ ܡܬܐ ܕܡܪܓ ܐܝܬ. ܘܐܝܟ ܦܢܝ ܠܓܘܢܝܐ ܕܡܫܡܫܝܢ: ܦܝ ܘܠܐ ܟܕ ܟܐܠܦܐ: ܐܠܐ ܦܝ ܘܐܪܥܐ. ܠܟܠ ܡܢܝ ܡܬܦܫܐ ܕܢܚܬܗ ܠܟܘܠܐ ܘܡܫܘܕܐ. ܘܡܢ ܗܘܐ ܐܦ ܡܢ ܠܐ ܡܝܬܐ ܕܠܐܘܪܚ ܐܚܪܢܘܣ. ܘܐܦܢ ܓܝܪ ܘܗܘܐ ܙܟܝܐ ܗܘ.

ܚܘܕ ܐܝܬ ܕܡܫܡܫܢܘܬܐ ܘܡܠܟ: ܕܡܢ ܠܐܬܡ ܦܢܝܢ ܐܝܟ ܟܗܢ. ܘܡܠܟ ܗܘܐ ܕܡܬܡܠܐ ܘܡܬܒܢܝܢܘܬܐ ܕܡܫܠܛܐ ܙܕܩܐ ܗܘ. ܐܠܐ ܘܦܢܝ ܕܢܐܡܪ ܟܢܘܫܝܐ ܕܬܠܡܝܕܐ ܣܘܟܠܐ ܠܐܫܬܘܕܝ ܐܝܟ ܦܝ ܘܠܐ ܡܫܬܪܝܐ ܐܝܟ ܕܟܪܝܗܐ ܢܐܡܪ ܘܡܬܐܡܪ ܡܢ ܡܫܠܠܐ ܘܐܘܟܝܬܐ ܘܦܟܝܠ ܡܫܠܛܐ ܗܘܐ ܐܝܬ. ܘܡܬܡܪܢܘܬܐ ܐܚܘܢܬܐ ܦܩܝܕܬ. ܟܕ ܛܒ ܠܗ ܟܠܠ ܡܢܗ ܡܫܬܠܛܝ ܕܢܦܩ ܩܢܐ ܩܠܐ. ܡܫܡܠܝܐ ܓܝܪ ܡܫܡܠܝܐ ܐܘܣܝܐ ܐܝܟ ܚܕܐ ܐܬܠܝܗ. ܚܘܬܐ ܗܘܠܐ ܡܫܡܠܝܐ ܡܘܬܐ. ܘܐܦ ܐܝܟ ܢܦܫ (102) ܗܘ ܘܡܫܬܠܛܐ: ܡܫܠܠ ܡܢ ܡܬܦܪܘܣ ܗܘ ܕܡܫܐ. ܐܘܣܝܘܬܐ ܕܝܢ ܠܗ ܟܝܢܝܬܐ ܐܠܐ ܡܘܕܝܐ ܘܗܘ ܕܣܝܡ ܐܝܬܝܗ. ܗܘ ܘܐܦ ܟܕ ܡܫܡܐ ܠܗܘܢܬܐ ܡܬܟܠ ܠܐܘܣܝܐ ܐܝܟ ܕܡܟܝܠ.

mean both nature and propriety, when he mingled the natures along with the proprieties. But (I say) this as a suggestion rather than a decree, for in what opinion should I be headstrong? Again, Masters, I pray that in this knowledge too I may be made perfect by you.

But where else do I fail in (your) letter? I shall make a defence against your fatherly rebuke with testimonia of the truth that I did not suddenly venture to discuss theology but approached the subject with much trepidation of mind and voice and I repeat the old saying 10,000 times "I am of a meagre voice and a slow tongue".[22] For we would teach by means of the written (word) every land and island, so to speak, even if some sort of lament should be necessary, and we will "go to Macedonia"[23] in word, (we) who recall the boldness of teaching of the Fathers. In those cases where it is required that I bring a mystery in writtten form I have drawn on your words in every respect and I am confident in a situation like this. But I shall accept your spiritual bridle with my whole tongue and will not bite it like an uncontrolled colt and make [a path][24] outside the proper sense. But you keep guard too, for you are a lamp (*Lebon p. 103*) of Israel like David[25] or a watchman like Ezekiel,[26] and do not lie hid under a measure,[27] but when you have ascended upon the candlestick of the Church shine again on us who are in the house of Christ, in order that "good will"[28] may touch us as we stretch out (our) mind again to you.

These things belong to the high priest of God. For my part, I (shall receive), so I believe, the reward of my labour, which from contempt I am ashamed that I should even call "labours", (which) will free the mind from every fleshly opinion. But through your divine prayers may I see here the peace of the Church with you true pastors, and may I go yonder with pure confidence that I shall be with you on the right hand side.

The Second Letter of Sergius the Grammarian to the Patriarch Lord Severus is ended.

Notes

1. 2 Kms. ix.8.
2. cf. 1 Kms. iii.1.
3. Ps. cxvii.20. There may be a word-play on ܬܪܥܐ "chapter" and "door".
4. Lebon suggests ὑπὸ ἀπειροκαλίας (from ignorance of the beautiful; want of taste) as underlying ܡܢ ܠܐ ܡܪܓܫܢܘܬ ܠܫܘܦܪܐ
5. ܣܦܝܩܘܬܐ: nothingness; a void; leisure; freedom. The underlying Greek may possibly be ἡσυχία.
6. cf. Dan. vii.11.

ܟܕ ܫܡܥܬ ܐܢܐ ܗܟܢܐܝܬ: ܠܘܬ ܛܘܪ ܗܠܝܢ ܕܡܣܡܟܬܐ ܡܘܬܒܗܘܢ ܕܡܫܝܚܝܐ: ܘܬܪܥܝܬܗ ܦܝܫ ܟܕ ܠܡܥܒܕܗ ܟܘܢܐ ܡܫܬܠܛ. ܠܐ ܕܝܢ ܟܕ ܡܬܟܠ ܠܗ ܕܐܗܘܐ ܡܠܝܚ. ܡܛܐ ܐܢܐ ܠܟܘܢ ܕܝܢ ܘܡܟܝܠ. ܕܒܬܟܠܬܐ ܐܢܫܝܬܐ ܠܘܬ. ܘܟܗܠܝܢ ܘܟܠܗ ܡܢ ܟܢܘܫܐ: ܟܕ ܡܕܡ ܗܘ ܕܡܥܪܒܬܐ ܡܪܡܕ ܡܫܬܡܥ ܘܐܡܪ ܐܬܐ: ܘܟܕ ܟܢܫܐ ܟܡ ܕܬܟܠܬܐ ܣܓܝ. ܣܒ ܡܢ ܡܟܝܘܡ ܡܟܠܬܐ ܕܡܟܫܪ ܐܠܗܘܗܝ. ܘܟܡܐ ܐܡܪ ܐܢܐ ܘܡܟܠܬܐ. ܗܘܐ ܟܕܘܢ ܐܢܐ ܐܢܐ ܠܐ ܦܫܦܫ ܐܢܐ. ܟܐܢܐ ܓܒܪ ܡܫܡܠܐ ܐܦ ܐܡܪܝܢ. ܠܘܬ ܡܛܠܐ ܐܢܐ: ܘܐܦ ܟܗܘܐ ܡܒܠܬܐ: ܡܟܝܘܢ ܬܘܕܝܐ ܐܠܗܝܐ.

ܡܢܐ ܕܝܢ ܡܫܬܠ ܣܦܪ ܠܗ ܟܐܓܪܬܐ ܟܠܐ ܡܪܡܘܬܗܘܢ ܐܟܘܬܐ ܟܡ ܡܫܘܐ ܘܡܪܘܐ ܐܦܘܗ ܟܢܘܫܐ: ܘܠܗ ܡܢ ܗܠܝܢ ܐܡܪܝܢܗ ܘܐܡܪ ܠܟܘܟܬܐ. ܦܝܫ ܕܝܢ ܟܠܪܘܚܬܐ ܘܪܟܐ ܘܟܪܐ ܡܠܐ ܡܫܒܠ ܐܢܐ ܟܠܐ ܓܒܪܐ. ܘܗܘܐ ܟܠܡܟܬܐ ܟܪ̈ܒܘ ܐܡܪ ܐܢܐ ܐܢܐ: ܕܡܟܦܢ ܟܪܐ ܡܠܐ ܐܠܗ ܘܡܫܪ ܟܡܠܐ. ܐܦ ܓܒܪ ܘܐܘܟܠܬܐ ܡܕܡ ܠܐܬܟܪ: ܟܠܐ ܡܟܘܡ ܕܝܢ ܐܘܟܠܬܐ ܘܓܒܪܬܐ ܐܡܪ ܕܟܠܐܡܪ: ܟܕ ܡܠܟܬܐ ܡܟܠܦܡ ܣܒ. ܘܟܠܐ ܡܡܕܘܢܐ ܟܡܟܠܬܐ ܐܬܐܡ ܣܒ. ܕܣܐܘܪܬܐ ܕܦܟܠܦܢܐ ܐܟܘܫܐ ܟܗܘܕ. ܟܗܠܝܢ ܬܬܟܠܐ ܕܐܠܬܐ ܡܠܝܠܝܬܗ ܘܐܬܐ ܡܢ ܦܢܗ ܩܠܟܘܢ ܡܢ ܟܠ ܦܪܘܫ ܓܪܦܗ. ܘܟܗܘܐ ܕܕܐܡܪ ܗܟܢܐ ܟܦܪܘܫܢܐ ܗܘܐ ܐܢܐ. ܟܪܡ ܕܝܢ ܦܓܘܕܐܟܘܢ ܘܡܫܚܠܬܐ ܟܠܟܠܗ ܟܡܢܐ ܡܫܬܠܛܐ. ܘܗܘܐ ܠܗ ܐܡܪ ܟܠܐ ܠܐ ܡܬܟܫܐ ܕܟܠ ܐܢܐ. ܘܡܟܪ ܡܢ ܡܪܬܐ ܘܦܬܐ ܟܕܦ ܐܢܐ ܕܗܬܐ. ܘܬܪ ܡܢ ܐܠܗ ܬܪ: ܕܡܪܓܠ ܐܠܗ (103) ܕܐܡܪܬܠܐܡܪ ܕܘܟܪ. ܐܘ ܕܘܡܐ ܐܡܪ ܣܪܦܝܠ. ܘܠܐ ܦܝܫ ܠܐܣܟ ܡܟܘܕܐ ܠܐܬܐ. ܟܠܐ ܕܝܢ ܡܟܪܬܐ ܕܟܕܬܐ ܟܕ ܫܡܥ ܐܠܗ: ܠܘܬ ܠܟ ܠܐܡܠܟ ܕܟܠܟܬܐ ܕܡܫܡܫܢܐ ܐܡܘܪ. ܐܟܝܐ ܕܟܕ ܠܘܬ ܟܠܐܡ ܬܘܟܠܬܐ ܡܟܠܣܡ ܣܒ: ܡܟܪܐ ܬܟܐ ܝܓܒܗ ܠܟ.

ܗܠܝܢ ܦܝܫ ܟܟܘܢܐ ܕܠܟܘܢ. ܟܠܗ ܪܟܐ. ܐܢܐ ܕܝܢ ܐܡܪܐ ܕܟܟܠܐ ܕܡܟܢ ܐܡܪ ܕܦܟܪ ܐܢܐ: ܐܡܠܟ ܘܐܦ ܟܩܠܐ ܐܡܪܐ ܡܟܠܟܒ ܐܢܐ ܡܬܠ ܡܣܬܠܐ: ܡܢ ܟܠ ܡܟܪܐ ܦܝܫ ܟܡܪܢܐ ܡܓܒܘܢ ܟܠܐܘܟܠܬܐ. ܟܕ ܕܝܢ ܟܟܠܬܐ ܘܡܟܘܢ ܠܟܘܟܬܐ: ܗܘܟܐ ܦܝܫ ܡܢܐ ܘܟܕܬܐ ܟܡܟܘܢ ܬܟܠܬܐ ܡܬܡܪܐ ܐܡܪܐ. ܟܗܠ ܕܝܢ ܟܡ ܦܪܘܫܢܐ ܘܟܡܟܬܐ ܐܙܠ: ܘܟܡܟܘܢ ܘܡܟܠܬܐ ܘܡܫܡܫܢܐ ܐܗܘܐ.

܀ܫܠܡܬ ܐܓܪܬܐ ܕܐܬܐܡ ܕܡܪܓܡܣ ܓܪܡܛܝܩܘܣ: ܟܠܐܘ ܕܦܬܪܓܡܐ ܡܪܝ ܫܠܘܡܐ܀

7. 1 Kms. iii.9. LXX ἀκούει.

8. ܥܒܕܐ.

9. cf. Jn. i.9.

10. cf. Judg. iii.21.

11. See p. 77 (Lebon) above, (Severus' *First Letter*). PG 76.85B. The Syriac translator attributes the participles to Cyril himself. On p. 77 ܡܣܚܦ is used to translate συγχέων, here ܡܚܠܛ is used.

12. The passage is difficult. Lebon suggests reading ܩܕܡܐܝܬ for ܩܪܡܐܝܬ: ". . . . the union is not *primarily* thought of when the natures are unmixed . . .", but this is probably less satisfactory.

13. So Sergius calls Gregory Nazianzen.

14. cf. PG 37.181C, line 7: τῷ λογῷ τῆς συμφυΐας. The Syriac is: ܫܘܬܦܘܬܐ ܕܐܟܝܢܐ. *Ep. CI, Ad Cled. Ep. I.*

15. ܚܕܝܘܬܐ ܕܠܘܬ ܣܝܡܐ The Greek is possibly ἕνωσις κατὰ θέσιν.

16. ܡܠܬܐ.

17. cf. below, p. 150.19–24.

18. Because of the gap in the ms. the place of this in the earlier letter of Severus is not known.

19. ܕܚܠܬ ܐܠܗܐ = εὐσέβεια.

20. cf. p. 86, line 8.

21. PG 76.1193B. This passage was quoted above by Severus, cf. p. 92.28 (= Pusey edn. Vol. 7, p. 134.13–14). *De Recta Fide ad Theod.*

22. Ex. iv.10.

23. cf. 1 Tim. i.3; Acts xvi.9.

24. Read ܐܗܠܐ for ܕܗܠܐ (misprint).

25. cf. 2 Kms. xxi.17 and 4 Kms. viii.19.

26. Ezek. iii.17; xxxiii.7.

27. cf. Mt. v.15.

28. cf. Lk. ii.14.

Letter II of Severus

Again the Second Letter of the Patriarch Severus to Sergius the Grammarian.

I now approve of your desire to learn, because when you received a letter which in it brought the words of scripture which is inspired by God, and (the words) of the revered teachers of mysteries in the holy Church who defined exactly the word of truth, you knew from them that it is right for those who are not beginners (in) confessing the faith to acknowledge and to profess the particularity according to natural quality of the natures from which there is the one and only Christ, (natures) I mean of divinity and of humanity: one person, one hypostasis, one nature belonging to the Word, meaning incarnate, and because you have chosen to set out again for discussion that which was difficult for your mind, and (because) you were not ashamed with the bashfulness which brings sin, and you were not afraid with the suspicion which brings (*Lebon p. 104*) destruction, but because you knew again to ask concerning the faith which is believed in because of the salvation of the soul, so that what belongs to truth might shine more brightly.

For it is very pleasant and welcome to me as well when I speak to a man who has a wisdom that investigates and not agreement only that does not test out and try—provided (of course) the range of the investigation does not transgress the measure. But even profane philosophy teaches that the measure is best in everything and the law of the fear of God confirms (it) when it forewarns (and) says "Do not remove the ancient limits which your fathers laid down".[1] As long as we retain these limits, it is good that we thrash out that which you have offered, or is in doubt. For holy scripture again teaches that iron sharpens iron,[2] (and) as one might say, when thoughts are sharpened, they are made more subtle and more acute.

Therefore when wise Cyril says in the Second Volume against the blasphemies of Nestorius, "When the mystery of Christ is brought into the middle for us, the principle of the union on the one hand recognises difference, but on the other hand rejects division, while neither confusing nor mixing the natures with each other",[3] you say that you cannot otherwise understand the undivided union, unless

❖ܬܘܒ ܕܡܢܗ ܕܦܛܪܝܪܟܐ ܫܠܘܪܐ: ܐܝܟܢܐ ܕܐܬܩܢܝ ܙܘܘܗܘܢ ܕܡܪܩܝܘܤ
ܒܪܛܠܡܘܤ❖

ܦܠܓܗ ܘܗܘܐ ܙܢܕܩܐ ܡܠܟܝܢ: ܘܟܕ ܡܠܟܐ ܐܠܝܛܐ ܗܘ: ܗܘ ܕܡܫܡܠܐ ܒܗ ܩܢܬܗ ܩܠܐ ܘܛܠܒܐ ܢܦܫ ܡܢ ܠܚܘܕ: ܘܒܢܝܫܐ ܩܛܠܗ ܙܪܐ ܘܟܒܠܐ ܡܫܝܚܠܐ ܘܦܫܡܘ ܠܘܩܒܠܗ ܡܠܟܐ ܘܥܒܕܐ: ܢܚܬ ܡܢܗܘܢ ܕܗܘܘ ܠܥܠܡܝܢ ܕܠܗ ܘܡܠܟܘܬܗ ܡܛܘܠ ܘܡܫܘܬܐ: ܘܢܚܬܘܢ ܘܐܡܪܘ ܘܡܠܟܐ ܗܘ ܘܐܝܟ ܕܡܫܘܕܥܬܐ ܒܫܠܟܐ ܘܒܢܝܐ ܘܡܫܘܢ ܐܠܗܘܗܝ ܗܘ ܡܢ ܘܒܠܫܘܙܘܗܝ ܡܫܝܚܐ: ܘܠܗܘܬܐ ܐܡܪ ܐܢܐ ܘܕܐܝܫܘܬܐ: ܡܢ ܦܪܘܫܐ ܡܢ ܡܫܘܚܐ: ܡܢ ܟܝܢܐ ܗܘ ܕܡܠܗ ܘܡܠܟܐ: ܢܚܬܐ ܕܝܢ ܕܡܫܟܢ. ܘܕܗܘ ܘܡܠܟܫܐ ܗܘܐ ܠܠܦܘܠܡܝܢ: ܬܘܒ ܒܕܘܪܐ ܬܦܢܝܢ ܬܫܥܝܢ ܘܚܡܫ. ܘܠܐ ܐܬܚܙܝܬ ܬܚܝܬܐ ܗܘ ܘܡܠܟܘܬܐ ܢܣܝܒܬܐ. ܘܠܐ ܐܬܝܠܝܕܬ (104) ܡܢܝܢܐ ܗܘ ܘܡܠܟܐ ܠܐܒܢܐ. ܐܠܐ ܘܡܛܠ ܗܡܫܘܬܐ ܗܘ ܘܡܛܠ ܦܘܪܫܢܐ ܘܒܥܐ ܡܠܘܟܫܢܐ. ܬܘܒ ܢܚܬ ܠܥܠܡܐ. ܐܡܝܢܐ ܘܗܟܢ ܘܫܪܪܐ ܠܗܡܪ ܢܚܬܢ.

ܐܦ ܠܐ ܢܦܪ ܫܟܝܢ ܡܫܘܚܐ ܘܡܫܝܚܐ: ܐܡܠܟ ܘܟܠܐ ܐܝܟ ܡܫܠܠ ܐܢܐ ܕܐܝܬ ܒܗ ܢܨܝܚܬܐ ܡܫܡܫܢܝܬܐ: ܘܠܐ ܡܫܬܘܬܐ ܠܐ ܡܫܝܚܬܐ ܘܡܫܡܫܝܢܬܐ ܒܟܝܢܗ: ܐܝ ܒܟܪ ܡܢ ܡܫܘܚܬܐ ܕܗܟܢ ܘܒܫܡܝܐ ܠܐ ܐܬܝ. ܘܡܫܘܚܬܐ ܕܝܢ ܕܒܟܠܡܕܡ ܛܘܒܬܐ ܐܠܗܐ: ܐܦ ܡܠܟܐ ܗܘ ܕܒܪ ܙܒܢܐ: ܘܡܫܘܚܐ ܕܢܚܬ ܠܚܘܕ ܡܠܐܟܝܢ. ܘܟܕ ܡܦܩܝܢ ܡܕܘܙ ܐܡܪ. ܘܠܐ ܬܘܒܢ ܐܬܢܘܚܐ ܕܒܟܠܗܝܢ ܗܟܢ ܘܫܡܫܘ ܐܒܗ̈ܝܢ. ܒܬܘܒ ܬܚܘܝܬܐ ܗܟܢ ܘܡܫܠܡܝܢܝܢ: ܫܡܪܐ ܘܢܚܘܫ ܗܘ ܘܡܫܝܢ ܐܬܠܘܡܛܟ ܐܘ ܐܬܦܫܛ. ܘܦܪܙܠܐ ܟܪ ܠܦܪܙܠܐ ܠܛܘܫ: ܗܘ ܘܐܝܢ ܐܝܟ ܢܐܡܪ ܒܝ ܢܛܠܛܘܫܝ ܫܩܛܠܐ: ܘܡܢܝܢ ܘܢܛܪ ܛܛܢ ܘܢܛܪ ܢܨܝܦ ܡܫܠܝܢ: ܬܘܒ ܛܠܒܐ ܡܫܝܚܐ ܠܠܦ.

ܒܝ ܗܘܟܠܐ ܢܣܝܒܐ ܡܘܪܠܟܘܫ: ܠܛܘܫܡܐ ܘܐܬܩܝܢ ܘܠܘܟܠܐ ܒܥܘܕܦܘܗܝ ܘܢܛܘܪܘܫ ܐܡܪ. ܘܟܕ ܡܫܠܐ ܠܝ ܠܥܒܕܐ ܙܐܪܐ ܗܘ ܘܡܫܝܚܐ: ܡܠܟܐ ܗܘ ܘܢܚܘܬܐ ܢܚܠܐ ܦܝ ܗܘܢܟܐ: ܘܢܥܐ ܘܝܢ ܦܘܠܓܐ: ܒܝ ܠܐ ܡܟܠܟܠܐ ܐܘ ܡܫܡܪܓܐ ܠܟܬܒܐ ܟܬܝܒܐ❖ ܐܡܪ ܐܢܐ ܐܢܐ: ܘܟܕ ܠܝ ܐܫܪܝܢܐ ܘܐܫܬܟܚ ܟܠܐ ܦܫܡܐ ܘܢܚܘܬܐ: ܐܝ ܡܫܪܓܐ ܡܢܝܢ ܘܡܫܟܚܬܐ ܠܐ ܡܫܡܠܠܐ ܘܟܬܒܐ ܢܛܐܡܪ. ܘܐܝ ܗܘܐ ܠܐ ܬܬܗܘܐ ܠܝ: ܫܡܫܐ ܘܦܪܢܘܬܐ ܡܫܡܗ ܐܢܐ ܠܢܚܘܬܐ. ܗܘ ܘܐܦ ܟܢܝܫ ܐܢܐ ܠܟܠܗ.

some mixing and indescribable mingling of the natures is professed, and if this is not granted to you, you call the union "juxtaposition", and mock it.

Therefore what shall we say about this, unless we quote again the words of the Fathers and following scriptures we say to you: "Apply your ear to the words of the wise, and hear my words, and set your heart that you may know that they are beautiful. And if you cast those things into your heart, they will make you rejoice at the same time (*Lebon p. 105*) in your lips, that your hope may be upon the Lord and he may make known his path for you."[4] For why, when the Doctor did not present his doctrine (only) this far, (namely), "not confusing or mixing the natures amongst each other",[5] but wisely added, "But with the Word of God becoming a partaker in flesh and blood, one Son is understood and named in this way as well,"[6] do you not learn from (this) addition the inexpressible nature of the union? For we learn the fact that God the Word became a participator in blood and flesh like us from the Apostle who wrote: "Therefore because the children participated in blood and flesh, he also in the same way participated in the same things".[7]

And so if the divine Apostle brought our construction, I mean that which is from soul and body (and) is inexpressible, as an example (for) the understanding of Emmanuel which is particularly inexpressible, and (which construction of ours) is neither a mixture nor a juxtaposition, why should we apply these things[8] which do not fit to the mystery? Is the soul of a man changed that it should become flesh, or vice versa, the flesh that it should become soul? For this is the peculiarity of mixture. Or is the *συμφυΐα*[9] and union of rational soul with its body to be interpreted in terms of bodies which cleave to each other or are stuck? In no way at all. For we confidently say that it is a natural coming together, for it transcends our comprehension to specify how the human mind is composed with its own body. And hear Cyril the Theologian in his *Scholia* clearly teaching this to us: (CYRIL): "The fact of union is accomplished in many ways. For (example), when men are divided in affection and opinion and are thinking at variance with each other, they are said to be united through reconciliation of affection as they remove (their) differences (*Lebon p. 106*) out of the centre. (Again) for (example), we say that those things which cleave to each other or come together in different ways, whether by juxtaposition (*παράθεσις*)[10] or mingling (*μίξις*)[11] or mixture (*κρᾶσις*),[12] are united. Therefore when we say that the Word of God was united to our nature, the mode of union is recognised to be above human compre-

ܡܢܐ ܗܘܠܝܢ ܠܗܘܢ ܗܘܐ ܐܡܪܝܢ. ܐܠܐ ܟܕ ܠܐܘ ܠܟܠܢܫ ܩ̈ܠܐ ܕܐܒ̈ܗܬܐ ܡܢ ܕܘܟܐ ܡܫܟܚܝܢ. ܘܡܬܠܐܡ ܠܡܐܡܪ ܠܟܘܢ: ܕܠܟܠܐ ܕܫܡܝܐ ܦܪܘ ܐܝܟ: ܘܡܫܒܚ ܩܠܗ. ܠܟܘܢ ܕܝܢ ܐܡܝܢ. ܐܡܝܢܐ ܕܠܐܘܚܐ ܘܡܫܬܐܠܐ ܐܠܗܘܬܝ. ܘܐܦ ܠܐܘܚܐ ܐܢܬܘܢ ܟܠܟܘܢ. ܡܫܝܚ ܠܟܘܢ ܐܚܝܕܐ (105) ܒܩܦܘܠܝܢ: ܐܡܝܢܐ ܕܗܘܐ ܡܫܪܝܢ ܟܠ ܡܪܝܐ: ܘܢܘܕܥܘܢ ܐܘܪܚܗ. ܠܡܢܐ ܓܝܪ ܟܕ ܡܟܫܦܐ ܠܗ ܒܝܕܐ ܠܗܘܐ ܐܡܝܢ ܡܠܠܗ: ܕܠܗ ܘܡܬܠܒܠܒܝܢ ܡܫܬܟܝܢ ܠܚܝ̈ܐ ܒܢܝܗܘ: ܐܘܦ ܕܝܢ ܡܫܬܥܠܝܢ: ܐܠܐ ܕܟܕ ܒܒܣܪܐ ܘܝܕܥܐ ܐܠܗܘܬܗ ܡܠܠܬܐ ܕܠܐܠܐ: ܡܢ ܠܐܘ ܘܗܘܝܐ ܒܪܐ ܡܫܬܟܠܠ ܘܡܫܬܠܡܗ: ܠܐ ܡܬܕܪܟܐ ܐܝܟ ܡܢ ܠܐܘܫܦܬܐ ܠܐ ܡܬܡܠܠܢܘܬܗ ܕܝܚܝܕܝܘܬܐ. ܗܘ ܓܝܪ ܕܐܠܗܘܬܗ ܒܝܕܐ ܘܒܒܣܪܐ ܐܚܝܕ ܡܠܬܐ ܕܠܐܠܐ: ܡܢ ܡܚܝܐ ܡܠܬܟ ܕܝܠܟ. ܡܛܠ ܗܘܠܝܢ ܕܐܚ̈ܝܢ ܐܠܗܘܬܗ ܒܝܕܐ ܘܒܒܣܪܐ. ܐܦ ܗܘ ܒܗ ܒܝܕܥܬܐ ܐܠܗܘܬܗ ܒܗܘܢ ܟܕ ܒܗܘܢ.

ܐܢ ܗܘܠܝܢ ܙܘܥܐ ܕܡܢ: ܗܘ ܕܡܢ ܢܦܫܐ ܐܡܪ ܐܝܟ ܘܦܓܪܐ: ܕܐܠܗܘܬܗ ܠܐ ܡܬܡܠܠܐ ܡܚܝܐ ܠܐܠܗܐ ܠܡܬܚܘܝܘ ܕܐܬܪܐ ܗܘ ܕܟܠ ܒܫܘܐܝܠܘܬ: ܕܡܢ ܠܐ ܡܬܡܠܠܢܘܬܐ ܐܠܗܐ ܐܠܗ: ܘܠܐ ܡܬܦܠܓ ܘܠܐ ܫܡܫܐ ܕܡܪܟܒܬܐ ܐܠܗܘܬܗ: ܡܛܠ ܡܢܐ ܚܕ ܗܠܝܢ ܘܠܐ ܠܫܡܫܐ ܠܒܪܐ ܡܫܪܟܝܢ. ܐܘܕ ܓܝܪ ܢܦܫܐ ܕܒܪܢܫܐ ܐܬܦܫܛ ܕܐܗܘܐ ܒܣܪܐ: ܐܘ ܒܦܓܪܐ ܒܣܪܐ ܠܗܘܢ ܕܗܘܐ ܢܦܫܐ: ܗܘܐ ܗܘ ܓܝܪ ܕܡܠܬܐ ܕܡܬܦܠܓ. ܐܘ ܐܟܝܢ ܕܠܗܠ ܠܦ̈ܝܫܐ ܕܕܟܝܢ ܠܒܢܝ̈ܐ ܐܘ ܡܬܢܦܫܢ ܡܫܬܒܠܐ ܡܫܚܠܦܐ ܕܐܚܝܕܐ ܘܡܚܝܕܘܬܐ ܕܢܦܫܐ ܡܬܡܠܠܐ ܠܗܘܐ ܦܓܪܐ ܕܡܢܗ: ܘܠܐ ܠܦܓܪ. ܕܡܬܬܐܬܐ ܦܘ ܓܝܪ ܒܣܪܐ ܕܐܚܝܕܐ ܐܠܗܘܬܗ: ܟܕ ܠܐܟܠܝܢ ܐܡܪܝܢ. ܕܠܐܡܪ ܓܝܪ ܙܝܐ ܕܐܟܘܬܗ ܢܦܫܐ ܐܢܫܬܐ ܠܗܘܐ ܦܓܪܐ ܕܡܢܗ ܡܪܟܒܐ: ܒܒܪܐ ܠܡܦܪܘܫܘܬܝ. ܘܡܫܒܚ ܠܦܘܪܫܢܗ ܡܫܡܠܠ ܠܐܠܗܬܐ: ܕܒܩܦܘܠܝܢ ܕܡܢܗ ܓܠܝܐܠܐ ܗܘܐ ܦܠܟ ܠܟ. ܦܘܪܫܢܗ ܕܫܘܒܪܐ ܕܝܚܝܕܘܬܐ ܩܪܝܐ ܦܫܝܛܬܐ ܡܫܬܡܫܢܐ. ܟܕ ܡܫܠܓܝܢ ܓܝܪ ܐܢܫܝܢ ܒܫܘܒܐ ܘܒܬܪܟܝܒܐ: ܘܡܫܬܠܓܐܠܗ ܠܗܘܐ ܚܕܝܐ ܡܬܪܟܒܝܢ: ܕܡܬܚܫܒܝܢ ܡܬܐܡܪܝܢ ܒܬܪܟܝܒܘܬܐ ܕܝܫܘܥܐ. ܟܕ ܡܪܫܝܢ (106) ܡܢ ܡܪܟܒܬܐ ܗܘܝ̈ܬܐ: ܡܬܚܫܒܝܢ ܓܝܪ ܐܡܪܝܢ: ܘܗܘܠܝܢ ܕܕܟܝܢ ܠܚܝ̈ܐ: ܐܘ ܐܬܝܢ ܠܟܘܢ ܚܝ̈ܐ ܩ̈ܝܡܐ ܐܢܬܐ ܐܘ ܒܫܡܝܐ ܕܡܪܝܢ. ܐܘ ܒܫܘܠܛܢܐ ܐܘ ܒܡܫܪܟܐ. ܐܡܠܝܢ ܗܘܠܝܢ ܕܐܬܝܚܕ ܐܡܪܝܢ ܠܚܝܐ ܕܡܢ ܡܠܬܐ ܕܠܐܠܐ ܘܡܫܟܚ ܡܢ ܬܪܟܒܬܐ ܕܒܪܢܫܐ ܡܬܝܚܕܐ ܐܝܟ ܕܝܚܝܕܘܬܐ. ܠܗ ܓܝܪ ܐܝܟ ܚܕܐ ܡܢ ܗܠܝܢ ܕܐܬܐܡܪܘ ܐܠܗܘܬܗ: ܠܐ ܡܬܡܠܠܐ ܘܗ

hension for it is not like one of those (ways) which were mentioned, but is completely inexpressible and not known by any man who lives, but to God who alone knows everything. And it is not at all astonishing that we are worsted in this way by such concepts, (since) when we enquire about how it is as regards our own situation we confess that comprehension is beyond the understanding that is in us. Now in what way do we believe that the soul of a man is united to his body? Who is there who is able to say? But if we (who) are accustomed to think and speak with difficulty (even) of small things, attain, if it is right, to imagine things so subtle and beyond understanding, we say that it is proper to think—yet the expression is inferior to the truth in every respect—that of such sort is the union of Emmanuel as one would think that the soul of a man has with its own body".[13]

Therefore how can you charge this inexpressible and truly divine union which the Word of God has miraculously accomplished, and this by condescending to us, with being that (union) taught by Nestorius which is a conjunction by relationship,[14] and believe that we are obliged to speak of two natures unless we confess, as you say, that at one time Christ had one ousia or quality? But this is nothing other than a real confusion[15] of ousia: therefore what you otherwise delude your hearers with is a persistent deception, (namely) your saying that you agree with us in confessing difference and particularity in accordance with (*Lebon p. 107*) natural quality of the natures from which Emmanuel is. For you think it is impossible to say that he is one unless he changes into one ousia, even when he is made up from two things of a different kind, and you propound for us that extraordinary (saying), and say: SERGIUS THE GRAMMARIAN: "Therefore unless the natures from which Christ is were inconfusedly mixed, how shall I say that these things which have thus remained unmixed were united hypostatically with each other? How will I retain the term "composition" when the natures are retained unmixed as you have said?"[16] For what is that at one time, according to your own words, "mixture without confusion"? For when you ask "How?" and in no other way are restrained from uncertainty, wise Cyril again supplies an answer, that not a mixture of natures but a composition took place, and once it took place the composition persisted, from which was completed one nature and hypostasis of the incarnate Word.

For in the Second Letter to Succensus he wrote as follows: (CYRIL): "For it is not the case that "one" is truly predicated only of things which are simple in nature, but (it may) also (be predicated)

ܕܝܢ ܟܠ ܡܠܬܗ. ܐܘ ܐܦ ܠܐ ܠܐܝܬ ܚܕ ܡܢ ܗܠܝܢ ܕܐܡܝܢܝܢ ܚܝܐ. ܒܪܡ ܠܐܒܗܐ ܗܘ ܕܒܠܚܘܕܘܗܝ ܡܠܟܝܢ ܚܝܐ. ܘܐܡܝܢܐ ܘܠܐ ܒܛܝܠ: ܐܢ ܡܢ ܦܘܫܩܐ ܕܐܝܟ ܗܘܢܐ ܡܕܘܟܝܢ: ܐܡܠܟ ܕܗܠܝܢ ܕܠܟ ܕܐܝܟܢܐ ܐܝܬ ܠܗܠܝܢ ܟܕ ܟܪܝܢ: ܠܟܠ ܡܢ ܬܘܟܠܬܐ ܕܐܝܬ ܒܝ ܡܕܘܝܢ ܕܐܠܗܐ ܡܕܘܟܝܢܬܐ. ܬܐܒܐ ܕܝܢ ܐܢܐ ܡܫܟܚ ܕܡܫܝܚܐ ܢܟܐ ܕܒܪܢܫܐ ܠܟܪ̈ܘܗܐ. ܡܛܠ ܗܘ ܕܡܫܡܫ ܕܠܐܡܪ. ܐܢ ܕܝܢ ܟܕ ܐܒܘܬܟܐ ܘܠܡܣܡܡ ܡܕܒܪܝܢ ܕܢܫܬܡܠܠ ܘܠܐܡܪ: ܡܡܫܟܝܢ ܐܢ ܙܘܡ ܕܫܘܒܚ̈ܐ ܕܗܘܟܐ ܡܗܝܡܢ ܘܠܟܠ ܡܢ ܗܘܐ ܒܝܬܐ: ܐܡܪܝܢ ܕܟܐܢܐ ܕܢܫܬܡܠܠ. ܟܪܝܙܐ ܕܝܢ ܡܢ ܡܠܦܢܘܗܝ ܡܢ ܫܪܪܐ ܡܠܟܬܐ. ܕܕܐܝܟ ܗܟܢܐ ܐܠܗܢ ܚܝܘܬܐ ܕܟܢܘܫܬܐ: ܐܝܟ ܗܘ ܕܢܫܬܡܠܠܝܘ ܕܐܝܟ ܠܗ ܘܠܟܢܫܐ ܕܒܪܢܫܐ ܟܠܗ ܦܪܝܫܐ ܕܡܠܬܗ܀

ܟܠܗ ܗܘܐ ܗܟܢܐ ܚܝܘܬܐ ܠܐ ܡܫܡܠܝܢܬܐ ܘܠܟܘܠܗܬܐ ܕܒܫܪܪܐ: ܗܘ ܕܡܟܠܬܐ ܕܠܗܐ ܒܠܘܡܫܬܐ ܟܕܝܢ: ܘܗܘܐ ܟܕ ܐܬܝܠܗ ܙܐܘܡ: ܐܝܟܢܐ ܗܘ ܕܡܢ ܢܬܦܫܘܩ ܡܠܟܪܐ ܡܟܠܬܐ ܐܝܠܗ: ܘܐܠܗܐ ܢܫܟܘܬܐ ܐܝܬܝܗܐ: ܘܡܫܟܚ ܐܝܟ ܕܐܘܡ ܟܪܝܢ ܡܠܐܟܝܢ ܚܝܢ ܕܢܐܡܪ: ܐܠܐ ܡܕܘܝܢ ܠܡܫܝܚܐ ܐܡܝܢܐ ܘܐܡܪ ܐܝܠܗ: ܕܚܝܐ ܗܘܐ ܐܘܫܠܐ ܚܝܐ ܐܟܝ. ܐܘ ܡܡܫܘܕܟܘܬܐ. ܗܘܐ ܕܝܢ ܘܠܐ ܡܕܝܡ ܐܚܪܢ ܐܠܗܢ: ܐܠܐ ܚܟܘܟܐ ܚܠܠܬܐ ܘܐܘܫܠܐ. ܡܗܝܡܢܘܬܐ ܗܟܢܐ ܫܪܟܬܐ ܐܠܗܢ: ܘܗܘ ܕܐܝܪܢܝܬܐ ܡܡܠܟܠ ܐܝܟ ܟܗܠܝܢ ܕܡܟܒܝܢ: ܗܘ ܕܐܡܪ ܐܝܟ ܕܡܠܟܟ ܠܝ ܕܐܘܪܐ ܗܘܢܟܐ ܘܢܟܠܬܐ ܗܘ ܘܐܝܟ (107) ܕܟܡܫܘܕܟܘܬܐ ܚܝܠܬܐ ܕܟܢ̈ܝܐ ܕܡܢܗܘܢ ܟܢܘܫܬܐ. ܫܦܪ ܐܝܟ ܚܢܢ ܘܐܝܬܝܗܝܢ ܟܠܗ ܠܡܫܡܫܘ ܠܡܐܡܪ: ܘܚܕ ܐܠܗܘܬ: ܐܠܐ ܗܘ ܕܟܝܕܐ ܐܘܫܠܐ ܫܦܪ. ܘܐܦ ܡܢ ܬܘܡ ܡܕܡ ܦܫܝܩܐ ܐܙܠܐ ܡܟܝܠ. ܘܡܫܪܐ ܐܝܟ ܠܝ ܗܘ ܬܡܝܗܬܐ ܘܐܡܪ ܐܝܟ ܫܪܝܪܐ ܒܪܫܠܝܡܘܬܐ. ܐܢ ܗܟܢܐ ܟܢ̈ܝܐ ܕܡܢܗܘܢ ܡܫܝܚܐ ܠܐ ܡܬܟܠܬܐ ܠܐ ܬܬܡܪܚ ܐܚܝܕܐ: ܐܡܝܢܐ ܕܝܢ ܗܘܘ ܠܐ ܡܬܦܪܫܐ: ܘܬܐܝܬܘ ܠܟܪܝܕܐ ܝܘܬܪܢܝܬ ܐܡܪ: ܐܡܝܢܐ ܕܝܢ ܬܐܘܡܐ ܕܡܪܟܒܘܬܐ ܐܠܗܐ: ܟܕ ܢܗܘܐ ܐܡܝܢܐ ܘܐܒܪܢܐ ܠܐ ܡܬܦܪܫܐ ܟܢ̈ܝܐ. ܡܛܠ ܒܪܢ ܚܝܐ ܟܪܟ ܐܝܟ ܦܠܐ ܘܡܠܟ ܡܬܦܪܫܐ ܘܠܐ ܒܟܠܗ. ܟܕ ܡܫܬܠܠܐ ܒܪܢ ܘܐܡܪ: ܘܐܝܬܝܗܝܢ ܠܐ ܡܬܠܝܐ ܐܝܟ ܡܢ ܦܘܫܠܐ: ܬܘܒ ܡܫܝܚܐ ܦܠܓܘܬܐ ܡܘܪܟܒܘܬ ܚܝܘܬܐ: ܕܠܗ ܡܬܦܪܫܐ ܕܟܢ̈ܝܐ ܐܠܐ ܙܘܟܐ ܗܘܐ. ܘܟܕ ܗܘܐ ܗܘ ܙܘܟܐ ܕܡܢܗ ܐܬܡܠܟ ܚܕ ܟܝܢܐ ܘܩܢܘܡܐ ܕܡܠܟܬܐ ܕܡܟܫܪ.

of those which have come together in composition, an example being the situation of man, (composed) from soul and body. For these (elements) which are of different type like this and are not consubstantial[17] with each other, completed one nature of man when they were united, even if the difference in nature of those things which have come together to union exists in discussion of the composition. Therefore those who say that, if the Word incarnate is one nature it follows in everything (and) in every respect that there will be confusion and mixture, as if the nature of (the) man were decreased and stolen away, speak needlessly, for it is not decreased, nor as they say, (*Lebon p. 108*) stolen away. For it suffices for the complete demonstration of the fact that (the Word) became man to say that he was incarnate. For if this had been kept quiet by us, there would be some place for their slander, but because it is added necessarily in what way is there lessening or stealing away?"[18] And in the Treatise of question and answer in which (he shows) that Christ is one, proceeding in the same considerations and exact measures of teaching, he says as follows: (CYRIL): "It is not the case that in everything and from every respect only what is simple and of one type is called 'one', but also those compounded from two or from many things of different types. And that that is the case seems right to those wise in these matters."[19] And in his Treatise concerning the Holy Trinity which he addressed to a certain Hermias he wrote as follows: (CYRIL): "For he who is the undying beauty of God the Father and (his) likeness and aspect, God the Word who is of him and in him, abased himself to emptiness, not that he was compelled to this by anyone, but in the will of the Father, in his own will he became man, and without damage in any way he preserved the glory of his nature unchanged in himself, but took up manhood according to the economy. And he is understood one Son from two, a divine and human nature, which have run and come together to one, inexpressibly and inexplicably composed to union, and in such a way that cannot be understood."[20]

Since therefore, as you have heard many times, composition possesses the (quality) of being above reason and inexpressible, why do you resort to mixture and damaging confusion, and openly attribute inexpressibility to that? For if the divine union of inhomination and incarnation, and those two (natures) from which there is one Christ indivisibly, suffered the same thing as bodies which are mixed, (*Lebon p. 109*) or (if) one of them departed from its own natural quality[21] and ceased being that which it was, I do not see what is then remarkable and inexpressible.

ܟܕ ܓܝܪ ܥܠ ܓܒܪܐ ܕܐܬܚܙܝ ܕܟܠܗ ܡܫܝܚܘܬܐ ܗܘܬ. ✣ܦܪܘܩܠܘܣ✣ ܠܗ ܓܝܪ ܠܐ ܦܩܚ ܟܝܢܐ ܠܟܝܢܗ ܡܬܐܡܪ ܚܕ ܒܡܙܓܐ: ܐܠܐ ܐܦ ܠܐܠܗܝܢ ܕܒܪܘܚܐ ܐܟܚܕܐ ܐܬܘ. ܕܐܝܟ ܐܡܪ. ܕܐܬܠܘܗܝ ܡܬܒܪܢܐ ܕܒܪ ܐܢܫܐ: ܡܢ ܢܦܫܐ ܘܦܓܪܐ. ܡܫܟܚܐ ܓܝܪ ܐܟܘܬܐ ܗܟܢ ܕܕܐܝܟ ܗܟܢ: ܘܠܗ ܚܠܘܦ ܟܝܢܐ ܕܢܦܫܐ. ܟܕ ܐܬܚܝܕ ܘܢ: ܚܕ ܟܝܢܐ ܕܒܪܢܫܐ ܡܫܬܟܠܠ: ܐܦ ܗܘ ܕܒܡܠܬܐ ܕܙܘܘܓܐ ܐܝܬ ܡܫܬܟܚܐ ܕܟܝܢܐ ܕܗܠܝܢ ܕܐܬܘ ܐܟܚܕܐ ܠܚܝܕܘܬܐ. ܠܬܪ̈ܬܐ ܗܟܝܠ ܡܫܬܟܠܠܝܢ ܗܠܝܢ ܕܐܡܪܝܢ: ܕܐܦ ܗܘ ܕܚܕ ܟܝܢܐ ܐܠܗܘܗܝ ܕܡܠܬܐ ܕܒܣܪܐ: ܒܟܠܗܝܢ ܡܢ ܡܠܦܢ̈ܘܗܝ ܢܦܫܐ ܕܒܘܠܒܠܐ ܗܘܐ ܘܡܬܒܠܒܠ ܐܝܟ ܦܝ ܕܐܡܪ ܘܡܬܬܓܝܪ ܟܝܢܐ ܕܒܪܢܫܐ. ܠܐ ܓܝܪ ܢܦܫܐ: ܘܠܐ ܐܝܟܢܐ ܕܐܡܪܝܢ (108) ܡܬܬܓܝܪ. ܗܟܢܐ ܓܝܪ ܠܗܘܢܝܐ ܡܫܡܫܢܐ ܕܗܘ ܕܒܗ ܗܘܐ ܟܝܢܐ: ܗܘ ܕܠܐܡܪ ܕܐܬܒܣܪ. ܠܗ ܓܝܪ ܗܘܐ ܐܬܐܬܝܬ ܗܘܐ ܡܢܗ: ܗܘܐ ܗܘܐ ܐܬܪܐ ܩܕܡ ܠܬܠܡܝܕܘܗܝ. ܡܛܠ ܕܝܢ ܕܐܬܒܪܝܬ ܡܬܘܡܝܐ: ܐܝܟܘ ܐܢܐ ܕܒܪܘܙܐ ܐܘ ܕܚܘܟܡܬܐ ܘܒܡܬܐܡܪܐ ܕܡܢ ܕܡܬܠܐ ܘܦܘܚ ܦܠܓܘܬܐ: ܟܕ ܘܚܕ ܗܘ ܡܫܝܚܐ: ܟܕ ܐܬܐ ܟܠܗܘܢ ܟܕ ܒܗܘܢ ܒܩܘܛܠܐ: ܘܩܛܠܐ ܢܛܠܬܐ ܘܩܛܝܠܐ: ܗܟܢܐ ܐܡܪ. ✣ܦܪܘܩܠܘܣ✣ ܘܠܗ ܒܟܠܗܝܢ ܘܡܢ ܡܠܦܢ̈ܘܗܝ ܗܘ ܦܘܠܚܢܐ ܘܚܕ ܐܟܘܬ ܡܬܐܡܪ ܠܟܝܢܗ ܚܕ: ܐܠܐ ܘܗܠܝܢ ܕܡܢ ܬܪܝܢ ܐܘ ܡܢ ܩܢܘ̈ܡܐ ܬܐܒ ܡܫܟܚ ܐܟܘܬܐ ܡܙܕܘܓ. ܫܦܝܪܐ ܕܝܢ ܕܗܘܝܐ ܐܬܝܗ ܠܟܝܢܗ ܕܡܫܡܫ ܒܗܠܝܢ✣ ܘܒܦܓܘܕܝܬܐ ܕܝܢ ܕܠܗ ܕܡܛܠ ܠܐܠܗܘܬܐ ܡܕܡܬܐ ܗܘ ܕܐܡܪ: ܒܗܝ ܐܝܟ ܐܟܘܬܐ ܟܕ ܗܟܢ. ✣ܦܪܘܩܠܘܣ✣ ܗܘ ܓܝܪ ܕܐܬܠܘܗܝ ܡܘܕܐ ܠܐ ܡܫܘܐ ܕܐܠܗܐ ܐܟܐ: ܘܡܫܘܬܐ ܘܚܝܐ: ܗܘ ܕܡܢܗ ܘܒܗ ܡܬܬܐ ܐܠܗܐ ܚܝܐ ܢܦܫܗ ܠܡܫܘܐ: ܠܗ ܟܕ ܡܢ ܐܝܟ ܟܠܐ ܗܘܐ ܐܬܐܡܪ: ܐܠܐ ܒܪܟܝܢܐ ܕܐܟܐ: ܒܟܝܢܐ ܕܠܗ ܗܘܐ ܟܝܢܐ. ܘܠܐ ܡܫܪܝܢܐ ܦܝ ܠܓܒܪ: ܘܠܐ ܡܫܟܚܐ ܒܗ ܐܡܪܐ ܕܚܝܘܬ ܡܫܘܒ. ܡܛܠ ܕܝܢ ܐܝܟܘܬܐ ܡܒܪܢܝܬܐ: ܘܚܕ ܡܢ ܬܪܝܢ ܡܫܬܟܠܠ ܒܪܐ: ܕܙܘܓܗ ܘܐܬܐ ܐܟܚܕܐ ܠܚܕ: ܟܕ ܟܝܢܐ ܠܐܠܗܐ ܘܐܢܫܐ: ܠܐ ܡܬܡܟܠܢܝܬ ܘܠܐ ܡܬܦܫܝܬ ܘܐܝܟ ܕܠܗ ܠܡܦܬܚܘܬܗ: ܠܚܝܕܘܬܐ ܬܐܪܟܗ✣

ܟܕ ܗܟܝܠܬ ܠܗ ܠܒܪܘܟܐ ܐܟܚܕܐ ܕܒܪܝܫ ܦܓܪܐ ܡܫܟܚܬ. ܗܘ ܕܠܗ ܡܛܠ ܡܢ ܡܠܬܐ ܘܠܐ ܡܬܡܟܠܐ. ܠܟܝܢܐ ܙܦܪ ܐܝܬ ܠܗ ܡܘܪܒܐ ܘܡܬܠܟܠܐ ܕܡܫܬܪܝܐ. ܘܚܕܐ ܐܝܬ ܠܗ ܕܒܪܝܬܗ ܗܘ ܕܠܐ ܡܬܡܟܠܐ. ܐܢ ܓܝܪ ܚܝܕܘܬܐ ܠܐܠܗܘܬܐ ܘܡܬܒܪܢܝܬܐ ܘܡܬܟܫܪܢܘܬܐ: ܗܝ ܟܕ ܗܝ ܚܝܬ ܠܓܫܡܐ ܕܡܬܡܬܓܝܪ:

But great Athanasius, whom if one were to call "The law of Orthodoxy", as did Gregory the Theologian, it would not swerve from what is proper, in his Treatise concerning faith calls the incarnation "composition", while showing it is truly inexpressible by forbidding unmeasured investigation. For he wrote as follows: (ATHANASIUS): "From (their questions) 'How?' and 'In what way?' and 'What follows?' even they have arrived at unfaithfulness. And they have prepared a dwelling-place instead of an incarnation, and instead of union and composition, a human activity, and instead of one hypostasis of our Lord Jesus Christ, two hypostases and persons, and in place of the Holy Trinity, unfittingly and unlawfully, they have thought of a quaternity. Unfittingly (indeed) in that they join a man with God, and number a servant with the Lord, and place a created person together with uncreated persons; and unlawfully, in that they make one hypostasis two, introducing to the Trinity a fourth hypostasis, which is foreign in everything, and of a different rank, and the last and least of all rational spirits."[22]

How alike, then, to these are the (doctrines) of Nestorius? For those who held that God the Word assumed our composition and participated like us in blood and flesh do not say, like Nestorius, that first of all an infant was formed in the womb, and thus through the love of friendship and through kindness (the Word) dwelt (in him) in (*Lebon p. 110*) a brotherly way,[23] and gave (him) the title and rank of Son, and the equality of an equal name. And see how wise Cyril quotes Diodore saying this: (DIODORE): "While the flesh was of Mary (and) when it was not yet taken up, it was from the earth and was in no way different from other flesh. For as Levi was tithed in the loins, but when he was born he assumed the rank, so also our Lord, while he was in the womb of the Virgin and of that ousia, did not have the rank of Sonship. But when he was formed and became the temple to God the Word, which receives the Only-Begotten, he assumed the rank of the name, and participated also in the rank itself."[24] And against these things, confuting him, (Cyril) learned and wise in the Spirit says: (CYRIL): "O excellent Sir, I say that you spew forth for us words which are unschooled and much infected with absurdity. For the holy body was from Mary, but, then, in the first beginnings of the becoming firm or constitution in the womb, it was holy as the body of Christ, and one sees no time in which it did not belong to him but rather was in common, as you said, and in equality with other flesh."[25]

And so how are we not cast outside of the truth, when we treat a conjunction by relationship in honour and an (in) dwelling and an

ܘܬܪܝܗܘܢ ܗܠܝܢ ܕܡܢܗܘܢ ܗܘ ܚܕ ܡܫܝܚܐ ܐܝܬܘܗܝ ܠܐ (109) ܡܫܬܘܕܝܢܝܬ: ܐܘ ܚܕ ܡܢ ܗܠܝܢ: ܡܢ ܡܫܘܕܥܘܬܐ ܟܝܢܝܬܐ ܕܠܗ ܐܩܢܘܡ: ܘܦܫ ܡܢ ܕܢܗܘܐ ܐܝܬܘܗܝ ܗܘ ܗܘ ܕܐܝܬܘܗܝ ܗܘܐ: ܡܛܠ ܗܝ ܗܝ ܕܡܫܝܚܐ ܡܫܟܚ ܘܠܐ ܡܬܡܫܟܚܢܐ: ܠܐ ܚܙܐ ܐܢܐ.

ܘܪܒܐ ܕܝܢ ܐܬܢܣܝܘܣ: ܗܘ ܕܢܨܚܢܐ ܕܗܝܡܢܘܬܐ ܬܘܪܐ ܐܢ ܢܐܡܪ: ܐܝܟ ܕܐܡܪ ܠܐܦܘܠܝܢܪܝܘܣ ܡܫܟܚ ܠܟܝܢܬܐ: ܠܐ ܦܐܫ ܡܢ ܗܝ ܕܦܐܝܐ: ܟܡܐܡܪܐ ܗܘ ܕܡܫܟܠ ܗܡܫܘܬܐ: ܙܘܟܝܐ ܡܫܡܫܘ ܠܡܬܟܫܪܢܘܬܐ ܟܕ ܡܫܘܐ ܠܗ ܠܐ ܡܬܡܫܟܠܢܝܬܐ ܕܚܝܘܬܐ: ܟܕ ܕܛܠܐ ܗܝ ܕܠܐ ܡܫܘܚܬܐ ܘܡܘܡܬܐ. ܦܓܪ ܓܝܪ ܗܘܝܐ. ܀ܐܬܢܣܝܘܣ܀ ܘܐܦܐ ܡܢ ܗܝ ܕܐܡܪܐ ܘܟܐܡܬܐ ܐܝܟ ܘܟܐܒܐ ܢܦܫܢܝܐ: ܟܠܠ ܗܡܫܘܬܐ ܐܦ ܗܠܝܢ. ܘܡܫܘܕܥܐ ܢܦܫ ܡܬܟܫܪܢܘܬܐ ܠܗܘܢ: ܘܢܦܫ ܚܝܘܬܐ ܙܘܟܝܐ: ܡܟܟܝܘܬܐ ܐܢܫܝܐ. ܘܢܦܫ ܚܕ ܦܘܫܐ ܕܡܪܢ ܢܦܫܗ ܡܫܝܚܐ: ܬܪܝܢ ܩܢܘܡܝܢ ܘܦܪ̈ܨܘܦܐ. ܘܢܦܫ ܠܐܠܗܘܬܐ ܦܝܫܬܐ: ܙܟܝܘܬܐ ܠܐ ܦܐܬܐ ܘܠܟܪ ܡܢ ܢܦܫܐ ܐܬܝܠܗ. ܠܐ ܦܐܬܐ ܦܡ: ܕܗܡ ܠܐܠܗܐ ܣܠܩܝܢ ܒܪܢܫܐ: ܘܒܟܝܐ ܦܝܫ ܒܗܡ ܡܪܐ: ܘܦܪ̈ܨܘܦܐ ܒܪܢܫܐ ܒܗܡ ܦܪ̈ܨܘܦܐ ܒܢ̈ܝܐ ܐܟܝܢܐ ܗܫܟܝܢ. ܠܒܪ ܡܢ ܢܦܫܐ ܕܝܢ: ܕܠܒܪ ܦܘܫܐ ܬܪܝܢ ܒܒܪܝܢ. ܟܕ ܡܫܬܠܡ ܠܐܠܗܘܬܐ ܦܘܫܐ ܙܒܝܢܐ: ܘܐܦܫܘ ܒܟܠ ܡܕܝܢ ܘܡܫܪܟܐ ܐܢܫܐ. ܘܐܢܫܝܐ ܘܟܪܝܐ ܕܠܗܘܢ ܪ̈ܘܚܐ ܦܫܝܛܬܐ܀

ܠܗܠܝܢ ܗܟܢܐ: ܐܡܟܝܐ ܐܝܬܝܗܝ ܕܕܡܝܢ ܗܠܝܢ ܕܢܣܛܘܪܝܘܣ. ܗܠܝܢ ܓܝܪ ܕܠܡܠܬܐ ܠܐܠܗܐ ܡܚܝܘ ܕܡܟܠ ܙܘܟܝܐ ܕܡܢ: ܘܐܬܬܠܘܐܦ ܐܟܘܬ ܒܢܦܫܐ ܘܒܒܣܪܐ. ܠܗ ܐܝܟ ܢܣܛܘܪܝܘܣ ܐܡܪܝܢ: ܕܠܘܩܒܠ ܐܬܚܒܠ ܒܘܠܐ ܒܡܪܟܒܐ: ܘܗܘܝܐ ܒܣܘܟܐ ܕܢܫܡܬܐ ܘܒܪܢܫܘܬܐ (110) ܒܡܪ ܐܝܬܝܗ. ܘܗܘܝ ܒܘܝܐ ܘܐܡܪܐ ܕܒܪܐ ܘܡܘܡܬܐ ܕܡܘܡܬܐ ܡܡܐ. ܘܒܪܗ ܐܡܟܝܐ ܗܘܕܝܠܘܣ ܢܣܒܚܐ ܡܫܝܚܐ ܠܕܝܘܕܘܪܘܣ ܕܗܘܐ ܐܡܪ. ܀ܕܝܘܕܘܪܘܣ܀ ܟܕ ܐܝܬܘܗܝ ܗܘܐ ܕܡܪܝܡ ܒܡܪܐ ܗܘ: ܐܡܬܝ ܕܒܟܠ ܠܐ ܐܬܡܟܠ ܗܘܐ: ܡܢ ܐܘܟܠ ܐܝܬܘܗܝ ܗܘܐ: ܘܠܐ ܡܫܟܚ ܗܘܐ ܡܕܡ ܡܢ ܒܫܪ̈ܐ ܐܢܫܝܐ. ܐܟܘܬ ܓܝܪ ܕܠܗܝ ܐܬܚܫܒ ܚܣܝܐ: ܟܕ ܐܬܟܪ ܕܝܢ ܦܝܠܛܘܣܐ: ܗܟܢܐ ܘܡܪܝ ܟܕ ܒܚܙܘܐ ܕܠܘܩܒܠܐ ܐܝܬܘܗܝ ܗܘܐ: ܘܕܝܢ ܐܘܣܝܐ: ܠܟܠ ܗܘܐ ܠܗ ܐܡܪܐ ܕܒܪܬܐ. ܟܕ ܕܝܢ ܐܬܩܪܒ ܘܐܘܣܐ ܠܡܠܟܘܬܐ ܠܐܠܗܐ ܗܘܐ: ܕܡܟܠ ܠܚܣܝܐ: ܦܝܠܛܘܣܐ ܕܡܠܐ: ܘܐܬܠܘܐܦ ܘܟܗ ܟܠܐܡܪܐ܀ ܠܗܐ ܗܟܢܐ ܐܦ ܟܕ ܡܟܫ ܠܗ ܗܘ ܢܘܟܪܝܐ ܘܢܣܒܝܢ ܒܪܘܚ ܐܡܪ. ܀ܢܣܛܘܪܝܘܣ܀ ܐܘ ܡܫܬܪܐ ܐܡܪ ܐܢܐ: ܕܟܠܝܐ

equality of the name of sonship as equal to hypostatic union, and speaking against (the words) of the holy and theological Fathers, we call the incarnation an inhabiting, and composition a human activity which takes place for a man clothed with God, who is impelled and enriched (with) divine partnership from the inspiration of the Spirit? For in the case of a conjunction by relationship, the independently existing infant has its own person (*Lebon p. 111*) and hypostasis, and similarly, the Word which dwelt in him is seen in his own hypostasis and person, and a union by relationship of the two persons takes place, which is only yoked by equality of name and by the honour of sonship. But in the case of hypostatic union and natural composition which is proper to God as well, because the flesh endowed with a reasonable soul had existence in very union with the Word, (namely, the flesh) which was assumed from the Holy Spirit and from Mary the Mother of God and perpetual Virgin, and it did not exist independently before the union with the Word, (therefore) the Word himself is believed immutably and without change to have become a child, while he remained that which he was and did not change or convert that which he took up, and he humbled himself to gradual growth, and exit, and full conception. And thus he was gloriously born from the holy Virgin, who remained a virgin even after the birth and was reckoned among mothers without lapsing from the boast of virginity. For now, how will anyone dare to say that he is two natures or two hypostases, he who was gloriously completed one Christ from two? For we will see no time, after (the time) when the Word "rested" on the Virgin according to the word of the Gospel,[26] in which that body endowed with a rational soul, which was united to him, did not belong to him.

Because of this Athanasius, (who is) wise in these divine matters, said that there is one nature incarnate of the Word, so that by means of this utterance which is utterly secure we may acknowledge the indisseverability of the union. For the Word himself, who had existence before the ages and is forever together with the Father, and is seen in his own hypostasis and is simple in ousia, became composite in the economy, and (that) word "incarnate" ensures that it is understood that the flesh endowed with a reasonable soul existed in relationship to the Word himself, and was not independently completed in its own hypostasis. (*Lebon p. 112*) For in the Treatise of Address to the God-fearing emperor Theodosius, Cyril, wise in all things, says as follows: (CYRIL): "Therefore being impelled towards the truth from every direction, (and) being particularly careful to tread in the footsteps which seem right to the divine scriptures,

ܩ̈ܠܐ ܓܒܐ ܐܝܬ ܠܟ ܠܐ ܡܬܢܦܠܬܐ: ܘܪ̈ܘܫܡܝܢ ܟܬ̈ܝܒܝ ܒܡܟܝܪܘܬܐ. ܗܘܐ ܓܝܪ ܡܢ
ܡܢܗܘܢ ܓܘܫܡܐ ܩܕܝܫܐ. ܐܠܐ ܗܟܢܐ ܒܡܥܪܬܐ ܩ̈ܕܝܫܬܐ ܕܒܝܬܐ ܐܘ ܕܡܕܝܢܬܐ ܕܡܪܒܝܬܐ:
ܩܕܝܫܐ ܐܝܬܘܗܝ ܗܘܐ: ܐܝܟ ܓܘܫܡܐ ܕܡܫܝܚܐ: ܘܟܕܝܢ ܘܠܐ ܚܕ ܡܢܗ ܐܒܕ. ܕܒܗ ܓܝܪ
ܟܠܗ ܐܝܬܘܗܝ ܗܘܐ ܕܡܠܬܐ: ܕܓ̈ܒܐ ܕܝܢ ܡܠܬܗ، ܐܝܟ ܕܐܡܪܢܐ ܘܟܣܝܘܬܐ ܕܟܝ̈ܢܐ ܐܠܗ̈ܝܐ܀
ܐܡܟܝܠ ܗܘܟܢܐ ܠܗ ܠܒܪ ܡܢ ܥܘܙܐ ܕܓܡܝܢ: ܕܒܡܫܘܬܐ ܕܐܠܗܘܬܐ ܗܘ ܐܝܬܝܬܐ:
ܘܡܟܡܢܐ ܘܡܫܘܬܐ ܥܡܐ ܕܒܪܘܬܐ ܡܫܬܡܫܝܢ ܠܝܕܘܬܐ ܦܘܫܩܬܐ. ܘܟܕ ܕܟܡܘܬܐ
ܘܐܬܘܬܐ ܩ̈ܕܝܫܬܐ ܘܡܫܡܠܝܢ ܠܐܠܗܘܬܗ ܐܡܪܝܢ: ܠܡܬܟܫܦܢܘܬܐ ܕܝܢ ܒܡܥܪܬܐ ܦܪܝܫ:
ܠܪܘܚܐ ܕܡܢ ܡܬܚܒܝܢܘܬܐ ܐܝܟܢܝܬܐ: ܗܘ ܕܪܘܚܐ ܠܒܪܢܫܐ ܠܟܠܗ ܠܐܠܗܘܬܐ: ܘܡܬܐܠܟܝܢ
ܘܡܬܦܫܬܐ ܠܐܠܗܘܬܐ ܡܢ ܡܫܘܚܬܐ ܕܪܘܚܐ ܒܠܒܪ. ܟܕܐ ܕܝܢ ܓܝܪ ܢܗܫܘܬܐ
ܘܐܝܟܘܬܐ: ܟܕܘܠܐ ܕܒ ܡܢܗ ܘܠܗ ܡܬܐܡܪ: ܦܪܨܘܦܐ (111) ܕܠܗ ܘܩܢܘܡܐ ܐܝܬ
ܠܗ: ܘܒܗ ܒܝܚܝܕܘܬܐ ܡܠܬܐ ܗܘ ܕܐܒܐ ܒܗ: ܒܩܢܘܡܐ ܘܒܦܪ̈ܨܘܦܐ ܕܠܗ ܡܬܝܚܕܐ.
ܘܚܝܘܬܐ ܐܢܫܝܬܐ ܕܐܝܟ ܦܪ̈ܨܘܦܐ ܗܘܬ: ܕܒܩܢܘܡܐ ܥܡܐ ܡܬܐܡܪܐ ܒܠܚܘܕ
ܘܕܐܡܪܐ ܕܒܪܘܬܐ. ܟܕܐ ܕܝܢ ܚܝܘܬܐ ܦܘܫܩܬܐ: ܘܪܘܟܒܐ ܚܝܐ ܐܠܗܝܐ ܘܚܕܐ
ܠܐܠܗܐ: ܡܬܠܐ ܕܒܗ ܚܝܘܬܐ ܕܟܕܐ ܡܠܬܐ ܗܘܐ ܠܗ ܠܗ: ܠܒܫܪܐ ܘܢܦܫܗ
ܡܬܚܠܦܝܢ: ܗܘ ܕܐܬܢܣܒ ܡܢ ܪܘܚܐ ܩܕܝܫܐ: ܘܡܢ ܡܢܗ ܡܠܝܐ ܠܐܠܗܐ
ܘܡܬܚܠܦ ܒܟܠܗܝܢ: ܘܠܐ ܐܬܦܢܝ ܡܢܗ ܘܠܗ ܡܢ ܩܕܡ ܚܝܘܬܐ ܕܟܕܐ ܡܠܬܐ:
ܗܘ ܡܠܬܐ ܠܐ ܡܫܬܚܠܦܢܘܬܐ ܘܠܐ ܡܬܗܦܟܢܘܬܐ ܡܬܐܡܪܝܢ: ܕܗܘܐ ܒܘܠܐ: ܒ
ܦܘܫ ܗܘ ܕܝܢ ܕܐܝܬ ܗܘܐ. ܘܠܐ ܒܚܕܘ ܕܝܢ ܕܢܩܒܠ ܗܕܡ ܐܘ ܫܘܢܝܐ. ܘܠܡܬܪܟܒܘܬܐ
ܕܟܡܠܝܢ ܡܠܘܠ ܘܡܫܡܫܐ ܘܡܬܚܙܝܐ ܡܫܬܡܥܢܐ ܐܬܚܝܒ. ܘܗܟܢܐ ܡܫܬܡܠܝܐ ܐܬܐܡܪ
ܡܢ ܟܠܗܘܢ ܩܕܝܫܐ: ܘܡܘܠܝܐ ܐܦ ܟܠܗ ܡܠܝܐ ܟܠܗܘܢ: ܘܠܐܝܩܪܘܬܐ ܐܠܗܝܬܐ:
ܘܠܐ ܢܦܩܘ ܡܢ ܥܘܡܪܐ ܕܟܠܗܘܢ. ܗܘܝܐ ܓܝܪ ܐܡܟܝܠ ܐܝܟ ܢܡܪܘܣ ܕܐܝܟ ܟܝܢܝ
ܐܘ ܐܝܟ ܦܘܢܩܝܢ ܢܐܡܪ: ܠܗܘ ܕܡܢ ܐܝܟ ܡܫܬܡܠܝܐ ܚܕ ܡܫܝܚܐ ܐܬܡܠܟܢ. ܟܕܝܢ
ܓܝܪ ܘܠܐ ܚܕ ܢܦܫܐ ܡܢ ܒ ܐܝܟ ܡܠܬܐ ܒܟܠܗܘܢ ܐܝܟ ܒܪܢܐ ܟܠܐ ܕܐܘܝܘܬܗ.
ܕܒܗ ܟܠܗܘܢ ܗܘܐ ܕܡܠܬܐ: ܦܓܪܐ ܗܘ ܕܐܬܢܣܒ ܠܗ: ܕܢܦܫܐ ܐܝܬ ܠܗ ܡܫܡܠܝܬܐ.
ܡܬܠܐ ܗܘܐ ܓܝܪ ܘܫܡܝܢ ܒܗܘܠܝܢ ܠܟܝ̈ܢܐ ܐܢܫܝܘܬܗ: ܚܕ ܐܡܪ ܕܐܝܬܘܗܝ
ܚܕ ܕܡܠܬܐ ܕܡܫܒܪ: ܐܡܟܝܠ ܕܒܗ ܗܘܐ ܒܪܢܐ ܟܠܐ ܕܗܘܪܢܐ ܡܢ ܟܠ: ܠܐ
ܡܬܦܫܩܬܐ ܕܚܝܘܬܐ ܢܦܫ. ܗܘ ܓܝܪ ܡܠܬܐ ܕܠܐ ܐܝܬ ܠܗ ܩܕܡ ܠܟܠܗ:
ܘܐܚܝܕܐ ܥܡ ܐܦܐ ܠܟܠܗܘܢ ܐܝܬܘܗܝ: ܒܩܢܘܡܐ ܕܠܗ ܡܬܝܚܕܐ: ܘܦܫܝܛܐ ܐܝܬܘܗܝ

and following the opinions of the Fathers, we believe that he who is from the root of Jesse, he who is from the seed of David, he who is from woman according to the flesh, he who is under the law with us as man, and above us, above the law as God, he who for our sake and with us (was) among the dead, he who above us on his own account is Lifegiver and Life, is in truth Son of God. And we do not make the manhood stripped[27] of divinity, nor do we divest the Word of humanity after the inexpressible and inexplicable union, but we confess one and the same Son, one thing from two objects, who was seen inexpressibly from two, meaning in a union of the supreme kind and not in a change of nature."[28] And above, in the same Treatise, he says again in a similar way: (CYRIL): "For he who is with him who begot him from eternity and (is) Son from before all ages, because he descended to the nature of man—not that he lapsed from being God, but rather he took up manhood—is rightly understood to have become also from the seed of David and had a birth (as) a child in his manhood. But what was assumed is not foreign to him, but his own in very truth: it is reckoned therefore as one[29] with him, just as one sees the composition of a man, for it is intertwined from things which are unlike in nature, I mean, soul and body; but thus one man is understood from two."[30, 31] (*Lebon p. 113*)

But because you brandish up and down the word "mixture", (on the grounds) that it is spoken by Gregory the Theologian, know that he used the word as well when he wanted to establish the supreme union, being completely unafraid of the danger of confusion[32] or mingling[33] which usually takes place with moist and fluid bodies. None of this happens to the nature of divinity so long as God remains, and he will remain for ever, nor will he involve himself that he should suffer change. And on this hear as well the instructive voice of holy Cyril, in the First Volume against the blasphemies of Nestorius, answering as follows: (CYRIL): "For some of the holy Fathers as well have used the word 'mixture', but because you say you are afraid lest it be thought that some confusion has taken place, as in the case of liquids which are mixed with each other, I set you free from (this) fear. For (the Fathers) did not think in this way: how could they? But they use the word when they are at pains to indicate the supreme union of those things which have come together. Now we say they were united in an inseparable union, and the Word from God has his own flesh unchangeably. And we find that even the Scripture inspired by God does not use the word very judiciously, but places it rather as is useful and simply.[34] Thus Paul the Theologian wrote about some people, 'But the word of the report did not

ܒܠܘܚܝܗ: ܡܪܕܘܬܐ ܗܘܬ ܒܡܕܝܢܬܐ. ܘܡܠܟܘܬܐ ܗܝ ܕܐܬܟܫܪ ܚܘܒܐ ܕܢܦܠܘܠ: ܕܒܠܗ ܕܡܠܟܘܬܐ ܐܬܐܡܪ ܒܣܦܪܐ ܗܢܐ ܕܡܫܝܚ ܚܕܒܫܒܬܐ: ܘܠܗ ܡܫܘ ܘܠܗ ܒܥܘܡܕܐ ܕܠܗ (112) ܐܬܠܡܕܘ. ܗܟܝܠ ܓܝܪ ܒܬܠܡܝܕܐ ܦܪܘܣܦܛܝܩܘܢ ܕܒܠܗ ܕܢܦܠ ܠܐܠܗܐ ܠܐܘܣܝܣ ܦܠܚܐ: ܐܡܪ ܚܣܝܐ ܒܟܠ ܩܘܪܝܠܠܘܣ. ÷ܩܘܪܝܠܠܘܣ÷ ܟܕ ܡܢ ܡܠܟܘܬ ܗܘܝܬܐ ܡܬܝܠܕ ܒܗܠ ܚܙܘܐ: ܒܝܘܡܬܐ ܗܝ ܕܡܦܪܐ ܠܡܠܬܐ ܠܠܐܦܐ ܕܪܘܡܐ. ܟܕ ܦܓܥ ܗܦܟ ܡܦܩܝܢ. ܘܟܕ ܢܦܩܝܢ ܠܡܠܬܚܡܐ ܘܐܬܦܬܚܐ ܠܗܘ ܕܡܢ ܒܣܪܐ ܕܐܡܗ: ܠܗܘ ܕܡܢ ܪܘܚܐ ܕܩܘܕܫ: ܠܗܘ ܕܡܢ ܐܠܗܐ ܒܒܣܪ: ܠܗܘ ܕܐܬܝܗܒ ܢܡܘܣܐ ܒܗܢ ܐܝܟ ܒܪܢܫܐ: ܘܠܟܠܗ ܡܢܗ ܠܟܠܗ ܡܢ ܢܡܘܣܐ ܐܝܟ ܐܠܗܐ: ܠܗܘ ܕܡܫܬܡܠܝܢ ܘܡܢ ܒܡܠܟܘܬܐ: ܠܗܘ ܕܠܟܠܗ ܡܢ ܡܫܬܡܠܝܢܘܗܝ ܡܠܟܝܢ ܚܝܐ ܘܡܝܬܐ: ܕܒܪܐ ܐܠܗܘܬܗ ܕܐܠܗܐ ܒܥܪܬܐ ܡܘܥܝܝܢ. ܘܠܐ ܠܐܢܫܘܬܐ ܚܣܝܕܬ ܡܢ ܐܠܗܘܬܐ ܒܕܝܢ ܚܕ: ܘܠܐ ܠܡܠܟܘܬܐ ܡܢ ܐܢܫܘܬܐ ܡܦܠܓܝܢ: ܟܠܗ ܚܕܝܘܬܐ ܠܐ ܡܬܡܠܟܝܢܬܐ ܘܠܐ ܡܬܦܫܝܢܬܐ. ܐܠܐ ܚܕ ܗܘܘ ܟܕ ܗܘ ܒܪܐ ܡܘܕܝܢ: ܕܡܢ ܬܪܝܢ ܡܘܒܠܝܢ ܚܕ ܡܫܝܚ: ܗܘ ܕܡܢ ܬܪܝܢ ܠܐ ܡܬܦܪܫܢܝܬ ܐܬܝܕܥ. ܚܝܠܐ ܕܝܢ ܕܚܕܝܘܬܐ ܗܝ ܕܟܠܗ ܡܢ ܟܠ: ܘܠܗ ܒܡܘܣܟܐ ܕܚܝܐ÷ ܘܟܠܗ ܬܘܒ ܒܗ ܒܬܠܡܝܕܐ ܒܪܝܐ ܕܗܦܟܐ ܐܡܪ ÷ܩܘܪܝܠܠܘܣ÷ ܗܘ ܓܝܪ ܕܒܗ ܗܘ ܕܡܠܒܫ ܡܢ ܒܟܠ ܐܠܗܘܬܗ: ܘܡܢ ܦܓܪ ܟܠܗ ܒܠܒܫ ܒܪܐ: ܡܬܡܠܠ ܕܢܣܒ ܠܒܣܪܐ ܕܒܪ ܐܢܫܐ: ܠܗ ܕܦܪܘܩ ܡܢ ܗܝ ܕܗܘܬ ܐܠܗܘܬܗ ܠܐܠܗܐ: ܡܟܠ ܕܝܢ ܐܢܫܘܬܐ: ܕܡܠܬ ܡܫܡܠܝܐ ܕܗܘܬ ܐܦ ܡܢ ܪܘܚܐ ܕܩܘܕܫ: ܘܡܠܝܗ ܕܠܐ ܐܝܬ ܠܗ ܗܝ ܕܒܐܝܩܪܗ: ܐܠܗܘܬܗ ܕܝܢ ܗܝ ܕܐܬܝܠܕ ܠܗ ܢܘܟܪܝܐ ܠܗ. ܐܠܐ ܕܝܠܗ ܒܒܣܪܐ: ܟܕ ܓܝܪ ܐܚܝܕ ܡܫܝܚ ܒܠܐܗ: ܐܝܟ ܡܐ ܕܐܦ ܙܘܒܐ ܕܒܪܢܫܐ ܚܕܐ ܐܝܬ. ܡܬܕܪܫ ܦܢ ܓܝܪ ܡܢ ܗܠܝܢ ܕܠܐ ܕܬܦܪܫ ܒܒܣܪܐ. ܢܦܫܐ ܐܡܪ ܐܢܐ ܘܦܓܪܐ. ܐܠܐ ܗܟܢܐ ܚܕ ܒܪ ܐܢܫܐ ܡܫܡܠܝܐ ܗܘ ܕܡܢ ܬܪܝܢ÷

(113) ܡܛܠ ܕܝܢ ܕܡܠܟܘܬܐ ܕܡܫܝܚܐ ܠܟܠܗ ܘܠܡܫܝܚ ܡܫܕܪ ܐܢܬ: ܐܝܟ ܦܢ ܘܐܡܪܐ ܠܦܪܢܛܘܣܩܘܣ ܡܫܡܠܝܐ ܠܠܘܩܒܠܐ: ܕܟܕ ܕܐܦ ܗܘ ܟܕ ܦܠܐ ܕܢܡܘܣ ܚܝܕܘܬܐ ܢܡܢܬܐ ܐܬܡܣܟ ܒܡܠܟܘܬܐ: ܟܕ ܡܢ ܡܕܝܢܬܐ ܕܟܘܪܗܢܐ ܐܘ ܕܫܘܠܛܢܐ ܠܦܓܪ ܠܐ ܕܢܠܠ: ܗܘ ܕܡܟܕ ܦܓܪܐ ܠܗܠ ܒܡܫܝܚܐ ܡܬܦܠܐ ܘܐܬܦܫܪ. ܕܒܝܘܡ ܡܢ ܗܠܝܢ ܠܐ ܦܓܪ ܒܚܝܐ ܕܐܠܗܘܬܐ: ܚܝܐ ܕܡܘܬܐ ܕܐܠܗܐ. ܡܘܬܐ ܕܝܢ ܠܠܡܕ: ܘܡܘܚܠܐ ܢܦܫ ܠܐ ܡܬܩܠܐ. ܘܡܛܠ ܐܦ ܒܗܘܐ ܒܬܪܝܢ ܩܠܐ ܡܬܩܛܝܠܐ ܕܡܝܬܐ ܩܘܪܝܠܠܘܣ. ܕܠܗܘܬܐ ܡܝܬܐ ܕܒܘܡܠܠ ܠܦܓܪܗܘܢ ܕܢܛܘܪܘܢ ܦܢܐ ܗܘܝܐ.

profit those who were not mixed in faith with those who heard."[35] For were these about whom the saying is (written) about to be mixed with each other in the same way as wine with water, and will they suffer some sort of confusion of hypostases with each other? Or (*Lebon p. 114*) will they rather be united in mind, as is written in the Acts of the holy Apostles, that among the people of those who believed, there was one heart and one mind.[36] But I think the latter is true, not the former. Therefore be without fears concerning this, for the mind of the saints is certainly prudent."[37]

But Gregory the Theologian in the Sermon on the Feast of the Epiphany, wanting to establish the sublimity of the union which, as you have now heard, is supernatural, said: (GREGORY): "God went forth with the assuming: one out of two which were opposite, flesh and spirit, of which the one deified and the other was deified. O new mingling![38] O wonderful mixture![39] He who is, became, and the Creator is created, and that which is incomprehensible is comprehended by means of (the) mind as an intermediate, which is in the middle (between) divinity and the grossness of flesh."[40] But in the First Treatise on the Son, showing that he recognises the union of God the Word to flesh endowed with a soul and intelligence (as) composition and not mixture, he wrote as follows, quarrelling with the Arians who were attributing words which were humiliating and to do with the economy to the existence of the Word which was before the ages, and not applying them to it when it was emptied and incarnated and enduring humility for our sake: (GREGORY): "In short, attribute those things which are more exalted to the divinity and the nature which is superior to sufferings and the body; and those things which are more lowly to the composite (one), to him who was emptied for your sake and incarnate—and it is not worse to say, he was made man as well—and was afterwards exalted, so that you, letting go of what is fleshly and lowly[41] in doctrine, may learn to be more exalted and to mount up with the divinity, and not continue in these visible things, but ascend with these intellectual things, and may recognise what is the principle[42] of nature and what is the law[42] of the economy. He who now is disdained by you was once (*Lebon p. 115*) above you: he who now is a man, was (once) not composite. Therefore what he was he remained, but what he was not he assumed."[43]

See (now) that we have clearly learnt that (Gregory) recognised the incarnation (as) composition, and not (as) mixture and confusion, even if it should happen that he used the term "mixture" for the establishment of the supreme union. For if we are going to stick

܀ܦܘܫܩܗ܀ ܫܡܐ ܓܝܪ ܕܫܘܪܓܐ ܫܡܗ ܐܦ ܐܢܫܝܢ ܡܢ ܐܒܗ̈ܬܐ ܩܕܝ̈ܫܐ. ܡܛܠ ܕܝܢ ܕܐܡܪ ܐܢܬ ܕܕܝܢܬܟ ܘܠܐ ܢܫܬܒܩ ܕܒܥܠܕܒܒܐ ܡܕܡ ܓܝܪ܆ ܐܝܟ ܡܐ ܕܒܛܫܝܐ ܘܩ̈ܛܝܠܐ ܕܡܬܡܪܓܢ ܒܗܘܢ ܚ̈ܕܝܐ: ܡܛܠ ܐܢܐ ܠܟ ܡܢ ܕܚܛܝܬܐ. ܠܗ ܓܝܪ ܗܘܝܐ ܐܬܪܢܗ. ܡܢ ܐܚܪܐ. ܡܬܚܫܚܢ ܕܝܢ ܒܡܠܬܐ: ܟܕ ܐܝܬ ܠܗܘܢ ܫܩܠܐ ܛܥܢܐ ܘܢܣܒܘܢ ܚܝܘܬܐ ܙܢܝܬܐ: ܘܗܟܝܠ ܕܐܝܢܐ ܐܬܐ ܗܘ. ܕܐܬܝܚܕܘ ܕܝܢ ܐܡܪܝܢ ܒܚܝܘܬܐ ܘܠܐ ܡܫܬܘܕܝܐ: ܘܐܝܬ ܠܗ ܠܐ ܡܫܬܚܠܦܐ ܒܗܢܐ ܕܝܠܗ ܠܚܛܝܬܐ ܕܡܢ ܐܠܗܐ. ܡܚܣܢ ܕܝܢ ܐܦ ܠܗ ܠܚܛܝܬܐ ܐܠܗܝܐ ܢܦܩ ܡܢ ܐܠܗܐ: ܕܠܗ ܦܫܛ ܡܟܝܟ ܠܚܛܝܬܐ. ܫܐܠ ܠܗ ܕܝܢ ܡܠܟܐ ܐܝܟ ܕܒܚܫܝܫܘܬܐ ܘܡܣܬܒܪܢܘܬܐ. ܗܟܢ ܗܘܝܐ ܦܠܓܘܣ ܡܥܠܝܐ ܠܐܠܗܝܬܐ ܡܬܓܠܝܢ: ܐܠܐ ܠܐ ܐܬܐܡܪܬ ܐܝܟ ܡܠܬܐ ܕܡܠܐ: ܠܗܢܘܢ ܘܠܐ ܡܬܓܠܝܢ ܗܘܘ ܒܥܡܝܩܘܬܐ ܒܗ ܗܢܘܢ ܕܡܠܐ. ܐܬܐ ܓܝܪ ܒܐܝܕܝܢ ܗܘܘ ܕܒܐܝ ܗܟܢܐ ܢܬܡܪܓܘܢ܆ ܒܗ ܚܝ̈ܕܝܐ: ܐܝܟ ܡܐ ܕܐܦ ܚܡܪܐ ܒܥܒ̈ܝܐ: ܘܒܥܠܕܒܒܐ ܡܕܡ ܕܩܛܝܠܐ ܕܚ̈ܝܕܝܐ ܚܕܘܝ: ܗܟܝܠ ܕܡܬܠܟܠܢܘܗܝ ܡܠܬܐ: ܐܘ ܡܛܠܗ (114) ܕܠܐܚܪܢܐ ܒܢܦܫܐ: ܐܝܟ ܗܘ ܕܠܐܝܬ ܒܦܪܨܘܦܐ ܕܩܕܝܫܐ ܩܕܝܫܐ: ܕܕܝܠܗ ܕܗܘܝ ܘܗܘܝܘ: ܐܬܐܘܗ ܗܘܐ ܠܟܠ ܘܢܦܫܐ ܚܕܐ. ܐܠܐ ܡܫܟܚ ܐܢܐ ܕܗܘܐ ܐܬܐܘܗ ܚܙܘܐ ܘܠܗ ܗܘ. ܠܒܪ ܡܢ ܕܝܢ ܗܟܝܠ ܕܟܠ ܗܟܢ ܗܘܝ: ܗܘܐ ܗܘ ܓܝܪ ܦܫܛ ܗܘܐ ܕܩܕܝܫܐ܀

ܬܐܘܪܝܐ ܕܝܢ ܡܥܠܝܐ ܠܐܠܗܝܬܐ: ܒܬܐܘܪܝܐ ܓܝܪ ܗܘ ܕܟܠ ܒܗ ܕܢܐ: ܟܕ ܒܪܐ ܕܢܫܡ: ܡܬܚܙܝܐ ܕܚܝܘܬܐ ܕܟܠ ܡܢ ܚܝܐ ܐܝܟ ܕܗܘܐ ܫܒܒܗ ܐܒܪ. ܀ܬܐܘܪܝܐ܀ ܢܦܩ ܕܝܢ ܐܠܗܐ ܒܗ ܢܫܡܬܐ: ܚܕ ܡܢ ܬܪ̈ܝܢ ܕܒܝܬܐ. ܒܬܪܐ ܘܙܘܓܐ. ܘܡܢܗܘܢ ܗܘܐ ܦܢ ܠܗ. ܗܘܐ ܕܝܢ ܐܬܬܟܠ. ܐܘ ܠܒܘܫܝܐ ܚܕܬܐ. ܐܘ ܠܫܘܪܓܐ ܚܡܝܐ. ܗܘ ܕܐܬܐܘܗ ܗܘܐ. ܘܒܪܘܐ ܡܬܒܪܐ. ܘܗܘ ܠܐ ܡܬܒܪܝܐ ܡܬܒܪܐ. ܟܕ ܢܦܫܐ ܡܬܚܙܝܐ: ܘܡܬܚܙܝܐ ܠܐܠܗܘܬܐ ܘܠܚܝܘܬܐ ܕܒܪܐ܀ ܒܬܐܘܪܝܐ ܕܝܢ ܩܕܡܝܐ ܕܡܛܠ ܒܪܐ: ܟܕ ܡܫܘܚ ܕܚܝܘܬܐ ܕܟܠ ܒܪܐ ܡܢܫܐ ܘܡܫܬܚܝܐ ܕܡܠܬܐ ܐܠܗܐ: ܪܘܚܐ ܚܝܐ ܘܠܗ ܡܫܘܪܝܐ: ܟܕ ܠܟܠ ܐܪܡܝܗ ܢܪܐ: ܕܟܠܐ ܩܕܡܬܐ ܘܡܬܒܪܝܢܬܐ ܠܟܠ ܚܝܐ ܕܡܠܬܐ ܕܡܢ ܩܕܡ ܠܠܟ̈ܠܐ ܡܫܡܫܝܢ: ܘܠܐ ܡܬܦܪܫܝܢ ܗܟܝܠ ܠܗܘܢ ܕܐܬܬܪܝܡ ܘܐܬܒܪܝ: ܘܦܠܓ ܡܫܡܫܘܬܐ ܕܡܛܠܬܗܝܢ: ܫܐܠ ܗܟܝܠ. ܀ܬܐܘܪܝܐ܀ ܟܕ ܡܠܠܗ: ܗܘܢ ܦܝ ܕܐܡܪ ܩܕܡ ܦܪܫ ܠܐܠܗܘܬܐ: ܘܠܟܝܢܐ ܕܡܟܠ ܡܢ ܚ̈ܝܐ ܘܡܢ ܓܘܫܡܐ. ܗܟܝܠ ܕܝܢ ܕܐܡܪ ܩܕܡ ܠܒܪܝܬܐ: ܘܠܗܘ

to the exaggerated use of words and not search out the sound meaning which shines out plainly from all his treatises, we would say, by not following carefully and intelligently, that because he said "The one deified and the other was deified" the flesh was deified and was changed into the ousia of divinity. And again, because he said, "It is not worse to say that he also became man", we should go on to think that God the Word fell to the ousia of humanity and one and the same person undergoes opposite effects from the two sides, since the followers of Nestorius as well, bringing up the words of this Father theologian, and thinking that they can beg from them a defence of their wickedness, pervert what is written in this way in the Sermon on Epiphany, or Nativity: (GREGORY): "He was sent out, but as man: for he was double, because he was also tired, and hungered, and thirsted, and was afraid, and wept according to the law[44] of the body."[45]

But since we know that (Gregory) does not, like these unclean men, say that the Son is double in natures and in hypostases, we reject the stain on the honour of this holy Father. For he recognises God inhominate, one from two. Nestorius does not confess this, but shuns this (formula) "from two", which establishes composition and completes one hypostasis and nature of the Word incarnate. For in (*Lebon p. 116*) the Sermon on the Epiphany he says: (GREGORY): "God went out with the assuming, one from two which were opposite, of which the one deified, and the other was deified".[46] But this "was deified" is understood and is said because the flesh shone out with the glory proper to God, as wise Cyril says,[47] and not because it had fallen into the nature of divinity. For Gregory the Theologian himself rejects this inaccurate understanding, when he said as follows in the Letter to Cledonius: (GREGORY): "If someone should say that the flesh is now laid down, while the divinity is stripped of the body, and not that it both is with the assuming and is also coming, may he not see the glory of the advent. For where is the body now, unless it is with him who assumed (it)? For it was not placed in the sun, as is the folly of the Manichaeans, that it should be honoured through disgrace or be poured out and dissolved in the air, like the nature of speech and the pouring out of a scent and the impermanent course of lightning. But where is that which was touched after the resurrection, or which is to be seen by those who pierced (him)? For divinity on its own is not visible. But he will come with the body, as I said,[48] in such a way as[49] he was seen by the disciples on the mountain, or appeared with the divine element overcoming the fleshly."[50] For his face was radiant like the sun on the

ܘܡܫܬܠܛ ܐܦܛܪܘܦ ܘܐܬܟܒܫ. ܠܐ ܕܝܢ ܥܡܪܐ ܕܢܐܡܪ ܕܐܦ ܐܬܟܪܝܗ. ܒܬܪܘܡ ܘܐܬܪܘܡܡ. ܐܡܬܝ ܕܝܢ ܚܙܐ ܐܢܫ ܒܥܪܘܬܐ ܕܩܛܠܐ: ܗܘ ܕܠܥܠܡ ܪܥܝܐ: ܐܬܟܦ ܕܢܛܪ ܪܥܝܐ ܠܗܘܐ. ܘܐܣܩ ܒܗ ܠܟܘܬܐ: ܘܠܐ ܠܗܘܐ ܒܥܠܡ ܕܩܕܡܘܗܝ. ܐܠܐ ܠܐܣܩ ܒܗܡ ܗܠܝܢ ܕܡܛܪܝܢ. ܘܐܬܗܦܟ ܥܒܕܐ ܡܢ ܡܫܠܛܢܐ ܕܥܒܕܐ: ܥܒܕܐ ܕܝܢ ܢܟܦܘܬܐ ܘܡܟܝܟܘܬܐ. ܗܢܐ ܕܝܢ ܕܗܘܐ ܠܗ ܡܫܬܠܛܢܐ: ܐܝܟ (115) ܗܘܐ ܐܝܟܢ ܕܐܦ ܠܟܠ ܥܡܗ ܐܝܬܘܗܝ ܗܘܐ. ܗܢܐ ܕܗܘܐ ܒܪܢܫܐ: ܘܐܦ ܠܐ ܡܬܒܥܐ ܐܝܬܘܗܝ ܗܘܐ. ܗܘ ܡܢ ܗܒܠ ܕܐܝܬܘܗܝ ܗܘܐ ܡܢ. ܗܘ ܗܢܐ ܕܝܢ ܕܠܐܝܬܘܗܝ ܗܘܐ ܡܩܒܠ܀

ܗܐ ܒܫܢܬ ܬܠܬܝܢ. ܕܪܘܡܝܐ ܢܦܠ ܗܘܐ ܠܡܬܟܬܒܢܘܬܐ ܘܠܗ ܡܥܪܒܐ ܘܒܡܕܒܪܐ. ܐܝܟ ܢܗܘܐ ܕܒܥܡܠܐ ܘܡܥܪܒܐ ܒܟܠܐ ܡܘܡܐ ܕܚܝܘܬܐ ܕܫܡܝܐ ܐܬܝܗܒ. ܐܢ ܒܥܪ ܒܠܒܝܡ ܚܝ ܕܒܡܫܡܘܬܐ ܕܩܠܐ ܡܢܝܡ ܢܦܩ: ܘܠܗ ܗܘܐ ܡܠܡܐ ܢܟܝܦ: ܗܘ ܕܡܢ ܡܠܘܗܝ ܡܐܡܪܘܗܝ ܒܥܠܡܐ ܡܬܠܝܘܐ. ܐܡܪܝܢ ܒܪ ܠܐ ܒܥܪܐܝܬ ܘܡܫܡܫܢܘܬܐ ܡܫܬܠܡܝܢ. ܕܡܫܬܠ ܕܐܡܪ ܕܗܢܐ ܡܢ ܠܟܠܗ: ܗܢܐ ܕܝܢ ܐܬܐܠܗ: ܕܥܡܪܐ ܐܬܐܠܗ ܘܐܬܕܒܩ ܠܐܘܠܐ ܕܠܟܘܬܐ. ܘܐܘܒ ܡܫܬܠ ܕܐܡܪ. ܠܐ ܕܝܢ ܥܡܪܐ ܕܠܡܪ ܕܐܦ ܐܬܟܪܝܗ: ܢܦܠ ܘܢܣܒܪ ܕܒܗܠ ܐܘܫܐ ܕܐܝܟܘܬܐ ܢܩܠ ܡܟܠܐ ܠܟܘܐ: ܘܗܘ ܒܪ ܕܗܘ ܡܢ ܠܐܪܡ ܒܥܝܢ ܢܦܠ ܒܡܝܬܐ ܡܩܘܒܠܐ. ܕܡܫܬܠ ܕܐܦ ܗܢܘܢ ܕܡܬܪܓܡ ܗܠܝܢ ܕܢܫܬܘܕܥ. ܒܪ ܡܫܡܫܠܝܢ ܒܩܠܐ ܕܗܢܐ ܐܝܬ ܡܫܬܠ ܠܟܘܠܬܐ: ܘܡܫܡܫܝܢ ܕܡܬܒܪܘܬܐ ܕܒܥܠܡܗܘܢ ܡܫܡܝܢ ܚܕܪܝܢ. ܡܫܡܫܝܢ ܗܘ ܕܒܡܬܐܡܪܐ ܕܒܝܬ ܕܚܝܐ ܐܘ ܕܒܝܬ ܡܠܐ ܡܫܡܫܐ ܗܘܒܐ. ܀ܒܪܢܫܢܫܘܬ܀ ܐܬܦܪܥ ܡܢ. ܐܠܐ ܐܝܟ ܒܪܢܫܐ. ܒܫܡܐ ܒܥܪ ܐܝܬܘܗܝ. ܡܫܬܠ ܕܐܦ ܠܐ ܘܟܡ ܘܙܘܗܝ ܘܐܦܛܪܘܦ ܘܦܩܕ ܒܢܥܘܬܐ ܕܒܘܫܡܐ܀

ܐܠܐ ܚܝ ܒܪ ܚܒܝܒ: ܕܠܗ ܐܝܟ ܗܠܝܢ ܠܛܟܐ: ܒܫܡܐ ܒܒܢܝܐ ܘܒܩܝܘܡܐ ܐܡܪ ܠܒܪܐ: ܫܬܪܝܢ ܡܘܡܐ ܕܐܬܥܘܝܬܐ ܕܗܢܐ ܐܝܬ ܡܢܝܐ. ܚܕ ܒܥܪ ܡܢ ܬܪܝܢ ܢܦܠ ܠܠܗܐ ܕܐܬܟܪܝܗ. ܗܘ ܕܐܦ ܢܫܬܘܕܥܘܢ ܠܐ ܡܨܝܐ. ܐܠܐ ܚܕܐ ܡܢ ܗܘ ܕܡܢ ܬܪܝܢ. ܘܐܬܝܗ ܡܫܡܫܢܘܬܐ ܕܪܘܚܐ: ܘܡܫܡܫܢܘܬܐ ܕܚܕ ܩܘܡܐ ܘܚܝܠܐ ܘܡܠܬܐ ܕܡܥܡܪ. ܒܗ (116) ܒܥܪ ܒܡܬܐܡܪܐ ܗܘ ܕܠܟܠ ܒܝܬ ܕܚܝܐ ܐܡܪ. ܀ܒܪܢܫܢܫܘܬ܀ ܢܩܦ ܕܝܢ ܠܠܗܐ ܒܗܡ ܢܫܬܘܕܥ: ܚܕ ܡܢ ܬܪܝܢ ܕܒܟܘܠܐ. ܕܡܢܗܘܢ ܗܢܐ ܡܢ ܠܟܠܗ. ܗܢܐ ܕܝܢ ܐܬܐܠܗ܀ ܗܘ ܕܝܢ ܕܐܬܐܠܗ ܡܬܝܠܕܐ ܘܡܬܐܡܪܐ: ܡܫܘܠ ܕܒܬܥܘܝܬܐ ܦܝܫ ܠܠܗܐ: ܐܝܟ ܕܐܡܪ ܡܠܡܐ ܡܘܪܚܘܬܐ. ܐܬܝܠܕ

mountain, as we hear the Gospel, and his garments were white like light.[51] But these things do not indicate a change of ousia, far from it, but the brilliance and the multitude of the glory which is proper to God. For how was he going to be seen by those who pierced (him), if the flesh which was pierced is changed from being visible to being invisible?

And Cyril the Theologian in the First Letter to (*Lebon p. 117*) Succensus wrote as follows: (CYRIL): "It is equally nonsensical to say that the body was changed into the nature of divinity, and that the Word was changed into the nature of flesh. For just as the latter is impossible, for (the Word) cannot be transformed and is immutable, so also is the former. For none of the things which are comprehensible, (that is, none) of the creatures, is able to be changed to the ousia or the nature of divinity, and flesh belongs to the created order. Therefore we say that the body of Christ is divine because it is the body of God, and is brilliant with inexpressible glory, incorruptible, holy (and) life-giving. But that it was changed into the nature of divinity, no-one of the holy Fathers thought or said, nor do we affirm this."[52]

But the Fathers called (Christ) double because the study of Christ is twofold, and some things are written about him in a human way, and some things as is proper to divinity. And this wise Cyril, who proceeds exactly in everything, referred to holy Athanasius in the Letter to the Monks, quoting instructively as follows: FROM ATHANASIUS: "Therefore the aim and character of divine scripture, as we have frequently said, is this, that the teaching in it about our Saviour is twofold, that he was God for ever, and is Son and Word and the brilliance and the wisdom of the Father; and at the end he became man for our sake when he assumed flesh from the Virgin Mary who bore God."[53, 54] And (Cyril) himself writes as follows, making a defence against the complaint from Theodoret against the Fourth Chapter: (CYRIL): "But I say it would be far better and (*Lebon p. 118*) far more learned to attribute the human words not to another person, which is understood independently and apart[55] (as) Son, (namely) to the form of the servant as those men are accustomed to say, but to attribute them rather to the measure of his humanity; for it was right that being God and man at the same time, he should proceed by means of both words".[56]

You see that the form of the words is twofold, but Christ himself is not double in natures or hypostases, but is one from two. Hence, (Cyril) in the Second Volume against the blasphemies of Nestorius, completely forbids mention of "double", wanting to block all access

ܒܣܪܐ. ܘܠܗ ܠܟܝܢܐ ܕܐܠܗܘܬܐ ܢܦܠ. ܠܗܢܐ ܓܝܪ ܡܘܬܐ ܠܐ ܚܫܝܐ: ܕܢܦܫ ܘܗܘ ܡܫܬܠܠ ܠܐܠܗܘܬܐ ܓܪܝܓܘܪܝܘܣ. ܟܕ ܠܓܢܣܐ ܕܟܠܗ ܡܫܝܚܝܘܬܗ ܐܡܪ ܗܟܢܐ. ܀ܓܪܝܓܘܪܝܘܣ܀ ܐܢ ܐܝܟ ܕܐܬܬܣܝܡ ܗܟܐ ܒܣܪܐ ܐܦܢ: ܟܕ ܒܪܢܫܘܬܐ ܐܬܡܢܝ ܠܐܠܗܘܬܐ ܡܢ ܓܘܫܡܐ: ܐܠܐ ܠܗ ܟܡ ܢܫܟܚܘܬܐ ܘܐܬܡܢܝ ܐܦ ܐܬܐ: ܠܐ ܚܙܐ ܠܡܫܘܚܬܐ ܕܡܬܐܬܝܐ. ܐܝܟܐ ܗܘ ܓܝܪ ܓܘܫܡܐ ܗܟܐ: ܐܠܐ ܟܡ ܗܘ ܕܢܦܫ. ܠܗ ܓܝܪ ܐܝܟ ܚܫܘܬܐ ܕܩ̈ܢܝܢܐ ܒܡܫܡܫܐ ܐܬܬܫܝܡ: ܐܝܟܢܐ ܕܢܛܥܢ ܟܡ ܙܒܢܐ: ܐܘ ܒܐܬܪ ܐܬܬܚܡ ܘܐܬܬܠܝܫ ܠܟܡ ܟܝܢܐ ܘܒܪܢܐ ܟܠܐ: ܘܐܬܚܫܘܬܐ ܕܙܟܝܐ: ܘܪܘܚܬܐ ܕܒܪܢܐ ܘܠܐ ܒܐܝܡ. ܐܝܟܐ ܕܝܢ ܐܬܡܢܝ ܘܗܘ ܕܐܬܓܫܫ ܠܗܘ ܡܫܟܚܬܐ: ܐܘ ܕܡܬܚܙܝܐ ܡܢ ܗܢܘܢ ܕܕܒܪܘ. ܠܐܠܗܘܬܐ ܓܝܪ ܡܢܗ ܘܠܗ ܠܐ ܡܬܚܙܝܢܝܬܐ ܗܝ. ܐܠܐ ܐܬܐ ܕܝ ܟܡ ܓܘܫܡܐ: ܐܝܟ ܡܠܬܐ ܕܡܠܟ. ܕܐܝܟ ܗܟܢܐ ܕܝܢ: ܐܝܟ ܡܠܐ ܕܐܬܚܙܝ ܠܡܠܟ̈ܫܢܐ ܒܥܘܙܐ: ܐܘ ܐܬܚܙܝ: ܟܕ ܙܟܝܐ ܠܐܠܗܘܬܐ ܠܒܪܢܫܘܬܐ܀ ܐܠܦܝ ܓܝܪ ܦܪܨܘܦܗ ܒܥܘܙܐ ܐܝܟ ܫܡܫܐ. ܐܝܟ ܕܡܫܟܚܝܢ ܠܐܘܪܚܬܗܘܢ. ܘܡܐܢܘܗܝ ܗܘܘ ܚܘܪ̈ܐ ܐܝܟ ܢܘܗܪܐ. ܗܠܝܢ ܕܝܢ ܠܗ ܡܘܚܠܐ ܘܐܘܣܝܐ ܩܕܡ. ܠܐ ܝܗܒ. ܐܠܐ ܢܗܝܪܘܬܐ ܘܫܘܦܪܐ ܕܐܘܣܝܐ ܕܠܐ ܠܐܠܗܐ. ܐܝܟܢܐ ܓܝܪ ܠܗܝܢ ܗܘܐ ܕܢܬܚܙܐ ܡܢ ܗܢܘܢ ܕܕܒܪܘ: ܟܕ ܒܣܪܐ ܗܘ ܕܐܬܐܡܪ ܡܢ ܡܬܚܙܝܢܐ ܐܬܚܙܝ ܟܠܐ ܡܬܚܙܝܢܐ.

ܗܕܐ ܘܩܘܪܝܠܘܣ ܡܫܬܠܠ ܠܐܠܗܘܬܐ: ܠܓܢܣܐ ܩܕܝܫܬܐ (117) ܕܟܠܗ ܡܫܝܚܝܘܬܗ ܐܡܪ ܗܟܢܐ. ܀ܩܘܪܝܠܘܣ܀ ܗܟܐ ܗܘ ܓܝܪ ܒܡܠܬܐ ܕܒܪܢܫܘܬܐ: ܕܢܐܡܪ ܕܐܬܝܠܕ ܓܘܫܡܐ ܠܟܝܢܐ ܕܐܠܗܘܬܐ: ܗܢܘ ܐܢܫܐ ܕܐܬܝܠܕ ܡܠܬܐ ܠܟܝܢܐ ܕܒܣܪܐ. ܐܟܘܬ ܓܝܪ ܕܒܗܝ ܠܟܠ ܠܗ ܦܘܪܫܐ: ܠܐ ܡܬܗܘܦܟܐ ܓܝܪ ܘܠܐ ܡܬܚܠܦܢܐ ܐܝܬܘܗܝ. ܗܟܢܐ ܘܗܝ ܐܚܪܬܐ. ܠܟܝܢܐ ܓܝܪ ܡܢ ܗܠܝܢ ܕܡܬܝܕܥܝܢ: ܘܠܐܘܣܝܐ ܕܐܠܗܘܬܐ ܐܘ ܠܟܝܢܐ ܕܢܦܫ ܕܡܬܗܦܟ ܡܬܚܡ ܡܢ ܒܪ̈ܝܬܐ. ܒܪܝܬܐ ܕܝܢ ܐܦ ܒܣܪܐ. ܡܬܚܡ ܠܐܠܗܐ ܡܢ ܐܡܪܝܢ ܕܐܬܗܘܝ ܦܓܪܗ ܕܡܫܝܚܐ. ܡܛܠ ܕܐܦ ܦܓܪܐ ܐܬܗܘܝ ܕܐܠܗܐ: ܘܡܬܚܕܝ ܒܡܘܫܚܐ ܘܠܐ ܡܬܡܫܠܠ. ܠܐ ܡܬܡܫܚܢܐ. ܡܫܝܚܐ. ܦܓܪ ܚܕܐ. ܕܐܬܚܕ ܕܝܢ ܠܟܝܢܐ ܕܐܠܗܘܬܐ: ܘܠܐ ܐܝܟ ܡܢ ܐܚܪ̈ܢܐ ܩܕܝܫܐ ܐܬܪܒܝ ܐܘ ܐܡܪ. ܐܦ ܠܐ ܚܕ ܗܟܢܐ ܡܫܡܫܢ ܚܕ܀

ܘܡܫܬܐ ܕܝܢ ܐܡܪܗ ܐܚܪ̈ܬܐ: ܡܫܬܠܠ ܕܚܫܫܬܐ ܐܬܡܢܝ ܠܐܘܪܚܐ ܕܟܠ ܡܫܝܚܐ. ܘܗܠܝܢ ܬܘܒ ܐܝܬܝܗ. ܗܠܝܢ ܬܘܒ ܦܠܓܐ ܠܐܠܗܘܬܗ ܡܠ̈ܬܐ ܡܫܬܠܠܗ. ܘܗܕܐ ܠܦܓܪܐ ܐܬܚܫܒܬ ܐܬܘ: ܡܫܬܠܠ ܩܘܪܝܠܘܣ ܗܘ ܕܒܠܠܟܝܢ ܡܬܡܠܠܐ ܪܘܐ:

to those who divide (Christ), thus: (CYRIL): "It is not the case that because the Word from God the Father assumed flesh and went out a man like us, he is for this reason called double. For he is one and not without flesh, he who in his own nature is without flesh and body.[57] For just as if someone killed a man like us, he is not (then) justly accused of having committed wrong on two men, but only on one, even if perhaps (the man) should be understood (to consist) of soul and body, which were united with each other (and) which are not the same in nature, but different. The same thing should be understood in the case of Christ, for he is not double, but one sole Lord and Son, the Word who is from God and the Father, but not without flesh."[58] In the same way, in the Third Letter against Nestorius he says this: (CYRIL): "For the one and sole Christ is not double, even if he is understood (as brought together) from two different elements, having come to inseverable union, just as man is also understood from soul and body and is not then double, but one from two."[59] *(Lebon p. 119)*

Do you not perceive that we should use holy Cyril (as) a builder and establisher of divine teaching, if we are going to resist the Nestorian faction accurately with the words of the holy Fathers? For though I was able to cite many and various things which were written by Gregory the Theologian, and (which) were very seriously mutilated by those who divide the one Christ, I desisted, since I was unwilling to trouble your understanding, for doubtless you had renounced mixture and were wanting a defence against these things, which is not easy to those who are untrained, but to those who have taken into account all these things which were said by the Doctor, they appear accurate and clear of any blame and reprehension. Or did not also Peter, chosen first of the Apostles, write this about the compact and profound letters of Paul, thus: "There are in them things which are hard to understand, which unlearned and unstable men pervert, as also the rest of scripture, to their own destruction"?[60]

For it is possible to see as well those who have drunk from the cup of the error of Eutyches corrupting that saying of holy Gregory, which he wrote in the Sermon on Epiphany: (GREGORY): "That which was without flesh becomes incarnate, the Word becomes thick".[61] For they think, being beside themselves, that the Word has become thick like water when it condenses to ice, and as they mistakenly strive for the confirmation of this (idea), they quote as well that which is said in this way, in the Sermon on New Sunday[62]: (GREGORY): "And he becomes poor in becoming solid (as) flesh,[63] in

ܠܐܪ̈ܙܐ ܕܟܠܗ ܕܒܢ̈ܝܐ ܘܡܬܚܫܒܢܘܬܗ ܗܘܝܐ ܚܦܝܠ. ܡܢ ܕܐܬܚܫܚܘ܀ ܙܒܢܐ
ܗܘܝܐ ܘܣܘܦܝܐ ܕܟܠܗ ܠܐܠܗܐ: ܐܝܟܢܐ ܕܩܕܝܫ ܦܘܠܘܣ ܐܡܪ: ܗܢܐ ܗܘ. ܕܒܟܠܗ
ܐܠܗܘܬܗ ܒܗ ܡܬܒܥܝܐ ܕܡܬܬܠܝܐ ܦܪܘܩ. ܟܕ ܡܠܝܐ ܠܐܠܗܐ ܐܠܗܘܬܗ ܗܘܐ
ܘܐܠܗܘܬܗ ܒܪܐ. ܘܡܠܟܘܬܐ ܐܠܗܘܬܗ ܘܪܘܚܐ: ܘܡܫܡܫܢܘܬܐ ܕܐܒܐ. ܘܟܢܫܐ ܡܫܡܠܝܢ
ܒܪܢܫܐ ܗܘܐ: ܟܕ ܒܣܪܐ ܢܣܒ ܡܢ ܒܬܘܠܬܐ ܡܪܝܡ ܡܠܐ ܠܐܠܗܐ܀ ܗܘ ܕܐܦ ܗܘ
ܟܠܗ ܒܟܠܗ ܕܒܣܒܪܬܐ ܡܫܠܡ ܕܐܬܩܪܝ: ܕܗܘܐ ܡܢ ܬܘܠܕܬܐ: ܟܕ ܢܣܒ ܒܪܢܫܐ
ܡܠܟ ܗܘܝܐ. ܡܫܝܚܐ܀ ܕܡܬܬܪܝ ܕܝܢ ܐܡܪ ܐܢܐ (118) ܘܦܪܨܘܦ ܫܡܪ
ܒܡܠܟܝܐ: ܕܟܝܢܐ ܩܠܝܠ ܐܢܫܝܐ ܢܣܒ: ܠܐ ܒܦܘܪܫܢܐ ܐܚܪܢܐ ܡܢܗ ܕܡܬܝܠܕ
ܕܡܠܬܐ ܘܒܪܢܫܐ ܒܪܐ: ܒܪܘܚܐ ܕܩܘܕܫܐ ܐܝܟ ܕܐܡܪ ܠܗܘܢ ܡܠܐ ܕܐܡܪܘ. ܐܠܐ
ܡܢܗ ܠܒܪܢܫܐ ܘܐܢܫܐ ܢܣܒ. ܗܕܐ ܗܘܐ ܫܪܝ ܕܟܕ ܐܠܗܘܬܗ ܠܐܠܗܐ ܐܟܚܕܐ
ܘܒܪܢܫܐ: ܕܟܕ ܬܪܝܢܘܬܐ ܩܠܐ ܢܙܝܐ܀
ܚܕܐ ܐܝܬ ܕܒܟܠܐ ܐܠܗܘܬܗ ܐܘܫܐ ܒܫܡܐ: ܘܠܐ ܗܘ ܡܫܝܚܐ ܒܫܡܐ ܐܠܗܘܬܗ
ܒܬܪܝܢ ܐܘ ܒܩܢܘܡܐ: ܐܠܐ ܚܕ ܡܢ ܬܪܝܢ. ܡܢ ܗܘܝܐ ܗܘܠܠ ܒܫܘܡܠܝܐ ܕܬܪܝܢ
ܕܠܘܬܟܠ ܒܪܘܚܐ ܘܢܫܡܬܐ. ܟܠ ܡܠܬܐ ܦܫܛ ܠܗܘܢ ܘܢܐܡܪ ܒܫܡܐ. ܟܕ
ܪܓܐ ܕܟܠ ܡܬܚܙܝܢܐ ܘܗܘܝ ܘܡܬܩܢܝܢ ܢܦܫܗ ܗܘܝܐ. ܡܫܝܚܐ܀ ܠܗ
ܡܛܠ ܕܒܣܪܐ ܚܒܠ ܡܠܬܐ ܕܡܢ ܠܐܠܗܐ ܐܒܐ ܘܢܣܒ ܒܪܢܫܐ ܐܟܘܬܢ: ܡܛܠ
ܗܘܐ ܒܟܠܐ ܡܫܬܡܠܝ ܐܦ ܒܫܡܐ. ܚܕ ܓܒܪ ܐܠܗܘܬܗ ܘܠܗ ܫܡܪ ܡܢ ܒܣܪܐ:
ܗܘ ܕܒܪܢܫܐ ܘܡܠܗ ܫܡܪ ܡܢ ܒܣܪܐ ܘܓܘܫܡܐ. ܐܝܟ ܗܠ ܓܒܪ ܕܐܦ ܐܝܬ ܠܒܪܢܫܐ
ܘܐܟܘܬܗ ܒܡܛܠ: ܠܗ ܐܝܟ ܗܘ ܕܒܠܝܠ ܩܢܝܐ ܒܢܘܡ ܠܡܬܪܐܬ ܐܟܘܬܗ
ܡܬܡܛܪܢ ܘܪܝܫܗ: ܐܠܐ ܟܕ ܒܟܣܘ ܐܦ ܠܓܒܗ ܘܠܡܚܪ ܡܢ ܢܦܫܐ
ܘܦܓܪܐ: ܗܟܢ ܕܟܝܢܝ̈ܐ ܐܬܝܚܕܘ: ܕܒܟܝܢܐ ܠܗ ܗܘ ܟܕ ܗܘ ܐܠܗܘܬܗ ܡܢܗ. ܐܠܐ
ܡܫܝܚܐ: ܗܘܝܐ ܠܐܦ ܘܟܠܐ ܡܫܝܚܐ ܢܘܦ ܕܢܦܬܠܬܠ. ܠܗ ܓܒܪ ܒܫܡܐ
ܐܠܗܘܬܗ. ܐܠܐ ܚܕ ܘܒܟܝܢܘܬܗ ܡܪܢܐ ܘܒܪܐ: ܡܠܬܐ ܗܘ ܕܡܢ ܠܐܠܗܐ ܘܐܒܐ. ܠܗ
ܕܝܢ ܫܡܪ ܡܢ ܒܣܪܐ܀ ܒܗ ܒܪܘܚܐ ܘܦܠܓܘܬܐ ܕܐܬܠ ܘܒܟܠ ܢܫܬܘܬܦ ܗܘ
ܗܘܐ ܐܡܪ. ܡܫܝܚܐ܀ ܠܐܠܗܘܬܗ ܓܒܪ ܒܫܡܐ ܗܘ ܚܕ ܘܒܟܝܢܘܬܗ ܡܫܝܚܐ:
ܐܦ ܡܢ ܬܪܝܢ ܫܘܬܦܝܢ ܘܡܫܬܟܢܢ ܡܫܬܡܠܝܢ: ܘܒܚܕܝܘܬܐ ܠܐ ܡܬܦܠܓܝܢܐ
ܐܝܟ. ܐܚܕܐ ܕܐܦ ܒܪܢܫܐ ܕܡܢ ܢܫܡܐ ܘܦܓܪܐ ܡܬܝܕܥ. ܘܠܗ ܒܫܡܐ ܡܠܟܘ: ܐܠܐ ܚܕ
ܡܢ ܬܪܝܢ܀

order that we might be enriched by his poverty".[64] But they are quite evidently proved to be in the wrong, inflicted with utter madness, and chopping off little words like mice, and taking an attitude towards scripture in the Jewish way, even though (*Lebon p. 120*) the Doctor wrote in this way in the First Treatise on the Son: AGAIN FROM GREGORY: "At the beginning he was without cause: for what is the cause of God? But at the end he became for a reason, and that was that you, scoffer, might be saved, you who disparage the divinity because it assumed your grossness".[65] Hence, therefore, it is recognised in advance that (when) he says that the Word became thick with our crassness, that means that he united an *οὐσία*, not a *φαντασία*, to himself hypostatically and in truth. For he also said about this: (GREGORY): "The Word grows thick; that which was invisible becomes visible; that which was untouchable is handled; that which was without time takes a beginning".[66]

And I could cite very many words which those who quarrel with orthodoxy have used as weapons against us, having excerpted in various ways the sound teaching of the holy Fathers, and they are proved to be in the wrong and are shamefully worsted by the complete context of what has been said by these men. For they have even composed a book of up to 250 so-called testimonies (taken) from excerpts of the proven doctor Cyril, and introduced him as the advocate of the error of the two natures. And while God stretched out his hand in the capital, we too have published a book against the error, to which the title is *Philalethes*, as a weapon against them, having set out these words of Cyril, and (now) everyone will know what is the true meaning, and what is sacrilege and what an instance of a lie. It is not surprising then if some people have held my poor words worthy of mutilation too! Therefore let these things not disturb you in the slightest: but it is time to say, like Qohelet, about this too: "There is nothing new or fresh under the sun",[67] but there is a similar vanity in their anxieties and they are inflicted with a related lack of reason. (*Lebon p. 121*)

But because you also try to obtain your former opinion from this quotation of holy Cyril which he speaks about Emmanuel, "He is composed (so as to become) one in the middle, of human properties, and those which are above man",[68] and, explaining (it) in I do not know what way, you say "The Father seems to say that the Word incarnate made to cleave natures along with properties, and is one in every respect, I mean both nature and particularity", (then) I am quite astonished. For, while (Cyril) (uses) a plural word, and discriminates (between properties) by difference, and says, "Of human

(119) ܐܪܐ ܠܐ ܕܐܦ ܐܝܟ: ܕܒܟܝܢܐ ܡܘܪܟܒܘܬܗ ܦܠܐ ܕܢܦܫܗ ܡܚܝܢܐ ܘܡܡܟܢܐ ܘܡܟܫܦܐ ܠܐܠܗܐ: ܐܝ ܕܗܘ ܕܒܟܝܢܗ ܩܠܐ ܕܐܒܗ̈ܬܐ ܩܕܝܫܐ ܠܥܠܡ ܚܝ ܕܢܬܠܬܐܝܬ ܢܬܠܬ ܒܗܐ ܦܣܩܐ ܕܢܬܦܪܫܘܢ: ܟܕ ܡܫܬܐܠܐ ܡܢ ܘܐܫܬܘܝܬܐ ܕܠܐܬܒ ܓܪܝܓܘܪܝܘܣ ܡܡܠܠ ܠܐܒܗ̈ܬܐ: ܘܡܢ ܗܢܘܢ ܕܡܦܠܓܝܢ ܠܚܕ ܡܫܝܚܐ ܦܪܝܫ ܡܢܗܪܬܐ ܡܩܠܐܡܝܢ: ܡܡܟܣ ܗܘܬ ܐܝܬ ܠܡܦܠܓܘܬܐ ܡܟܫܦܬ: ܐܝܟ ܦܬ ܕܠܐ ܪܓܐ ܐܝܠܐ ܐܡܝܢܘܬ ܠܐܘܟܠܝܢ. ܟܕ ܓܪ ܡܪܢܐ ܗܘܬ ܡܢ ܡܫܬܘܕܝܐ: ܘܡܣܬܦܩ ܟܪܘܚܐ ܕܟܠ ܗܠܝܢ ܒܠܐ ܗܘܬ. ܗܘ ܕܠܗ ܕܟܠܐ ܐܝܬܘܗܝ ܠܗܠܝܢ ܘܠܐ ܡܣܬܟܠ. ܠܗܠܝܢ ܕܝܢ ܕܐܬܝܠܕ ܡܠܟ ܗܠܝܢ ܕܐܬܐܡܪ ܡܢ ܡܠܦܢܐ: ܐܦ ܡܬܚܬܬܐ ܘܡܫܬܥܐ ܡܢ ܟܠ ܕܒܟܠ ܘܠܟܠܢܫܐ ܩܕܡܝܢ. ܐܘ ܠܗ ܐܦ ܗܘܐ ܦܠܓܘܬ ܟܝܢܐ ܚܕܝܐ ܕܩܢܘܡܐ ܕܡܠܬܐ ܗܘܐ ܡܬܠܠ ܐܝܬܝܐ ܡܫܬܘܕܝܢܐ ܘܡܫܬܡܥܢܐ ܘܦܓܪܘܬܐ ܗܘܝܐ. ܕܟܝܢ ܐܝܬ ܡܬܚܡ ܕܢܣܒ ܠܡܫܬܡܠܝܘ: ܗܟܢ ܕܠܐ ܡܫܬܢܐ ܘܠܐ ܡܫܬܚܠܦܐ ܡܬܟܠܝܢ. ܐܡܝܢܐ ܕܐܦ ܡܠܬܐ ܕܡܪܝܐ ܠܗܐ ܐܝܬܝܗܘܢ.

ܡܛܠ ܕܐܦ ܠܗܢܘܢ ܕܐܡܪܘ ܓܝܪ ܕܒܝܬܐ ܕܐܘܪܫܠܡ ܐܝܟ ܠܡܫܝܚܐ: ܕܡܫܡܫܝܢ ܡܠܬܐ ܗܝ ܕܥܒܝܕܐ ܓܪܝܓܘܪܝܘܣ: ܗܝ ܕܐܡܪ ܒܡܠܦܢܐ ܕܟܠ ܚܕܐ ܕܚܝܐ. ܓܪܝܓܘܪܝܘܣ܀ ܗܘ ܕܠܐ ܒܣܪܐ ܡܬܒܣܪ: ܡܠܬܐ ܡܬܓܫܡܐ܀ ܡܬܪܢܝ ܠܗܘܢ ܓܪ ܪܘܚܐ ܕܡܠܬܐ ܐܬܐܡܪ: ܐܝܟ ܡܢܐ ܕܡܬܢܐ ܕܡܛܪܝܢ ܠܦܪܨܘܦܗܘܢ. ܘܟܕ ܡܬܬܠܡܝܢ ܠܦܓܪܐ: ܒܗܐ ܡܘܡܢܐ ܐܦ ܗܘ ܡܬܠܡ. ܗܘ ܕܒܡܠܦܢܐ ܕܟܠ ܢܕܒܪܐ ܚܕܐ ܐܡܪܐ ܗܘܝܐ. ܓܪܝܓܘܪܝܘܣ܀ ܘܡܬܬܡܣܟ ܗܘ ܕܒܣܪܐ ܠܐܒܘܗܝ. ܐܡܝܢܐ ܕܝܢ ܒܡܫܡܫܢܘܬܐ ܕܗܘ ܢܬܠܐ܀ ܐܠܐ ܡܬܬܡܫܡܫ ܦܪܝܫ ܚܕܢܝܐܝܬ: ܕܒܗܘܢ ܡܫܬܪܝܐ ܗܘܝܐ ܐܡܪܢܝܬܐ: ܘܦܠܘܣܦܘܬܐ ܐܝܟ ܒܡܫܪ̈ܬܐ ܡܫܪܝܢ: ܘܡܬܩܘܪܐܝܬ ܒܗܐ ܡܠܬܐ ܢܬܚܡ. ܟܕ ܓܝܪ (120) ܕܗܘ ܡܠܦܢܐ ܐܡܪ ܒܡܠܐܡܪܐ ܦܫܝܛܐ ܕܡܛܠ ܒܪܐ ܗܘܐ ܢܫܐ. ܘܐܘܦ ܕܡܠܗ ܕܓܪܝܓܘܪܝܘܣ܀ ܒܪܫܝܬ ܐܝܬܘܗܝ ܗܘܐ ܘܠܐ ܕܟܝܢܐ. ܐܢܫܐ ܗܘ ܓܪ ܕܟܝܢܐ ܕܐܠܗܐ. ܐܠܐ ܘܡܚܣܢܐ ܗܘܐ ܡܛܠ ܕܟܝܢܐ. ܗܘܐ ܕܝܢ ܐܝܬܘܗܝ ܗܘܐ: ܘܐܝܟ ܡܪܟܒܐ ܠܦܓܪ. ܐܝܟ ܕܡܛܠ ܗܘܐ ܡܟܣܝܐ ܐܝܟ ܟܠ ܐܠܗܘܬܐ: ܕܟܝܘܬܐ ܕܠܟ ܡܬܒܠܐ܀ ܦܫܝܛܐ ܗܘܝܐ ܐܠܗܐ ܡܢ ܗܘܢܐ: ܘܡܠܬܐ ܐܦܪ ܕܐܬܒܝܢ ܟܝܘܬܐ ܕܢܝ. ܗܘܐ ܕܐܝܬܘܗܝ: ܘܐܘܫܐ ܕܠܐ ܦܓܫܐ ܘܟܪܘܙܐ ܚܕ ܠܗ ܡܬܐܠܝܬ. ܡܛܠ ܗܘܐ ܓܪ ܐܦ ܐܡܪ. ܓܪܝܓܘܪܝܘܣ܀ ܕܡܠܬܐ

properties and of those which are above man", you mingle[69] everything to one particularity, as you have expressed it above, (namely) that at one time there took place one ousia or quality. For what are the properties which are above man? Certainly, divine in some way. And the human? It is already recognised that they are all the properties of flesh which is ensouled with a rational and intelligent soul. But the properties are of natural quality: for example, of divinity—the inability to be touched, and the inability to be seen; and of humanity—the ability to fall under sight, and the ability (to fall) under touch. But because the Word, which is invisible in ousia, was united in hypostasis to visible flesh, which has an intelligent soul, it is written that he was seen and touched, as we have said many times. For difference of natural quality stands firm and unchangeable, but the principle of the union allows that those things which in nature are properties of the flesh should be called properties of the Word because of the economy, and in the same way made the properties in ousia of the Word to be called properties of the flesh. (*Lebon p. 122*)

What then; should we tinker with the definition which is thus distinct and again present the message of true religion[70] (in terms of) confusion and blending?[71] And how, (when) the Doctor said, "Composed (so as to become) one in the middle", do you say in contradiction, "At one time, one ousia or quality has taken place", and again, "The Word incarnate is one in every respect, (I mean) both nature and particularity"? For if the Word incarnate became of one ousia and of one quality, as you have said, and of one particularity, he would be reduced, according to your definition, from being composite to something which would be simple, and wise (Cyril) made a mistake in that he still goes on calling him "composite", when he is like this.[72] But how do you say "one particularity", and not remember our saying that the Tome of Leo says: "Each one of the natures retains its particularity without diminishment",[73] so that we should think and say that these (natures and properties) adhere (to each other) in a division? For where (on the one hand) Christ is divided in a duality of natures after the union, each one of the natures proceeds without diminishment in those (properties) which are its own. But on the other hand, where the one nature of God the Word incarnate is professed—because he is Emmanuel, according to the word of holy Cyril—to be gloriously composed (so as to become) some one thing from two, it allowed the flesh—as is proper for the economy—sometimes also to suffer what belongs to it.[74] But this "sometimes" makes clear in every respect that it used as well properties which were above man, when he wished this. And also because

ܡܬܚܒܠ. ܗܘ ܠܐ ܡܬܚܫܢܐ ܡܬܚܫ. ܗܘ ܠܐ ܡܬܓܫܫܢܐ ܡܬܓܫܫ. ܗܘ ܕܠܐ ܙܒܢܐ ܡܙܕܒܢ܀

ܘܦܝܣ ܟܠܠ ܡܫܬܐܠܬܐ ܡܫܝܚܐ ܗܘܐ ܕܐܬܡܪ. ܐܝܟܢ ܕܦܢܝܘܗܝ ܕܪܝܫ ܟܡ ܠܐܘܪܚܐ ܗܘܟܢܐ: ܘܡܠܟܘܬܐ ܫܡܝܢܐ ܕܐܒܗ̈ܬܐ ܩܕܝܫܐ: ܟܕ ܢܬܠܘܢ ܡܫܬܘܬܦܝܢ ܐܝܟ ܠܟܘܢ. ܘܡܢ ܩܕܡ ܕܡܫܬܡܠܝܐ ܠܗܠܝܢ ܐܡܝܪ̈ܢ ܐܬܬܣܝܡܘ ܘܫܟܘ ܒܗܘܢܐ. ܡܛܠ ܕܐܦ ܡܢ ܒܬܪ ܡܠܟܘܬܐ ܡܘܪܝܟܘܬܗ ܚܕܝܐ ܠܥܠܡ ܘܫܡܥܝܢ ܐܝܟ ܕܠܥܠܡ: ܡܫܡܫܢܘܬܐ ܡܢ ܦܘܩܕܢܐ ܕܒܗ ܡܠܬܐ: ܘܐܬܠܘܗܝ ܐܝܟ ܡܫܠܡܢܐ ܕܓܒܝܢ ܘܐܩܝܡ ܒܢܝܢ. ܘܟܕ ܠܗܠܝܢ ܐܘܡܝ ܐܝܬ ܒܡܕܝܢܬ ܡܠܟܘܬܐ: ܟܠܐ ܓܒܝܢ ܡܫܝܚ. ܘܡܠܟܐ ܕܪܥܝܢ ܦܠܠܬܗ ܠܟܘܢ ܐܝܟ. ܟܕ ܗܠܝܢ ܩܕܡ ܟܠܐ ܕܡܘܪܟܘܬܐ ܡܫܝܚ. ܘܡܕܝܢ ܟܠܝܗ ܐܝܬ ܗܘ ܚܝܠܐ ܕܡܢܐ: ܘܐܝܬ ܠܐܚܪܢܐ ܕܡܘܕܝܐ ܘܕܘܡܝܐ ܕܝܠܗܘܢ. ܡܕܝܢ ܗܘܝܢ ܕܝܠ: ܐܝܟ ܕܐܦ ܠܟܠܟ ܡܫܬܘܬܦܬܐ ܐܠܗܐ ܐܝܟܢ ܕܢܗܘܘܢ. ܗܠܝܢ ܗܘܝܢ ܟܠ ܠܡܥܒܕ ܕܢܝܚܘ. ܕܟܠܐ ܗܘ ܕܝܢ ܕܢܐܡܪ ܐܦ ܟܠܐ ܗܘܐ ܐܝܟ ܣܘܟܠܐ: ܘܠܐ ܡܕܡ ܚܕܐ ܘܡܪܘܬܐ ܠܐܢܫ ܫܡܝܐ. ܐܠܐ ܡܪܘܡܘܬܐ ܕܕܡܝܐ ܐܝܬ ܒܬܪܝܨܘܬܗܘܢ ܘܒܫܡܪܘܬܐ ܗܘܝܐ ܐܝܟܢܐ ܒܪܘܚܡ.

(121) ܡܛܠ ܕܝܢ ܕܐܦ ܡܢ ܗܘ ܒܪܐ ܟܠܐ ܕܡܕܝܢܐ ܡܘܪܟܘܬܗ: ܗܘ ܕܐܡܪ ܡܛܠ ܒܡܘܬܒܐ: ܕܒܝܬܟܠܬܐ ܐܢܫܝܬܐ ܘܟܠܗܝܢ ܕܟܠܠ ܡܢ ܒܪܢܫܐ: ܠܚܕ ܡܕܡ ܕܒܡܟܠܬܐ ܡܪܘܒ. ܡܫܝܚܐ ܐܝܬ ܠܗܘܢ ܕܠܟܘܠܗܝܢ ܡܕܡܝܐ ܠܗܒܐ: ܘܟܕ ܡܫܡܫ ܐܝܬ ܠܐ ܢܦܠ ܐܢܐ ܐܡܝܢ ܐܡܪ ܐܢܐ: ܕܕܡܐ ܕܐܡܪ ܐܒܐ: ܕܒܢܝܐ ܒܗܘܢ ܕܒܝܬܟܠܬܐ ܐܡܪ: ܘܚܕ ܡܢ ܟܠ ܕܡܢ ܐܠܗܘܬܗ ܡܟܠܬܐ ܕܡܟܠܢ: ܘܟܠܐ ܐܡܪ ܐܢܐ ܘܡܟܠܬܐ: ܐܬܘܪܝܐ ܦܝܣ: ܟܕ ܗܘ ܓܒܪ ܡܫܬܐܠܬ ܫܡܗ: ܘܟܡܘܣܟܠܐ ܦܪܫ ܘܐܡܪ: ܒܝܬܟܠܬܐ ܠܐܒ ܐܢܫܝܬܐ ܘܟܠܗܝܢ ܕܟܠܠ ܡܢ ܒܪܢܫܐ: ܐܝܬ ܠܐܒ ܠܚܕܐ ܕܡܟܠܬܐ ܢܦܠ ܐܝܬ ܠܡܟܠܬܐ: ܐܝܟ ܗܘ ܕܟܠܠ ܐܡܪܐ ܠܗ: ܕܚܕܐ ܙܒܢ ܚܕܐ ܕܒܬܐ ܐܘܩܝܐ ܐܘ ܐܦ ܡܫܘܕܥܘܬܐ. ܐܝܟܢ ܓܒܪ ܐܬܝܗܝܢ ܕܒܝܬܟܠܬܐ ܕܟܠܠ ܡܢ ܒܪܢܫܐ. ܡܢ ܟܠ ܦܪܘܫ ܠܐܠܗܘܬܐ ܡܕܡ ܘܐܢܫܝܬܐ. ܡܕܝܢܐ ܚܕܐ: ܕܟܠܗܝܢ ܕܒܝܬܟܠܬܐ ܕܒܣܪܐ ܕܡܫܡܫ ܒܢܦܫܐ ܡܟܠܬܐ ܘܡܬܟܠܢܬܐ. ܕܒܝܬܟܠܬܐ ܕܝܢ ܕܡܫܘܕܥܘܬܐ ܒܫܝܢܬܐ: ܕܠܗܘܬܐ ܦܢ ܐܟܝܠܐ ܕܠܐ ܡܬܓܫܫܢܘܬܐ ܘܠܐ ܡܬܚܫܢܘܬܐ. ܕܐܝܬܘܬܐ ܕܝܢ ܗܘ ܕܐܦܠܐ ܒܣܪܐ ܘܓܫܡܐ. ܐܠܐ ܡܛܠ ܕܡܟܠܬܐ ܗܘ ܕܠܘܬܗܘܢ ܠܐ ܡܬܚܫܢܐ: ܒܡܘܬܒܐ ܐܬܝܕ ܠܡܫܪܐ ܗܘ ܡܬܚܫܢܐ: ܕܫܡܐ ܐܝܬ ܠܗ ܕܡܬܟܠܢܐ. ܗܘ ܟܠܗܘ

of this he used to walk over the crests of the waves, and he entered when the doors were closed and stood in the house with the apostles; and he allowed (them) to touch (him), and he did not deny handling of (his) body. For thus also, when he ascended bodily to heaven, the angels pointed as with a finger to the disciples, saying, "Men of Galilee, why do you stand looking (*Lebon p. 123*) into heaven? This Jesus who has been taken up from you to heaven is coming thus in the way that you have seen him go to heaven".[75] Therefore how will anyone with a Godfearing mind, and (who) cleaves to the teachings of the Apostles believe that the body which is subject to being seen, and so was seen and is expected to be seen, was changed to the divine ousia?

Therefore, because you ask us these things as a pupil and say that you have not assented to this within yourself,[76] but you ask if the Word incarnate is one in every respect, (I mean) both nature and particularity, as it was expressed by you above, "at one time there took place one ousia and quality", we give you advice, Beloved, in a brotherly and loving way, (and) we quote that scriptural passage, "Spring away from evil like this; do not delay, make your way far from it, for it does not follow the ways of life, but its paths are slippery and unknown".[77] For holy Cyril said in the Treatise against the Synousiasts: (CYRIL): "For if they say that the flesh of the Word was changed to the nature of divinity, it is fully necessary that it should be understood that he has renounced in every way his wish that he should become man. And see how Paul, who is wise in everything, says, 'For there is one God, and one mediator between God and men, the man Jesus Christ, who gave himself a substitutionary ransom on our behalf'.[78] For he is mediator as God and man at the same time, the same (person), who reconciles us to God and the Father through himself and in himself."[79] AND AGAIN AFTER A LITTLE: "And how will anyone dispute that, unless his still being and being thought like us is not suitable for him, it follows that he should say, 'When he comes, will the Son of Man find faith on the earth?',[80] and not rather, 'When the Word of God comes naked and without flesh, will he find faith in himself (*Lebon p. 124*) like this, among those on earth?' But because he openly and clearly calls himself Son of Man even at the time of the advent from heaven, it is evident that he has not changed the flesh into something else, but has it the more gloriously, incorruptible, without stain and adorned with unapproachable light. For he descends from heaven not in the former state of weakness—how could that be?—but in the glory of his Father with the holy angels."[81]

⌜But I am particularly astonished at how sometimes you call the

ܘܕܐܬܐܚܕ ܘܐܬܓܫܡ. ܐܝܟ ܡܐ ܕܟܬܝܒܝܢ ܒܓܠܝ̈ܢ ܐܡܪܝܢ. ܡܫܠܡܐ ܓܝܪ ܕܡܥܡܘܕܝܬܐ ܚܝ̈ܠܬܐ: ܡܫܡܠܝܬܐ ܘܠܐ ܡܬܬܘܥܝܢ ܩܐܡ. ܡܠܬܐ ܕܝܢ ܕܚܕܝܘܬܐ: ܗܟܢ ܕܒܟܝܢܐ ܕܬܡ̈ܠܬܐ ܕܒܣܪܐ: ܡܛܠ ܡܕܒܪܢܘܬܐ ܕܬܡ̈ܠܬܐ ܘܡܠܬܐ ܚܕܐ ܕܠܐܡܬܪ̈ܝ. ܘܗܟܢ ܒܡܥܒܕܐ ܕܐܘܣܝܐ ܕܬܡ̈ܠܬܐ ܘܡܠܬܐ: ܕܬܡ̈ܠܬܐ ܕܒܣܪܐ ܒܟܝܢܐ ܕܠܐܡܬܪ̈ܝ.

(122) ܗܢܐ ܗܟܝܠ ܚܠܝܦ ܠܡܠܬܐ ܕܗܘܐ ܡܫܪܝܐ: ܘܐܘܒ ܠܒܘܠܒܠܐ ܘܠܫܘܚܠܦܐ ܡܣܡܣܝܢ ܒܙܥܘܪܘܬܐ ܕܪܥܝܢܗ ܠܐܠܗܐ. ܐܝܟܢܐ ܕܝܢ ܡܠܟܝܐ ܐܡܪ: ܕܠܚܕ ܩܢܘܡ ܘܒܡܨܥܝܬܐ ܡܪܢ: ܡܫܘܛܠܐ ܐܦܢ ܐܝܟ ܐܝܟ: ܗܘ ܕܚܕ ܙܒܢ ܚܕܐ ܗܘܐ ܐܘܣܝܐ: ܐܘ ܐܦ ܡܫܘܕܝܬܐ. ܘܐܘܒ. ܚܕ ܡܢ ܩܢܘܡ̈ܐ ܐܠܗܘܬܐ ܡܠܬܐ ܕܐܬܒܣܪ: ܘܚܢܢ ܘܒܬܠܡܬܐ. ܐܢ ܓܝܪ ܕܚܕܐ ܐܘܣܝܐ ܡܠܬܐ ܕܡܥܒܪ ܗܘܐ: ܘܚܕܐ ܡܫܘܕܝܬܐ ܐܝܟ ܕܐܡܪܬ: ܘܚܕܐ ܕܬܠܡܬܐ: ܡܢ ܗܘܝܐ ܠܗܘܢ ܕܡܢܗ ܗܘܐ: ܫܪܝ ܐܝܟ ܡܠܬܐ. ܘܐܫܬܠܝ ܣܟܡܐ ܕܠܗܘ ܕܗܘܝܐ ܐܝܟ ܠܗ: ܕܒܗܢܐ ܗܘܐ ܡܪܟܒܐ ܚܢܢ. ܐܝܟܢܐ ܕܝܢ ܦܪܐ ܐܝܟ ܚܕܐ ܕܬܠܡܬܐ: ܘܠܐ ܡܫܡܠܝܐ ܐܝܟ ܒܚܕܢܘܬܐ ܕܐܡܪܝܢ: ܘܐܦܢ ܠܗܡܢܐ ܕܠܘܬܢ: ܕܢܗܘܐ ܠܚܕ ܡܢ ܬܪ̈ܝܢ ܕܠܐ ܒܘܪܟܐ ܕܚܕܝܘܬܐ: ܘܒܦܫܛܐ ܗܟܢ ܢܩܦ ܕܠܬܪܥܐ ܘܐܡܪ. ܒܪ ܡܦܩܝܢ ܓܝܪ ܡܫܝܚܐ ܠܬܪܝܢܘܬܐ ܕܬܪ̈ܝܢ ܠܟܠ ܚܕܝܘܬܐ: ܠܚܕ ܡܢ ܬܪ̈ܝܢ: ܒܗܠܝܢ ܕܠܗ ܘܠܐ ܒܪܢܫܘܬܐ ܙܪܐ. ܒܪ ܕܝܢ ܚܕ ܟܝܢܐ ܕܡܠܬܐ ܐܠܗܐ ܘܡܟܬܒ ܡܬܬܐܘܪܐ: ܡܛܠ ܕܡܫܘܬܦܐ ܐܠܗܘܬܗ ܐܝܟ ܒܪܐ ܗܠܐ ܘܡܒܝܢܐ ܡܪܟܒܘܬܗ: ܕܠܚܕ ܩܢܘܡ ܗܘ ܕܡܢ ܬܪ̈ܝܢ ܡܫܬܠܡܐ ܡܪܢ: ܡܟܝܠ ܗܘܐ ܠܟܝܢܐ ܐܝܟ ܕܩܐܐ ܠܡܒܕܪܢܘܬܐ: ܐܦ ܕܢܣܒ ܐܝܟ ܐܡܬܝ ܗܟܢ ܕܠܗ. ܗܘ ܕܝܢ ܕܐܝܬ ܐܡܬܝ ܡܥܘܕܐ ܡܢ ܠܡܦܪܘܫ: ܕܡܬܚܫܒ ܗܘܐ ܬܘܒ ܘܒܬܪ̈ܟܢܬܐ ܕܟܠܗ ܡܢ ܒܪ ܐܢܫܐ: ܐܡܬܝ ܕܗܘܐ ܙܒܢܐ ܗܘܐ. ܘܡܬܚܙܝܐ ܐܦ ܠܟܠܗ ܡܢ ܙܒܢܐ ܕܬܫܥܝܬܐ ܡܩܒܠ ܗܘܐ. ܘܟܕ ܐܫܬܩܝ ܠܐܘܪܚܐ ܚܕܐ ܗܘܐ: ܘܒܥܠܡܐ ܟܠܗ ܩܕܝܫܐ ܩܐܡ ܗܘܐ. ܘܡܬܚܙܐ ܗܟܢ ܗܘܐ: ܘܒܫܡܝܐ ܓܘܫܡܐ ܠܐ ܦܩܕ ܗܘܐ. ܗܟܢܐ ܓܝܪ ܘܩܠܝܠܐ ܒܪ ܗܘܝܐ ܓܘܫܡܢܝܐ ܠܫܡܝܐ. ܒܪ ܐܝܟ ܕܒܪܬܐ ܡܫܘܚ ܠܩܕܝܫܐ ܐܡܪܝܢ ܗܘܘ. ܒܬܪܐ ܬܚܬܝܐ: ܗܢܐ ܡܫܡܫ ܐܝܟܘܢ ܒܪ ܚܣܝܪ (123) ܐܝܟܘܢ ܒܫܡܝܐ. ܗܢܐ ܡܛܠ ܕܐܫܬܡܥ ܡܢܗܘܢ ܠܫܡܝܐ: ܗܟܢܐ ܐܬܐ: ܒܗܢܐ ܗܝ ܕܡܬܠܒܫܘܢ ܕܐܙܠ ܠܫܡܝܐ. ܓܘܫܡܐ ܗܟܝܠ ܕܢܦܠ ܒܚܝܠܐ: ܘܗܟܢܐ ܐܬܚܙܝ ܘܕܠܚܝܐ ܡܫܬܠܡܐ: ܐܝܟܢܐ ܐܝܟ ܕܐܝܬ ܠܗ ܗܘܝܐ ܕܕܢܚ ܡܢ ܠܐܠܗܐ: ܘܢܦܩ ܠܡܩܠܣܐ ܩܕܝܫܐ: ܕܐܬܗܦܟ ܠܐܘܣܝܐ ܠܐܠܗܝܬܐ ܡܫܟܢ.

incarnation a composition, and (then) again you say that "at one time there took place one ousia or quality". Did the union therefore begin with composition, but when composition ceased, was it reduced to one ousia, in order that, as you say, the holy Trinity should be kept a Trinity and not receive a superfluous person?⌉[82] But you have heard both the divinely inspired scripture and the God-clad teachers of holy mysteries say that the Word ascended to heaven endowed with a body, (the Word) who had previously descended from there without a body when he undertook to enter emptiness, and that he is composite and composed in a glorious way. For they taught us in various ways, with those terms which are now being used. For if we were to say like Nestorius, that a man complete in his own hypostasis adheres to the Word in honour and only benevolently, (then) they would be right to fear a quaternity. For that unclean man says somewhere: (NESTORIUS): "Let us confess God in (a) man, and let us worship the man who is worshipped along with God Almighty by means of a divine conjunction".[83] But because those who are reared on true religion confess and proclaim one hypostasis from two, the Trinity remains a Trinity, even if the Word was incarnate and inhominate, and is one in hypostasis even while incarnate; he who before was simple, but now (*Lebon p. 125*) is gloriously and inexpressibly composed to flesh endowed with a soul and with a mind, and is not divided into two, and remains without confusion: the same one consubstantial[84] both to God the Father and to us.

But you again equip (yourself) as with something which is mighty and inescapable and you introduce the term, which pleases you, of *συμφυΐα*, (because) Gregory the Theologian professes *συμφυΐα* of the natures in the case of the divine inhomination and you think that this brings to one ousia those things which are different in natural quality—divinity and manhood—from which neither confusedly nor defectively there is one Christ.

Recognise, then, that the truth is not like this. For in the case of the inhomination the Theologian called *συμφυΐα* what wise Cyril calls "a natural coming to be one",[85] and hypostatic union—which we say the soul of a man like us has with its own flesh—(and) which completes together one hypostasis from two. But (Gregory) used the term in the Treatise on Baptism as well about the one ousia and divinity which is seen in the holy Trinity, when he wrote as follows: (GREGORY): "The infinite *συμφυΐα* of three infinite things".[86] But above he called the equality of nature[87] of three hypostases "*συμφυΐα*", which cannot be understood in the same way in the case

ܡܛܠ ܗܟܝܠ ܕܗܟܢ ܐܝܟ ܡܠܦܢܐ ܡܫܠܡܐ ܐܝܬ ܠܢ: ܘܐܡܪ ܐܢܐ ܕܗܘܐ ܠܐ ܕܝܢ ܒܢܦܫܢ: ܡܫܠܡܐ ܐܝܬ ܕܝܢ ܕܐܦ ܚܕ ܐܠܗܘܬܗ ܡܢ ܟܠ ܕܒܗ ܡܟܝܠ ܕܐܬܒܥܝ: ܘܚܝܠܐ ܘܝܕܥܬܐ: ܐܝܟ ܗܘ ܕܟܬܝܒ ܕܐܬܐܡܪܬ ܥܠܝܢ: ܕܚܕܐ ܐܦ ܚܕܐ ܕܗܘܬ ܐܘܣܝܐ ܐܘ ܡܫܘܕܥܘܬܐ: ܡܬܚܙܝܢ ܠܗܘܢ: ܩܢܘܡܐ ܐܝܬܝܗ ܘܫܘܬܦܘܬܗ: ܟܕ ܐܡܪܝܢ ܗܘ ܠܡܠܬܐ. ܡܢܘ ܡܢ ܒܬܪ ܕܐܝܟ ܗܟܢܐ. ܠܐ ܢܬܬܙܝܥ. ܟܕ ܙܘܥܐ ܡܢܗ ܥܕܡ ܐܘܪܚܐ. ܐܘܪܚܬܐ ܓܝܪ ܕܚܝܐ ܠܐ ܙܕܩ: ܒܙܘܥܝܢ ܕܝܢ ܡܫܬܡܠܝܢ ܘܠܐ ܡܬܒܝܢ. ܐܡܪ ܓܝܪ ܡܪܝܐ ܡܙܡܘܪܗ ܒܦܬܓܡܐ ܕܠܡܫܠܡ ܡܫܡܫܢܘܬܐ. ܀ܡܙܡܘܪܗ܀ ܐܦ ܓܝܪ ܠܟܝܢܐ ܘܠܐܠܗܘܬܐ ܐܡܪܝܢ ܕܐܬܬܩܦ ܒܒܪܐ ܕܡܟܝܠ: ܡܛܠ ܐܝܟܐ ܕܢܫܬܡܠܐ: ܕܐܘܣܦ ܒܟܠ ܐܝܬ ܡܢ ܗܘ ܕܒܟܠ ܕܗܘܐ ܒܪܗ ܕܐܒܐ. ܘܗܘ ܐܠܗܐ ܚܟܝܡ ܒܟܠ ܦܘܠܚܘܗ ܐܡܪ: ܚܕ ܓܝܪ ܐܠܗܐ: ܘܚܕ ܡܪܝܐ ܕܐܠܗܐ ܘܕܟܝܢ ܐܒܐ: ܒܪܐ ܝܫܘܥ ܡܫܝܚܐ: ܗܘ ܕܢܦܩ ܢܦܫܗ ܐܝܟܢܐ ܦܘܪܫܢܐ ܕܩܢܘܡܐ. ܡܪܝܐ ܓܝܪ ܐܠܗܘܬܗ ܐܝܟ ܐܠܗܐ ܐܦܝܢ ܘܒܪܢܫܐ ܗܘ ܟܕ ܗܘ. ܕܡܪܢܐ ܠܝ ܠܐܠܗܐ ܘܐܒܐ: ܟܕ ܢܦܫܗ ܘܒܗ ܀ܘܒܬܪ ܕܗܘܝܘܬܐ ܠܐܒܘ܀ ܘܐܡܝܢܐ ܒܬܡܪܐ ܐܝܟ: ܕܠܗ ܐܬܡܪ ܗܘܐ ܘܠܐ ܡܟܝܠ ܠܗ ܗܘ ܕܗܘܐ ܐܠܗܘܬܐ ܒܝܕܥܬܐ ܘܡܫܠܡܢܘܬܐ ܐܒܘܗܝ: ܕܢܣܒܐ ܗܘܐ ܕܢܐܡܪ: ܐܢܐ ܗܢܐ ܕܐܢܐ ܒܪܗ ܕܐܝܟܐ ܡܫܡܫ ܗܘܡܢܘܬܐ ܒܟܠ ܐܘܪܚܐ: ܘܟܠܗ ܡܬܠܗ. ܐܢܐ ܗܢܐ ܕܐܢܐ ܒܪܬܐ ܘܠܐ ܒܒܪܐ ܡܟܝܠ ܕܐܠܗܐ: ܗܡܫܡܫܢܘܬܐ ܘܐܝܟ (124) ܗܟܝܠ ܢܦܫ ܒܟܠܗܘܢ ܒܟܠ ܗܟܢ ܕܒܟܠ ܐܘܪܚܐ. ܐܠܐ ܡܛܠ ܕܓܒܠܬܗ ܘܗܘܢܐܝܬܗ ܒܪܗ ܕܐܝܟܐ ܐܡܪ ܢܦܫܗ: ܘܒܟܝܢܐ ܘܡܬܬܠܬܐ ܕܡܢ ܡܫܝܚܐ: ܡܬܚܒܠ ܗܘܐ ܘܠܐ ܗܘܦܟ ܠܡܒܥ ܐܚܪܝܢ ܠܡܫܪܐ. ܐܠܗܘܬܗ ܠܗ ܕܝܢ ܡܫܝܚܐ ܠܡܬܝܕܥܘ ܠܐ ܡܬܚܒܠܢܐ: ܘܠܐ ܡܫܬܢܐ: ܘܡܛܠܬܐ ܒܗܘܢܝܐ ܘܠܐ ܡܬܐܡܪ ܣܢܝܐ ܓܝܪ ܡܢ ܡܫܝܚܐ. ܠܗ ܒܕܡܘܬܐ ܦܐܝܬܐ ܡܫܝܚܝܬܐ. ܡܢ ܐܡܬܝ: ܐܠܐ ܒܗ ܒܠܡܫܘܚܬܐ ܕܐܒܘܗܝ: ܒܗܝ ܩ̈ܠܝܠܐ ܩܕܡܝܐ܀

ܠܡܫܘ ܐܦ ܕܝܢ ܦܓܪ: ܕܐܡܝܢܐ ܐܦ ܙܘܥܐ ܡܫܡܫܗ ܐܝܟ ܠܡܬܠܡܕܢܘܬܐ ܐܝܟ ܐܡܝܢ: ܘܐܘܒ ܐܡܪ ܐܝܟ ܕܚܕܐ ܐܘܣܝܐ ܚܕܐ ܐܦ ܕܗܘܬ: ܐܘ ܐܦ ܡܫܘܕܥܘܬܐ. ܐܢܐ ܓܝܪ ܗܢܝܢ ܦܫ ܡܬܚܘܝܬܐ ܡܢ ܙܘܥܐ: ܟܕ ܦܫ ܕܝܢ ܙܘܥܐ ܒܚܕܐ ܐܘܣܝܐ ܗܢܝ: ܐܡܝܢܐ ܘܐܝܟ ܕܐܡܪ ܐܝܟ: ܠܐܚܪܢܘܬܐ ܡܫܝܚܝܬܐ ܠܐܒܗ̈ܬܐ ܠܐܚܪܢܘܬܐ: ܘܠܐ ܠܐܚܪܢܐ ܦܪܨܘܦܐ ܠܡܪܐ: ܐܠܐ ܡܫܒܚܐ ܘܟܠܠܐ ܢܦܫ ܡܢ ܐܠܗܐ ܘܒܟܝܢܗ ܐܠܗܐ ܩ̈ܠܝܠܐ ܙ̈ܘܥܐ ܩܕܡܝܐ. ܘܡܫܡܫܢܐ ܐܡܪܗ ܕܗܟܢ ܡܟܝܠ ܠܫܡܝܐ. ܗܘ ܕܠܘܩܕܡ ܚܝܠܗ ܡܢ ܠܥܠ ܘܠܐ ܓܘܫܡܐ: ܟܕ ܠܫܘܪܝܐ ܡܟܝܠ ܕܒܗܘܢ: ܘܡܫܪܝܐ ܐܠܗܘܬܗ: ܘܡܫܡܫܢܘܬܗ

of inhomination. For in (the case of) the Trinity, each hypostasis exists independently, and denotes its own person, but (there is) one and the same ousia of the nature according to which it is understood generically, and this he calls *συμφυΐα*. But no-one understands *συμφυΐα* in this way in the case of the inhomination, (*Lebon p. 126*) namely, that the hypostases would be separated to two, but that the two of them would have one ousia, or it would again be found that the Trinity is a quaternity, and from (this) formulation of an equality of nature[88] of the flesh in relation to the Word, nothing is gained. For the unity in the case of inhomination is from the composition of things of different type, and not consubstantial[89] with each other. But in the case of the divinity which is apparent in the Trinity, the union (is) not from composition—for each of the three hypostases is not composed with another—but is simple and not composite. But community of ousia and identity of divinity produces unity and lack of difference in everything, and an absence of division and separation, except for the distinction in hypostases.

Therefore there is one meaning of "*συμφυΐα*" in the case of (Trinitarian) theology, and another in the case of the economy and inhomination, and they are diametrically[90] opposed to each other. For Gregory the Theologian himself said as follows, writing in the First Letter to Cledonius: (GREGORY): "But I say *ἄλλο καὶ ἄλλο* in distinction to how it is in the case of the Trinity: for there it is *ἄλλος καὶ ἄλλος* lest we should confuse the hypostases; but not *ἄλλο καὶ ἄλλο* for the three of them are one and the same in divinity",[91] and in the case of the incarnation, he said the opposite before: FROM HIM AGAIN: "But these things from which our Saviour is are *ἄλλο καὶ ἄλλο* unless the invisible is to be the same as the visible, and the without (*Lebon p. 127*) time as that which is under time. But the Son is not *ἄλλος καὶ ἄλλος*: away with you".[92]

But the next thing that we shall learn is that in the case of the incarnation he calls the composition "*συμφυΐα*" and not "equality of nature".[93] For (Gregory) called *συμφυΐα* the coming together of our soul with the body, which is taken even by the Apostle for an example of the divine inhomination, in the Treatise on the funeral of Caesarius his brother, writing as follows: FROM THE SAME MAN: "But after a short time (the soul) will take up its kindred flesh, in which together it philosophised about the (life) beyond, from the earth to which she[94] had yielded and entrusted it, in what way God knows, who bound together and loosed these things, when alongside the flesh she takes possession of the glory from heaven, and just as she shared in its hardships, because of the *συμφυΐα* also

ܡܪܒܒ. ܗܠܝܢ ܓܝܪ ܡܡܫܟܚܢܐ ܒܬܪ̈ܝܢ ܒܩ̈ܠܐ: ܒܗܠܝܢ ܕܗܘܐ ܐܬ̈ܐ ܠܠܦܘ ܠܝ. ܠܗ ܓܝܪ ܐܝܟ ܢܣܛܘܪܝܘܣ ܐܡܪܝܢ ܗܘܘ: ܕܒܪܢܫܐ ܕܒܣܘܥܪܢܐ ܕܝܠܗ ܡܫܡܫܢ: ܓܡܝܪܐ ܘܒܠܚܘܕ ܘܢܣܒܬܗ ܢܦܩ ܠܡܥܠܬܐ: ܡܛܠ ܡܬܩ̈ܪܝܢ ܗܘܘ ܕܝܠܕܐ ܘܪܒܘܬܐ. ܗܘ ܓܝܪ ܠܡܠܐ ܐܡܪ ܒܪܘܚ. ܀ܢܣܛܘܪܝܘܣ܀ ܗܘܐ ܠܠܗܐ ܕܒܪܢܫܐ. ܘܢܣܒܗ ܠܒܪ ܐܢܫܐ ܗܘ ܕܒܡܫܡܫܢܘܬܐ ܠܐܠܗܘܬܐ ܒܗ ܠܠܗܐ ܐܝܟ ܟܠ ܡܫܡܠܝܢ܀ ܡܛܠ ܕܝܢ ܕܚܕ ܩܢܘܡܐ ܗܘ ܕܡܢ ܬܪ̈ܝܢ ܡܬܚܘܐ ܘܡܬܐܡܪ ܡܢ ܗܠܝܢ ܕܡܪܟܒ ܡܢ ܕܝܠܗ ܕܠܠܗܐ: ܡܫܘܐ ܠܐܢܫܘܬܐ ܠܐܠܗܘܬܐ: ܐܦ ܡܠܬܐ ܘܐܬܒܣܪ ܘܐܬܒܪܢܫ: ܘܐܬܚܘܝ ܒܩܢܘܡܐ ܚܕ ܘܟܕ ܡܒܣܪ ܗܘ ܘܡܬܚܙܐ ܦܝ ܦܓܪܐ: ܗܟܢܐ ܕܝܢ: (125) ܟܠܗ ܒܣܪܐ ܩܢܘܡܐ ܘܡܡܠܠܐ ܡܚܝܠܬܐ ܘܠܐ ܡܬܐܡܪܢܝܬ ܡܪܒܒ ܘܠܐ ܡܦܠܓ ܠܬܪ̈ܝܢ. ܘܡܫܬܐ ܘܠܐ ܒܗܠܟܐ. ܘܠܠܗܐ ܐܒܐ ܘܠܗ ܒܪ ܟܝܢܐ ܗܘ ܒܗ ܗܘ.

ܐܠܐ ܠܘܒ ܐܝܟ ܡܐ ܕܡܪܝܡ ܙܘܓܐ ܘܒܠܚܘܕ ܠܡܕܒܪܘ ܡܢܗ ܡܕܡ ܐܝܬ ܗܘ ܕܡܫܐܠ ܠܝ. ܐܦ ܡܢܐ ܕܡܘܣܦܬܐ ܘܐܚܝܕܐ ܡܠܬܐ ܐܝܟ ܠܡܥܒܕܐ: ܓܪܝܓܘܪܝܘܣ ܡܡܠܠ ܠܬܠܝܬܝܐ. ܡܘܣܦܬܐ ܘܐܚܝܕܐ ܘܒܬܠܐ ܐܡܪ ܟܠܗ ܡܬܒܪܢܫܘܬܐ ܠܐܠܗܘܬܐ ܘܡܩܒܠ ܐܝܟ ܕܗܘܐ ܟܠܐ ܚܕܐ ܐܘܣܝܐ ܡܫܡܠܝܐ ܠܗܠܝܢ ܕܒܡܫܡܫܢܘܬܐ ܚܝܠܐ ܡܩܒܠܝܢ ܠܐܠܗܘܬܐ ܘܐܢܫܘܬܐ: ܘܡܫܘܝܢ ܚܕ ܡܫܡܠܝܐ ܠܐ ܡܬܒܠܒܠܬܐ ܘܠܐ ܡܫܬܪܝܐ ܐܢܘܢ.

ܕܝܢ ܗܟܝܠ: ܕܠܗ ܗܟܢܐ ܐܝܬ ܠܡܦܪܘ. ܡܘܣܦܬܐ ܓܝܪ ܘܐܚܝܕܐ: ܟܠܐ ܡܬܒܪܢܫܘܬܐ ܚܕܐ ܡܫܡܠܝ ܠܬܠܝܬܝܐ. ܠܗܘ ܕܡܫܡܫܗ ܦܝ ܚܝܠܐ ܡܘܪܒܐܘܣ ܡܠܐܠܐ ܒܚܝܐ ܘܐܝܟ ܚܝܐ: ܘܡܚܝܘܬܐ ܡܘܣܦܬܐ ܗܘ ܘܐܡܪܝܢ ܘܐܝܟ ܐܦ ܠܒܢܝܐ ܕܒܪܢܫܐ ܕܐܝܟܢ ܟܠܗ ܒܣܪܐ ܘܢܦܫܗ: ܘܡܫܡܫܢܘܬܐ ܐܠܗܝܐ ܐܚܝܕܐ ܕܚܕ ܩܢܘܡܐ ܘܡܢ ܬܪ̈ܝܢ. ܐܬܒܣܪ ܕܝܢ ܒܡܠܬܐ: ܒܡܐܡܪܐ ܘܟܠ ܡܫܡܫܢܘܬܐ: ܐܦ ܟܠܗ ܚܕܐ ܐܘܣܝܐ ܘܠܐܠܗܘܬܐ ܘܡܬܚܙܝܐ ܠܡܫܡܫܢܘܬܐ ܩܢܘܡܝܐ. ܘܐܟܢ ܗܘܝܐ. ܀ܓܪܝܓܘܪܝܘܣ܀ ܕܠܐܠܗܐ ܘܠܐ ܦܘܩ: ܡܘܣܦܬܐ ܘܐܚܝܕܐ ܘܠܐ ܡܫܘܚܬܐ܀ ܐܠܐ ܠܟܠ ܡܘܣܦܬܐ ܘܐܚܝܕܐ ܡܪܐ: ܠܡܘܬܐ ܚܝܐ ܘܐܠܗܐ ܩ̈ܢܘܡܝܢ. ܗܘ ܘܠܐ ܡܫܡܫܢܐ ܘܟܠܐ ܡܬܒܪܢܫܘܬܐ ܒܗ ܒܪ ܒܗ ܒܪܐ ܢܦܠܘܬ. ܕܟܠܐ ܠܐܠܗܘܬܐ ܓܝܪ: ܟܠܐ ܩܢܘܡܐ ܡܢܗ ܘܠܗ ܡܠܐܝܢ: ܘܦܪܨܘܦܐ ܕܝܠܗ ܟܠܗ. ܚܕܐ ܕܝܢ ܐܘܣܝܐ ܘܗܘܐ ܒܝ ܒܗ ܕܟܝܢܐ. ܐܝܟ ܗܘ ܕܡܬܚܝܕܐ ܟܝܢܐܝܬ: ܠܗܘ ܕܐܦ ܡܘܣܦܬܐ ܘܐܚܝܕܐ ܡܪܐ. ܟܠܐ ܕܝܢ ܡܬܒܪܢܫܘܬܐ: ܘܐܦܠܐ ܐܝܟ (126) ܠܡܘܣܦܬܐ ܘܐܚܝܕܐ ܗܟܢܐ ܡܫܬܡܠܠ:

will she bestow her own pleasures".[95] Therefore shall we because of the term συμφυΐα foolishly think that the body with the soul of a man is completed to one ousia? And who with intelligence would venture to say this?

But we find the same Doctor also calling our composition "mixture" in the Treatise on love of the poor, thus: (GREGORY): "(Our) mixture is like this, and because of this it seems to me that when we are lifted up because of the image, we will be withdrawn because of the dust".[96] But he already applies the term "deification"[97] to us, and he wrote as follows in his Sermon on Epiphany about the glory which will be given us: FROM THE SAME MAN: "(There is) a living creature (which is) guided here, and journeys to another place, and (at) the fulfilment of the mystery, it is deified by (its) inclination to (God)".[98]

Therefore just as in the study of a man like us, (the terms of) συμφυΐα, and mixture and deification (*Lebon p. 128*) do not indicate that there is a change in him of ousia or identity, so also they do not in the case of inhomination for God the Word.

But take note of this, lest because of the term συμφυΐα you become too blind as regards the establishment of your former opinion, (that) it is also used of harmony and agreement[99] of the soul, and of the habitual leading of the ascetic life. For wise Basil said as follows, writing to Gregory the Theologian: (BASIL): "What is the συμφυΐα and unanimity of mind of the brothers who are deified and exalted by you? What is the emulation of the best and the incentive, that we are kept in the written precepts and rules?"[100]

But it is time to lead out a little stream from the waters of Athanasius, who is glorious in everything, against those who believe that the flesh has come to the same ousia as God the Word, so that the Trinity, as they think, should remain a Trinity, and with it to drown the cunning (argument). For he wrote as follows in the Letter to Epictetus: (ATHANASIUS): "Let those who even thought that it was possible that there would be a quaternity in place of the Trinity, if it should be said that there is a body from Mary, very much be put to shame. For (they say) if we say that the body is consubstantial with[101] the Word, the Trinity remains a Trinity since the Word introduces nothing foreign to it. But it we say there is a human body from Mary, there would necesarily be a quaternity in place of the Trinity because of the addition of the body, since the body is foreign in ousia and the Word is in it. But when they say these things like this, they do not understand how they contradict themselves. For, even if they do not admit the body which is from Mary (*Lebon*

ܐܡܝܢܐ ܕܩܢ̈ܘܡܐ ܗܘ ܒܠܚܘܕ ܠܦܪ̈ܨܘܦܐ: ܚܕܐ ܕܝܢ ܐܘܣܝܐ ܠܬܠܬܐ ܐܝܬ ܕܠܩ̈ܢܘܡܐ. ܘܐܠܐ ܠܘܬ ܡܫܠܡܢܐ ܠܐܠܗܘܬܐ ܪ̈ܚܡܘܬܐ: ܘܡܢ ܙܢܐ ܕܫܘܝܐ ܚܝܠܐ ܕܒܣܪܐ ܕܒܗ̇ ܡܫܠܡܐ: ܘܠܐ ܡܢܝܢ ܡܠܦܐ. ܕܒܗܝ ܡܫܠܡܢܘܬܐ ܓܝܪ ܚܝܘܬܐ ܕܡܢ ܙܘܥܐ ܕܐܢܫ̈ܝܢ ܐܘܪ̈ܚܐ ܘܠܗ ܕܟ̈ܠ ܚܝܐ ܕܢܦ̈ܫܐ ܡܢܗ. ܒܠܐ ܐܠܗܘܬܐ ܕܝܢ ܕܒܫܠܡܘܬܐ ܡܫܡܠܝܐ: ܠܗ ܡܢ ܙܘܥܐ ܚܝܘܬܐ. ܠܐ ܓܝܪ ܡܫܬܘܕܥ ܒܗ̇ ܗܘ ܐܝܢܐ ܕܚܝ ܡܢ ܠܐܠܗܐ ܩܢܘܡܝܢ. ܐܠܐ ܦܫܝܛܐ ܡܢܝܢ ܐܠܗܘܗܝ ܘܠܐ ܡܪܟܒ. ܒܫܘܝܘܬܐ ܕܝܢ ܕܐܘܣܝܐ ܘܚܕܐ ܒ ܗܝ ܕܐܠܗܘܬܐ: ܒܚܝܘܬܐ ܘܒܠܐ ܡܫܬܚܠܦܢܘܬܐ ܒܟܠ ܡܢܝܢ ܡܫܠܐ: ܘܗܝ ܕܠܐ ܡܬܚܠܦܐ ܘܠܐ ܡܫܬܢܝܐ: ܡܛܠ ܡܢ ܗܝ ܕܡܫܬܡܠܝܐ ܒܩܢ̈ܘܡܐ.

ܡܢܝܢ ܐܝܢܐ ܗܘ ܗܘܐ ܕܡܫܘܚܬܐ ܕܐܝܟܐ ܒܗܝ ܡܫܡܠܝܘܬܐ ܐܠܗܘܬܐ: ܘܐܝܢܐ ܐܠܗܘܗܝ ܒܗ̇ ܡܕܒܪܢܘܬܐ ܘܡܫܠܡܢܘܬܐ. ܘܡܢ ܕܡܫܬܪܪܐ ܒܗ̇ ܗܘ ܡܫܬܘܕܥܬܐ ܦܫܝܛ ܘܡܫܬܡܥ. ܗܟܢܐ ܓܝܪ ܐܦ ܗܘ ܓܪܝܓܘܪܝܘܣ ܡܡܠܠ ܬܐܘܠܘܓܐ ܐܡܪ: ܟܕ ܥܩܒ ܒܗ̇ ܠܬܘܬܒܘܬܐ ܠܟܪܙܐ ܥܒܝܕܬܐ. ܀ܓܪܝܓܘܪܝܘܣ܀ ܐܡܪ ܐܢܐ ܕܝܢ ܐܚܪܬܐ ܘܐܚܪܬܐ ܒܩܘܦܐ. ܐܘ ܒܗ̇ ܠܐܠܗܘܬܐ ܐܝܬ. ܒܗܠܝܢ ܓܝܪ ܐܚܪܢܐ ܗܘ ܘܐܚܪܢܐ: ܘܠܐ ܒܩܢ̈ܘܡܐ ܢܚܠܚܠ. ܠܗ ܕܝܢ ܐܚܪܬܐ ܘܐܚܪܬܐ. ܚܕܐ ܓܝܪ ܠܐܠܗܘܬܗ ܘܗܝ ܟܕ ܗܝ ܒܠܚܘܕܝܗ̇. ܒܗ̇ ܕܝܢ ܡܫܬܘܬܦܢܘܬܐ ܗܝ ܕܒܟܘܠܗ ܦܝܫ ܐܡܪ ܀ܠܘܬ ܕܠܗ܀ ܐܚܪܬܐ ܕܝܢ ܘܐܚܪܬܐ ܗܟܢ ܕܥܠܝܗ̇ ܦܪܘܩ. ܐܢ ܗܘ ܕܠܗ ܗܘ ܠܐ ܡܫܬܚܠܦܐ ܒܡܫܬܚܠܦܐ: ܘܠܐ (127) ܕܚܕܐ ܒܗܘ ܕܐܝܬܗ ܕܚܕܐ. ܠܗ ܕܝܢ ܐܚܪܢܐ ܘܐܚܪܢܐ ܒܪܐ ܠܐ ܠܗܘܐ܀

ܕܫܘܝܘܬܐ ܕܝܢ ܕܐܘܣܝܐ ܒܗ̇ ܡܫܬܘܬܦܢܘܬܐ ܒܙܘܥܐ ܦܪܐ: ܘܠܗ ܫܘܝܐ ܚܝܠܐ: ܦܪܝܫܐ ܕܡܢ ܗܘܦܟܐ ܢܠܟܐ. ܡܛܠܬ ܓܝܪ ܕܐܘܣܝܐ ܕܦܫܛܐ ܕܡܢ: ܒܗ̇ ܓܘܫܡܐ ܗܘ ܘܐܦ ܒܠܚܘܕܝܬܐ ܦܫܝܛ ܠܡܫܝܚܐ: ܘܡܫܬܪܪܢܘܬܐ ܕܐܠܗܘܬܐ: ܦܫܝܛܘܬܐ ܘܐܚܪܢܐ ܦܫܛܗ ܒܦܠܐܓܪܐ ܕܟܠ ܡܟܘܪܬܐ ܘܡܫܪܝܘܬ ܐܝܟܘܗܝ. ܡܠܟ ܗܕܝܐ. ܀ܘܡܠܗ܀ ܒܠܡ ܡܟܝܠ ܕܝܢ: ܘܦܫܪܐ ܐܝܟܢܐ ܫܠܠ: ܕܗܘ ܗܠܝܢ ܕܒܗܠܝܢ ܐܚܪܢܐ ܦܠܓܘܬܐ ܒܟܕܐ. ܡܢ ܐܘܪܚܐ ܕܡܘܟܟܐ ܘܐܬܐܘܦܢܝܐ: ܟܕܝܐ ܗܘ ܕܢܦܩ ܠܐܠܗܐ: ܗܘ ܕܗܠܝܢ ܘܐܚܪܢܐ ܐܡܪ ܘܡܢܐ. ܟܕ ܚܡ ܗܘܐ ܢܘܪܐ ܠܡܫܘܚܬܐ ܕܡܢ ܠܐܡܢ. ܘܐܟܝܢܐ ܕܒܩܢ̈ܘܡܝܗ ܡܫܬܘܬܦܐ ܗܘܐ: ܡܛܠ ܫܘܝܘܬܐ ܘܐܘܣܝܐ: ܗܟܢܐ ܐܦ ܡܢ ܩ̈ܝܠܬܐ ܕܡܢܗ ܢܦܩܬ܀ ܐܢܐ ܗܟܢܐ ܘܗܘܝܐ: ܡܛܠ ܫܡܐ ܕܫܘܝܘܬܐ ܘܐܘܣܝܐ: ܡܫܬܪܪܝܢ ܫܠܝܛܐ ܕܐܘܣܝܐ

p. 129) but (affirm) it is consubstantial[102] with the Word, they will be shown to affirm a quaternity according to their own doctrine nonetheless, whatsoever they pretend lest they should be thought so to think. For just as the Son, according to the Fathers, while he is consubstantial[102] with the Father, is not the Father, but the Son is said to be consubstantial[102] with the Father; so also, the body (being)[103] consubstantial[102] with the Word, is not the Word, but is other than the Word. But since it is other, according to their own argument, their Trinity will be a quaternity. For the true Trinity, which is truly completed and indivisible, does not accept an addition, but that which was found by them (will). How can they still be Christians, when they understand God to be other than he is?"[104]

Therefore, let us not bring the flesh to equality of nature[105] with the Word, on the pretext of these (words) of the Fathers, who have applied the term "mixture" without danger to the supreme union. For even if we should say that it took (its) origin from Mary, but afterwards changed to the divine ousia, we would end up in the same depth of wickedness (as) those who believed that not even at the beginning did the Word unite that (flesh) to himself from the ousia of the Virgin. For we find even holy Cyril, who thus explains to us that the term "mixture" was spoken of by the Fathers, used the term at the same time, without, as a result of this, raising up the flesh to the divine ousia and confusing the difference in ousia of those things which have run together inexpressibly to union, and have completed for us one Christ from two.

For in the Letter to the Monks, of which we have just made mention, he proceeded in this way, taking our composition for (*Lebon p. 130*) the provision of an example of the union in the incarnation or inhomination: (CYRIL): "But the mystery concerning him is somehow like our own birth. For the mothers of those who are on earth, waiting upon nature for child-birth, have in the womb flesh which gradually congeals and through some inexpressible actions of God comes and is completed to human birth.[106] But God placed the spirit in the living creature, in a way which he knows, for 'He creates the spirit of man in him',[107] according to the words of the prophet. But the principle of the flesh is one thing, and similarly (the principle) of the soul is another. But even though they were mothers only *of bodies from the earth*, because thus they brought forth the complete living creature, that is, I mean, from soul and body, they are not said to have brought forth a part. And no-one says, to give an example, Elizabeth bore the flesh, but consequently did not also bear the soul. For she bore the Baptist ensouled, and as one man from

ܐܘܣܝܐ ܡܫܟܠܠܐ ܒܓܘܫܡܐ ܥܡ ܢܦܫܐ ܕܒܪܢܫܐ܆ ܘܡܛܠ ܡܢ ܗܠܝܢ ܕܐܝܬ ܠܗܘܢ ܗܘܝܐ܆ ܡܬܒܪܝܢ ܕܗܘܐ ܐܡܪ.

ܡܬܚܫܒ ܕܝܢ ܠܗ ܟܕ ܠܗ ܠܡܫܟܚܘ܆ ܕܒܐܣܛܪܐ ܕܡܬܚܙܐ ܘܣܝܡܐ ܦܫܝܛܐ܆ ܐܦ ܡܕܡ ܡܫܟܚ ܒܪܘܚܐ ܕܠܐ ܗܘܐ. ܓܪܝܓܪܝܘܣ܀ ܕܐܝܟ ܗܘܝܐ ܡܕܡ. ܘܡܛܠ ܗܠܝܢ ܐܝܟ ܕܠܐ ܡܬܚܙܝܐ. ܐܝܟܢܐ ܕܗܐ ܕܡܬܚܫܒܝܢ ܚܢܢ ܡܛܠ ܓܘܫܡܐ܆ ܡܛܠ ܟܦܪܐ ܢܬܦܫܘܢ܀ ܡܢ ܟܕܘ ܕܝܢ ܘܡܫܐ ܕܡܬܐܠܗܘܬܐ ܘܫܡܝܢ ܠܗܝܢ܆ ܘܟܠ ܚܘܫܒܐ ܕܟܠܗ ܕܢܬܘܥ ܠܝ܆ ܒܡܠܦܢܐ ܕܡܠܗ ܕܟܠ ܟܡܐ ܕܢܐ ܡܕܡ ܗܘܝܐ. ܕܡܠܗ܀ ܚܝܘܬܐ ܕܗܘܢܐ܆ ܡܬܕܒܪܐ ܘܡܬܝܕܥܬܐ ܐܝܟܢܐ ܒܟܠܗ. ܘܡܫܟܚܐ ܕܙܕܩܐ܆ ܒܪܘܚܐ ܕܟܠܗ ܡܬܐܠܗܐ܀

ܐܝܟܢܐ ܗܘܝܐ ܕܡܬܐܪܐ ܕܒܪܢܫܐ ܘܐܦܠܐ܆ ܘܠܐ ܡܫܬܘܐܐ ܕܐܟܚܕܐ܆ ܘܠܐ ܡܫܟܚܐ ܘܠܐ (128) ܡܬܐܠܗܘܬܐ܆ ܡܫܬܟܚܐ ܐܝܬ ܠܗ ܕܐܘܣܝܐ܆ ܐܘ ܕܝܢ ܟܕ ܕܝܢ܆ ܗܘܝܐ ܐܦ ܟܠܐ ܡܬܒܪܝܢܘܬܐ ܕܟܠܐ ܡܛܠܬܐ ܠܟܠܐ.

ܐܝܟܢܐ ܕܝܢ ܕܠܐ ܦܓܪܢ ܠܗܘܐ ܫܡܫܐ ܐܝܬ ܟܠ ܫܡܐ ܕܡܫܘܚܬܐ ܕܐܟܚܕܐ܆ ܟܠܐ ܦܫܝܛܐ ܕܡܪܟܒܐ ܡܫܬܪܝܢܘܬܐ ܕܐܝܬ ܠܟܝ܆ ܕܟܝ ܕܗܘܐ܆ ܐܦ ܟܠܐ ܐܘܣܝܐ ܕܒܣܝܡܐ ܘܫܘܡܐ ܕܐܟܚܕܐ ܡܬܢܚܬܐ. ܘܐܦܣܘܬܐ ܕܦܠܚܘܬܐ ܕܐܟܚܕܐ. ܒܫܡܠܝܘܬ ܓܒܪ ܢܦܫܐ ܟܕ ܦܠܚܢ ܟܠܐ ܓܪܝܓܪܝܘܣ ܡܫܟܠܠ ܠܠܘܬܐ ܗܟܢܐ ܐܡܪ. ܀ܒܫܡܠܝܘܬ܀ ܐܢܐ ܗܘ ܡܫܘܚܬܐ ܕܐܟܚܕܐ ܘܫܡܐ ܘܐܢܫܐ܆ ܐܝܠܝܢ ܕܡܢܝܢ ܡܬܐܠܗܝܢ ܘܡܬܩܪܒܝܢ. ܡܛܠ ܗܘ ܡܫܪܝܢܘܬܐ ܕܡܬܚܙܝܢܘܬܐ ܘܠܒܝܫܘܬܐ܆ ܕܡܠܝܘܬܐ ܡܠܬܐ܆ ܘܦܩܕܘܬܐ ܐܬܦܪܫܢ܀

ܟܠܐ ܦܘܠ ܕܝܢ ܕܫܒܪܢ ܕܟܠܗ ܟܕ ܟܠܗ ܠܐܘܣܝܐ ܕܡܛܠܬܐ ܠܟܠܐ ܐܝܟ ܫܒܪܐ܆ ܟܠܐ ܦܘ ܕܐܝܬܐ ܠܐܠܗܘܬܐ܆ ܐܝܟܢܐ ܕܡܫܬܒܪܢ܆ ܐܢܐ ܗܘ ܕܡܢ ܩܕܡ ܘܐܬܝܗܒ ܡܢ ܟܠܗ܆ ܙܕܝܐ ܐܝܟ ܓܒܪܐ ܕܘܟܬܐ. ܘܡܢ ܦܘ ܢܦܩ ܠܒܝܬܐ. ܦܠܚ ܓܒܪ ܕܠܓܒܪܐ ܕܟܠܐ ܐܦܠܛܘܢ ܗܟܢܐ. ܀ܐܬܝܫܘܥ܀ ܢܬܚܙܝ ܕܝܢ ܙܘܕܩܐ܆ ܦܘܠ ܕܫܒ ܐܬܝܗܒ܆ ܕܡܫܟܚܐ ܕܚܕܐ ܠܐܠܗܘܬܐ ܠܗܘܐ ܙܕܝܩܘܬܐ܆ ܐܝ ܗܘ ܕܡܬܐܡܪ ܕܡܢ ܩܕܡ ܐܬܘܗܝ ܓܘܫܡܐ. ܐܝ ܗܘ ܟܕ ܓܒܪ ܕܢܐܡܪ ܒܪ ܟܝܢܐ ܕܡܛܠܬܐ ܠܦܓܪܐ܆ ܡܫܘܚܬܐ ܠܐܠܗܘܬܐ. ܟܕ ܠܐ ܡܕܡ ܐܦܫܝܛܐ ܡܛܠܬܐ ܟܗ ܡܛܠܬܐ. ܐܝ ܕܝܢ ܐܝܟܢܐ ܢܐܡܪ ܠܦܓܪܐ ܕܡܢ ܩܕܡ܆ ܐܝܟܢܐ ܕܟܕ ܐܦܫܝܛܐ ܐܬܘܗܝ ܦܓܪܐ ܠܐܘܣܝܐ܆ ܘܐܬܘܗܝ ܟܗ ܡܛܠܬܐ܆ ܙܕܝܩܘܬܐ ܚܕܐ ܠܐܠܗܘܬܐ

two, from soul, I mean, and body. Let us accept that something like this took place in the birth of Emmanuel. For he was born, as I have said, from the ousia of God and the Father, his only-begotten Word. But because he assumed flesh, and made it his own, and was also called Son of Man and became like us, it does not seem shocking to me that we should say—rather we are compelled to confess—that he was born in the flesh by means of a woman, just as also the soul of a man is born with its flesh, and is counted as one with it, although in nature it is understood to be other than it, and is according to its own principle. And if someone should wish to say that some mother is 'flesh-bearer' and consequently not 'soul-bearer' as well, he talks far too much. For, as I have said, she bore the living creature, (*Lebon p. 31*) skilfully composed from things which are unlike. And from two, yet there is one man, while each one of them remains what it is, but they have run together to a natural union, and, as it were, mix with each other that thing which each one of them has as its own."[108]

How do you understand, in the cases of the structure of a man like us, how (Cyril) says a living creature is composed from things which are unlike each other, and not consubstantial[109] with each other, but the two of them have run together to natural union, and as it were mixed with each other that thing which each one of them (had) as its own naturally in ousia? Because of this, when there is a mortal body the whole living creature is called mortal, and when there is a rational soul, the whole living creature is called rational, as we said when we were writing before as well. It is the same therefore in the case of Emmanuel too: in some places all of him is called man, when our Saviour says, "Why do you seek to kill me, the man who told you the truth?"[110] and in others it is written that all of him descended from heaven.[111] And Julius the Theologian also said as follows in the Treatise of the title[112] "Concerning the union of the body to the divinity of the Word": (JULIUS): "Thus also, he is consubstantial[113] with God in invisible spirit, the flesh being included in this description, because it is united to him who is consubstantial[113] with God. And again, he is consubstantial[113] with men, the divinity also being included with the body because it was united to him who is consubstantial[113] with us, while the nature of the body is not changed in the union with (the Word who is) consubstantial[113] with God, or by sharing the title of being 'consubstantial',[113] just as the nature of the divinity is not changed either in sharing the human body (*Lebon p. 132*) and in the title of 'flesh consubstantial[114] with us'."[115] And in the Book of Treasures, wise Cyril says as follows

ܠܐܘܪܐ: ܡܛܠ ܠܐܘܣܛܐ ܕܥܡܡܐ. ܟܕ ܗܟܢ ܕܝܢ ܗܘܝܐ ܐܡܬ̈ܝ: ܠܐ
ܡܫܬܠܛܝܢ ܕܐܝܟܢܐ ܢܫܠܛܝܢ ܒܢܦܫܗܘܢ. ܐܦ ܓܝܪ ܠܐ ܐܡܪܝܢ ܡܢ ܡܕܡ (129)
ܠܦܓܪܐ: ܐܠܐ ܒܪ ܟܝܢܐ ܠܗ ܠܡܠܬܐ: ܠܗ ܡܕܡ ܕܒܝܪ ܗܘ ܡܢܐ ܕܡܕܡܝܢ ܗܘܘ:
ܘܠܐ ܐܪܐ ܢܫܬܒܪܘܢ ܐܝܟ ܡܢܐ ܕܡܫܬܘܕܝܢ. ܗܕܐ ܐܝܟ ܠܪܥܝܬܗܘܢ ܡܫܬܝܚ ܘܐܡܪܝܢ
ܪܚܡܘܬܐ. ܐܡܝܢܐ ܓܝܪ ܕܒܪܐ ܐܝܟ ܐܒ̈ܗܬܐ: ܟܕ ܐܠܗܘܬܗ ܒܪ ܟܝܢܐ ܕܐܒܐ: ܒܐܠܗܘܬܗ
ܕܗܘ ܐܒܐ: ܐܠܐ ܒܪܐ ܒܟܠ ܐܒܐ ܡܬܐܡܪ ܒܪ ܟܝܢܐ. ܗܘܝܐ ܘܦܓܪܐ ܒܪ ܟܝܢܐ ܕܡܠܬܐ
ܒܐܠܗܘܬܗ ܕܗܘ ܡܠܬܐ. ܐܠܐ ܐܚܪܢܐ ܒܟܠ ܡܠܬܐ. ܟܕ ܐܚܪܢܐ ܕܝܢ ܐܠܗܘܬܗ ܗܘܬ ܐܝܟ
ܡܠܬܗܘܢ ܠܐܠܗܘܬܐ ܕܡܠܘܗܝ ܪܚܡܘܬܐ. ܒܟܠ ܓܝܪ ܠܐܠܗܘܬܐ ܗܘ ܫܪܝܪܬܐ:
ܘܒܫܪܪܐ ܡܫܡܫܢܘܬܐ ܘܠܐ ܡܬܦܠܓܢܘܬܐ ܡܫܡܠܝܐ ܠܐܘܣܛܐ. ܐܠܐ ܗܘ ܕܡܢ ܗܢܘܢ
ܐܠܗܘܬܗ. ܘܐܡܝܢܐ ܡܛܠ ܒܬܫܡܫܬܐ: ܟܕ ܐܚܪܢܐ ܠܐܠܗܐ ܠܒܪ ܡܢ ܗܘ
ܘܐܠܗܘܬܗ ܡܫܬܠܛܝܢ܀
ܠܐ ܗܟܝܠ ܡܢ ܗܟܢ ܕܐܒ̈ܗܬܐ ܘܠܐ ܡܬܝܕܥܐ ܒܡܠܐ ܕܡܘܕܝܢ ܠܫܝܢܘܬܐ ܪܚܡܬܐ
ܒܝܗ: ܢܝܬܐ ܠܒܪܢܫܐ ܠܡܠܘܬܐ ܟܝܢܐ ܕܟܠ ܡܠܬܐ. ܐܦ ܓܝܪ ܢܐܡܪ ܕܡܢ ܡܕܡ
ܡܛܠ ܫܘܪܝܐ: ܒܠܚܘܕ ܕܝܢ ܕܠܐܘܣܛܐ ܠܐܠܗܘܬܐ ܚܕ: ܒܐܒܐ ܘܒܪܗ ܕܡܘܡܠܝܐ
ܕܒܠܐ ܫܘܚܠܦ: ܕܗܢܘܢ ܕܐܦܠܐ ܒܫܘܪܝܐ ܡܢ ܐܘܣܛܐ ܕܠܐܠܗܘܬܐ ܐܡܪܘ ܕܚܕ ܒܗ
ܡܠܬܐ ܟܝܢܐ. ܡܛܠ ܕܐܦ ܠܒܪܝܬܐ ܡܫܬܡܠܝܐ: ܗܘ ܕܗܘܝܐ ܢܦܩ ܠܝ ܚܫܐ
ܕܡܘܕܝܢ ܕܡܢ ܐܒ̈ܗܬܐ ܐܬܐܡܪ: ܡܫܡܫܝܢ ܕܒܗ ܒܫܡܐ ܐܚܝܕ ܐܬܝܚܕ. ܘܠܗ
ܡܛܠ ܗܕܐ ܒܟܠ ܐܘܣܛܐ ܠܐܠܗܘܬܐ ܠܒܪܐ ܐܫܟ ܘܠܟܠܗ. ܡܫܝܚܐ ܕܐܘܣܛܐ
ܕܗܟܢ ܘܠܐ ܡܬܐܡܪܢܘܬܐ ܐܚܝܕ ܙܗܝܪ ܠܫܝܢܘܬܐ: ܘܡܢ ܡܫܡܫܢܐ ܗܘ ܕܡܢ ܠܐܪܝܡ
ܡܫܠܡܐ ܠܝ.
ܛܠܝܪܬܐ ܓܝܪ ܕܒܟܠ ܕܚܢܢܐ: ܗܘ ܕܗܘܝܐ ܒܗܘܕܝܐ ܒܟܕܝ. ܡܛܠ ܗܢܐ ܕܝܢ: ܟܕ
ܠܪܘܫܐ ܕܡܢ ܡܛܠ (130) ܒܫܪܬܐ ܕܐܠܗܘܬܐ ܕܫܝܢܘܬܐ: ܗܘ ܕܡܬܒܪܢܘܬܐ ܐܘ
ܡܬܒܪܢܘܬܐ. ܫܡܘܕܥܘܢ܀ ܕܡܢ ܕܝܢ ܟܕܘܡ ܠܡܟܒܐ ܕܡܢ ܙܪܥܐ ܕܒܝܬܗܘܢ: ܐܡ̈ܗܬܐ
ܓܝܪ ܕܗܟܢ ܕܬܪܒܝܬܐ: ܟܕ ܡܫܡܫܝܢ ܠܒܝܬܐ ܒܟܠ ܡܕܐ: ܐܝܟ ܒܢܝܢ ܦܢ
ܒܡܪܒܝܬܐ: ܒܫܪܪܐ ܕܒܡܠܬܐ ܡܛܠ ܦܢܝ ܘܒܡܫܘܕܥܘܬܐ ܡܕܡ ܠܐ ܡܬܦܠܓܢܘܬܐ
ܕܐܠܗܐ: ܐܠܐ ܘܡܫܬܡܠܝܐ ܠܡܠܝܘܬܐ ܐܢܫܝܬܐ. ܙܥܐ ܕܝܢ ܒܚܝܘܬܐ ܙܥܝܐ ܠܐܠܗܐ: ܟܕ ܐܝܬ
ܗܘ ܕܢܒܥ. ܒܪܐ ܓܝܪ ܙܥܝܐ ܕܒܪܢܫܐ ܒܗ ܐܝܟ ܒܪܐ ܡܠܐ ܕܢܒܐ. ܐܚܪܬܐ ܗܝ ܕܝܢ
ܡܠܬܐ ܕܒܫܪܐ: ܘܒܗ ܟܕ ܡܠܘܬܐ ܐܚܪܬܐ ܕܢܫܐ. ܐܠܐ ܐܦ ܬܘ̈ܒ ܗܟܢ ܐܩ̈ܘܬܐ

when he used the term "mixture": (CYRIL): "For the body did not become that of some other man but his own, and because of this it is reckoned as his own. For there is one Christ, from humanity and from God the Word as it were mixed, not as a result of change into what was not (before), but as a result of assuming the temple from the Virgin."[116]

But do not suppose that what you said the opposition cites is new. For what they say is old and foolish and laughable in a variety of ways, for instance, their claim that, when we say "One nature of God the Word" and add "incarnate", we are introducing the other nature.[117] They have become many times over foul by the denial of the flesh[118] and the confession of the Word as simple after the union.[119] But it is well known that the word "incarnate" indicates composition, and one hypostasis from two, and removes distinction of the hypostases and natures. For we have already quoted that in *That Christ is One*, holy Cyril said as follows: "It is not the case that in everything and from every respect only what is simple and of one species is called 'one', but those things as well which are composed from two or more and of different species. For so those who are skilled in these matters think is right."[120]

Thus those who divide Emmanuel to overthrow this wise Doctor have attempted something that is the daughter of stupidity itself, and the sister of contradiction.[121] For in the Eighth Chapter or Anathema he said as follows: (CYRIL): "If someone should venture to say that the man who was assumed should be worshipped along with God the Word, (*Lebon p. 133*) and should be co-glorified or together should be called God, as if (they were) one with another, and does not rather honour Emmanuel with one worship and offer one hymn of praise, in that the Word became flesh, let him be anathema".[122] But Andrew of Samosata, (one) of the chief authorities in that time, finding fault with the Chapter, said against holy Cyril: (ANDREW): "But you will be caught, fallen into the same (errors). For you have written in one of your Treatises, that the Son sat with[123] the Father, along with his flesh. How can you then find fault with someone who says that the man and God the Word are worshipped together, seeing that 'σύν' and 'μετά'[124] have the same import and meaning."[125] And Cyril makes a defence against this and shows (Andrew) to have erred with the ultimate error, equating a duality of hypostases with one hypostasis and person and nature from composition. And he wrote as follows: (CYRIL): "For the opposition says, 'Truly even you will be caught somewhere, for you have written in a letter that the Son sits with the Father, along with

ܕܦܘܩܕܢܐ ܒܠܚܘܕ ܕܡܢ ܐܘܪܚܐ: ܐܠܐ ܗܟܝܠ ܒܗܘ ܕܒܟܠܗ ܣܘܓܐܐ ܡܠܝܢ: ܗܘ ܕܡܢ ܢܟܝܐ ܐܡܪ ܐܢܐ ܘܦܪܢܐ: ܠܗ ܡܫܝܚܐ ܡܫܐܡܪ̈ܢܝ ܕܢ̈ܟܝܢ. ܘܠܐ ܐܡܪ ܐܝܟ ܐܠܗܐ ܠܡܐܡܪ ܠܐܠܗܘܬܗ ܡܕܝܢܐ ܒܣܪܐ ܦܝ: ܠܐ ܕܝܢ ܡܫܝܚܐ ܘܡܕܝܢܐ ܢܟܝܐ. ܡܕܝܢܬܗ ܓܝܪ ܠܡܡܠܠܘ ܒܗ ܡܢܗܘܢ. ܘܐܝܟ ܚܕ ܡܢ ܬܪܝܢ ܠܒܪܢܫܐ. ܡܢ ܢܟܝܐ ܐܡܪ ܐܢܐ ܘܦܪܢܐ. ܡܕܡ ܕܐܝܟ ܗܟܢܐ ܢܦܠܛ ܘܐܬܦܠܓ ܘܡܫܝܚܐ ܕܡܫܘܬܦܘܬ. ܡܟܝܠ ܓܝܪ ܐܝܟܢܐ ܘܡܪܢܐ ܡܢ ܐܘܦܝܐ ܕܠܐܠܗܐ ܘܐܢܐ ܡܫܝܚܐ ܡܣܝܒܪܘ. ܡܛܠ ܕܝܢ ܕܢܦܠܛ ܒܣܪܐ ܘܒܒܪܗ ܕܡܠܬܐ: ܘܐܬܐܡܪ ܐܦ ܒܪ ܐܢܫܐ ܘܗܘܐ ܐܒܘܗܝ: ܠܐ ܡܕܡ ܚܣܝܪܐ ܡܫܬܟܚܐ ܒܗ ܕܢܐܡܪ: ܡܬܐܡܪܐ ܕܝܢ ܐܦ ܐܠܗܐ ܕܗܘܐ: ܕܐܬܝܠܕ ܒܒܣܪ ܡܢ ܐܢܬܬܐ: ܐܝܟ ܡܐ ܕܐܦ ܢܟܝܐ ܕܒܪܢܫܐ ܒܗ ܒܒܣܪܗ ܡܬܝܠܕ: ܘܐܝܟܢܐ ܡܫܝܚܐ ܠܐܠܗܐ: ܒܪ ܛܒ ܒܒܝܬܐ ܐܡܪܐ ܗܟܢ ܡܢܗ ܡܬܝܕܥܐ: ܘܐܬܝܠܕ ܐܝܟ ܡܫܝܚܐ ܕܡܠܬܐ. ܘܐܦ ܐܝܟ ܢܒܝܐ ܕܠܐܠܗܐ ܕܦܫ ܢܐܡܪ: ܕܐܬܝܠܕ ܦܝ ܡܕܝܢܐ ܒܣܪܐ: ܠܗ ܕܝܢ ܡܫܝܚܐ ܘܡܕܝܢܐ ܢܟܝܐ: ܡܬܐܡܪܐ ܐܡܪ ܦܝܠܝܦ. ܡܕܝܢܐ ܓܝܪ ܐܝܟ ܕܐܡܪܐ ܠܚܘܬܐ: ܒܗ (131) ܡܪܢܒܐ ܚܦܝܪ ܒܐܘܡܢܘܬܐ ܡܢ ܗܟܢ ܘܠܐ ܕܫܠܡ. ܘܡܢ ܬܪܝܢ ܦܝ. ܒܪܡ ܕܝܢ ܚܕ ܒܪܢܫܐ. ܒܗ ܡܫܝܚܐ ܦܝ ܟܠ ܚܕ ܡܢܗܘܢ ܗܘ ܕܢ ܕܐܬܐܡܪ: ܦܝܠܝܦ ܕܝܢ ܐܡܪܐ ܠܚܕܝܘܬܐ ܡܫܝܚܐ. ܘܐܝܟ ܗܘ ܕܡܫܬܟܚܝܢ ܠܦܪ̈ܨܘܦܐ. ܗܘ ܡܕܡ ܕܐܝܟ ܕܡܟܝܠ ܠܡܟܠܒ ܡܢܗܘܢ ܐܝܬ ܗܘܐ܀

ܡܫܬܡܠܝ ܐܝܬ ܐܝܟܢܐ ܒܗܘ ܦܘܩܕܐ ܕܒܪܢܫܐ ܘܐܠܗܐ: ܡܢ ܦܪܘܨܘܦܐ ܡܢ ܠܐ ܕܫܠܡ ܠܦܪ̈ܨܘܦܐ: ܘܠܗ ܬܪܝܢ ܒܢ̈ܝܐ ܕܬܪ̈ܝܢ ܐܡܪ ܕܡܪܢܒܐ ܚܕܝܘܬܐ: ܠܐܘܡܗܘܢ ܕܝܢ ܐܝܟܢܐ ܦܝܠܝܦ ܠܚܕܝܘܬܐ ܡܫܝܚܐ: ܘܐܝܟ ܗܘ ܕܦܪܨܘܦܐ ܠܦܪ̈ܨܘܦܐ: ܗܘ ܡܕܡ ܕܐܝܟ ܕܡܟܝܠ ܠܡܟܠܒ ܡܢܗܘܢ ܒܐܘܦܝܐ ܡܢܝ. ܡܛܠ ܗܘܐ ܒܗ ܦܘܩܕܐ ܐܝܟܢܐ ܡܫܘܬܦ: ܟܠܗ ܚܕܝܘܬܐ ܡܬܐܡܪܐ ܡܫܘܬܦܐ. ܘܒܗ ܢܟܝܐ ܐܝܟܢܐ ܡܫܬܡܠܝܐ: ܟܠܗ ܚܕܝܘܬܐ ܡܫܬܡܫܐ ܡܫܬܡܠܝܐ. ܗܘ ܕܐܦ ܡܢ ܩܕܡ ܒܗ ܚܠܡ ܗܘܐ ܐܡܪܝܢ. ܗܟܢܐ ܗܟܝܠ ܐܦ ܒܗܢܐ ܒܡܫܘܬܦܘܬ. ܒܕܘܟ ܦܝ ܟܠܗ ܒܪܢܫܐ ܡܫܬܡܫܐ. ܒܗ ܐܡܪ ܗܘ ܦܪܘܩ: ܡܢܐ ܦܪܫ ܐܠܗܐ ܕܐܬܚܠܛ: ܠܒܪܢܫܐ ܕܦܪܘܢ ܡܫܬܟܚ ܠܗܘܢ. ܒܕܘܟ ܕܝܢ: ܕܟܠܗ ܢܒܥ ܡܢ ܚܣܝܐ ܟܠܗ. ܗܘ ܕܐܦ ܡܫܝܚܐ ܠܐܠܗܘܬܐ ܘܠܗܘܢ ܒܠܡܐܡܪܐ ܕܪܥܝܢ ܡܛܠ ܚܕܘܬܐ ܕܦܪܢܐ ܒܗܐ ܠܐܠܗܘܬܐ ܕܡܠܬܐ ܗܟܢܐ ܐܡܪ. ܘܠܗܘܢ܀ ܗܟܢܐ ܘܠܐܠܗܘܬܐ ܒܪ ܟܝܢܐ ܒܪܘܚܐ ܗܘ ܠܐ ܡܬܚܫܒܐ: ܒܗ ܡܫܬܡܠܝ ܒܗ ܚܝܐ ܐܦ ܒܣܪܐ: ܕܟܠܗ ܗܘ ܒܪ ܟܝܢܐ ܕܠܐܠܗܐ ܡܫܝܚ: ܘܐܦ ܠܐܢܫܐ ܒܪ ܟܝܢܐ: ܒܗ ܡܫܬܡܠܐ ܘܠܐܠܗܘܬܐ

his flesh, and how after that will you find fault with someone who says that it is right that God the Word and the man should be worshipped together, and together called God? For it is the same thing to say 'σύν' and 'μετά'.' Let us therefore rebuke those who do not know the meaning of what was said, and who do not look at the nature of the facts. For on the one hand, when the discussion is making an examination about one person, or nature, or hypostasis, and those things from which it is, or is naturally composed, then the term 'σύν' or 'μετά' ensures for the thing signified the fact of its being one through composition, and it does not define it dividedly into two. And on the other hand, when hypostases are previously divided into two, and (are so divided) that each one of them should be independently and individually known, (when) 'σύν' or perhaps 'μετά' is applied, (*Lebon p. 134*) then we say that (the term) has given a sign (that) (they) are two or more still, and not one through composition. For example, if I should say, perhaps, that the soul of a man and his body are honoured together if some honour should come from someone to one man, who is from two, or if someone should say the soul is one living thing along with its body, he would in no wise be defining the one (man) as two men, but rather is seen not to be ignorant of those things from which he is, or is naturally composed. But when he says that Peter and John are together called men, or that along with Peter also John went up to the temple, it is not consequently the case that there 'σύν' or 'μετά' gives a sign of one man. For Peter is not composed with John, nor do the two of them complete the constitution of one man. Therefore why do they doctor the truth, in an unlearned way dividing the one to two Christs?"[126]

Therefore since there is a great and immeasurable difference, and, if we speak scripturally,[127] (as great a difference) as the east is removed from the west, between natural composition or hypostatic union, and a conjunction of honour, which binds two hypostases by an equality of name, how should we be obliged by the followers of Nestorius to take refuge in one ousia (resulting) from a confusion of ousiai, in order that we might turn aside from a [duplication][128] of natures, as you are saying. It is not so: it is not! Let no-one make you err by the persuasion of words, as the Apostle says.[129]

I pleasantly asked your Chastity: when one ousia and quality has come into being at one time, as you say, how do you then say there (still) remained a difference in ousia of the natures from which Christ is? For if there should be one quality and ousia, then (the marks) of the difference have taken to flight. For at any rate you say—because your intention is to hint at (lit. hints at) (*Lebon p. 135*) what has been

ܒܗ ܦܓܪܐ܆ ܕܟܠܗ ܒܪ ܚܝܢ ܐܬܚܙܝ. ܟܕ ܠܐ ܡܫܬܚܠܦ ܚܝܐ ܕܦܓܪܐ ܒܚܕܝܘܬܐ ܕܟܠܗ ܒܪ ܚܝܐ ܕܐܠܗܐ܆ ܘܒܡܫܬܘܬܦܘܬܐ ܕܫܡܐ ܕܒܪ ܚܝܐ. ܐܡܟܢܐ ܕܐܦܠܐ ܚܝܐ ܕܐܠܗܘܬܐ ܡܫܬܚܠܦ܇ ܒܡܫܬܘܬܦܘܬܐ ܕܦܓܪܐ (132) ܐܝܟܢܐ܆ ܘܒܡܘܡܗܘܐ ܕܒܣܪܐ ܒܪܢܫ܀ ܘܒܟܠܟܐ ܕܝܢ ܕܫܪ̈ܟܬܐ܆ ܟܕ ܒܫܡܐ ܕܡܥܘܪܓܐ ܐܬܚܫ ܚܫܫܐ ܡܘܪܟܒܘܬ ܐܡܪ ܗܟܝܠ. ܀ܡܘܪܟܒܘܬ܀ ܠܘ ܓܝܪ ܕܐܝܟ ܐܚܪܢ ܐܠܐ ܕܝܠܗ ܗܘܐ ܒܥܡܐ. ܡܛܠ ܗܘܐ ܘܐܝܟ ܕܝܠܗ ܚܫܝܒ. ܚܕ ܓܝܪ ܡܫܝܚܐ ܡܢ ܐܝܬܘܬܐ ܘܡܫܠܡܬܐ ܕܐܠܗܐ܆ ܐܝܟ ܡܐ ܕܡܫܪܪ. ܠܗ ܡܢ ܗܘ ܕܐܬܚܙܝ ܟܠܐ ܗܘ ܕܒܟܠܗܘܢ ܗܘܐ. ܐܠܐ ܡܢ ܗܘ ܕܢܣܒ ܗܝܟܠܐ ܕܡܢ ܒܬܘܠܬܐ܀

ܐܦ ܗܘ ܕܝܢ ܕܐܡܪܢܐ ܕܗܘܝܘ ܕܒܣܘܟܠܐ ܡܫܬܡܥ܆ ܠܐ ܬܬܕܡܪ ܕܚܕܐ ܗܘ. ܡܛܠ ܕܠܗ ܓܝܪ ܟܕ ܚܝܐ܆ ܘܡܫܬܟܚܐ ܡܬܓܫܡܐ ܗܘ ܕܐܡܪܢ. ܕܟܠܗ ܕܐܡܪܝܢ ܚܕ ܚܝܐ ܕܐܠܗܐ ܡܠܬܐ܆ ܘܡܬܩܢܝܢ ܡܬܚܙܝܐ܆ ܠܗܘ ܚܝܐ ܐܚܪܢܐ ܡܬܠܝܢ. ܒܫܘܝܘ ܓܝܪ ܕܩܢܝܢ ܗܘܘ ܦܓܪܐ܆ ܗܘ ܕܒܫܘܪ ܒܒܣܪܐ܆ ܘܟܠܗ ܚܕܝܘܬܐ ܬܘܒ ܦܓܪܐ ܗܘܐ ܒܡܠܬܐ. ܐܠܐ ܡܫܪ ܚܕܐ܆ ܕܡܠܬܐ ܗܘ ܕܒܒܣܪ ܪܘܚܐ ܪܡܙܐ܆ ܘܚܕ ܩܢܘܡܐ ܡܢ ܬܪܝܢ܆ ܘܟܠܦܪܨܘܦܐ ܕܩܢܘܡܐ ܘܟܝܢ̈ܐ ܕܢܦܫܐ. ܐܝܟܢ ܓܝܪ ܡܢ ܒܪܘ ܕܐܡܪ ܩܕܝܫܐ ܡܘܪܟܒܘܬ ܒܗܘ ܕܚܕ ܗܘ ܡܫܝܚܐ ܗܟܝܠ. ܀ܡܘܪܟܒܘܬ܀ ܠܗ ܒܟܠ ܘܡܢ ܡܠܦܢܘܬܐ ܚܕ ܡܬܐܡܪ ܒܚܘܝܕܐ ܗܘ ܦܓܪܐ ܘܒܢܘܦܫܐ ܐܪܥܐ. ܐܠܐ ܓܝܪ ܘܗܠܝܢ ܕܡܢ ܬܪܝܢ ܐܘ ܦܓܪܐ ܘܡܫܬܡܠܝܐ ܐܪܥܐ ܡܪܒܝܢ. ܕܗܟܢܐ ܓܝܪ ܡܫܪ ܐܝܟ ܠܗ ܡܫܬܠܒܪܐ ܠܗܘܢ ܕܒܪܐܡܪ ܗܠܝܢ ܚܫܒܝܢ܀

ܗܟܢܐ ܕܗܠܝܢ ܕܒܪܬܐ ܕܠܗ ܟܕ ܕܠܗ ܕܡܫܬܪܪܐ ܗܘܬ. ܘܚܠܬܐ ܕܗܦܟܬܐ ܢܩܫܘ ܗܢܘܢ ܕܡܦܠܓܝܢ ܠܚܕܝܘܬܐ. ܕܢܘܦܩܘܢ ܠܡܫܝܚܐ ܗܘܐ ܡܠܦܢܐ. ܐܡܪ ܓܝܪ ܒܡܦܠܓܘ ܕܐܦܢܐ ܐܘ ܚܪܫܐ ܗܟܝܠ. ܀ܡܘܪܟܒܘܬ܀ ܐܢ ܐܝܟ ܡܡܪܚܝܢ ܕܐܡܪ ܠܒܪ̈ܝܬܐ ܕܐܬܚܫܒ܇ ܘܠܐ ܕܢܫܬܦܝ ܒܗ ܡܠܬܐ ܕܐܠܗܐ (133) ܘܐܦܢܐ ܢܬܠܚܫ ܐܘ ܐܦܢܐ ܢܬܦܪܐ ܕܐܠܗܐ܆ ܐܝܟ ܐܚܪܢܐ ܒܗ ܐܚܪܢܐ܆ ܘܠܐ ܢܬܦܪܫ ܒܚܕܐ ܦܓܪܬܐ ܡܫܡܫ ܠܚܕܝܘܬܐ ܘܚܕܐ ܬܬܚܫܒ ܩܠܐ ܡܦܪܫ܇ ܒܗܘ ܕܗܘܐ ܡܠܬܐ ܒܣܪܐ܆ ܚܪܫܐ ܢܗܘܐ܀ ܐܠܐ ܐܝܪܐܘܣ ܗܘ ܡܥܡܠܐ ܕܡܢ ܗܢܘܢ ܕܒܪܝܫܐ ܠܗܠܝܢ ܒܗܘ ܕܚܝܐ܆ ܟܕ ܓܒܠ ܠܡܦܠܘܢ ܐܡܪ ܟܠܐ ܦܪܝܫܐ ܡܘܪܟܒܘܬ. ܀ܐܝܪܐܘܣ܀ ܘܐܝܟ ܒܗܘܢ ܟܕ ܒܗܘܢ ܡܬܐܡܪ ܐܝܟ ܕܒܥܠܡ. ܡܛܠ ܓܝܪ ܒܥܠܡܐ ܡܢ ܡܠܦܢܝܢ܆ ܕܝܠܗ ܒܪܐ ܘܐܦܠܐ ܐܚܪܢܐ ܗܘ ܒܥܒܕܘ. ܐܡܟܢܐ ܠܗܘ ܗܘܦܠܐ ܓܒܠ ܐܝܟ ܠܗܘ ܘܐܡܪ

said on this point all over the place—the lesser was changed to the more exalted, and the whole of Emmanuel is divinity in ousia, (and) how then will he be seen at the time of the second and glorious coming by those who pierced (him)? For when the visible ousia has once changed to the invisible, he is reduced to what does not fall under sight, and the divine scriptures deceive, which established that he is to be seen by those who pierced (him). But in this matter, it is time that I give a few words, and I come not, as the Apostle said, to visions and revelations of the Lord,[130] (but) to the words of the wisdom spoken by God, and I shall say, like (Paul): "I have become a fool: you drove me (to it)".[131]

For I said as follows in what was written to you before: "But to say that Emmanuel was composed from two properties or from two activities[132] is foolish and unlearned. For, because 'to understand' is a property of a rational mind, but 'blackness' or perhaps 'whiteness' (is a property) of a body, do we say because of this that a man is composed from 'understanding' and from 'whiteness' or 'blackness'? But no-one of intelligence says this: but he says that man exists from the natures of body and soul, to which (natures) those (properties) which were mentioned adhere and are visible and do not exist in isolation."[133] But when you read these things, you quoted the passage, saying that [we said][134] "from 'being rational' and from 'blackness'".[135] But "to understand" and "being rational" are not the same.[136] For "being rational", which is a reasonable mind, exists in a hypostasis, but "to understand" (is) a movement and activity of a rational mind. Therefore, when we have said "from 'understanding'", how do you answer "from 'being rational'", (*Lebon p. 136*) and in this have perverted the truth? But after this you thought that we were speaking about blackness which is smeared on a tablet, and takes place, and again does not take place, and in this way you have said that a quality is that which leaves an ousia just as it is naturally, when it fades to whiteness. But we were speaking about the blackness which is seen in a human body (and) which is an inseparable accident, as for example that [137] of the Ethiopian, which it was right for us to learn from the words of Jeremiah does not naturally happen to change. For he says, as if about something which is impossible, "If the Ethiopian should change his skin, and the leopard his spots".[138] But be sure that we are not seeking accurately to define what a propriety is according to the definitions of pagan philosophy. For those things are set at naught and are outside our court. For who does not know that the faculty of laughter is the propriety of "man", and neighing of "horse"? But we have one care, namely

ܘܡܫܡܠܝܢ ܒܪܢܫܐ ܐܣܝܐ ܘܡܫܡܠܝܐ ܠܐܠܗܐ. ܟܕ ܗܘ ܕܐܣܝܐ ܘܒܥܐ: ܗܘ ܟܕ ܗܘ
ܚܠܠ ܘܐܬܪܚܡܬܐ ܐܝܬ ܠܗ̇. ܘܢܦܩ ܒܪܘܚܐ ܠܗܠ ܗܘܐ ܘܡܫܬܐ: ܘܛܒܐ ܗܘܐ ܛܘܒܢ
ܐܣܝܘܬܐ: ܕܐܬܪܣܝܘܬܐ ܕܩ̈ܘܡܬܐ ܡܫܬܢܝܢ ܗܘܐ. ܠܚܕ ܩܘܡܬܐ ܘܦܪܨܘܦܐ: ܘܚܝܠܐ ܕܡܢ
ܙܒܢܐ. ܥܠܬ ܕܝܢ ܗܘܝܐ. ܀ܡܬܪܚܡܬܗ܀ ܐܠܐ ܓܒܪ ܐܡܪܝܢ ܫ̈ܩܘܒܠܐ: ܐܝܟ ܡܬܠܐܚܕ
ܐܝܬ ܐܦ ܐܝܬ ܒܝܘܡ ܘܡܬܒܥܐ ܠܡܝܬܐ: ܘܡܬܥ ܒܪܐ ܘܐܚܐ ܐܣܝܐ ܟܡ ܒܦܪܘ.
ܘܐܡܚܠ ܠܡܬܘܡ ܚܕܠܐ ܐܝܬ ܠܗ̇ܘ ܘܐܡܪ: ܘܠܐ ܘܡܫܡܠܝܐ ܠܐܠܗܐ ܘܒܪܢܫܐ ܐܣܝܐ
ܢܫܡܠܝܢ ܘܐܣܝܐ ܢܡܪܐ ܠܐܠܗܐ. ܗܘ ܓܒܪ ܟܕ ܗܘ ܐܠܗܘ: ܕܢܐܡܪ ܐܣܝܐ ܘܟܡ.
ܡܢܝܢ ܢܫܟܢ ܘܠܐ ܚܪܡܝܢ ܚܠܠ ܘܗܘܠܝܢ ܕܐܬܐܡܪ. ܘܠܐ ܚܙܝܢ ܒܚܝܠܐ ܕܡܫܬܢܐ. ܐܡܠܐ
ܦܘ ܓܒܪ ܕܟܠ ܚܕ ܦܪܨܘܦܐ ܐܘ ܚܝܠܐ ܐܘ ܩܘܡܬܐ ܚܕ ܡܚܝܠܐ ܡܫܡܠܝܐ: ܘܗܘܠܝܢ
ܕܡܩܘܡ ܐܠܗܘܬܐ ܐܘ ܡܪܟܒ ܒܚܝܠܗ: ܘܡܫܡܠܝܐ ܗܘ ܕܐܚܪܢܐ ܐܘ ܗܘ ܕܟܡ ܢܛܪܐ
ܠܗܘ ܕܡܬܚܝܒ ܐܦ ܗܘܝܐ ܗܘ ܕܚܕ ܢܗܘܐ ܐܠܗܘܬܐ ܒܙܒܢܐ: ܘܠܗ ܠܡܬܘܡ
ܡܫܬܟܚܐ ܡܬܚܫܒܐ. ܐܡܠܐ ܕܝܢ ܕܟܕ ܡܚܡܝܢ ܡܫܬܟܚܝܢ ܩ̈ܘܡܬܐ ܠܡܬܘܡ:
ܘܠܗܠ ܗܘ ܕܠܐ ܕܠܡܚܕ ܡܚܘܐ ܘܠܗ ܡܬܚܝܒ ܘܡܬܟܠܐ: ܗܘ ܕܐܣܝܐ ܐܘ
ܟܡܐ ܗܘ ܕܟܡ ܡܬܐܡܪܐ: (134) ܗܝܕܝܢ ܕܐܬܝܢ ܐܘ ܕܩ̈ܝܡܬܐ ܠܐܘܟ: ܘܠܐ ܕܚܕ
ܒܪܘܚܐ ܐܡܪܝܢ ܚܝܢ ܕܒܥܐ ܠܗ ܠܫܘܘܕܝܐ: ܐܝܟ ܡܐ ܕܐܦ ܐܡܪ ܐ̱ܢ ܠܓܒܪܗ:
ܘܡܬܐܡܪܐ ܢܫܐ ܕܒܪܢܫܐ ܘܦܓܪܗ ܐܣܝܐ: ܐ̱ܢ ܐܡܪܐ ܡܕܡ ܢܗܘܐ ܡܢ ܐܝܟ ܠܗܠ ܚܕ
ܒܪܢܫܐ: ܗܘ ܘܐܠܗܘܬܐ ܡܢ ܠܐܘܟ: ܐܘ ܢܐܡܪ ܐܝܟ ܠܢܦܫܐ ܘܐܠܗܘ ܚܕܐ ܚܝܘܬܐ ܟܡ
ܓܘܫܡܗ. ܠܗ ܡܢ ܡܠܦܪܘܫ ܠܡܬܘܡ ܩܢܝ ܐܢܫܐ: ܡܬܚܝܡ ܠܗܘ ܚܕ: ܡܬܚܝܕܐ
ܕܝܢ ܡܬܐܡܪܐ: ܘܠܐ ܠܐ ܢܒܥ ܗܟܢ ܕܡܗܘܡ ܐܠܗܘܬܐ ܐܘ ܡܪܟܒ ܒܚܝܠܗ: ܐܡܠܐ
ܕܝܢ ܕܐܡܪ ܦܛܪܘܣ ܘܡܘܚ ܐܣܝܐ ܡܬܐܡܪܝܢ ܩ̈ܢܘܡܐ: ܐܘ ܕܟܡ ܦܛܪܘܣ ܐܦ
ܢܘܚ ܫܠܡ ܗܘܐ ܠܚܡܠܐ: ܠܐ ܡܫܡܠܐ ܗܘ ܕܐܣܝܐ ܐܘ ܕܟܡ ܫܘܘܕܝܐ ܘܚܕ ܐܝܟ
ܚܒܪܐ. ܠܐ ܓܒܪ ܡܪܟܒ ܦܛܪܘܣ ܟܡ ܢܘܚ: ܐܦܠܐ ܠܫܘܡܠܐ ܘܚܕ ܒܪ ܐܢܫܐ
ܡܫܡܠܝܢ ܠܐܘܡܗܘܢ: ܡܢܐ ܗܘܠܐ ܡܬܛܒܥܝܢ ܠܡܪܘܐ: ܟܕ ܡܫܬܟܚܝܢ ܠܐ ܡܬܚܫܒܐ
ܠܡܬܘܡ ܡܫܡܫܝܢ ܠܗܘ ܚܕ܀
ܟܕ ܗܘܠܐ ܦܓܪܐ ܐܠܗܘܬܐ ܫܘܟܠܠܐ ܘܠܐ ܡܫܘܡܠܐ ܘܐܝܟ ܡܐ ܕܪܘܚܐ ܡܚܝܢܐ
ܡܢ ܡܕܒܪܐ ܘܡܬܒܐܬܐ ܢܐܡܪ: ܙܘܒܐ ܚܝܠܐ: ܐܘ ܚܝܘܬܐ ܩܘܡܬܢܝܬܐ: ܠܗܠ
ܢܣܩܘܬܐ ܘܐܡܪܐ: ܕܠܡܬܘܡ ܩܘܡܝܢ ܒܫܘܡܠܐ ܫܡܐ ܐܡܪܐ: ܐܡܝܢܐ ܡܢ ܩܢܘܡܗ
ܕܢܫܬܪܘܫ ܠܐܬܪܝ: ܘܠܗܠ ܚܕܐ ܐܘܫܡܐ ܗܘ ܕܡܢ ܡܚܘܒܐ ܕܐܘܫܡܫ ܠܓܘܫܡ:

that we should establish and demonstrate plainly that where a composition and natural coming together of ousiai or natures is constituted, as in the case of the constitution of a man like us, it is superfluous and quite senseless to say that the living creature is composed from those things which appear in the ousiai.

But you are also learning and very clearly, from these things which are said, that the definitions and laws of pagan philosophy do not help you at all in the case of this which was previously set down. For the wise men in these matters say that the propriety of the human mind is to learn, to err, to remember; but the propriety of the human body is to be composed with organs in such a way so as to serve the activity of a rational mind, and as holy Basil said, to be created upright, and apart from the other living creatures, to be provided with a direction of gaze towards heaven.[139] For just as (*Lebon p. 137*) a man experienced in the craft of music does not otherwise fashion the preparation of a reed (-pipe), which is equipped to receive the blowing of a tune of this sort or of a properly controlled breath, except in such a way that it is (fashioned) appropriately to the tune which is blown, so that he will not have to change the instrument, which is equipped to serve the motion of the player; so too the Creator moulded the human body in such a way that it would be fitting and be appropriate for the dwelling-place and staying of a rational soul, so that it should not have any difference whatsoever from the bodies of the other living creatures which do not serve the interests of rational souls. Therefore, because to learn, to err, and to remember is the propriety of a human soul, and to be moulded in such a way (the propriety) of a human body, shall we say that a man is composed from learning and remembering (and) from a fashioning of the body in such a way? We would be mocked, and quite rightly, since it is right to say that a composite living creature is composed from ousiai or natures, and we would be saying (that) the composition (came) from the properties existing in them. And this is the case in the instance of a man like us.

But note that in the case of the divine nature it is impossible for us to speak precisely (of) propriety, for God is not receptive of these, but we are obliged to say something of this thus only in a metaphorical way. Because of this, Evagrius, being very capable in these matters, says in one of his Chapters: (EVAGRIUS): "If either genus or species or difference or property or accident or what is composed from these is affirmed for every enquiry, we find that none of these which were mentioned (*Lebon p. 138*) (applies) in the case of the holy Trinity. Let us worship in silence what is inexpressible."[140] And he

ܐܡܝܢܐ ܕܡܢ ܣܗܕܘܬܐ ܕܟܬ̈ܒܐ ܐܝܟ ܕܐܡܪ ܐܢܐ ܢܣܒܬ. ܠܐ ܐܬܚܙܝ ܗܟܝܢ ܠܐ ܐܬܚܙܝ. ܠܐ ܐܝܟ ܒܥܡܐ ܩ̈ܠܐ ܢܬܚܙܘܢ. ܐܝܟ ܕܐܡܪ ܡܫܝܚܐ.

ܗܢܝܬ ܡܛܠ ܦܘܩ ܠܒܥܒܕܘܗܝ: ܕܟܕ ܚܕܐ ܐܘܣܝܐ ܚܕܐ ܐܦ ܗܘܬ ܐܝܟ ܕܐܡܪ ܐܢܐ ܘܡܫܘܕܥܘܬܐ. ܐܡܝܢܐ ܡܛܠ ܐܡܪ ܐܢܐ: ܕܗܘ ܡܥܠܝܐ ܕܐܘܣܝܐ ܕܫ̈ܢܝܐ ܕܩܢܘ̈ܡܐ ܡܫܬܠܡ. ܐܦ ܓܝܪ ܚܕܐ ܡܫܘܕܥܘܬܐ ܘܐܘܣܝܐ ܠܐܬܩܝܡ: ܡܛܠ ܕܒܪܐ ܘܐܒܐ ܕܡܥܠܝܐ. ܡܢ ܡܠܦܢܘܬܐ ܓܝܪ ܐܡܪ ܐܢܐ: ܡܛܠ (135) ܕܟܠܐ ܗܘܐ ܠܟܠ ܘܡܬܚܙܐ ܠܗܘܢ ܕܡܬܐܡܪ̈ܝܢ، ܘܦܪ ܪܚܡܝ: ܗܘ ܕܒܪܝܬܐ ܐܬܦܪܣܬ ܠܗܘܢ ܗܘ ܕܡܥܝܪܐ: ܘܥܠܘ ܠܡܫܘܐܝܬ: ܠܗܘܢܬܐ ܐܬܚܘܝ ܒܐܘܣܝܐ. ܐܡܝܢܐ ܗܟܝܠ ܠܚܕܐ ܡܢ ܗܘܝ̈ ܕܥܠܘ ܒܪܝܬܐ ܕܬܬܐܠܗܬܐ ܕܐܬܪܐ ܘܡܢܚܬܐ. ܟܕ ܚܕܐ ܐܦ ܓܝܪ ܟܠܐ ܡܬܚܙܝܢܘܬܐ ܥܒܕ ܐܘܣܝܐ ܡܬܚܙܝܢܬܐ: ܡܪܝܐ ܠܗܘܢ ܘܠܐ ܢܦܠ ܒܚܕܐ. ܘܓܠܝܢ ܡ̈ܠܐ ܠܟ̈ܢܘܬܐ: ܕܡܠܬܗ ܕܡܬܚܙܝܐ ܠܗܘܢ ܕܒܪܗ: ܘܟܠܗ ܗܘ ܕܝܢ ܪܚܡܐ ܗܘ ܕܐܬܬܠ ܡܠܬܐ ܪܚܘܡܬܐ: ܘܐܬܐ ܠܗ ܐܝܟ ܕܐܡܪ ܡܫܝܚܐ: ܠܟܢܘ̈ܫܐ ܕܡܪܢܐ ܘܠܩ̈ܢܝܢܐ. ܠܚ̈ܝܠܐ ܕܡܥܠܝܬܐ ܗܘ ܕܐܬܡܠܠܬ ܡܢ ܠܠܗܐ. ܘܐܡܪ ܐܝܟ ܗܘ: ܗܘܝܬ ܡܛܠ ܕܐܠܗܘܗܝ ܠܟܝܢܐܘܬ.

ܐܡܪܬ ܓܝܪ ܒܗܠܝܢ ܕܡܢ ܩܕܡ ܒܠܥܕ ܐܬܚܙܝ ܗܟܢܐ. ܗܘ ܕܝܢ ܕܠܐܡܪ ܕܡܢ ܐܬܪܐ ܕܬܒܥܬܐ ܐܘ ܡܢ ܐܬܪܐ ܡܬܟܢܫܘܬܐ ܐܬܘܣܦ ܒܡܫܘܐܝܬ: ܡܛܠ ܘܠܐ ܙܕܩ. ܐܢܐ ܓܝܪ ܕܡܛܠ ܕܗܘ ܕܢܫܬܟܚ ܕܥܒܕܬܐ ܗܘ ܕܢܦܫܐ ܡܬܟܢܬܐ: ܕܦܓܪܐ ܕܝܢ ܐܘܪܚܘܬܐ ܐܘ ܚܘܙܬܐ ܐܢ ܬܓܪܫ: ܡܛܠ ܗܘܐ ܐܡܪܢܢ ܠܒܪܢܫܐ ܕܡܢ ܗܘ ܕܢܦܫܬܐ ܘܡܢ ܚܘܙܬܐ ܡܪܒܒ: ܐܘ ܡܢ ܐܘܪܚܘܬܐ: ܐܠܐ ܠܐ ܐܝܟ ܕܐܝܬ ܠܗ ܗܘܬ ܐܡܪ ܗܘܐ. ܐܠܐ ܡܢܗܘܢ ܕܫ̈ܢܝܐ ܕܦܓܪܐ ܘܢܦܫܐ ܐܡܪ ܕܡܬܚܡ ܒܪܢܫܐ. ܠܐܬܚܡ ܕܗܟܢ ܘܐܬܐܡܪ ܘܢܦܫ ܘܦܓܪܐ: ܘܠܐ ܡܬܦܪܫܐ ܡܢܗܘܢ. ܐܝܟ ܕܝܢ ܟܕ ܡܪܢܐ ܗܟܢ ܐܬܐܡܪ ܠܡܠܬܐ. ܟܕ ܐܡܪ ܐܢܐ ܕܐܡܪܝܢ: ܕܡܢ ܡܠܬܐ ܘܐܘܪܚܘܬܐ: ܠܗ ܓܝܪ ܗܘ ܟܕ ܗܘ ܗܘ ܕܢܫܬܟܚ ܘܡܠܬܐ. ܡܠܬܐ ܓܝܪ ܗܘ ܕܐܬܚܙܝ ܢܦܫܐ ܚܘܝܢܬܐ ܒܡܫܘܚܬܐ ܐܬܚܙܝ. ܗܘ ܕܝܢ ܕܢܫܬܟܚ ܕܒܪܐ ܘܡܬܟܢܫܘܬܐ ܕܢܦܫܐ ܡܬܚܝܢܬܐ. ܐܡܝܢܐ ܗܟܝܠ ܟܕ ܚܕ ܡܢ ܗܘ ܕܢܦܫܬܐ ܐܡܪܝܢ: ܐܝܟ ܟܕ ܡܫܘܚ ܐܝܟ (136) ܐܬܪܐ ܡܢ ܡܠܬܐ. ܘܟܗܘܐ ܐܝܟܢܐ ܒܚܙܘܐ. ܒܬܪ ܗܟܢ ܕܝܢ ܐܬܚܙܝܐ: ܕܡܛܠ ܐܘܪܚܘܬܐ ܗܘ ܕܡܬܚܙܝܢܐ ܒܟܠ ܡܫܬܟܚܝܢ ܚܝ: ܕܓܘܫܡܐ ܘܦܓܪܐ ܠܐ ܓܘܫܡܐ: ܗܟܢܐ ܘܐܬܪܐ ܕܡܫܘܕܥܘܬܐ ܐܬܚܙܝ: ܗܘ ܕܟܕ ܐܝܟܢ ܒܚܘܙܬܐ: ܠܐܘܣܝܐ

says these things rightly, because God is understood to be above ousia or nature. For in the Treatise entitled "εἰς τὸν κατάπλουν"[141] to those (who came) from Egypt, Gregory the Theologian says as follows: (GREGORY): "I recognise two supreme differences in the things which exist, which are Lordship and servitude. It is not what, amongst us, either tyranny has ordained, or [poverty][142] has separated out, but what nature defines, if it should seem good to someone so to call it. For what is first is also above nature."[143] Holy Cyril as well, in the First Book of the Commentary on the Gospel of John said as follows: (CYRIL): "But God will again be above this, in that he is above ousia, and there is nothing in creation which is supremely comparable to him so that a picture might be taken of the Holy Trinity, which (picture) has no difference, [as to exactness] of doctrines".[144] For we also do not know what God is in ousia or nature.

Henceforth, in the case of (Trinitarian) theology, and in the case of the economy of the inhomination of the only-begotten God the Word, we do not use terms in a precise way, but, as a result of the poverty of the terms at our disposal, we make the demonstrations of the things which are understood. Because of this, when we make terms about the inhomination, we say that it is the propriety of the humanity to hunger, or to thirst, or to be weary, but we do not say this in any precise way, for this is not the propriety only of man, but also of the other living creatures, which by nature breathe the air, and live lives subject to the senses and are nourished. Because a propriety, expressed precisely, is that thing which (*Lebon p. 139*) belongs to something alone, and without sharing with another. But because to hunger and to thirst or to be tired are not properties of the bodiless God, because of this, in a comparison in relation to him, we call these "properties of humanity". But, even if they are in nature properties of (humanity), they are also properties of God the Word, because of the economy. And he is said to have hungered, and thirsted, and to have been weary from a journey, because he was united hypostatically to a body whose nature it was to suffer these things. And he who divides them, and assigns these separately to the humanity, and estranges them from the only-begotten God—although he is in no way diminished according to the principle of his own impassibility—unties the economy and estranges him who is in the likeness of God, and who did not think it robbery that he should be equal with God, from voluntary emptying and humiliation for love of man, which he accepted that he should undergo for our sake. On which Cyril, (who is) wise in everything, in the Treatise of question and answer, *That Christ is One*, said these things: (CYRIL):

ܡܬܩܪܐ ܐܝܟ ܕܡܫܝܚܐ. ܡܢ ܕܝܢ ܡܛܠ ܐܘܟܡܘܬܐ ܐܡܪܢ: ܗܘ ܕܡܬܚܙܝܐ ܒܓܘܫܡܐ ܐܝܬܝܐ. ܗܘ ܕܒܟܝܢܗ ܐܠܗܘܬܗ ܘܠܐ ܡܬܦܪܫ. ܐܝܟ ܡܐ ܐܦ ܠܟܝܢܗ ܗܘ ܘܒܫܡܐ. ܗܘ ܕܐܦ ܡܢ ܒܬܪ ܥܠܠܐ ܕܐܘܣܡܐ ܙܘܥ ܗܘܐ ܕܢܬܙܘܥ: ܘܠܐ ܡܫܬܢܐ ܘܐܬܗܦܟ ܠܐ ܠܟܝܢܗ. ܐܡܪ ܓܝܪ ܐܝܟ ܡܐ ܕܡܛܠ ܗܘ ܘܠܐ ܡܫܬܚܠܦ. ܐܦ ܗܟܢ ܒܓܘܫܡܐ ܡܫܝܚܐ: ܘܦܪܘܫ ܒܟܠܗܘܢ: ܒܪܡ ܕܝܢ: ܕܢܣܒ ܠܗ ܐܝܟ ܠܒܘܫܐ ܕܦܓܪܢܝܘܬܐ ܕܠܒܪ ܡܢܗ ܕܡܬܬܠܬܠ ܠܗܢܘܢ: ܕܗܢܐ ܐܠܗܘܬܗ ܕܡܫܝܚܐ. ܗܠܝܢ ܓܝܪ ܘܕܝܢ ܘܠܒܪ ܡܢ ܕܘܟܬܐ ܕܡܢ ܐܠܗܘܬܗ. ܡܛܠ ܓܝܪ ܠܐ ܡܬܚܙܐ: ܕܕܡܫܝܚܐ ܗܘ ܕܒܪܢܫܐ ܒܓܘܫܡܐ: ܕܡܫܝܚܐ ܕܝܢ ܐܦ ܠܟܝܢܗ ܕܐܠܗܘܬܐ. ܐܠܐ ܟܕ ܗܘܐ ܠܢ ܡܛܠ ܦܓܪܐ ܘܢܦܫ ܘܢܫܡܬܐ ܒܟܝܢܗ: ܘܐܝܟ ܕܘܟܬܐ ܘܓܘܫܡܐ ܟܝܢܐ ܕܐܣܝܩܘ ܐܘ ܕܒܢ̈ܝܐ ܫܡܫ: ܐܝܟ ܡܐ ܕܟܠܗ ܟܠܐܘܪ ܕܒܪܢܫܐ ܕܐܒܘܗܝ. ܠܡܬܚܙܝܘ ܗܘ ܘܦܢܝܘܬ ܘܠܐ ܗܘܝܐ. ܗܘ ܕܡܢ ܗܠܝܢ ܕܡܬܚܙܝܢ ܒܐܘܣܝܐ ܢܐܡܪ ܕܡܬܒܪܝܐ ܐܘܣܬܐ.

ܕܐܦ ܠܒܪܢܫܐ ܕܝܢ ܘܢܦܫܐ ܕܦܓܪܢܝܘܬܐ ܕܠܒܪ: ܟܠܗ ܗܘܐ ܕܡܫܝܚܐ ܫܡܝܐ: ܘܠܐ ܡܢܝܢ ܡܬܒܥܝܢ ܠܗ: ܐܦ ܡܢ ܗܠܝܢ ܕܡܬܐܡܪܢ ܡܛܠ ܐܢܬ: ܘܦܪܘܫ ܢܬܚܙܐܬ. ܣܒܪܝܢ ܓܝܪ ܕܟܠܗ ܗܠܝܢ: ܕܡܛܠܬܐ ܕܢܫܐ ܐܠܗܘܬܐ ܐܡܪܝܢ ܕܐܠܗܘܬܗ: ܗܘ ܕܐܬܟܢܝ ܗܘ ܕܐܠܗܐ. ܗܘ ܕܐܬܒܢܝ. ܕܡܫܝܚܐ ܕܝܢ ܕܦܓܪܐ ܐܢܫܐ: ܗܘ ܕܗܘܝܐ ܠܡܘܕܥ ܒܐܘܪ̈ܚܐ: ܐܡܝܢܐ ܕܢܦܫܗ ܠܡܫܬܘܕܥܘܬܐ ܕܢܫܡܐ ܡܫܬܠܡܢܐ. ܘܐܝܟ ܕܡܫܝܚܐ ܒܡܫܝܚܘܬܗ ܐܡܪ: ܗܘ ܕܐܘܪܚܐ ܠܡܒܪܐ: ܘܡܛܪ ܡܢ ܫܢܘܬܐ ܐܣܛܘܟܣܐ ܡܬܟܡܠܐ ܢܗܘܐ ܐܝܬ ܠܗ ܫܘܪܐ ܟܠܗ ܫܡܝܐ. ܐܡܝܢܐ (137) ܓܝܪ ܕܗܘ ܕܡܬܢܣܒ ܒܐܘܣܝܘܬܐ ܘܡܪܢܘܬܐ: ܠܗ ܐܫܪܝܬܗ ܡܬܦܫܛ ܒܐܘܪܐ ܕܫܡܝܐ: ܕܗܘ ܕܒܠܥܒ ܕܢܦܩܠ ܢܫܡܐ ܘܫܡܝܐ ܕܐܝܟ ܗܘܝܐ: ܐܘ ܕܡܬܩܘܣܬܐ ܘܡܦܢ ܡܬܚܣܢܐ: ܐܠܐ ܗܘܝܐ ܐܡܝܢܐ ܕܒܗܘܝܘܬܗ ܢܗܘܐ ܐܝܬ ܠܗ ܟܠܗ ܫܡܝܐ ܗܘ ܕܡܬܢܫܝܐ: ܐܡܝܢܐ ܘܠܐ ܢܗܘܐ ܒܠܥܒ ܕܡܫܝܚܐ ܐܘܪ̈ܚܬܗ: ܗܘ ܕܒܠܥܒ ܕܢܫܡܐ ܠܪܘܚܐ ܕܗܘ ܕܦܢܐ. ܒܗ ܒܪܝܐ ܐܦ ܒܒܘܪܐ ܠܓܘܫܡܐ ܐܝܬܝܐ ܓܒܠܐ: ܐܡܝܢܐ ܕܕܒܝܩ ܘܒܗ ܢܗܘܐ ܐܠܗܘܗ ܠܒܝܬ ܡܫܪܝܐ ܘܕܘܪܐ ܕܢܫܡܐ ܡܫܬܠܡܢܐ. ܐܡܝܢܐ ܕܠܗ ܒܘܣܡܐ ܐܝܬܐ ܕܓܘ ܢܗܘܐ ܐܝܬ ܠܗ: ܟܠܗ ܓܘܫܡܐ ܕܫܘܬܐ ܐܣܛܘܟܣܐ: ܐܝܟܢ ܕܠܗ ܠܒܫܩܬܐ ܫ̈ܠܡܬܐ ܡܫܡܫܝܢ. ܐܦܐ ܗܟܢ ܡܛܠ ܕܕܡܫܝܚܐ ܕܢܫܡܐ ܦܝ ܐܝܬܝܬܐ: ܗܘ ܕܐܬܟܢ ܘܗܘ ܕܐܬܒܢܝ ܐܠܗܘܬܗ: ܘܗܘ ܕܐܬܒܢܝ: ܕܓܘܫܡܐ ܕܝܢ ܐܝܬܝܐ ܗܘ ܕܗܘܝܐ ܠܡܓܒܠ: ܢܐܡܪ ܕܡܢ ܗܘ ܕܐܬܟܢ ܘܠܐܬܒܢܝ: ܡܢ ܓܒܝܠܘܬܐ ܕܕܐܝܟ ܗܘܝܐ ܕܓܘܫܡܐ ܡܪܟܒ ܒܪܢܫܐ: ܐܠܐ

"Therefore along with the principles of the incarnation, there enter as well those things which because of it, according to the economy, came upon him who endured voluntary emptying, for example, to be hungry and to be weary. For just as he could not be weary, seeing he is all-powerful, and it could not be said that he was hungry, (seeing) he is the nourishment and life of all, unless he made his own a body which would naturally hunger and be weary, so too he could not be counted among sinners; for thus we say he became sin. And he would not have become a curse, when he underwent the cross for our sake, unless he had become flesh, that is, was incarnate and inhominate."[145] (*Lebon p. 140*)

But while these things are explained by us in this way as we understand (them), it is also necessary that I should add this, lest someone should run to the types of the law, and thence should fail because of ignorance and besmear the hypostatic union with an inadequate meaning. For our Lord is prefigured there in many ways, now as in a golden ark, now as in manna kept in a pot, now as in the composition of incense, now as in fine linen and jacinth, and in things like this, (and) in garments from there, and in sacrifices of calves and of rams, and of meal and in confections. For these things were foresigns of the shadows of the legal scripture, which were making partial and obscure suggestions of the truth and were quite deficient and inferior in exactness.

Holy Cyril also wrote in this way about the "averter of evil" in the Letter to Acacius: (CYRIL): "But (examples) are inferior to what is true, and sometimes (only) give partial illustrations of the things which are signified. But we say the law was a shadow and a type, and (is like) a picture which is placed as an illustration for those looking at the realities. But shadows are the first delineations of the skill of those who paint on boards."[146] But he taught these things in the Second Volume against the blasphemies of Nestorius, and rebuking the madness of that man, he says:[147] (CYRIL): "Tell me again: how do you describe inseparable conjunction? As union—namely, of course, the hypostatic (union) which we teach, struggling on behalf of the doctrines of truth,—or (as) that (conjunction) which is estimated in terms of juxtaposition,[148] and which is (*Lebon p. 141*) understood as being the proximity of something to something else? For the scripture inspired by God thus accepts the expression, and says to the consecrated Moses as he composed the description of the former tabernacle: 'And you shall make fifty rings of gold, and you shall fasten the curtains[149] one with another with the rings'.[150] For there were five of them and each one of them has something special

ܡܠܓܡܝܢ ܘܦܠܓܝܢ ܙܘܓܐܝܬ: ܟܕ ܙܘܓ ܕܡܢ ܐ̈ܢܫܝܢ ܐܘ ܡܢ ܟܝ̈ܢܐ ܢܐܡܪ
ܘܡܪ̈ܟܒܐ ܚܘܝܐ ܡܪܟܒܬܐ: ܘܐܡܪܝܢ ܡܢ ܕܬ̈ܟܝܠܬܐ ܕܡܟܝܢ ܒܗܘܢ ܠܪ̈ܘܟܒܐ. ܘܟܠܗ
ܦܡ ܒܪܢܫܐ ܕܐܟܘܬܗ ܗܠܝܢ.
ܘܟܕ ܕܝܢ ܕܟܠܐ ܚܝܐ ܠܐܠܗܐ: ܐܦ ܠܐ ܐܝܬ ܕܢܐܡܪ ܡܪܟܒܬܐ ܕܡܟܝܠܬܐ. ܡܛܠ ܕܐܦܠܐ
ܡܫܟܚܐ ܕܗܠܝܢ ܐܠܗܘܬܗ ܠܐܠܗܐ. ܐܠܐ ܥܠܬܐ ܟܠܗܘ ܩܕܝܡ ܡܢ ܗܠܝܢ ܕܐܡܪ
ܗܘܝܢ ܡܬܐܡܪܝܢ ܕܢܐܡܪ. ܡܛܠ ܗܢܐ ܘܐܘܪܝܓܢܣ ܟܕ ܟܠܗ ܗܠܝܢ ܦܠܓ
ܐܡܠܦܢ: ܗܘܐ ܐܡܪ ܟܕ ܡܢ ܡܠܘܗܝ ܕܝܠܗ. ܘܐܘܪܝܓܢܣ܀ ܐܢ ܟܠ ܡܨܐܐ ܐܘ
ܟܢܫܐ ܐܝܬ ܕܡܬܡܛܝܢ: ܐܘ ܐܘܪܚܐ ܐܘ ܡܫܟܢܐ: ܐܘ ܕܡܟܬܐ: ܐܘ ܟܘܪܝܐ: ܐܘ
ܗܘ ܕܡܢ ܗܠܝܢ ܡܪ̈ܟܒܢ: ܟܠܗ ܕܝܢ ܕܩܕܝܡ ܡܢ ܗܠܝܢ ܕܐܬܐܡܪ (138) ܢܫܟܚ
ܟܠܐ ܠܐܠܗܘܬܐ ܦܫܝܛܬܐ: ܟܠܗܐ ܢܬܠܟܕ ܗܘ ܕܠܐ ܡܬܐܡܪ܀ ܘܙܘܓܐܝܬ ܗܠܝܢ
ܐܡܪ: ܡܛܠ ܕܐܦ ܟܠܗܠ ܡܢ ܐܘܣܝܐ ܐܘ ܟܝܢܐ ܡܫܬܠܡܠ ܠܐܠܗܐ. ܗܟܢܐ ܓܝܪ
ܘܟܬܒܐ ܕܙܡܝܢ ܟܠ ܓܘܫܡܐ ܟܠܗ ܗܠܝܢ ܕܡܢ ܡܕܡ: ܒܪܢܝܓܘܣ ܡܫܡܠܠ
ܠܬ̈ܠܬܐ ܐܡܪ. ܒܪܢܝܓܘܣ܀ ܠܘܩܝ ܦܘܣܩܐ ܩ̈ܕܡܝܐ ܚܕܐ ܐܝܬ ܒܗܠܝܢ
ܘܐܬܠܝܗܝ. ܡܪܟܒܬܐ ܘܟܘܢܬܐ. ܠܗ ܗܠܝܢ ܕܟܠܗܝ: ܕܐܘ ܠܪܘܟܒܬܐ ܦܫܝܛܬܐ: ܐܘ
ܡܫܟܚܢܘܬܐ ܦܫܝܛܬܐ. ܐܠܐ ܗܠܝܢ ܕܟܝܢܐ ܠܐܝܢ. ܐܢ ܠܐܝܬ ܡܫܟܚܐ ܕܗܘܐ ܢܗܘܐ. ܗܘ
ܓܝܪ ܦܫܝܛܐ ܐܦ ܟܠܗܠ ܡܢ ܟܝܢܐ܀ ܗܘܐ ܐܦ ܦܫܝܛܐ ܡܬܪܟܒܢ: ܟܠܗܠ ܦܫܝܛܐ
ܘܦܘܫܩܐ ܘܐܘܪܝܓܢܣ ܕܗܘܝܢ ܐܡܪ ܗܟܢܐ. ܡܬܪܟܒܢ܀ ܢܗܘܐ ܕܝܢ ܠܐܘܟ: ܘܟܠܗܠ
ܡܢ ܗܘܐ ܠܐܠܗܐ. ܟܢܘ ܕܐܦ ܟܠܗܠ ܡܢ ܐܘܣܝܐ ܐܠܗܘܬܗ. ܘܗܘ ܙܘܓܐ ܙܘܓܐܝܬ
ܟܠܗ ܠܗ ܒܟܝܢܐ. ܐܟܢܐ ܕܐܦ ܪܘܚܐ ܩܕܝܡ ܠܡܫܟ ܕܐܠܗܘܬܐ ܦܫܝܛܬܐ:
ܕܟܠܗ ܠܗ ܩܕܝܡ ܕܡܫܟܚ ܠܟܝܢܘܬܐ ܕܦ̈ܠܓܘܬܐ܀ ܐܦ ܠܐ ܓܝܪ ܕܡܢܐ ܐܠܗܘܬܗ
ܗܘ ܠܐܠܗܐ ܠܐܘܣܝܐ ܐܘ ܟܝܢܐ ܦܫܝܛ.
ܡܢ ܗܪܟܐ ܐܦ ܟܠܗ ܡܫܟܠܠܐ ܠܐܠܗܘܬܐ ܘܟܠܗ ܡܦܪܫܢܘܬܐ ܕܡܬܦܪܫܢܘܬܐ ܕܚܝܘܬܐ
ܡܬܠܐ ܠܐܠܗܐ: ܠܗ ܒܟܠܠ ܡܬܝܠܕܬܐ ܡܬܚܫܚܢ. ܟܠܗ ܕܝܢ ܡܫܟܚܢܘܬܐ ܕܦܫܝܛܘܬܐ
ܕܟܠܗܝܢ: ܒܟܕܝܡ ܚܕ ܠܐܩܢܘܡܐ ܕܗܠܝܢ ܕܡܬܡܠܝܢ. ܡܛܠ ܗܢܐ ܘܐܡܪܬ ܕܒܟܕܝܡ
ܩܠܐ ܡܛܠ ܡܬܦܪܫܢܘܬܐ ܐܡܪܢܢ ܚܕ: ܕܡܬܠܬܐ ܕܐܦܫܐ ܐܠܗܘܬܐ ܗܘ ܕܐܟܒܝ: ܐܘ
ܕܠܙܘܓܐ: ܐܘ ܕܠܐܐ: ܘܠܗ ܡܬܝܠܕ ܗܘܐ ܐܡܪܝܢ: ܠܗ ܓܝܪ ܕܡܬܠܬܐ ܗܘ ܕܒܪܢܫܐ
ܟܠܗܘ ܗܘܐ: ܐܠܐ ܘܗܠܝܢ ܡܬܘܬܐ ܐܬܬܝܢܬܐ: ܕܡܟܝܢ ܕܢܩܘܡ ܐܐܙ ܘܚܝ̈ܐ ܡܬܩܪܝܢܐ
ܚܝ̈ܐ ܘܡܬܬܪܚܡ. ܡܛܠ ܕܕܡܬܐ ܗܘ ܕܡܬܐܡܪܐ (139) ܡܪܟܒܬܐ: ܗܘ

of its own, so that it would be different, apart from the others, (and) it was fastened with rings. But we do not say that there was a union like this in the case of Christ. For it is not the case that, just as one thing cleaves to another, or as in the manner of mental agreement, or in the way of proximity of bodies, so also he is (joined). For, as I have said many times already, the Word from God made his own the body taken up from the holy Virgin, and we assert that he was in truth (thus) united, and not to flesh that has no soul."[151]

But because I have heard that some men have read the letter which I sent to you earlier, who, from ignorance and a presumptuous lack of culture, do not much agree with the words of holy Cyril, may they know that they have set themselves outside the holy conflicts which (are waged) against the council which was at Chalcedon. For Dioscorus, a witness of Christ, who alone did not bend the knee to Baal at (that) assembly of vanity, wrote thus to Domnus who formerly presided (over the church) in Antioch, about those who presumed to compose evil treatises against certain compositions of wise Cyril: DIOSCORUS: "They are therefore composing writings for which they should be blamed, which do not agree with, but are opposed to the holy scriptures, and to the (writings) of our blessed brother the Bishop Cyril, who is praised in everything. For this in truth demonstrates that they are blameworthy (*Lebon p. 142*) and are not in agreement with the holy treatises. For our wise and prosperous Father was an ecumenical Doctor, and he, if anyone, wrote correctly and without blame. For he was not only a skilled workman with words, for nature gave him this glory along with the others, as it were from the cradle, but also, as he was enriched with a gift from above, he made known as much as he was able the mystery of the inhomination of the only-begotten Son of God. And there is no-one of his writings which does not exceed all admiration, whether you mention a book, or a letter, or a commentary made off the cuff, or a public homily, or the chapters or anathemas: all are proven and accurate, and have a beautifully polished sense, and agree with the divine words, so that aptly we may say about them, 'Who is wise, that he knows these things? And intelligent, that he understands these things? For the ways of the Lord are straight, and the righteous walk in them, but the wicked will lose strength in them.'"[152]

Therefore, how are they not condemned to shame, those who boast that they are zealous in opposition to the Council of Chalcedon, but because of inexperience[153] are not able to put on the armour[153] of the (battle-) rank, which is the teaching of holy Cyril? But you chaste brother, remain in this (armour),[154] and lay low the

ܕܠܥܒܕܝܢ ܒܠܚܘܕܘܗܝ ܐܝܬ: ܘܠܝܬ ܠܗ ܫܘܬܦܘܬܐ ܥܡ ܐܚܪܢܐ. ܐܠܐ ܡܛܠ ܕܗܠܝܢ ܠܗ ܕܬܚܠܬܐ ܕܐܠܗܐ ܘܠܐ ܠܫܡ ܐܠܗܘܬ: ܗܘ ܕܒܟܠ ܥܒܕܐ ܐܘ ܕܠܐ: ܡܛܠ ܗܝ: ܠܡܫܝܚܐ ܕܠܥܠܡ ܐܡܪܝܢ ܕܬܚܠܬܐ ܕܐܝܬܘܬܐ ܠܗܠܝܢ. ܐܠܐ ܐܦ ܒܚܝܠܐ ܕܬܚܠܬܐ ܘܡܢܗ ܐܠܗܝܢ: ܐܦ ܕܡܚܠܬܐ ܕܐܠܗܐ ܡܛܠ ܡܕܒܪܢܘܬܐ: ܕܬܚܠܬܐ ܐܠܗܝܢ. ܘܗܘ ܡܬܐܡܪ ܕܟܠ ܘܕܝܢܗܘܢ ܘܠܐܘ ܡܢ ܐܘܪܚܐ: ܡܛܠ ܕܡܫܬܡܠܝܐ ܡܢܝܢ ܗܘܐ ܠܫܘܡܠܝܐ ܕܡܢ ܕܗܠܝܢ ܚܢܢ. ܘܗܘ ܕܡܫܬܠܛ ܠܗܘܢ: ܘܗܠܝܢ ܡܫܬܠܛ ܡܢܗ ܘܡܢܗ ܠܐܝܬܘܬܐ: ܘܡܬܒܪܝܐ ܠܗܘܢ ܡܢ ܡܣܝܒܐ ܐܠܗܐ: ܟܕ ܠܐ ܡܕܡ ܢܚܣܪ ܒܡܠܟܘܬܐ ܘܠܐ ܫܘܫܘܬܐ ܕܡܠܗ: ܚܪܐ ܡܕܒܪܢܘܬܐ: ܘܡܬܒܪܝܐ ܠܗܘܢ ܘܐܠܗܘܬܗ ܒܕܡܘܬܐ ܕܐܠܗܐ: ܘܠܗ ܫܘܠܛܢܐ ܚܝܒ ܠܗܘܢ ܕܗܘܐ ܐܠܗܘܬܗ ܓܒܐ ܠܐܠܗܐ: ܡܢ ܡܦܘܩܐ ܕܚܝܠܐ ܘܡܫܘܚܬܐ ܪܫܝܡ ܐܝܟܐ. ܗܘ ܕܡܫܬܠܛ ܡܢܗ ܕܒܗܘܢ ܠܗ. ܒܗܘܐ ܡܫܝܚ ܒܟܘܠ ܡܫܘܠܡܘܗܝ: ܕܒܡܬܐܡܪܐ ܕܡܬܐܠܐ ܘܦܘܩ ܦܠܓܘܬܐ ܕܝܢ ܗܘ ܡܫܝܚܐ ܗܟܢ ܐܡܪ. ܀ܡܫܘܠܡܘܗܝ ܥܠܝܢ ܗܟܝܠ ܡܢ ܩܠܐ ܕܡܬܟܪܙܢܘܬܐ: ܐܦ ܗܠܝܢ ܕܡܫܬܠܛܢܘ ܡܕܒܪܢܘܬܐ ܐܠܗܝܐ. ܠܗܘ ܕܡܫܪ ܫܘܪܝܐ ܕܚܝܠܐ. ܐܡܪܐ ܕܗܘ ܕܒܟܠ ܘܗܘ ܕܠܐ. ܐܝܟ ܡܐ ܕܝܢ ܘܠܐ ܠܐ ܗܘܐ: ܟܕ ܗܘ ܐܠܗܘܬܗ ܡܠܟܗ ܚܝܠܐ: ܘܠܐ ܡܬܐܡܪ ܗܘܐ ܕܒܟܠ: ܘܐܘܪܚܐ ܘܡܢܐ ܕܟܠ ܗܘ ܐܠܗܘܬܗ: ܐܠܐ ܠܐ ܕܡܠܗ ܒܒܪܗ ܠܫܘܡܠܝܐ ܗܘ ܕܡܢ ܕܒܟܠ ܘܕܠܐ: ܗܟܝܠ ܘܠܐ ܡܢ ܒܬܠܐ ܒܪܘܚ ܡܬܬܝܗܒ ܗܘܐ. ܗܟܝܠ ܟܢ ܐܡܪܝܢ ܠܗ ܕܗܘܐ ܡܫܝܚܐ. ܘܠܐ ܗܘܐ ܗܘܐ ܒܠܚܘܕܐ: ܟܕ ܙܟܝܐ ܫܟܠ ܗܘ ܕܡܫܬܠܛ: ܐܠܐ ܠܐ ܕܗܘܐ ܒܫܪܐ: ܗܘ ܕܝܢ ܐܬܒܪ ܘܐܬܟܪܙ܀ (140) ܟܕ ܗܟܝܠ ܕܝܢ ܗܟܢܐ ܐܝܟ ܕܐܘܪܚܝܢ ܡܫܬܡܠܝܢ ܠܢ: ܘܐܦ ܗܘ ܐܘܪܚ ܘܡܢ ܗܟܝܠ ܕܐܝܟ ܐܠܗܘܬܗ. ܐܝܟܢܐ ܕܠܐ ܐܢܫ ܒܗܠܝܢ ܠܦܘܩܕܢܐ ܢܦܘܩ: ܘܡܢ ܠܘܩܒܠ ܡܢ ܠܐ ܡܬܟܬܒܐ ܚܙܐ: ܘܠܘܬܗ ܘܠܐ ܡܛܠ ܕܡܬܐ ܡܘܗܒܬܐ ܢܗܘܐ. ܡܛܠ ܗܘ ܕܡܢܝ ܒܪܢܫܐ ܕܫܬܐ ܠܐܡܢ ܡܫܒܚ ܡܬܐܡܪ. ܒܟܠ ܗܢ ܐܝܟ ܕܒܫܘܒܚܐ ܘܡܕܡܘܬܐ. ܒܟܠ ܕܝܢ. ܐܝܟ ܕܒܚܝܠܐ ܘܐܝܟ ܒܫܘܠܛܢܐ. ܒܟܠ ܕܝܢ. ܐܝܟ ܕܒܪܘܚܐ ܕܒܢܝܢܐ. ܒܟܠ ܕܝܢ. ܐܝܟ ܕܒܥܘܕܪܢܐ ܘܡܫܝܚܐ: ܘܒܗܠܝܢ ܕܕܝܢ ܠܗܘܢ: ܒܚܝܠܐ ܕܡܢ ܗܘܢܐ: ܘܒܕܝܢܐ ܕܐܘܪܚܐ ܘܕܪ̈ܫܐ ܘܫܘܒܚܐ. ܘܒܡܠܟܘܬܐ. ܗܟܢ ܗܟܢ ܕܘܟܝܐ ܡܕܝܢܐ ܕܡܠܟܘܬܐ ܘܡܠܟܐ ܢܦܫܢܐ ܐܠܗܝܢ ܗܠܝܢ. ܕܫܘܒܚܐ ܩܕܝܫܐ ܘܡܫܘܡܠܝܐ ܕܚܙܐ ܟܠܗܝܢ ܗܠܝܢ. ܘܡܢ ܡܫܬܠܛܢܘܬܐ: ܦܪܘܩ ܡܫܝܚܝ̈ ܗܠܝܢ ܘܒܢܝ̈ܢ.

enemy, and the Lord will fight on your behalf,[155] for the battle belongs to the Lord. And may no-one venture to revile the ranks of the living God,[156] as someone who proceeds outside the laws of the battle ranks, and turns aside to the right or to the left, while seeing him guarding himself from all sides against the arrows of the enemy.[157]

But it is good that your Holy Wisdom should know that for a long time we have been praying that you may receive the rewards of your toils, both in this (*Lebon p. 143*) world, and in that to come. And it is not our custom in a fleshly way to fawn upon those about whom we pray, but we honour the ordinance of the gospel and the example which our Lord handed down, saying to his disciples, "Truly I tell you, there is no-one who forsaking houses or brothers or sisters or father or mother or wife or sons or fields for my sake and for the sake of the gospel will not receive an hundred times now at this time houses and brothers and sisters and mothers and sons and fields with persecution, and in the world to come, everlasting life".[158] We in no way say that when our Lord said these things, he promised in a fleshly way, or otherwise provocatively, or led the disciples to the point where they would crave these things and be scornful of what is good in truth and is never given up, but as he said in another place, "Seek the kingdom of God and his righteousness, and all these things will be added to you",[159] in the same way here, wanting to confirm the importance of the promises, he says, as a way of addition, that these things are given an hundred times in the present time.

But I rejoice along with you at your fuller understanding, and that you have wholly come to belong to the future hope. And I say, exulting at the same time, what was said by God to those of the Israelites who said to Moses, "Everything which the Lord God has said to you, we shall obey and do",[160] (namely), "I have heard the words of this people, everything which they have said to you. They have said rightly all (that they have spoken). Who will grant that they will have a heart like this, so that they will fear me, and keep my commandments all their days, so that it will go well for them?" Come then in the same opinion, and apply yourself to progress, (*Lebon p. 144*) "forgetting what is behind, and reaching out to what is ahead".[161] And leap clear from that foolish doctrine, which brings to one ousia the (elements) from which there is without confusion the one Lord and God and our Saviour Jesus Christ; and tell it you have recovered, and especially so, if you are about to "write to Macedonia"[162] about the faith. For when you said that you confess at the same time particularity, and difference as regards natural

ܗܘ ܕܐܦ ܩܕܝܫܐ ܦܘܠܘܣ ܟܬܒ ܠܥܒܪ̈ܝܐ ܕܟܠܗ ܐܡܪ ܕܡܛܠ ܡܫܬܘܕܝܢܐ ܗܘܝܬ ܐܢܐ. ܀ܦܘܠܘܣ܀ ܩܪܝܒܝܢ ܕܝܢ ܡܢ ܗܠܝܢ ܕܚܙܐ ܘܐܬܩܝܡܬ ܩܢܘܡܐܝܬ. ܐܝܟ ܐܡܬܗ ܕܒܢ̈ܝ ܗܠܝܢ ܕܩܠܝܠܝܢ: ܐܡܪܝܢ ܕܝܢ: ܕܠܚܘܒܐ ܘܦܘܩܕܢܐ ܐܝܬܘܗܝ ܗܘܐ ܢܡܘܣܐ ܘܐܦ ܙܕܩܐ ܡܕܡ ܕܫܡܥܐ ܟܠܗ ܚܘܐ ܠܗܠܝܢ ܕܚܪܝܢ ܠܡܫܬܥܒܕܢܘܬܐ. ܠܚܝܠܬܐ ܕܝܢ ܘܐܘܡܢܘܬܐ ܕܗܠܝܢ ܕܪܚܡ ܠܡܫܬܒܚܘ: ܗܠܝܢ ܡܕܝ̈ܢܬܐ ܕܬܘܩܢܐ ܐܝܬܝܗܝܢ܀ ܘܡܬܦܣܩܐ ܕܝܢ ܕܐܬܘܢ ܕܠܘܩܒܠ ܢܩܘܦܐ ܕܢܬܦܢܘܢ ܡܢܗ ܗܠܝܢ. ܘܟܕ ܡܛܘܠ ܠܚܣܝܘܬܐ ܕܗܘ ܐܡܪ. ܀ܦܘܠܘܣ܀ ܐܡܪ ܠܢ ܕܝܢ ܠܘܬ. ܡܢܐ ܕܝܢ ܐܦ ܢܡܘܣܐ ܠܐ ܡܬܦܠܚܢܘܬܐ ܐܡܪ ܐܝܟ. ܐܘܐ ܠܡܫܝܚܘܬܐ: ܐܝܟܢܐ ܕܝܢ ܕܗܘ ܡܘܡܣܬܐ ܗܘ ܕܚܝ ܡܬܦܫܝܢ: ܟܕ ܡܬܬܡܫܝܢ ܚܠܦ ܢܩܦܬܐ ܕܚܙܐ. ܐܘ ܗܘܐ ܗܘ ܕܒܫܡܝܐ ܡܬܦܫܩܐ: ܘܗܘ ܕܟܠܗ ܡܕܡ (141) ܕܢܡܘܣܐ ܕܦܠܚ ܡܬܓܪܐ. ܡܫܡܠܝ ܓܝܪ ܗܘܝܐ ܠܡܫܡܠܝܘܬܐ ܡܠܬܐ ܢܫܝܢ ܡܢ ܠܥܠ. ܘܐܡܪ ܕܝܢ ܟܠܗ ܡܕܡܐ ܗܘ ܕܢܘܚܐ: ܟܕ ܡܢܗܪ ܩܠܐ ܡܛܠ ܡܫܡܥܐ. ܗܘ ܩܕܡܐ. ܘܐܝܟܢ ܡܘܪܐ ܡܫܡܫ ܕܕܘܟܐ. ܘܐܦ ܠܡܢܗܪܢܘܬܐ ܐܚܪܢܐ ܟܠܗ ܐܚܪܢܐ ܠܡܘܪܐ. ܡܫܡܫ ܓܝܪ ܐܝܬܝܗܝܢ ܗܘܝ. ܘܦܘܠܘܣ ܚܕܐ ܡܫܡܥ ܟܠܗ ܗܘ ܕܐܦ ܐܬܪܐ ܐܚܪܢܐ ܡܕܡ ܕܡܫܬܐܠ ܐܝܟ ܠܗ. ܡܛܪ ܡܢ ܗܠܝܢ ܐܚܪ̈ܢܝܬܐ: ܢܡܘܣܐ ܗܘܐ ܠܡܘܪܐ. ܚܝܢ ܕܝܢ ܠܗ ܗܘܝܐ ܐܡܪܝܢ ܕܗܘܐ ܚܝܘܬܐ ܕܟܠܐ ܡܫܝܚܐ. ܠܗ ܓܝܪ ܐܝܟ ܡܠܐ ܕܦܠܚ ܠܦܠܚ ܢܦܩ: ܐܘ ܟܝܢܐ. ܕܡܘܫܐ ܢܡܘܣܐ. ܐܘ ܟܗܘ ܡܢܗܪܘܬܐ ܕܟܘܡܪ̈ܐ: ܗܘܝܐ ܐܦ ܗܘ. ܐܠܐ ܓܝܪ ܐܡܝܢܐ ܕܡܢ ܟܝܘ ܪ̈ܚܡܝܢ ܩܦܝܠ ܐܡܪܬ: ܕܠܗ ܟܕ ܠܦܬܪܐ ܗܘ ܕܐܬܢܣܒ ܡܢ ܟܠܗܘܢܬܐ ܩܕܝܫܬܐ. ܘܒܟܬܒܐ ܐܡܪܝܢ ܚܝܢ ܕܐܬܚܝܒ ܡܫܠܡܐ ܕܡܢ ܠܥܠ: ܠܗ ܠܟܬܒܐ ܠܐ ܡܫܬܡܥܐ܀

ܡܛܠ ܕܝܢ ܕܫܡܥܬ ܕܐܬܩܢ ܡܢܗ ܠܦܬܪܐ ܕܡܢ ܩܕܝܫ ܦܘܠܘܣ ܠܘܬܗ: ܕܠܗ ܦܝܫ ܡܠܦܝܢ ܠܟܢ̈ܫܐ ܩܠܐ ܕܩܕܝܫܐ ܦܘܠܘܣ: ܡܢ ܠܐ ܡܬܦܫܩܐ ܘܠܐ ܙܕܩܘܬܐ ܡܢܗܪܢܘܬܐ: ܢܒܥܘܢ ܕܠܟܪ ܡܢ ܬܘܪ̈ܨܐ ܩܕܝܫܐ ܗܠܝܢ ܕܠܘܩܒܠ ܦܘܩܕܢܘܗܝ ܕܒܗܘܢ ܒܒܠܥܕܘܬܐ ܐܝܟ ܢܦܫܗܘܢ. ܕܡܦܪܫܝܢ ܓܝܪ ܦܘܪܫܢܐ ܕܫܡܥܐ: ܗܘ ܒܠܚܘܕܘܗܝ ܠܐ ܡܢ ܒܘܪܟܐ ܠܟܠܠ ܒܢܘܫܐ ܕܡܬܩܪܐ: ܗܘܝܐ ܟܕ ܟܠܗ ܕܢܘܚܘܢ ܗܘ ܕܒܟܠ ܒܪܝܐ ܟܕ ܒܐܝܕܘܬܐ: ܡܛܠ ܗܢܘܢ ܕܐܡܪܝܢ ܕܫܡܥܘܢ ܡܠܦܢ̈ܐ ܒܩܠܐ ܟܠ ܡܫܟܢܐ ܡܕܡ ܕܢܡܘܣܐ ܦܘܠܘܣ. ܀ܕܫܡܥܘܢܘܣ܀ ܟܕ ܓܝܪ ܘܡܠܟ̈ܘܬܐ ܕܪ̈ܚܡܬܐ ܫܡܥܝܢ ܘܠܐ ܩܠܝܢ: ܘܫܡܥܘܢܬܐ ܐܝܟ ܠܗܘܢ ܠܡܠܟ̈ܐ ܩܕܝܫܐ. ܘܠܗܘܢ ܕܢܘܚܐ ܘܡܫܡܠܐ ܒܟܠܗܘܢ ܐܦܝܣܩܘܦܐ ܦܘܠܘܣ: ܗܘܐ

quality, and not that which individually and in every way distinguishes the natures from which there is the one and undivided Christ, and you also proceeded to confuse everything into one ousia and quality and particularity, both I am found extracting from your confession, as scripture says, a sheaf inadequate to make flour,[163] and you (are found) collecting your wages in a purse full of holes,[164] of which the prophet Hosea teaches[165] the former, and Haggai the latter.

But these things were added only jokingly because of love, lest the message have an undiluted[166] astringent, but that it should be gently mixed with pleasure and some sweetness. For we would be thought to do wrong, if we removed you, even by this, from the mixture. But the apostolic word bids and commands saying: "All the time let your talk in grace be seasoned with salt".[167] But may it apply to us, as we share in the apostolic salt, and since we adhere to their doctrine, let us scorn these superfluous things of debate. But let us ratify (our) reasonings with faith, so that thus we may acquire wisdom from there. For the prophetic word says, "Unless we believe, we shall not understand".[168]

The Second Letter of the Patriarch Severus to Sergius the Grammarian is ended.

Notes

1. Prov. xxii.28.
2. Prov. xxvii.17.
3. PG 76.85A–B. Also cf. above, p. 77.23–26, and p. 99.12–13 (= Pusey edn. Vol. 6, p. 113.11–14).
4. Prov. xxii.17–19.
5. PG 76.85B (= Pusey edn. Vol. 6, p. 113.14). *Adv. Nest. Lib. II.*
6. PG 76.85B (= Pusey edn. Vol. 6, p. 113.14–16).
7. Heb. ii.14.
8. i.e. concepts of mixture and juxtaposition.
9. [illegible] cf. Syriac text p. 99, line 22, above.
10. [illegible].
11. [illegible].
12. [illegible].
13. PG 75.1376C–1377A (= Pusey edn. Vol. 6, p. 510.8–512.6).
14. [illegible].
15 [illegible].
16. cf. p. 100 above.
17. [illegible] = ὁμοούσια. (Harvard syr. 22 = [illegible]).
18. PG 77.241B–C (= ACO I, 1, 6a, p. 160.2–13).
19. PG 75.1285C (= Pusey edn. Vol. 7, p. 360.9–12).

ܓܝܪ ܒܡܪܕܐ ܕܒܢܝ̈ܢ (142) ܡܫܘܚܐ ܠܗܘܢ: ܘܠܐ ܩܠܝܠ ܠܡܐܡܪ̈ܬܐ ܡܕܝ̈ܢܝܐ. ܗܕܐ ܓܝܪ ܡܠܟܐ ܠܐܚܝܕܐ ܚܟܝܡܐ ܘܡܬܪܓܫܢܐ ܐܒܘܗܝ. ܐܠܘ ܕܝܢ ܐܢ ܗܘ ܕܐܝܟ ܐܚܪܝܢ ܠܬܘܪܝܬܗ ܘܠܐ ܒܒܠܝܘܬܗ: ܠܗ ܒܠܚܘܕ ܕܟܠܗ ܙܒܢܐ ܐܬܠܘܗܝ ܗܘܐ ܕܩܠܐ: ܐܦ ܗܢܐ ܓܝܪ ܡܘܟܟܐ ܒܗ ܗܢܘ ܐܝܬܝܗ̇: ܐܝܟ ܗܘ ܕܡܢ ܒܪܘܪܐ ܚܝܐ ܐܘܪܚܐ ܒܗ: ܐܠܐ ܘܕܒܝܩ ܒܡܘܟܟܬܐ ܕܡܢ ܟܠܟܠ ܒܥܙ ܓܠܐ ܐܝܟ ܕܡܡܟܢܐ ܠܡܙܐܠܗ: ܙܪܐ ܕܡܬܒܪܝܢܘܬܐ ܘܡܣܒܪܐ ܒܪܗ ܕܐܠܗܐ. ܘܟܠܗ ܡܕܡ ܡܢ ܗܠܝܢ ܕܗܘ: ܗܘ ܕܠܐ ܐܬܐ ܠܒܗܠܠ ܡܢ ܟܠ ܠܕܡܘܪܬܐ. ܐܘ ܟܠܒܐ ܠܐܡܪ: ܐܘ ܠܚܙܬܐ: ܐܘ ܦܘܡܐ ܕܡܢ ܗܠܝܢ ܒܟܝܢ. ܐܘ ܠܐܘܪܚܐ ܕܟܘܬܐ. ܐܘ ܩܛܠܐ ܐܘ ܣܬܪܐ. ܟܠܗܘܢ ܐܬܠܗܘܢ ܒܣܬܪ̈ܬܐ ܘܡܬܟܢ̈ܫܬܐ. ܘܗܘܝܐ ܕܡܫܪ ܠܟܦ ܐܝܟ ܠܗܘܢ. ܘܡܠܟܝܢ ܠܩܛܠܐ ܠܐܟܘܠܬܐ. ܐܡܝܢܐ ܕܠܚܡܐ ܕܠܐܡܪ ܡܬܥܒܕܢܘܬܗܘܢ: ܕܡܢܗ ܡܚܡܝܢܐ ܕܢܕܪ ܗܠܝܢ: ܘܡܬܒܩܝܢܐ ܕܢܫܬܘܐܠܘܢ. ܕܠܐܘܝ ܐܘܪܚܬܗ ܕܡܕܝܢܬܐ: ܘܪܘܝܚܐ ܡܬܟܠܝܢ ܒܗܘܢ: ܒܩܠܐ ܕܝܢ ܢܬܡܠܟܘܢ ܒܗܘܢ܀

ܐܡܝܢܐ ܗܟܢܐ ܠܗ ܠܐܡܪܬܐ ܚܘܒܗ: ܗܢܘ ܕܙܕܩܘ ܦܢ ܠܗܘܢܝܐ ܗܘܠܗܘܕܗ ܘܡܢܘܕܥܝܢܐ ܡܬܟܢܘܫܝܢ: ܙܒܢܐ ܕܝܢ ܕܡܕܒܪܐ ܐܟܢ ܕܐܬܠܗܘܢ ܡܩܪܒܢܐ ܘܡܕܝܢܬܐ ܡܘܕܥܘܗ: ܡܬܟܠ ܠܐ ܡܫܡܫܢܘܬܐ ܕܢܬܟܢܫܘܢ ܠܐ ܡܬܚܫܚ. ܐܝܟ ܕܝܢ ܐܝܬ ܕܢܐܡܪ: ܒܗܠܝܢ ܐܠܗܐ: ܘܠܡܬܡܠܟܢܐ ܐܘܪܚܐ. ܘܡܕܝܢܐ ܕܢܥܒܕ ܚܠܦܝܗܘܢ: ܕܡܕܝܢܐ ܗܘ ܡܕܒܪܐ. ܘܠܐ ܢܥܒܕ ܐܝܟ ܠܡܬܚܫܒܘ ܚܕܪܐ ܕܐܠܗܐ ܚܝܐ: ܐܝܟ ܦܢ ܕܠܒܪ ܡܢ ܢܦܫܗܐ ܘܚܕܪܘ ܡܕܝܢܐ ܐܬܐ: ܘܡܫܬܠܛ ܒܚܝܠܐ ܐܘ ܒܡܫܠܐ: ܒܝ ܚܝܐ ܒܗ ܕܡܢ ܟܠ ܕܒܪ ܒܒܥܬܐ ܕܟܘܠܗ̇ ܡܕܒܪ.

ܐܦ ܗܟܢ ܕܝܢ ܕܡܫܪ ܕܐܬܝܗ ܡܬܡܠܟ ܢܦܫܬܐ: ܡܢ ܡܕܡ ܙܒܢܝܢ ܕܢܬܒܥܘܢ ܒܗ ܐܚܪ̈ܐ ܕܩܛܠܐ ܘܒܗܘܢ (143) ܒܒܥܐ ܘܒܗܘ ܕܟܠܗ. ܘܠܗ ܒܡܙܝܢܬܐ ܐܝܟ ܠܝ ܒܚܝܐ ܕܢܚܡܘܢ ܠܐܠܗܝܢ ܕܡܬܟܢܝܢ ܒܗܘܢ. ܐܠܐ ܒܝ ܡܡܠܟܝܢ ܠܡܟܬܒܐ ܐܘܪܚܬܐ: ܘܠܡܦܩܢܐ ܗܘ ܕܡܢܝ ܐܡܠܟ ܒܝ ܐܡܪ ܠܡܠܟܝܢܘܗܝ. ܐܡܝܢ ܐܡܪ ܐܢܐ ܠܟܘܢ: ܕܟܠ ܐܝܟ ܕܡܟܦ ܒܢܬܐ ܐܘ ܐܡܗܬܐ ܐܘ ܐܚ̈ܘܬܐ: ܐܘ ܐܒܐ ܐܘ ܐܡܐ: ܐܘ ܐܢܬܬܐ: ܐܘ ܒܢܝܐ: ܐܘ ܠܒܘܫܐ ܡܬܠܟܠ ܘܡܬܠܐܘܪܚܘܗܝ: ܘܠܐ ܢܦܩ ܒܒܬܐ ܒܢܝܢ ܗܘܐ ܒܒܝܬܐ ܗܘܐ: ܒܢܬܐ ܘܐܡܗܬܐ ܘܐܚܘܬܐ ܘܒܢܝܐ. ܘܠܒܘܫܐ ܒܗ ܙܕܘܩܐ. ܘܒܒܠܝܐ ܕܐܬܐ ܚܝܐ ܕܒܠܒܗ. ܒܝ ܗܠܝܢ ܐܡܪ ܡܪܝ: ܠܐ ܒܕܘܡ ܐܡܪܝܢ ܚܝ ܕܒܡܙܝܢܬܐ ܐܬܠܘܗܝ: ܐܘ ܐܚܪܢܝܬܐ ܡܡܪܚܢܘܬܐ: ܐܘ ܠܡܠܟܝܢܐ ܡܟܠܐ ܗܘܐ ܒܟܠܐ ܗܘ ܕܢܗܘܘܢ

20. PG 75.692D–693A.
21. Note in margin: Where there is ܡܫܘܚܘܬܐ it is ποιότης (in Greek).
22. Lietzmann, *op. cit.*, p. 296.3–15. *Quod unus sit Christus.*
23. H. syr. 22 = ܐܣܟܝܐܝܬ: "in a relational way".
24. PG 76.1449D–1450A. Latin only. The text is preserved in Syriac: cf. Severus, *Philalethes*, CSCO 133 (Syr. 68), p. 140.2–12.
25. PG 76.1450A. Latin only. For the Syriac, cf. *Philalethes*, *op. cit.*, p. 140.14–21.
26. Lk. i.35.
27. The Syriac is ܪܚܡܬ ܡܢ ܐܠܗܘܬܐ. Greek: οὔτε φιλοῦντες θεότητος.
28. PG 76.1200B–C (= Pusey edn. Vol. 7, p. 149.14–150.9).
29. ܐܟܚܕ. Greek: ὡς ἕν.
30. Note in margin: The interpreter put "from two" (ܡܢ ܬܪܝܢ) here in place of συναμφότερον.
31. PG 76.1169C–D. (cf. Pusey edn. Vol. 7, p. 81.12–82.1).
32. ܡܘܣܒܐ.
33. ܚܘܠܛܢܐ.
34. i.e. for convenience.
35. cf. Heb. iv.2.
36. Acts iv.32.
37. PG 76.33B–C (= Pusey edn. Vol. 6, p. 72.21–73.12).
38. ܚܘܠܛܢܐ = μίξις.
39. ܡܘܙܓܐ = κρᾶσις.
40. PG 36.325B–C.
41. The Greek is χαμερπές.
42. The Greek for both is λόγος.
43. PG 36.97B–100A.
44. νόμῳ.
45. PG 36.328C.
46. PG 36.325B–C.
47. cf. Cyril, *Scholia*, ch. 9 (Pusey edn., Vol. 6), p. 516.1–14.
48. ὡς ἐμὸς λόγος.
49. τοιοῦτος δὲ οἷος.
50. PG 37.181A–B.
51. Mt. xvii.2.
52. PG 77.236C–D (= ACO I, 1, 6a, p. 156.11–18).
53. τῆς θεοτόκου.
54. PG 26.385A and PG 77.13C–D (= ACO I, 1, 1a, p. 12.5–8).
55. ܕܝܠܢܐܝܬ ܘܡܢܬܢܝܬܐ ܠܒܪܐ = Greek: ἰδικῶς καὶ ἀνὰ μέρος Υἱῷ . . . .
56. PG 76.416A (= Pusey edn. Vol. 6, p. 428.24–430.3).
57. The Greek in Migne reads αἵματος.
58. PG 76.84D–85A (= Pusey edn. Vol. 6, p. 112.26–113.7).
59. PG 77.116A (= Pusey edn. Vol. 6, p. 26.26–28.2).
60. 2 Pet. iii.16.
61. PG 36.313B.
62. i.e. Sunday after Easter, Low Sunday (καινὴ κυριακή).
63. καὶ πτωχεύει τῷ σὰρξ παγῆναι.
64. PG 36.612B.
65. PG 36.100A.
66. PG 36.313B. *Or. XXXVIII, In Theophania.*
67. cf. Eccles. i.9.
68. PG 76.1193B, line 13. Also cf. above, p. 92.28 and p. 102.8. (= Pusey edn. Vol. 7, p. 134.13–14). *De Recta Fide ad Theod.*
69. ܫܠܡ.
70. ܕܚܠܬ ܐܠܗܐ = Greek: εὐσέβεια.
71. ܠܚܘܠܛܢܐ ܘܠܡܘܙܓܐ Elsewhere I translate both roots as "confuse".
72. i.e. he is as you, Sergius, assert.

ܦܪܝܫ ܒܗܕܐ ܗܟܝܠ: ܘܢܚܫܘܢ ܥܠ ܛܥ̈ܝܘܬܐ ܕܩܢܘܢܐ: ܘܠܐ ܡܫܬܡܥܝܢ ܡܫܬܠܡܝܢ. ܐܠܐ ܐܝܟܢܐ ܕܐܡܪ ܒܪܘܟܬܐ ܐܚܪܢܐ: ܕܒܗ ܡܬܟܣܝܐ ܘܟܠܗܘܢ ܘܡܬܗܦܟ. ܘܗܟܢ ܡܟܝܠ ܡܫܬܘܕܥ ܠܟܘܢ: ܗܟܢܐ ܘܗܘܝܐ ܒܝܬ ܒܢܝܐ ܕܢܦܩ ܩܕܡܝܐ ܕܟܘܠܝܐ ܐܡܪ. ܕܐܝܟ ܕܟܬܝܒܐ ܕܐܬܦܫܛܬ: ܘܗܢܐ ܚܫܒ ܐܢܘܢ ܕܒܝܬܐ ܕܢܐܡ ܡܫܬܐܡܪ.

ܒܪܡ ܕܝܢ ܒܟܠ ܚܕܐ ܐܝܬ ܒܬܘܟܠܢܐ ܕܠܐܪ ܡܫܡܠܝܐ. ܘܕܒܗܠܝܢ ܗܘܐ ܕܫܪܝܐ ܕܠܟܝ: ܘܐܡܪ ܐܝܬ ܐܚܪܝܐ ܘܙܕܩ ܐܝܬ. ܗܘ ܕܐܬܐܡܪܬ ܡܢ ܐܠܗܐ ܒܗܕܐ ܗܟܝܠ ܕܡܢ ܐܫܬܪܝܠ ܕܐܡܪܗ ܠܡܣܟܢܐ: ܕܟܠ ܡܐ ܕܡܫܡܠܠ ܡܪܝܐ ܐܠܗܐ ܠܗܕܐ ܘܢܫܒܚ ܘܢܒܥܐ. ܫܦܝܪܬ ܒܪܬܐ ܛܠܐ ܕܩܠܐ ܕܒܥܐ ܗܘܐ ܟܠ ܡܐ ܕܐܡܪܗ ܠܗܕܐ: ܠܬܪܝܢܬ ܡܟܝܠ ܗܟܝܠ ܕܡܠܠܗ. ܡܛܠ ܢܛܠܠ ܕܢܗܘܐ ܗܘܐ ܠܟܘܢ ܒܗܘܢ: ܐܡܬܝ ܕܢܗܘܘܢ ܕܫܠܝܢ ܡܢܚ: ܘܢܛܪܝܢ ܦܘܩܕܢ ܡܢܗܘܢ ܢܩܫܬܐ. ܐܡܬܝ ܕܫܦܝܪ ܢܗܘܐ ܠܟܘܢ. ܐܠܐ ܗܟܢܠ ܒܗ ܒܝ ܒܗ ܒܬܘܟܠܢܐ ܘܡܫܡܫܢܐ ܐܬܡܪܗ: ܒܝ (144) ܗܘܝܢ ܗܘ ܘܒܫܬܪܐ ܛܥܢܐ ܐܝܬ: ܒܗܕܐ ܗܟܝܠ ܕܝܢ ܕܠܫܪܪܐ ܡܬܡܠܝܐ ܐܝܬ. ܘܡܢ ܠܡܫܘܚܬܐ ܗܘ ܕܡܫܡܠܝܐ: ܗܘ ܕܒܗܕܐ ܚܕܐ ܐܘܣܝܐ ܡܬܡܠܝܐ: ܒܗܟܢ ܕܡܢܗܘܢ ܠܐ ܒܟܠܗܝܢ ܐܬܝܗܝ ܗܘ ܚܕ ܡܪܝܐ ܘܐܠܗܐ ܘܦܪܘܩ ܢܦܫܢ ܡܫܝܚܐ: ܗܢܘ ܒܪܢܫܐ ܘܕܘܝܕ ܫܠܝܡܐ ܐܝܬ ܐܡܪ ܠܗ: ܘܡܬܒܪܐܝܬ ܐܦ ܗܘ ܕܒܠܒܪ ܐܝܬ ܕܐܬܝܗܒ ܠܒܡܫܪܝܐ ܡܛܠܠ ܗܡܝܢܘܬܐ. ܒܝ ܓܒܪ ܐܝܬ ܐܒܪܬܐ ܕܡܛܘܐ ܐܝܬ ܐܚܪܝܐ ܕܒܠܬܐ ܘܡܫܝܚܐ ܗܘ ܕܐܝܟ ܕܒܡܫܘܕܥܘܬܐ ܚܝܠܬܐ: ܘܠܗ ܗܘ ܕܡܢܗܘܢ ܘܠܗܘܢ: ܘܒܟܠ ܕܝܠ ܡܦܪܫ: ܠܒܢ̈ܝܐ ܕܡܢܗܘܢ ܐܬܝܗܝ ܗܘ ܚܕ ܘܠܐ ܡܬܦܠܓܢܐ ܡܫܝܚܐ: ܘܠܗܒ ܠܚܕܐ ܐܘܣܝܐ ܘܡܫܘܕܥܘܬܐ ܘܕܝܠܝܘܬܐ ܥܠ ܡܕܡ ܐܦܠܐ ܘܢܒܥܬ: ܘܐܦܠܐܒܝܬ ܦܫܛܬܐ ܡܢ ܬܘܕܝܬܐ ܕܟܠ ܐܢܫ ܕܡܫܡܥܐ: ܒܗܝ ܕܟܠܬ ܠܗ ܚܠܐ ܕܐܒܢ ܦܫܝܛܐ. ܘܐܓܪܐ ܡܒܝܢ ܐܝܬ ܒܙܪܥܐ ܕܢܝܫܒ. ܐܝܟܢ ܕܗܘܐ ܦܢ ܢܚܠ ܗܘܢܐ. ܒܗܘܐ ܕܝܢ ܚܝܝܢ ܦܠܫܘܦܘܬܐ ܚܒܝ.

ܗܟܝܠ ܕܝܢ ܡܛܠ ܚܘܒܐ ܗܘ ܒܟܝܢܗ ܡܦܪܫܐܝܬ ܐܬܐܘܣܦ. ܒܗܕܐ ܗܘ ܕܠܐ ܗܘ ܕܡܪܘܬܐ ܠܐ ܡܫܬܟܚܐ ܐܝܬ ܒܥܠܬܐ. ܐܠܐ ܒܗܘܠܝܗ ܘܒܦܘܪܫܢܐ ܘܒܗܝܡܢܘܬܐ ܡܕܡ ܠܗܘܐ ܡܬܒܪܝܐ. ܡܫܬܒܪܝܢ ܗܘܝܢ ܓܒܪ ܕܡܬܗܠܟܝܢ: ܐܦ ܗܘ ܕܠܝܬ ܐܦ ܒܗܘܐ ܡܢ ܡܬܒܪܝܐ ܢܝܫܢ. ܘܡܛܠܬܐ ܕܝܢ ܗܟܝܢܬܐ ܡܦܪܫܢܐ ܘܦܫܝܛ ܒܝ ܐܡܪܐ. ܕܡܛܠܬܗܘܢ ܥܠ ܗܢܐ: ܒܫܟܘܬܐ ܒܥܠܝܐ ܠܗܘܐ ܡܬܒܪܝܐ. ܠܗܘܐ ܠܝ ܕܝܢ ܕܒܝ ܒܡܬܦܘܬܐ ܕܥܠܝܐ ܗܟܝܠܬܐ ܗܘܝܢ: ܘܒܝ ܐܚܝܕܝܢ ܡܠܟܐ ܕܗܟܝܠ: ܢܗܘܐ ܫܠܝܛ ܡܢ

73. PL 54.765A.
74. cf. PG 76.1413C. (= *Ad Reginas de Recta Fide Oratio Altera*, Pusey edn. Vol. 7, p. 328.4–5).
75. Acts i.11.
76. cf. p. 102.12 ff. above.
77. cf. Prov. ix.18A; v.8, 6.
78. cf. 1 Tim. ii.5–6.
79. PG 76.1431B (Latin only). The passage is preserved in Syriac. cf. *Philalethes*, *op. cit.*, p. 49.3–11.
80. Lk. xviii.8.
81. PG 76.1431C–1432A (Latin only). The passage is preserved in Syriac: cf. *Philalethes*, *op. cit.*, p. 50.6–19.
82. Preserved in Greek in Leontius of Jerusalem. PG 86.1848A–B. *Contra Monophysitas*.
83. Friedrich Loofs, *Nestoriana* (Halle, 1905), p. 249.2–4. ܢܩܝܦܘܬܐ translates the Greek συνάφεια.
84. ܒܪ ܟܝܢܐ.
85. Lebon suggests this is σύμβασις φυσική.
86. PG 36.417B.
87. ܫܘܬܦܘܬ ܟܝܢܐ.
88. ܫܘܬܦܘܬ ܟܝܢܐ.
89. ܩܕܡ ܟܝܢܐ.
90. Note in margin: A diameter is where there are two things which confront each other in a primary sense, as is the case of the position at full-moon, when the moon is in the eastern side of the sky and the sun in the western.
91. PG 37.180A–B.
92. PG 37.180A.
93. ܫܘܬܦܘܬ ܟܝܢܐ.
94. i.e. the soul.
95. PG 35.781C–784A.
96. PG 35.865C.
97. θεοποίησις.
98. PG 36.324A.
99. ܫܘܝܐ ܕܪܥܝܢܐ. Dr S. P. Brock has suggested ὁμόπνοια as the underlying Greek.
100. Severus' reference is wrong. It is Gregory Nazianzen, *Ep. VI To Basil*, PG 37.29C. I owe this reference to Dr Lionel Wickham and Bishop Kallistos of Diokleia.
101. ܒܪ ܟܝܢܐ = ὁμοούσιον.
102. ܒܪ ܟܝܢܐ = ὁμοούσιον/ος.
103. *sc.* according to them.
104. PG 26.1064B–1065A.
105. ܫܘܬܦܘܬ ܟܝܢܐ.
106. The Greek is: εἰς εἶδος τὸ ἀνθρώπινον.
107. Zech. xii.1.
108. PG 77.21B–D (= ACO I, 1, 1a, p. 15.12–33).
109. ܩܕܡ ܟܝ̈ܢܐ.
110. cf. Jn. viii.40.
111. cf. Jn. vi.38.
112. Lietzmann, *op. cit.*, p. 185.
113. ܒܪ ܟܝܢܐ = ὁμοούσιος/ον/ου.
114. ܒܪ ܟܝܢܢ = τῆς ἡμῖν ὁμοουσίου σαρκός.
115. Lietzmann, *op. cit.*, p. 188, lines 9–18.
116. PG 75.333A.
117. cf. p. 99.30, above.
118. i.e. leaving out σεσαρκωμένη.
119. i.e. again without the addition σεσαρκωμένη.
120. PG 75.1285C (= Pusey edn. Vol. 7, p. 360.9–12).

ܐ ܒܪ̈ܬܐ ܕܡܪܝ ܒܗܘ ܒܪܨܘܡܐ ܘܕܐܘܪܝܐ ܕܐܣܛܒܝܐ

ܘܠܟܢ ܠܡ̈ܪܝܐ ܕܒܟܬܐ: ܒܩܘܒܠܐ ܕܝܢ ܚܠܦܝܗܘܢ ܡܫ̈ܒܚܬܐ: ܐܡܝܢ ܕܗܘܝܢ ܢܛܘܦ
ܫܒܚܬܐ ܕܡܢ ܠܥܠ. ܐܠܐ ܓܝܪ ܢܘܚܡ: ܐܦܠܐ ܚܕ ܐܡܪܐ ܡܟܬܐ ܢܚܣܬܐ.
܀ܘܫܒܚܬ ܠܒܪ̈ܐ ܕܐܒܘܢ ܕܦܬܓܡ̈ܐ ܫܦܝܪܐ ܒܗ ܡܪܢ ܒܪܨܘܡܐ܀

121. Lebon comments here: Sensus harum vocum haud clarus.
122. PG 77.121A–B (= Pusey edn. Vol. 6, p. 36.20–26).
123. *συνήδρευσεν*. Syriac: ܝܬܒ ܐܟܚܕܐ.
124. ܐܟܚܕܐ/*σύν*/ together, and ܥܡ/*μετά*/with.
125. cf. PG 76.352C (= Pusey edn. Vol. 6, p. 322.11–16). *Apol. pro XII Cap. Contra Orient.*
126. PG 76.352C–353A. (= Pusey edn. Vol. 6, p. 322.11–324.15). *Apol. pro XII Cap. Contra Orient.*
127. Ps. cii.12.
128. Reading [Syriac] (= H. syr. 22) for [Syriac].
129. Col. ii.4.
130. cf. 2 Cor. xii.1.
131. 2. Cor. xii.11.
132. H. syr. 22 reads [Syriac] for [Syriac]. This reading would seem to be supported by Sergius, p. 155.4, above.
133. cf. above, p. 86. cf. also, p. 72.23 and p. 101.24.
134. Reading [Syriac] (= H. syr. 22) for [Syriac].
135. cf. p. 101 above of Lebon's edition.
136. *τὸ λογίζεσθαι* and *τὸ λογικόν*. cf. Lebon, CSCO 120 (Syr. 65), p. 102, note 5.
137. *sc.* blackness.
138. Jer. xiii. 23.
139. *Homilia in illud, Attende tibi ipsi.* PG 31.216C.
140. This is from the *Gnosticus* of Evagrius, §143 (ed. Frankenberg, p. 550). For the Greek, see Socrates, *H. E.* III, 7 (PG 67.396B). The use of this text by Severus is mentioned by J. Muyldermans, *Evagriana Syriaca* (Louvain 1952), p. 170, note 138. I owe this reference to Bishop Kallistos of Diokleia.
141. PG 36.241, note 51.
142. Reading [Syriac] (= H. syr. 22 = *πενία*) for [Syriac].
143. PG 36.248D.
144. PG 73.85A. This is taking Lebon's suggested emendation, reading [Syriac] [Syriac] for [Syriac], which follows the Greek *ὡς εἰς δογμάτων ἀκρίβειαν*. (= Pusey edn. Vol. 3, p. 72.5–9).
145. PG 75.1264B. (= Pusey edn. Vol. 7, p. 341.28–342.8).
146. PG 77.217B–C.
147. Note in margin: Take note.
148. The Greek is *τὴν κατὰ παράθεσιν*.
149. Note in margin: In place of "curtains" (*τὰς αὐλαίας*) which is here, it says "court" (*αὐλήν*) in the Greek. (PG 76.84C reads *αὐλαίας*).
150. Ex. xxvi.6.
151. PG 76.84B–C (= Pusey edn. Vol. 6, p. 111.30–112.16).
152. Hos. xiv.10. For Dioscorus' Letter, see "Akten der Ephesinischen Synode vom Jahre 449", ed. J. Flemming, *Abh. der Kgl. Ges. der Wiss. zu Göttingen*, Phil.-hist, Kl., n.s. 15, Berlin 1917, p. 137 (of translation). I owe this reference to Dr Lionel Wickham.
153. cf. 1 Kms. xvii.39.
154. cf. 2 Tim, iii.14.
155. cf. Ex. xiv. 14.
156. cf. 1 Kms. xvii. 36.
157. The sense of this passage is far from clear.
158. Mk. x.29–30.
159. Mt. vi.33.
160. Deut. v.27.
161. cf. Phil. iii.13.
162. cf. 1 Tim. i.3, and p. 102 above.
163. cf. Hos. viii.7.
164. cf. Hag. i.6.

165. This is taking ܥܒܕ ܦܝܠܘܣܘܦܘܬܐ to represent just the verb φιλοσοφέω. cf. p. 127 above, and PG 35.781C.
166. The Syriac is [illegible].
167. Col. iv.6.
168. cf. Is. vii.9.

Letter III of Sergius

The Third Letter of Sergius the Grammarian to holy Severus the Patriarch. (*Lebon p. 145*)

Only late have I become aware of my ignorance. And at first I did not attend to my artifice, which I did not know: for "honour lies still where there is no danger", as one of our number said. But I was not steadfast in relation to the divine laws, nor did I hear the cither[1] when he prayed: "Lord, place a watchman on my mouth, and a door, a keeper on my lips".[2] Then I pushed aside the doctrines of the wise, and made a mock of these various texts: "Who will give a guardian upon my mouth, and a seal of shrewdness upon my lips lest I should fall as a result of them, and my tongue should fight with me?"[3], and "A slip from the floor is better than one from the tongue",[4] (and) "The folly of one who is silent was searched for, and it was not found".[5] Therefore I have learned this sin, (I) who am a man with a babbling tongue. You did not agree that with evil I would cure evil, and I have received a sentence of double ignorance. But I am grateful to those who give rebuke, and I acknowledge thankfulness to God that I am corrected, again with a frank mind, among those who counsel wisely, for "The haters of correction die in disgrace",[6] and "The ear which hears the correction of life shall dwell in the midst of the wise",[7] and "He who keeps corrections loves his own soul",[8] and "He who kept correction will be glorified".[9] My soul was admonished by all these good (words); (and) thus I have borne your holy and divine letter.

But at once from the beginning, I was cut off in (mid) speech—for I shall repeat the whole disputation—when I heard that iron sharpens iron. You commanded that I should look a little within myself, and I induced my gaze within, and saw my reasoning (was made) of clay, and very frail. And afterwards I turned quickly to the parable, for I will not forsake (*Lebon p. 146*) the wise, "How can the (clay) pot associate with the (iron) kettle? It will knock and itself be broken".[10] Then with difficulty I recollected that I should act wisely, and I was descending to the remaining words. Then, but then, the beginning of the whole marvel happened to me: (my) eyes cringed back from the light, and were completely unable henceforth to en-

(145) ✤ܐܓܪܬܐ ܕܬܠܬ ܕܠܗ ܕܣܪܓܝܣ ܓܪܡܛܝܩܘܣ: ܠܘܬܗ ܕܩܕܝܫܐ ܣܘܝܪܐ ܦܛܪܝܪܟܐ✤

ܡܬܡܣܟܢܘܬܟ ܡܪܓܫ ܐܢܐ ܟܠ ܡܟܝܟܘܬܐ ܕܝܠܟ. ܘܡܬܕܡܪ ܡܢ ܐܘܡܢܘܬܐ ܕܝܠܟ ܕܠܐ ܢܦܠ. ܐܝܟܢܐ ܓܝܪ ܕܠܐ ܡܣܝܒܪܢܘܬܟ ܕܗܟܢܐ. ܐܡܝܢܐ ܕܐܡܪ ܐܝܟ ܡܢ ܗܠܝܢ ܕܟܬܒܬ. ܠܐ ܥܒܕܬ. ܗܘܝܬ ܕܝܢ ܘܟܠܗ ܢܦܫܐ ܠܟ̈ܬܒܐ ܠܐ ܡܫܬܡܫܢܐ. ܘܠܐ ܠܡܫܬܪܐ ܥܒܕܬ ܟܕ ܡܕܡ: ܕܣܝܡ ܡܪܝܐ ܢܛܘܪܬܐ ܠܦܘܡܝ: ܘܐܚܘܕܐ ܬܪܥܐ ܥܠ ܣܦ̈ܘܬܝ. ܒܬܪ ܡܢ ܘܐܬܘܚܝܬܐ ܕܢܩܡܫܐ ܘܢܦܠ. ܘܒܟܝܢܐ ܩ̈ܠܐ ܗܠܝܢ ܡܦܠ̈ܬܐ ܐܦܠܛܘܢܝܬ: ܕܦܫ ܢܬܠܠ ܟܠ ܦܘܡܝ ܢܛܘܪܬܐ: ܘܟܠ ܩ̈ܦܘܠܝ ܠܬܪܥܐ ܣܦܘܬܝ ܘܠܐ ܐܦܠ ܡܢܗܘܢ: ܘܠܥܝܢ ܠܐ ܢܦܪܘܟ ܟܦܟ. ܘܡܬܘܪܒܬ ܡܢ ܐܘܪܚܐ ܡܬܡܪܢܬ ܐܘ ܡܢ ܟܣܝܐ. ܐܬܟܢܫ ܡܫܬܥܠܝܬܐ ܟܬܡܝܬܐ ܘܠܐ ܐܬܟܫܦܬ. ܗܕܐ ܗܘܝܢܐ ܣܦܝܩܘܬܐ ܡܫܟܚ ܐܢܐ: ܗܘ ܕܟܣܐ ܘܠܐ ܠܐܘܪܚܐ: ܠܐ ܕܢܬ ܘܟܬܝܒܬܐ ܟܬܝܒܬܐ ܐܦܠܐ: ܘܦܣܩܐ ܘܠܐ ܐܣܪܟܬܐ ܒܦܝܣܬܐ ܥܒܕܬ. ܡܬܒܥ ܐܢܐ ܕܝܢ ܒܗܠܝܢ ܕܡܟܬܒܢ ܣܘܟܐ. ܘܛܥܢܬ ܢܦܫܝ ܐܢܐ ܠܐܠܗܐ ܕܡܬܪܘܐ ܐܢܐ. ܘܒܗܠܝܢ ܕܡܫܬܡܠܢ ܡܟܬܒܢ ܠܐܦ ܒܗܘܢܐ ܚܐܪܐ. ܕܦܫܝܩ ܟܡ ܡܬܩ̈ܢܘܬܐ ܡܫܠܡ ܡܬܡܪܢܬ. ܘܐܘܪܚܐ ܕܥܡܠܐ ܡܬܚܫܒܢܘܬܐ ܕܝܢܐ: ܟܡܕܡܝܬܐ ܘܫܦ̈ܝܪܐ ܠܟܠܐ. ܘܗܘ ܕܢܛܪ ܡܬܩ̈ܢܘܬܐ: ܙܡܝܢ ܢܩܡܗ. ܘܗܘ ܕܢܛܪ ܡܬܚܫܒܢܘܬܐ ܢܠܐܒ. ܒܗܠܝܢ ܡܠܝܢ ܠܦ̈ܬܐ ܐܬܐܬܐ ܢܩܒ. ܗܟܝܠ ܐܓܪܬܐ ܕܡܠܘܢ ܡܕܝܢܬܐ ܘܡܠܘܐܬܐ ܣܢܝܩܬܐ.

ܐܠܐ ܡܣܒܐ ܡܢ ܥܘܕܪܢܐ: ܡܠܦܣܣ ܗܘܠܟ ܒܟܪܝܐ ܗܠܐ. ܐܬܐ ܓܝܪ ܡܠܗ ܡܪܝܐ ܒ ܥܒܕܬ ܕܦܪܙܠܐ ܠܛܘܦ ܠܦܪܙܠܐ: ܐܝܟܘ ܒܢܩܫ ܡܟܠܠ ܩܝܢܐ: ܘܠܓܘ ܢܓܪܐ ܠܚܒܪܐ ܕܝܠܗ. ܘܡܣܬܟܠ ܠܣܝܒܬܐ ܕܦܝܓܝܣ ܒܚܘܪܐ ܚܒܝܒܐ. ܘܡܠܘܐ ܠܘܬܐ ܕܡܬܠܠ ܗܘ ܕܗܦܛܠ. ܠܐ ܡܪܢܫ ܐܢܐ (146) ܓܝܪ ܡܢ ܚܒܝ̈ܒܬܐ: ܕܡܢܐ ܡܫܬܠܡܢܘܬܐ ܡܕܝܢܐ ܟܠܐ ܡܕܝܢܐ: ܕܗܘ ܢܦܫܐ ܘܗܘ ܡܬܬܟܪܐ. ܠܡܣܡܝܢ ܗܠܝܢ ܟܢܫܬ ܗܘ ܕܐܬܚܝܢ. ܘܟܠܐ ܩ̈ܠܐ ܗܘܝܢ ܘܡܢܐ ܢܝܚܐ ܗܘܝܬ. ܗܡܝܢ ܕܝܢ ܗܡܝܢ: ܗܘ ܕܥܘܪܢܐ ܟܠܗ ܠܐܘܡܢܘܬܐ ܓܒܝܬܐ ܠܟ. ܘܟܬܒܐ ܦܣ ܡܦܩ ܡܢ ܢܘܗܪܐ. ܘܟܠ ܡܠܗ ܡܬܡܠܠ ܠܐ ܡܩܦܚ ܩܘܡ ܕܢܬܝܠ ܒܢܟܡܐ. ܠܐܘܪܚܬܐ ܙܡܝܪܐ ܗܘܬ. ܗܘ ܕܐܦ ܠܡܟܝܟܬܐ ܕܚܢܘܬܐ ܡܣܝܒܪܢܘܬܐ ܒܗܝܪܐ ܗܘܬ. ܘܐܝܟ ܐܝܟܐ ܕܝܢ ܘܐܝܟ ܐܝܟܐ ܠܡܚܘܝܢܘܬܐ ܡܢ ܠܐ ܡܬܚܫܒܬܐ ܦܛܝܠܬ: ܙܪܩܬܐ ܕܦ̈ܘܩܕܢܐ ܐܬܦܫܩ ܐܘܪܚܐ. ܐܢܐ ܗܘܬܠܐܘܡܐ ܡܬܠܠ ܗܠܝܢ ܐܝܟ

lighten (my) mind. (My) understanding was dizzy, (my mind) which was in danger of (lapsing into) the sleep of despondency. But what, what opinion have I reaped from (my) lack of learning? I shall be accused of the teaching of the changers of ousiai. Therefore I shall make a defence about what my opinion is concerning them, taking God as a witness of the statement, (to show that) those men are reckoned foolish by me, and followers of the madness of Eutyches.

First they trample underfoot the mysteries of the divine birth (that was) for our sake. For when the flesh has been dissolved into divinity, it is no great thing that the virginity should be preserved, when the Spirit only passed through her. Therefore let us come to Father Cyril (that we may enquire) about this true saying. For she gave birth to the Word from God the Father according to the flesh, when he became flesh. For the marvel is seen in this, that while the laws of birth are preserved, God is born in a fleshly way, while (at the same time) nature is overcome, for virginity is not done away with, even though bodily birth took place. But how have these (accusations) of an impure doctrine befallen me, when I confess composition (just) like the Fathers? For if a man takes completely pure gold, and another (takes) debased (gold), (and) when he purifies it, unites it (to the other), in this way this (constitutes) an addition of ousia and not a composition. But who would be so bold as (to say) like a young man, that in the case of the perfect Trinity, there is an addition of divinity, taking what did not exist before, but came into existence at the end? (Such an attempt would belong) either to the audacity (*Lebon p. 147*) of Nestorius, which strives in the pagan way to deify, or to the empty-mindedness of Arius, which drunkenly (moves) the creature into divinity. All things which belong to the Word are settled and superior to all change. For in the beginning was the Word, and (he was) with God and was God, and became flesh.[11]

But just as he was embodied, and has not endangered the ousia of divinity and is even now true God as well, so too he has preserved his own true flesh. Thus the prophets did not deceive about the advent, saying that God comes visibly. Thus we do not err in the direction of illusion because we have become among the perceivers of the Word, and touched him with (our) hands.[12] For if we should blaspheme (saying) that, like a cloud and every vapour which went up into the air from the earth, and is dissipated by the rays of the sun, this happened also to the body of our Lord by the mingling with divinity, (then) God was not seen, was not touched, did not hunger, did not thirst, was not weary, and undertook none of these things which are

ܠܗ ܛܪܘܦܝܐ: ܟܕ ܠܐܠܗܐ ܚܫܐ̈ܝܬ ܫܘܐ ܕܡܠܬܐ ܢܩܦ ܐܝܬ ܒܪܘܚܐ. ܕܩܛܠܐ ܣܡܟܝܢ ܠܗ ܘܟܠܗ ܚܫܐ ܕܢܦܫܐ ܘܦܓܪܐ.

ܡܕܡ ܦܫ ܕܕܪ̈ܐ ܕܡܬܩܪܒܘܬܐ ܠܐܠܗܘܬܐ ܕܡܬܚܫܚܢ ܕܝܠܗ. ܟܕ ܓܝܪ ܒܒܪܐ ܐܫܬܘܝ ܠܐܠܗܘܬܐ: ܗܘ ܕܐܬܒܛܢ ܒܡܘܠܕܐ ܠܐ ܙܘܓܐ. ܕܪܘܚܐ ܒܟܠܗ ܒܒܪܢܐ ܒܗ. ܢܟܢ ܗܘܠܐ ܠܐܦ ܡܘܕܝܢܘܬܗ: ܘܡܬܚܫܚ ܗܘܐ ܒܪܐ ܦܠܐ ܡܢ ܥܢܢܐ. ܡܟܝܠ ܓܝܪ ܒܒܪܢܫܘܬܗ: ܟܕ ܒܒܪܐ ܗܘܐ: ܡܠܬܐ ܕܡܢ ܐܠܗܐ ܐܒܐ. ܒܗܘܐ ܓܝܪ ܡܬܚܫܚܢܘܬܐ ܠܐܘܪܚܘܬܐ ܘܡܬܬܪܝܡ ܢܦܫܗ ܦܫ ܕܡܬܒܐ: ܒܒܪܢܫܐ ܕܝܢ ܡܬܚܫܒ ܠܐܠܗܐ. ܘܟܕ ܡܙܘܓܐ ܒܚܝܐ. ܒܡܘܠܕܐ ܓܝܪ: ܘܟܕ ܗܘܐ ܡܟܝܠ ܓܘܫܡܐ ܠܐ ܡܬܚܙܝܢܐ. ܐܝܟܢܐ ܕܝܢ ܟܕ ܪܘܒܐ ܒܡܫܐ ܐܟܘܬܐ ܡܫܘܐ ܐܝܬ: ܗܟܢ ܕܐܬܚܘܝܬ ܠܡܬܐܬܐ ܒܒܪ ܒܒܪ. ܐܦ ܓܝܪ ܕܗܘܐ ܐܝܟ ܢܦܫ ܗܘ ܕܪܘܚܐ ܡܢ ܒܠܐ: ܐܡܪܐ ܕܝܢ ܡܫܒܚܐ ܒܡ ܡܒܪܐ ܚܝܢ: ܠܘܩܒܠܐ ܗܘ ܕܐܘܫܐ ܗܘܐ ܕܐܝܟ ܗܘܐ ܘܠܗ ܪܘܒܐ. ܡܢܗ ܕܝܢ ܢܒܪܝܢ ܕܠܘܩܒܠ ܠܐܠܗܘܬܐ ܡܫܡܫܢܝܬܐ: ܢܬܒܝܢ ܠܘܩܒܠܐ ܕܐܠܗܘܬܐ. ܢܦܫ ܕܝܢ ܕܝܢ ܗܘ ܕܠܐ ܐܠܗܘܬܗ ܗܘܐ ܡܢ ܩܕܡ. ܒܒܪܐ ܕܝܢ ܗܘܐ. ܐܪܐ ܕܡܢܪܘܬܐ (147) ܕܡܬܛܦܪܘܬܗ ܗܘ ܕܡܫܚܐ ܕܐܬܚܘ ܚܠܦܝܗ ܐܠܗܐ: ܐܘ ܕܡܫܬܪܝܐ ܗܘܝܐ ܕܐܪܘܥܗ. ܗܘ ܕܪܘܚܐ ܒܐܠܗܘܬܐ ܒܪܬܐ. ܡܠܗܘܢ ܗܟܝܢ ܕܡܠܬܐ ܡܬܩܪܝܬܐ. ܘܡܢ ܟܠ ܡܘܫܚܬܐ ܩܕܝܫܝܢ. ܒܪܢܫܐ ܓܝܪ ܐܠܗܘܢ ܗܘܐ ܡܠܬܐ. ܘܟܕ ܐܠܗܐ ܘܠܐܠܗܐ ܐܠܗܘܢ ܗܘܐ. ܘܒܒܪܐ ܗܘܐ.

ܐܦܢܐ ܕܝܢ ܕܐܬܚܙܝ ܘܠܐܘܟܐ ܠܐܠܗܘܬܐ ܡܫܕܢܘܬܗ ܠܐ ܒܟܕ: ܘܐܠܗܘܢ ܗܘܝܐ ܘܠܐܠܗܐ ܒܪܢܫܐ: ܗܘܝܐ ܘܒܒܪܐ ܕܡܠܗ ܢܛܪ ܒܙܪܐ. ܗܘܝܐ ܢܟܝܐ ܠܚܫܐ̈ܝܬܐ ܠܐ ܕܓܠܗ: ܘܐܡܪ ܕܡܬܚܫܚܐ ܐܬܐ ܐܠܗܐ. ܗܘܝܐ ܚܝ ܒܟܠ ܗܓܓܘܬܐ ܠܐ ܛܥܝܢ: ܕܕܡܘܬܗ ܢܦܫܐ ܕܡܠܬܐ ܕܩܡ. ܘܒܗܝܐ ܒܐܦܝܐ ܓܝܪ. ܐܦ ܓܝܪ ܐܝܟ ܒܪܦܠܐ ܘܟܘܠ ܒܓܘܢܐ ܕܡܢ ܐܪܓܐ ܗܟܢ ܒܟܠ ܐܐܪ: ܘܦܪܓܠܐ ܡܦܫܝܐ ܡܬܚܙܝܐ: ܐܦ ܠܓܘܫܡܗ ܕܡܢܗ ܒܣܘܟܠܐ ܕܐܠܗܘܬܐ ܗܘܐ ܓܝܪ ܠܗ ܡܓܝܣܢ. ܠܐ ܐܬܚܝܢ ܐܠܗܐ. ܠܐ ܐܬܓܫܫ. ܠܐ ܒܥܐ. ܠܐ ܙܥܐ. ܠܐ ܠܐܐ. ܘܠܐ ܡܕܡ ܡܢ ܗܠܝܢ ܕܠܗ ܕܦܪ: ܘܠܐ ܒܗ ܒܓܠܝܐ ܐܬܚܙܝ. ܘܦܓܪܗ ܡܫܡܪ ܐܝܬ ܕܐܦܪ ܕܡܠܬܐ: ܒܗܘ ܕܠܐ ܡܬܚܫܚܐ ܓܘܫܡ ܓܘܫܡܐ ܡܫܘܬܐ. ܠܐ ܢܩܡܩ ܦܓܪܗ ܐܬܚܪܐ ܘܛܘܦܣܐ ܕܪܝܪܐ ܢܟܝܐ. ܠܐܝܕܐ ܓܝܪ ܕܩܝܐ ܡܦܪܫ ܐܝܕܐ. ܢܬܐܚܕ ܠܪܓܠܐ. ܘܡܫܬܟܚܐ ܗܘ ܡܫܡܫ ܢܬܚܐ. ܘܠܐ ܢܬܕܡܪ. ܐܦ ܕܝܢ ܘܐܦܪ ܕܓܘܫܡܢ ܘܚܝܘ: ܕܒܪܘܚܐ ܒܒܪܐ ܘܓܪܡܐ ܒܠܗ ܠܗ: ܐܝܟ ܡܐ ܕܚܝܢ

ours, nor was he fastened to the cross, and I am quite unentitled to say that he died, he who no longer was embodied with a mortal body. Nor would Thomas carefully seek out and look for the mark of the nails: for to what side would he place (his) hand? The doors would be closed, and Jesus would be seen in the middle: and we would not be astonished. And if he says, "Touch me and see, for a spirit does not have flesh and bones, as you see I have",[13] will we shut our ears to the truth? But who is astonished when a spirit hastens to heaven? For God is spirit,[14] and we know his wisdom is an ethereal spirit, passing through every intelligible spirit, pure (and) most ethereal.[15] As far as these first principles go, we are not mad in them, blessed Father of Fathers—and we do not learn these from your accurate voice! (*Lebon p. 148*)

But I believe that there is one nature of the Word incarnate after the inexpressible union, and I do not vitiate the incarnation in any way. You find fault with me, on the grounds that I change the body of the Word. But I acknowledge along with that (body) the soul as well, in that I fully attend to and accept that he says, "He who eats my flesh and drinks my blood has life for ever".[16] I also attend to these words: "I have power to lay down my soul and take it up again",[17] and there was no confusion of the humanity. Let us grant to God that he was truly incarnate, so that he should be able even to suffer on our behalf, so that death might be despoiled in that God died. Let us believe that he rose in a fleshly way from the dead, lest we renounce[18] the resurrection of our own flesh. This Jesus, in the same way in which he was seen by the disciples going up to heaven, will come at the second advent, and he will sit upon the throne of his glory, while the holy angels stand by him: thus he will separate out the goats and the sheep, to the right and to the left. For the [judge][19] endured to be embodied on our behalf—he who accepted the form of a servant, and in shape was found as a man[20]—and that he should display related parts: for which are the right hands and which the left, to an uncontained spirit? But in accordance with your teaching, the quotation, "They shall look on him whom they pierced",[21] (shows) that the Word still keeps in the body the marks of the sufferings (undergone) for love of man.

Therefore I name the whole Jesus God, but incarnate. I acknowledge Israel went down to Egypt with seventy-five souls,[22] but not with (souls) only, but I understand (with souls) which were embodied. And I give heed truly to these words: "There is one mediator of God and men: the man Jesus Christ",[23] but I do not lapse into a debased[24] opinion in this. For I acknowledge (*Lebon p. 149*) "the

ܐܠܗܐ܆ ܠܢ ܕܐܡܪ ܠܢ: ܢܫܒܘܩ ܐܘܪܚ ܠܒܐ ܚܙܘܐ. ܡܢܗ ܕܝܢ ܡܬܝܕܥ: ܒܗ ܪܘܚܐ ܪܗܛ ܠܒܐ ܚܟܝܡܐ. ܪܘܚܐ ܗܘ ܓܝܪ ܕܐܠܗܐ. ܘܪܘܚܐ ܠܚܟܡܬܐ ܕܗܘܬ ܡܕܒܪܢ ܡܛܝܒܘܬܐ. ܕܟܕ ܟܠ ܪܘܚ ܡܕܒܪܢܘܬܐ ܕܟܠܬܐ. ܡܛܝܒܐ ܠܗ̇ ܡܢ ܟܠ ܚܛܝܢ. ܒܟܠ ܒܗܘܢ ܠܐܬܥܛܦܘܬܐ ܠܗ ܗܠܝܢ ܚܣܝܢ ܚܝܢ ܐܘ ܛܘܒܬܐ: ܐܝܟ ܕܐܡܪܬ. ܘܠܐ ܗܠܝܢ ܡܢ ܒܪܐ ܡܠܘ ܚܠܝܡܬܐ ܡܠܒܫ.

(148) ܟܕ ܕܝܢ ܒܝܬܐ ܕܡܠܟܘܬܐ ܡܒܣܪܐ ܡܥܡܕܢ ܐܢܐ ܒܠܚܘܕ ܚܝܡܘܬܐ ܠܐ ܡܬܡܠܟܢܘܬܐ: ܘܠܐ ܡܕܡ ܦܪܝܫ ܐܢܐ ܡܢ ܡܬܒܣܪܢܘܬܐ. ܪܡܐ ܐܡܪ ܠܢ: ܕܓܘܫܡܐ ܕܡܠܟܘܬܐ ܡܫܡܠܐ ܐܢܐ. ܐܢܐ ܕܝܢ ܒܗ ܗܘܝܐ ܢܦܫ ܐܢܐ ܐܦ ܒܢܦܫܐ. ܕܡܫܢ ܐܢܐ ܦܓܪܝ ܘܡܫܡܠܝܐܝܬ ܕܐܡܪ: ܗܘ ܕܐܦܠܐ ܒܣܪܟܐ ܘܦܠܓܐ ܕܝܢ: ܐܡܪ ܠܗ ܚܝܐ ܕܠܥܠܡ. ܡܦܩ ܐܢܐ ܘܠܗܘܢ ܩܢܐ ܩܠܗܘܢ. ܘܡܬܠܡܕܐ ܐܡܪ ܠܢ ܕܐܝܟܢ ܢܫܒ ܘܐܘܒ ܐܫܟܚܗ. ܘܠܐ ܡܕܡ ܐܬܒܠܒܠ ܘܐܫܬܢܝ. ܡܛܠ ܠܐܠܗܐ ܕܐܬܒܪ ܒܪܢܫܐܝܬ. ܐܝܟܢܐ ܘܐܦ ܚܫ ܡܬܛܠܠ ܢܦܫܐ. ܐܝܟܢܐ ܕܢܬܒܪ ܡܘܬܐ ܕܡܝܬ ܐܠܗܐ. ܢܘܡܣ ܕܒܪܢܫܐ ܩܡ ܡܢ ܩܒܪܐ. ܘܠܐ ܠܡܫܡܠܝܘܬܐ ܕܒܣܪܐ ܕܡܢ ܢܦܪ. ܗܘܐ ܡܘܬܐ: ܗܘܐ ܐܢܐ ܘܐܬܚܙܝ ܠܡܠܟܝܘܬܐ ܘܦܠܛ ܠܒܣܪܐ: ܗܘܐ ܘܡܫܬܐܠܬܐ ܘܐܬܩܝܡ ܐܬܐ. ܘܡܛܠ ܟܠ ܒܘܪܚܐ ܕܡܘܒܠܗ. ܟܕ ܡܛܠܬܐ ܩܪܝܒܐ ܡܫܡܫ ܠܒܐܝܗ. ܗܘܐ ܠܒܐ ܡܫܝܚܐ ܘܡܫܡܠܐ ܡܦܪܫ: ܒܪܢܫܐ ܘܒܪܒܐ. ܕܐܬܓܫܡ ܒܪ ܡܛܠܬܗ ܡܫܒܪ ܕܒܗܐ: ܗܘ ܕܡܫܒܠ ܘܡܘܬܐ ܕܒܣܪܐ: ܘܠܐܚܫܚܫܐ ܐܠܗܝܐ ܐܝܟ ܒܪܢܫܐ. ܘܩܒܠܬܐ ܐܢܫܝܬܐ ܢܦܐ. ܠܪܘܚܐ ܒܪ ܠܐ ܡܫܬܡܠܝܢܘܬܐ ܐܝܟܢ ܩܢܘܡܐ ܘܐܝܟܢ ܡܫܠܠܐ. ܗܘ ܕܝܢ ܕܐܝܟ ܡܫܬܘܬܦܘܬܗ ܚܙܝܢ ܒܗܘ ܕܝܕܗ: ܕܒܟܠ ܢܛܪ ܡܠܬܐ ܕܛܘܦܣܐ ܕܟܝܢܐ ܩܢܘܡܝܐ ܐܢܫܐ ܒܓܘܫܡܐ.

ܡܫܡܗ ܐܢܐ ܗܟܝܠ ܠܟܠܗ ܡܫܘܚ ܐܠܗܐ. ܐܠܐ ܕܡܒܣܪ: ܢܦܫ ܐܢܐ ܘܠܐܡܫܪܐܝܬ ܕܒܡܒܝܢ ܘܡܫܡܫ ܢܫܩ ܚܝܠܗ ܠܡܪܝܡ. ܠܗ ܒܡ ܗܟܝܢ ܕܝܢ ܒܟܠܗܘܢ: ܐܠܐ ܘܦܪ̈ܨܘܦܝܢ ܡܫܬܡܠܝܢܘܬܐ. ܘܒܗܠܝܢ ܩܢܗ ܟܠܐ ܚܪܝܪܐܝܬ ܚܙܐ ܐܢܐ: ܕܟܕ ܗܘ ܡܕܒܪܢܐ ܕܐܠܗܐ ܘܦܬܓܡܐ: ܒܪܢܫܐ ܡܫܘܚ ܡܫܝܚܐ. ܐܠܐ ܒܗܘܐ: ܠܗ ܠܒܐ ܡܫܝܚܬܐ ܡܫܝܚܬܐ ܚܙܝܢ ܐܢܐ. ܢܦܫ ܐܢܐ (149) ܓܝܪ ܠܦܓܪܐ ܕܡܢ ܐܠܗܐ ܐܬܝܠܕ ܠܢ. ܘܠܗ ܐܠܗܐ ܡܫܡܫܢܐ: ܕܡܫܬܡܠܝܢܘܬܐ ܐܬܒܪܝ: ܘܒܪܢܫܐ ܕܐܠܗܘܬܐ ܡܕܒܪ: ܘܐܦ ܡܢ ܪܘܚ ܟܠ ܟܠ ܒܫܪ. ܘܠܗ ܒܫܪܝܪܘܬܐ ܦܓܪܐ ܒܟܝܢܗ ܡܫܬܡܠܝܢܘܬܐ:

man attested by God for us",[25] wholly perfect God, who was perfectly made man, and the prophet calling out in a divine way, "I shall pour out from my Spirit onto all flesh".[26] Nor do I uselessly understand only the body, but I accept the whole constitution of men, even when a part customarily indicates a whole: as sometimes I call the world τὸ πᾶν even though I have learned that the heaven is called this.

This true doctrine has run into my mind with pure wonder, in relation to all the words of the holy Fathers, and I run, and lawfully and religiously I keep within bounds. Therefore let Gregory the Theologian say confidently (now) mixture (κρᾶσις) (now) mingling (μίξις), now composition (σύνθεσις):[27] for through equality of name, I recognise one fact, which was made known to me from many names. For I understand the supreme union of God to flesh endowed with a soul, and without confusion maiming the meaning, for (the flesh) has not changed to that which is eternal. And let him also say these words which are worthy of wonder: "Of them, the one deified, but the other was deified".[28] These teach neither a change nor a confusion. For even if iron is said by us to be hot, it is not thought that it was changed into fire itself. For once united to fire, it still even thus remains iron. For if the fire that we know rejects the ousia of matter, it is destroyed, since it does not naturally persist in another way than by being mingled with some ousia of matter. And in the case of that (quotation): "The Word became thick, and congealed",[29] I utterly reject (the idea) that I should be lame in my understanding (of it). For since I enquired about (those) words, I have explained (them) according to your pious opinion, (in saying that the Word) received our thickness of body. And (*Lebon p. 150*) as far as I was able, (I) who am propped up now with a feeble mind, I resisted before the Assembly those who again seize doctrines contrary to this from the Father.[30] And that, "He became double",[31] I have resolved according to your examples. And I have unravelled those sayings which are published by them, "It is (to be) understood (as referring to) his Father, and not to him who is seen"; "(What) is understood, is not of him".[32] Therefore we are not overthrown by those putting forward these (opinions), and ones like these, because God directs (us). But how is it astonishing that these men borrow the (sayings) of the holy Fathers in the cause of what is evil, when they even oppose the divine scriptures, and imagined that from there they would strengthen their wickedness?

But now it is time that I make a defence of (some) statements which are criticised, and assist with a staff those things which are

ܐܠܐ ܦܘܫܩܐ ܕܠܗ ܕܬܪܝܨܐ ܡܫܟܚܢܐܝܬ. ܘܟܕ ܡܫܟܚܐ ܡܟܝܠ ܕܢܐܘܕܐ ܗܘ ܕܡܫܡܫܢܐ: ܗܟܝܠ ܒܝܘܡ ܒܟܠܗܝܢ ܡܫܡܫܐ ܐܢܐ ܠܟܠ. ܘܗܐ ܠܡܫܡܠܝܐ: ܕܗܘܐ ܡܬܬܒܥܢܐ ܢܦܫܝ.

ܗܘܐ ܠܡܫܝܚܝܐ ܡܪܢܝܬܐ ܕܢܩܦ ܒܢܦܫ ܒܗܘ ܠܐܘܪܚܘܬܐ ܕܫܠܝܐ: ܒܗܐ ܕܠܗܘܢ ܟܢܫ ܩܠܐ ܕܐܟܘܬܐ ܩܕܝܫܐ. ܘܪܘܫ ܐܢܐ: ܘܢܩܦܘܬܐ ܘܫܦܝܪܘܬܗ ܕܐܠܗܐ ܡܠܒܫ ܐܢܐ. ܢܐܡܪ ܗܟܝܠ ܟܕ ܠܐܟܠܐ ܘܡܘܕܝܢ ܘܡܫܒܚܝܢ ܘܡܙܡܪܝܢ: ܒܪܝܟܘܬܗ ܡܫܬܒܚܐ ܕܐܠܗܐ. ܒܫܘܠܡܐ ܗܟܢܐ ܓܝܪ ܚܙܐ ܐܢܐ ܚܕ ܗܘܒܢܐ. ܘܟܕ ܥܣܪܐ ܢܦܠܐ ܐܬܝܗܒ ܠܝ. ܚܝܘܬܐ ܓܝܪ ܕܫܡܝܐ ܕܐܠܗܐ ܒܗܐ ܒܣܪܐ ܡܢܦܫܐ ܡܫܬܡܠܝܐ: ܘܒܥܠܡܐ ܠܐ ܡܫܬܟܚ ܒܗܘܢ. ܠܐ ܓܝܪ ܗܘܦ ܐܘ ܒܗܘ ܕܒܟܠܗ. ܢܐܡܪ ܕܝܢ ܗܘܠܝܢ ܟܢܫ ܩܠܐ ܕܩܘܡ ܒܠܐܘܪܚܘܬܐ. ܕܡܛܘܠ ܗܢܐ ܦܝ ܠܗ. ܗܢܐ ܕܝܢ ܐܬܐܠܗ. ܒܗ ܡܫܝܚܐ ܩܠܝܦ ܗܠܝܢ ܘܫܒܘܚܐ. ܦܪܬܐ ܓܝܪ ܐܚܘܗ ܕܕܡܟܝܢ ܢܐܡܪ ܡܢܝ: ܒܗ ܕܐܬܐܘܦܝ ܒܗ ܒܢܘܪܐ ܡܫܬܠܒ. ܡܫܚܕ ܓܝܪ ܚܕܐ ܙܒܢ ܒܢܘܪܐ: ܡܛܠ ܓܝܪ ܐܦ ܗܟܝܠ ܦܪܬܐ. ܠܗ ܓܝܪ ܒܐܘܫܐ ܕܗܘܬ ܒܦܪܐ ܢܘܪܐ ܕܒܗܠܝ: ܡܫܬܠܘܚܐ ܕܠܐ ܡܟܝܠ ܘܐܫܬܢܝܬ ܠܦܘܐ: ܐܚܘܗ ܕܒܐܘܫܐ ܡܕܡ ܕܗܘܬ ܠܐ ܐܬܚܙܝ. ܘܟܠܐ ܗܘ ܕܐܬܒܟܝ ܡܟܠܬܐ ܘܟܠܗܝܢ: ܦܓܪ ܕܢܦܫ ܐܢܐ ܕܐܣܬܪ ܒܗܘܢ. ܟܕ ܓܝܪ ܐܬܒܠܥ ܟܢܫ ܩܠܐ: ܐܝܟ ܠܐܘܪܚܬܗܘܢ ܕܫܒܩ ܐܠܗܐ ܦܦܫܗ. ܕܒܫܘܬܐ ܕܡܢ ܕܒܗܪܐ ܡܟܠ. ܒܗܠܝܢ ܕܝܢ (150) ܕܒܠܡܩܒܠܢܐ ܕܩܝܡܝܢ ܫܘܫܛܠܗ: ܡܢ ܗܘܐ ܠܐܘܒ ܓܪܣܝܢ ܡܢ ܐܒܐ: ܐܝܟ ܕܡܫܡܫ ܗܘܝܬ ܐܢܐ: ܗܘ ܕܒܗ ܢܦܫܐ ܕܒܘܪܬܐ ܠܐܠܐ ܗܘܐ: ܡܕܡ ܒܝܘܡܐ ܐܬܠܒܫ ܗܘ ܕܒܫܡܝܐ ܗܘܐ: ܐܝܟ ܡܩܝܡܐ ܕܠܒܗܘܢ ܚܪܝܬ. ܘܗܝܕܝܢ ܩܠܐ ܕܡܬܒܥܝܢ ܡܢ ܗܢܘܢ ܦܠܚܝܬ. ܕܐܠܐ ܕܗܘ ܕܡܫܬܠܡܠ. ܒܗ ܕܝܢ ܕܗܘ ܡܠܚܝܐ. ܒܗ ܕܝܢ ܕܗܘ ܕܡܫܬܠܡܠ. ܟܕ ܗܠܝܢ ܗܟܝܠ ܘܕܐܝܟ ܗܠܝܢ ܡܫܬܟܚܝܢ ܠܐ ܢܦܠܝܢ ܚܕ: ܕܐܠܗܐ ܡܠܘܢ ܡܫܐ ܕܝܢ ܠܡܫܘܐ: ܐܘ ܒܗ ܕܗܠܝܢ ܕܐܟܘܬܐ ܩܕܝܫܐ ܒܗܐ ܗܘ ܕܒܝܫܐ ܫܡܠܝܢ: ܐܠܝܢ ܕܐܦ ܒܟܠ ܡܠܟܐ ܕܐܠܗܐ ܫܘܪܝ: ܘܒܗܘܢ ܡܢ ܗܪܟܐ ܐܬܘܠܟܘ ܕܢܫܪܘܢ.

ܐܠܐ ܕܝܢܐ ܗܘ ܒܝ ܡܫܡܠܐ ܕܐܦܣ ܒܪܘܚܐ ܚܠܦ ܟܢܫ ܩܠܐ ܕܡܬܩܪܝܢ. ܘܒܗܠܝܢ ܕܫܠܝܛܝܢ ܡܢܝܢ ܒܫܘܠܛܢܐ ܐܚܪ̈ܢܐ. ܫܘܒܚܐ ܗܘ ܕܝܢ ܒܫܡܝܐ: ܕܒܗܠܝܢ ܕܗܘܝܐ ܡܬܠܝܢ ܐܬܐܠܦ ܢܦܫܐ. ܐܠܐ ܟܕ ܒܪܟܬܗ ܩܕܝܫܬܐ ܡܫܚ ܐܢܐ: ܒܗܐ ܠܐܠܗܘܬܐ ܐܚܒ ܗܫܐ. ܒܗܝܕܝܢ ܦܝ ܟܕ ܐܦܪ ܠܐܘܫܐ ܕܙܘܒܢܐ. ܠܐ ܕܝܢ ܒܪܝܟܠ ܟܕ ܫܦܠܐܝܬ ܡܛܠ ܕܐܪܐ ܐܬܐܘܣܦ ܒܩܠܐ. ܟܕ ܗܟܝܠ ܐܦܪܐ. ܗܟܝܠ ܕܝܢ ܢܦܫܗ ܕܐܝܟ ܠܫܡܝܐ

lying sadly low. And it is a difficult business, that I should impart life to those things which are thus dead, but anointed by your holy prayers, I shall make an attack upon the conflict, giving first a definition of composition. For as I deal with the mystery, I have not yet used (defined) terms, although I have spoken in this way. But I have learned that the principle of composition is like this: (namely) the coming together from two or more simples, which have come to some one thing, in which also what is complete (in itself) is a part, (and) afterwards the parts are not investigated with regard to the principle of duality, since once and for all there has come into being one ousia or quality.[33] (Please) understand me about this too, that what was said as regards ousiai, (namely) that some are simple, and some are composite, (should be said) in the same way as regards the signs of ousiai, that we know some simple and some composite. But because I also confess composition in the case of the divine inhomination, I shall introduce (it), so that we may debate about it as well. (*Lebon p. 151*) And you, Doctor (and) Father, bear patiently the words of my poor understanding, for I do not contradict (what you have said)—far be it that I should act so madly—but since I wish to escape from a false opinion, I confidently venture to undertake such a contest.

The words *φύσις* and *οὐσία* mean the same as far as we are concerned, the one being derived from *πεφυκέναι* and the other from *εἶναι* and you, O Theologian, agree with me (on this). For you have said somewhere in (your) letter, "Where composition and natural coming-together of ousiai or of natures is constituted".[34] Therefore, if we teach "from two natures, one nature of the Word incarnate", how do we sin against the mystery, if, by means of words with the same meaning, we fulfil the same doctrine, (in saying) that from two ousiai there is one ousia of the Word incarnate? But this "incarnate" I have omitted, in as much as it is frequently declared, but I do not dissolve the composition because of this. And I turn (my) mind to mere surmise, and I urge you, O Father, to endure for a little my presumption with regard to the precision of the philosophers; even if they are outside our fold, we shall greatly clarify the explanation. Among these philosophers, Aristotle, who is called *ὁ νοῦς* said these words somewhere, as he provides an illustration of ousia: ARISTOTLE: "But ousia is, if we will speak with an example, such as man, horse."[35] But it is not the case that he does not acknowledge the composition of the living creature because of this. For everything which is simple is understood, rather than falling under the senses. Therefore how do I defraud the truth, when I call the incarnate Word

ܕܙܘܥܐ. ܒܣܘܦܐ ܕܡܢ ܠܬܚܬ. ܐܘ ܕܡܢ ܡܨ̈ܥܝܬܐ ܦܢ̈ܝܬܐ ܕܐܝܟ ܡܢܗ ܠܗ. ܕܒܗ ܗܘ ܕܡܫܡܫ ܡܫܠܐ ܐܠܗܘܬܗ. ܒܠܚܘܕ ܠܐ ܡܫܟܚ ܩܢܘܡܐ ܒܗܝ ܡܠܬܐ ܕܐܘܣܝܬܐ ܡܬܬܚܡ. ܕܚܕܐ ܐܝܟ ܚܕܐ ܐܘܣܝܐ ܕܗܘܬ ܐܘ ܡܣܬܘܕܥܐ. ܘܗܘܐ ܐܦܠܛܘܢ ܠܗ: ܗܘ ܕܬܬܡܪܐ ܒܗܝܐ ܐܪ̈ܣܛܘܣ. ܘܩܢܝܢ ܓܝܪ ܐܝܬܝܗܘܢ ܦܢ̈ܝܬܐ: ܗܠܝܢ ܕܝܢ ܡܬܬܒܥܝܬܐ. ܘܒܗܝ ܡܩܘܕܫܐ ܕܐܪ̈ܣܛܘܣ ܒܗ ܒܪܝܫܘܬܐ. ܒܗܠܝܢ ܓܝܪ ܦܢ̈ܝܬܐ. ܒܗܠܝܢ ܕܝܢ ܡܬܬܒܥܐ ܕܒܝܫ. ܐܠܐ ܡܛܠ ܕܟܠ ܐܦ ܒܗܝ ܡܬܒܪܢܝܢܘܬܐ ܠܐܠܗܘܬܐ: ܡܛܘܠ ܟܠ ܕܙܘܥܐ. ܐܝܟܐ ܕܐܦ ܒܗܝ ܗܘܬ (151) ܒܥܠܡܐ ܕܝܠܗ. ܘܐܝܟ ܡܟܬܒܢܐ ܐܚܪܢܐ: ܒܡܥܒܕܐ ܡܩܒܠܐ ܗܘܝܢ ܟܠܗ ܥܠܐ ܕܐܬܒܪܝܘ ܡܢ ܫܘܠܛܢܐ. ܒܗ ܓܝܪ ܡܫܬܘܕܥܐ ܐܡܪ ܐܝܬ ܠܗܘܟܠ ܗܠܝܢ ܕܠܝܢ. ܠܐ ܠܗܘܐ ܕܟܠܗ ܗܝ ܐܟܝܐ. ܐܠܐ ܒܕ ܟܠ ܐܝܬ ܐܟܢܘܣ ܡܢ ܠܡܘܢܝܐ ܗܢܝܐ: ܡܡܪܢܣ ܐܝܬ ܕܟܘܠܗ ܗܝ ܠܐܠܗܘܬܐ ܒܦܪܘܫܘܬܐ ܐܟܝܢ.

ܘܡܩܕܡܐ ܕܝܢ ܕܒܝܬ ܘܐܪܘܣܝܐ: ܐܣܝܪܐ ܐܝܬܝܗܘܢ ܒܗܘܢ. ܕܗܘ ܕܝܢ ܡܢ ܗܘ ܕܡܢ: ܗܘ ܕܝܢ ܡܢ ܗܘ ܕܐܝܬܘܗܝ ܡܬܬܒܥܐ: ܘܐܝܟ ܐܘ ܡܫܡܠܠ ܠܟܝܢܝܬܐ ܐܡܪ ܐܝܟ ܗܟܢ. ܐܡܪܝܢ ܓܝܪ ܒܕܘܡ ܕܐܠܝܢܐ: ܕܐܝܟ ܕܙܘܥܐ ܘܒܣܘܦܐ ܒܣܝܐ ܕܐܪ̈ܣܛܘܣ ܐܘ ܕܩܢ̈ܝܐ ܗܢܘܢ: ܡܢܝܢ ܐܢ ܡܢ ܠܬܚܬ ܒܬ̈ܪܝܢ ܚܕ ܒܝܬܐ ܘܡܠܬܗ ܕܡܫܡܫܬܐ ܘܡܫܡܫ ܡܫܬܡܫܝܢ: ܐܝܟ ܒܬܘܠܐ ܡܫܬܟܚܝܢ ܒܪܐܙܐ: ܐܢ ܒܕ ܩܢܝܢ ܩܠܐ ܕܦܘܡܐ ܚܕܐ: ܗܘ ܒܕ ܗܘ ܠܬܪܝܢܐ ܡܫܡܫܝܢ ܚܕ: ܕܡܢ ܠܬܚܬ ܐܪ̈ܣܛܘܣ ܚܕܐ ܐܘܣܝܐ. ܘܡܠܬܗ ܕܡܫܡܫܬܐ ܘܡܫܡܫ. ܗܘ ܕܝܢ ܕܡܫܡܫܢܐ ܒܗܘ ܕܦܢ̈ܝܢ ܡܬܐܡܪܐ ܒܪܫܐ. ܐܠܐ ܟܕ ܒܗܘܐ ܡܪܐ ܐܝܬ ܒܙܘܥܐ: ܘܒܗܝ ܡܫܡܫܢܘܬܐ ܦܢ̈ܝܬܐ ܡܫܡܫ ܐܝܬ ܒܟܘܠ ܘܡܫܡܫ ܐܝܬ ܘܡܫܡܠܠ ܠܡܪܢܝܬܐ ܐܘ ܐܟܐ: ܗܡܫ ܒܫܠܡܘܬܐ ܘܦܢ̈ܝܬܐ. ܘܐܦ ܒܗܝܢ ܐܢܝܢ ܡܢ ܕܘܟܬܐ ܕܥܠ: ܦܢ̈ܝܢ ܒܦܘܣܩܐ ܡܫܬܦܝܢ. ܡܢ ܗܠܝܢ ܦܠܣ̈ܘܦܐ ܐܪܝܣܛܛܠܝܣ ܗܘ ܘܡܬܐܡܪ ܗܘܝܐ: ܒܕ ܢܦܫ ܠܐܣܘܢܝܬܐ ܘܐܘܣܝܐ: ܗܠܝܢ ܩܢ̈ܝܢ ܩܠܐ ܐܡܪ ܒܕܘܡ. ܀ܐܪܝܣܛܛܠܝܣ܀ ܐܝܟܢܐ ܕܝܢ ܐܘܣܝܐ ܗܝ ܕܐܝܟ ܒܛܘܦܣܐ ܢܐܡܪ: ܐܝܟ ܡܐ ܕܒܪܢܫܐ ܗܘܫܝܐ. ܐܠܐ ܒܗ ܡܬܛܒܥܐ ܠܐ ܢܦܩ ܡܢܒܥܘܬܐ ܕܝܠܗ. ܦܠܝܓܐ ܓܝܪ ܘܦܠܝܓܐ ܡܫܬܠܡ: ܡܬܚܬܢܐ ܠܐ ܢܦܠ ܒܗܝ ܩ̈ܢܝܐ. ܐܝܟܢܐ ܗܟܢܐ ܒܕ ܦܪܐ ܐܝܬ ܐܘܣܝܐ ܠܡܫܡܫܐ ܘܐܬܒܪܝܬ: ܗܘܐ ܕܡܫܡܫܐ ܡܫܬܡܫܢܝܬܐ: (152) ܓܠܝܡ ܐܝܬ ܫܪܝܐ. ܗܘܝܐ ܘܗܠܝܢ ܕܡܫܬܘܕܥܢܘܬܐ ܙܘܓ ܒܗ ܕܐܫܪܐ. ܘܐܡܪ ܐܝܬ ܕܡܫܬܘܕܥܢܘܬܐ ܕܐܘܣܝܐ ܕܡܠܬܐ: ܐܡܬܘܡ ܒܗ ܒܡܫܪܐ ܘܒܕܝܐ: ܘܒܡܫܬܘܕܥܢܘܬܐ ܠܡܫܬܡܫܢܘܬܐ ܐܡܬܘܡ. ܒܕ ܗܠܝܢ ܡܬܐܡܪ̈ܝܢ ܡܢ ܠܬܪܝܢܐ ܕܒܪܢܫܐ ܕܐܡܪ ܫܪܝܐ ܠܐ ܡܬܐܒܕ.

"ousia", and understand this (ousia) (to be) incarnate? (*Lebon p. 152*) Thus it is right for me to explain as well the matters concerning quality, saying that the quality of the ousia of the Word who shared with me in flesh and blood,[36] also shared in the corporeal signification. Since these things are said by a mind which desires to speak the truth, they will not be called to account. For it is right that we should judge words in relation as well to the persons who make the sayings, and we ought to examine a few of the many (statements).

But now we will take up again that statement with regard to making a defence. We know that the things which belong to a genus also extend to species.[37] And we say that a living creature is an ousia endowed with a soul and sensation. And we know that a man and a horse and a bull are (instances of) this (ousia) along with some different propriety which belongs to each one of them. Therefore using the same name we call simples and composites and all these things which are mentioned "living creatures", and in this, the generic name of the ousia is applied by means of the hypostases which are particular ousiai, as it seems right to Father Basil as well.[38] Therefore, if we call the simple Son, even though he became composite for our sake, one hypostasis, and we are completely sure that he is endowed with a body, why may we not also take the name of the highest genus, and call the Son "ousia", while defining that this was incarnate? For even Father Cyril, as you yourself quote him, asserts that "one" is predicated not only of simples, but also extends to composites. For he says as follows: CYRIL: "For 'one' is not said in truth, only as regards things (which are) simple in nature, but also as regards those which are brought together in composition, as is the case with man".[39]

I am saying these things because of rebukes. But henceforth I come to the second rebuke. (*Lebon p. 153*) I was considered, O Father, to be a fraud, because sometimes I marvel at properties, and sometimes I eschew them. And in myself I appeared (as) a many-footed man,[40] because I take on a variety of colours. But I, in truth, on the contrary, will be neither of these things: it is not the case that I have spoken with (my) neighbour, while evil (is) in (my) heart. For I studiously shun the curse which by day and by night is sung on the cither. But I, from (my) first words, was of the same mind, and in *every respect* have believed that the invisible and intangible God the Word, along with the flesh also accepted the properties of the flesh, and became visible and tangible on our behalf. These are not (the properties) of simple divinity, but of (divinity) embodied, (which) because of the economy, also endured these (properties) of ours. But

ܙܘܥ ܓܒܪ ܕܒܝܬܗ̇ ܬܒܗ ܩܠܠ ܐܦ ܠܘܬ ܦܪ̈ܘܫܐ ܕܫܡܫܝܢ ܠܟܠܐ: ܘܡܢ ܗܠܝܢ
ܕܡܫ̈ܟܠܝ ܦܠܐ ܢܫܡܥ ܗܠܝܢ ܕܙܠܝܠܝܢ.
ܬܘܒ ܕܝܢ ܘܗܘ ܡܛܠܬܐ ܠܘܬ ܡܦܩ ܒܪܘܚܐ ܢܫܡܥܘܢ ܡܫܪܪܢ. ܘܗܠܝܢ ܕܐܝܬ
ܠܓܢܣܐ: ܕܐܦ ܠܘܬ ܐܪ̈ܙܐ ܒܒ̈ܬܝ ܡܒܕܩ. ܘܐܡܪܝܢ ܡܢ ܠܫܘܬܐ ܐܘܫܐ ܡܫܡܫܬܐ
ܡܪܓܫܢܝܬܐ: ܘܠܒܪ ܐܝܟܐ ܘܠܫܘܫܐ ܘܠܬܘܪܐ: ܗܘܐ ܡܒܕܩ. ܟܕ ܕܡܠܬܐ ܡܒܝܢ
ܐܡܪܬ: ܗ̇ܘ ܕܒܟܠ ܚܕ ܡܢܗܘܢ ܐܝܬ. ܚܝ̈ܠܐ ܗܠܝܢ ܘܡܬܐܡܪܝܢ ܒܟܠ ܫܘܝܐܝܬ
ܠܦܓܪ̈ܐ ܘܠܡܪ̈ܟܒܐ. ܘܠܟܠܗܘܢ ܗ̇ܢܝܢ ܕܡܬܐܡܪ̈ܝܢ. ܘܒܗ̇ܘ ܗܘܐ ܫܡܐ ܕܓܢܣܐ
ܘܐܘܫܐ ܡܬܐܡܪ. ܟܕ ܩ̈ܢܘܡܐ ܐܠܝܢ ܕܐܪ̈ܗܫܐ ܩ̈ܢܠܬܐ ܐܠܗܘܬܐ: ܐܝܟ ܕܐܦ
ܠܐܬܐ ܒܡܢܝܢܗܘܢ ܡܦܪܐ. ܐܢ ܗܘܝܘ ܠܒܪܐ ܦܫܝܛܐ: ܘܒܗ ܗܘܐ ܡܪ̈ܟܒܐ ܡܬܚܫܒܝܢ:
ܚܕ ܩܢܘܡܐ ܡܫܡܠܝܐ ܘܕܝܠܢܝܢ ܡܢ ܡܠܦ̈ܢܘܗܝ ܡܒܕܩ ܚܕ: ܡܛܠ ܚܝܐ
ܘܫܡܐ ܗ̇ܘ ܕܓܢܣܐ ܡܢ ܟܠ ܠܐ ܡܫܬܚܠܦ: ܘܠܒܪܐ ܐܘܫܐ ܐܡܪܝܢ. ܘܟܕ ܡܬܚܫܒܐ
ܗܘܐ ܡܬܚܫܒ. ܘܟܕ ܗܘܝܠ ܠܗ ܒܟܠܗ ܠܘܬ ܦܫܝܛܐ: ܐܠܐ ܐܦ ܠܘܬ ܡܪ̈ܟܒܐ
ܡܬܐܡܪ: ܘܡܫܬܡܠܝܢ ܐܠܐ ܟܕ ܠܡܢܝܢܗ̇ ܓܒܪ ܡܦܪܫ: ܗܘܝܠ ܓܒܪ ܐܡܪ.
ܘܡܫܬܡܠܝܢ܀ ܠܗ ܓܒܪ ܠܘܬ ܦܫܝܛܐ ܗܠܝܢ ܕܟܒܝܐ ܠܟܠܗܘܢ ܚܕ ܒܡܪ̈ܟܒܐ
ܡܬܐܡܪ: ܐܠܐ ܘܠܘܬ ܗܠܝܢ ܕܒܪ̈ܘܟܒܐ ܡܬܚܫܒܝܢ. ܐܝܟ ܡܐ ܕܐܡܪܘܗܝ ܫܡܥܢܐ ܡܒܝܢ
ܕܒܪܢܫܐ܀
ܗܠܝܢ ܗ̇ܢ ܚܠܦ ܡܪ̈ܝܫܘܬܐ ܐܡܪ ܐܢܐ. ܐܢܐ ܐܢܐ (153) ܕܝܢ ܡܛܠ ܘܠܘܬ ܡܪܝܫܘܬܐ
ܘܐܘܩܝܡ. ܐܣܛܘܟܣܐ ܐܘ ܐܬܐ ܕܡܬܚܫܒܐ ܐܝܬܝܗ̇ ܕܟܕ ܗ̇ܢ ܡܬܝܕܥ ܐܢܐ ܒܪ̈ܬܝܬܐ:
ܟܕ ܕܝܢ ܡܬܡܠܐܬܐ ܡܢܗܘܢ. ܘܐܝܟ ܗ̇ܝܢ ܩ̈ܛܠܐ ܐܣܛܘܟܣܐ ܒܫܡܐ: ܕܩ̈ܛܠܐ
ܩ̈ܦܠܐ ܡܫܬܡܠܝܬܐ. ܐܢܐ ܕܝܢ ܟܕ ܫܪܪܐ: ܡܫܬܘܕܥܬ ܗ̇ܘܐ ܕܝܠܗܝܢ ܠܗܠܝܢ. ܠܗ
ܡܛܠ̈ܐ ܟܕ ܡܢ̈ܝܐ ܡܫܠܠܢ: ܟܢܫܬܐ ܕܝܢ ܠܟܠܢܐ. ܒܪܗ ܐܢܐ ܓܒܪ ܦܫܝܛ ܡܢ
ܠܘܛܬܐ ܕܐܝܬܝܘܬܐ ܘܟܠܝܠܐ ܡܒܘܕܪܐ ܒܡܠܘܬܐ. ܐܠܐ ܐܢܐ ܗ̇ܢ ܡܢ ܬܒܗ ܩܠܠ ܡܒܝܢ̈ܬܐ
ܕܡܢܗ ܒܗܘܢ. ܘܡܢ ܡܠܦ̈ܢܘܗܝ ܗܢܝܢܐ. ܘܡܛܠܬܐ ܠܐܠܗܐ ܠܐ ܡܬܚܫܒܐ ܘܠܐ
ܡܬܓܫܫܐ. ܟܕ ܒܒܪܐ ܘܬܟ̈ܝܬܐ ܕܒܒܪܐ ܡܛܠ. ܘܗܘܐ ܡܬܚܫܒܐ ܘܡܬܓܫܫܐ
ܡܬܚܫܒ. ܗܠܝܢ ܕܠܐ ܐܝܬܝܗܝܢ ܕܠܗܘܬܐ ܦܫܝܛܬܐ. ܘܡܬܓܫܫܬܐ ܕܝܢ: ܡܛܠ
ܡܒܪ̈ܘܬܐ ܣܓܝ̈ܐܬܐ ܘܗܠܝܢ ܕܡܢ. ܘܐܣܛܘܟܣܐ ܕܝܢ ܡܛܠܬܐ ܠܐܝܟܢ ܕܐܡܪ ܒܟܝܢܗ
ܐܠܐܡܪܬܐ. ܦܓܪܗ ܕܐܬܦܫܛ ܡܢܗܘܢ. ܘܗܘܐ ܠܗ ܗܘܐ ܟܕ ܠܐܠܗܐ ܘܒܪܐ ܟܠܐ ܘܡܟܘܢ:
ܘܠܗ ܗܘܝܐ ܐܝܟܢܐ: ܕܐܝܬܗ ܠܘܬ ܕܦܫܝܛ ܡܬܚܫܒ ܐܢܐ. ܘܡܛܠ ܡܢ

because the saying seemed to some to have been said in too clumsy a way, I earnestly desired to be made acute by you. And this happened to me through God and your word, that condescended to such an extent, that it should descend upon me, who am particularly of small account. And thenceforward in every respect I had a formula which could not be contradicted, as it will be kept orthodox in every way. But it is good for me again to have regard for (some) one of the experts, and from that (source) send for a word of instruction. I have enlightened it like the dawn, and declared it afar. I have affirmed the "teaching as prophecy, and bequeathed it for other generations".[41] But confidently I add, "I have not toiled for myself alone, but for all those who are seeking it".[42]

But what is this third thing which as it were stares at me, and violently seizes on my heart? For I was believed to have understood that the lower was changed into the higher.[43] But this is completely renounced by those who still confess composition. (*Lebon p. 154*) For if I had attempted by boiling water through the continued application of fire, to change the wet ousia to air, that which is said would have been thought to have been in my mind. But now I shall give my opinion on this point as far as I am able. On all accounts, according to exact terms, body is considered that which is without soul; while we acknowledge flesh only (as) that which is alive. We learn that that[44] which is present to all things which breathe, both to us and to composed living creatures, is mixed from four elements. Therefore, (there is) on the one hand flesh and blood to the rational and irrational (alike). But on the other hand, the quality of soul is thought to introduce a change, and this indicates something rather significant, but it is not the case that the nature of the flesh of men is changed. Likewise, I acknowledge on the one hand that the ensouled flesh which is united to the Word—for I fear after this to say "mixed"!—is human and of our nature, but on the other hand, in so far as it is composed to (be one with) God, it exists (with) those special (properties) in comparison to our flesh. For it did not accept sin (as a result) of transgression; it was not obliged to hunger and thirst and sleep, but to be occupied with the Word to which it was united, which willed to suffer these things for the sake of the confirmation of the inhomination.

Therefore, this is not to change (an) ousia, but accurately to wonder at the mystery, that when the Word was composed in union to dense flesh, he made it more glorious than anything. For he is born without a seed, and a virgin is (his) mother. And he is fed, not needing it, but desiring it. But he is without all sin, and walks among

ܡܠܦܢܘܬܗ. ܐܝܟ ܟܕ ܡܠܟܐ ܕܟܢܫ ܠܥܠܡܐ ܠܡܘܟܠܗ. ܘܒܥܠܗ ܕܝܠ ܡܫܪܐ ܠܐܬܝܢ. ܛܒ ܟܕ ܕܝܢ ܠܘܒ ܕܐܣܘܪ ܠܗܠ ܐܝܟ ܡܢ ܣܒܝܥܐ: ܘܡܢ ܗܘܕܐ ܐܥܕܪ ܡܠܟܐ ܕܡܕܝܢܬܐ. ܐܝܟ ܕܦܫܐ ܐܝܘܒܐ ܘܡܘܠܟܗ ܒܝܬܐ ܒܪܘܚܐ. ܠܡܠܟܘܬܐ ܐܝܟ ܢܒܝܠܘܬܐ ܐܚܪܐ. ܘܡܒܥܠܗ ܠܡܪܒܠܐ ܐܣܬܝܒܠܐ. ܡܘܣܦ ܐܝܠ ܕܝܢ ܟܕ ܠܐܦܠܐܝܬ: ܕܠܗ ܟܕ ܒܠܚܘܕ ܒܒܠܠ: ܐܠܐ ܘܠܟܠܗܘܢ ܗܢܘܢ ܕܟܢܫ ܠܗ.

ܐܠܐ ܐܚܐ ܗܘܐ ܘܗܘܐ ܕܐܬܠܠ ܘܐܝܟ ܡܢܗܐ ܟܕ ܘܦܘܓܐ ܒܗ ܒܟܠܟܝܢ ܡܫܝܠܠ. ܐܦܠܛܪܐ ܓܒܪ ܕܐܦܠܛܘܢ: ܕܗܘ ܕܒܪܝܪ ܠܗܐ ܗܘ ܕܡܬܓܪ ܐܠܗܘܬ. ܗܘܐ ܕܝܢ ܕܦܓܝܢ ܪܣܡܐ ܡܢ ܗܠܝܢ ܕܡܘܕܝܢ ܒܪܡܠܠ (154) ܪܘܚܐ. ܠܗܘ ܓܒܪ ܐܝܟ ܗܘܐ ܟܕ ܡܡܠܛܝܢ: ܕܟܕ ܡܢܐ ܡܫܡܠܠ ܗܘܝܟ ܒܚܝܐ ܫܓܝܐܐ ܕܢܘܪܐ: ܘܠܐܘܣܝܐ ܙܛܒܠܐ ܠܐܬܪ ܐܘܦܝ. ܠܓܘ ܡܢ ܠܪܒܠܐ ܕܡܟܐ ܡܫܠܟܪܐ ܗܘܐ ܗܘ ܕܡܠܐܦܪܐ. ܗܟܐ ܕܝܢ ܘܟܠܐ ܗܘܐ ܠܠܪܒܠܝ ܐܝܟ ܕܐܝܟ ܟܕ ܐܦܪ ܐܝܠ. ܡܢ ܒܠܠ ܦܪܘܣ ܒܘܡ ܐܝܟ ܡܠܟܐ ܒܐܝܠܐ: ܦܓܪܐ ܡܠܪܝܐ ܐܦ ܗܘ ܘܠܐ ܢܦܫ. ܒܫܪܐ ܕܝܢ ܒܠܚܘܕ: ܠܗܘ ܕܚܣ ܡܒܥܝܢ. ܗܝܠ ܠܟܠܗܘܢ ܗܠܝܢ ܕܫܡܫܝܢ: ܘܟܠ ܘܠܝܫܘܬܐ ܡܪܒܒܠܐ. ܘܡܢ ܐܪܒܥܐ ܐܣܛܘܟܣܝܢ ܡܡܙܓ ܡܠܦܝܢ. ܠܡܫܝܚܐ ܗܘܒܠ ܘܟܠܐ ܡܫܝܚܐ: ܒܫܪܐ ܦܢ ܘܪܘܚܐ. ܡܡܘܪܒܘܬܐ ܕܝܢ ܕܢܦܫܐ ܡܫܠܟܪܐ ܕܡܟܐ ܡܘܣܒܐ. ܘܗܘܐ ܕܠܗܢ ܡܘܫܐ ܠܡܠܟܐ ܡܣܘܝܐ ܘܟܠܗ ܕܡܣܒܟ ܒܝܐ ܠܒܫܪܐ ܕܫܝܢܐ. ܗܒܝܐ ܘܠܒܫܪܐ ܕܡܢܦܫ ܗܘ ܕܡܣܒܪ ܠܡܠܟܐ: ܕܢܠܐܝܠ ܓܒܪ ܡܒܠܐܦܪ ܕܡܣܪܟ: ܐܢܫܐ ܦܢ ܢܒܗ ܐܝܠ ܘܒܪ ܒܝܢ. ܒܗܘ ܕܝܢ ܕܡܪܘܒ ܠܗܐ ܠܐܠܗܐ: ܗܠܝܢ ܠܠܪܘܬܐ ܠܗܘܒܠ ܒܫܪܐ ܕܠܝܢ ܡܒܝܢ. ܣܛܒܠܐ ܓܒܪ ܕܡܢ ܡܠܒܒܪܘܬܐ ܠܐ ܦܒܠ. ܕܒܦܘ ܘܒܪܘܐ ܘܒܡܘ ܠܐ ܐܓܪ ܕܠܒܝܐ ܕܝܢ ܠܡܠܟܐ ܕܡܣܒܪ ܠܗܐܗ: ܕܗܠܝܢ ܡܛܠ ܡܘܪܪܐ ܘܡܠܒܪܢܫܘܬܐ ܙܒܢ ܕܚܫ.

ܗܘܐ ܗܘܒܠ ܠܗ ܕܢܡܣܒܟ ܐܘܫܝܐ ܐܠܗܝܐ. ܐܠܐ ܕܠܗܘܡܪ ܣܠܠܐܝܠ ܒܪܐܪܐ. ܕܟܕ ܠܗܐ ܒܫܪܐ ܒܚܝܐ ܐܬܪܒ ܡܠܟܐ ܒܣܝܡܘܬܐ ܕܠܗܐܗ: ܠܗܝܐ ܕܡܒܚܣ ܡܢ ܒܠܠ ܒܒܝ. ܫܠܛ ܡܢ ܪܘܚܐ ܓܒܪ ܡܠܡܠܒ ܘܒܠܘܒܠܐ ܐܠܗܝܐ ܐܝܟܐ. ܘܡܠܐܪܫܐ ܦܢ ܠܗ ܕܫܡܫ ܐܠܐ ܕܦܒܐ. ܠܒܪ ܡܢ ܡܠܗ ܕܝܢ ܣܛܒܠܐ ܐܠܗܘܗ. ܘܡܘܠܒ ܒܝܢܠ ܢܩܘܒܐ ܒܝ ܠܐ ܡܠܝܐܐ. ܘܒܝܐ ܕܙܛܒܐ ܐܝܟ ܡܒܝܐ ܒܬܒܠܠ ܡܡܡܡ. ܘܟܕ ܡܪܒ ܡܘܬܐ ܠܠܒܠܒܐ ܐܘܪܚ. ܘܐܬܪ ܦܢ ܡܘܒ ܡܒܒܪܬܐ ܒܝ ܫܠܗ. ܗܘ ܕܝܢ ܕܪܘܚܐ ܡܢ

the Jews without being seen. And the nature of wet things serves (his) feet like the dry land. And when death drew near, he removed it on the third day. And the air provided a crossing when he ascended. But that which is beyond all speech (is this): he sits in heaven God incarnate at the right hand of majesty. For he established us along with him, and made us sit (*Lebon p. 155*) along with him with his Father. Thus he is coming at the second advent.

And a fourth saying has become a risk to me, so that (I am) again called to judgement, on the grounds that I have set aside ousiai, and interweave composition from signs. But I do not acknowledge that I suffered (from) this ignorance. For a quality does not exist without an ousia, nor should we recognise ousiai without signs. Therefore when I said that two ousiai were composed, along with them I was also uniting the signs.[45] But accurate speech determines that we should speak of God as being above ousia. But when God, the cause of all, says to Moses, and (Moses) wrote this word in place of a name, "He who is, sent me",[46] I make so bold—but I have taken my cue from him—to call God "ousia" as well: for God is, and is above those things which are. Therefore let us call him "ousia", and "above ousia". But you have defined, and very clearly, that the propriety of God (is) grace:[47] "Why do you call me good? No-one is good, except one, God".[48] For if a propriety is that thing which belongs to someone and to him alone—(and) now according to the quotation above it belongs to God alone to be good—(then) clearly something of this sort is a definition of a propriety. Nevertheless it is necessary that we reverence these great matters in silence. For God is in truth above ousia and propriety.

I have ventured (to say) these things to you, O Father of Fathers, and I have run far from my rank: not because I did not know myself at all, but because I was afraid that I might be trapped in (your) written accusations. And I prostrate myself at your holy feet, that you enact a law on those who have your second letter, (*Lebon p. 156*) that they read my defence as well, lest as time takes up these words of yours—for it keeps everything securely—it will tell posterity that I stumbled with an opinion like this, and this be thought to be the common rebuke of all the churches of God which have used the spark of my feeble tongue because of the remoteness of bishops in the *east*. But certainly some people, wanting to find fault, (will) think the matter is presumption. But I define ignorance as the death of the soul, and since I very much want to be alive, I fear to fail (in) this. But for those who in astonishment deride my search, I shall read again the wise law: "If you will invoke wisdom, and will give up your

ܥܠ ܡܠܟܐ܃ ܠܐܠܗܐ ܡܣܒܪܐ ܒܡܫܝܚܐ܂ ܒܡܫܝܚܐ ܕܪܒܘܬܐ ܢܛܪ܂ ܐܡܫܝ ܓܝܪ ܒܗܘܢ܃ ܘܐܘܦ (155) ܒܗܘܢ ܒܗܠ ܐܒܗܘܗܝ܂ ܗܒܠ ܒܫܠܝܛܘܬܐ ܕܐܬܝܗܒܬ ܐܬܐ܂

ܘܡܠܟܐ ܕܐܬܒܥܝ ܒܡܫܝܚܘܬܗ ܗܘܐ ܠܗ܃ ܕܐܘܦ ܒܗܠ ܕܝܠܗ ܡܬܚܫܒܐ܂ ܕܒܪܢܫܐ ܐܩܢܘܡ܃ ܘܡܢ ܦܓܘܪܐ ܡܬܪܟܒܐ ܘܢܦܫܐ܂ ܐܢܐ ܕܝܢ ܠܐ ܝܕܥ ܐܢܐ ܕܝܕܥܬ ܗܘܐ ܠܐ ܡܬܚܫܒܐ܂ ܡܫܘܕܥܘܬܐ ܓܝܪ ܕܠܐ ܐܘܣܝܐ ܠܐ ܗܘܝܐ܂ ܘܠܐ ܐܩܢܘܡ ܕܠܐ ܦܓܘܪܐ ܙܕܩ ܕܢܫܬܟܚ ܠܝ܂ ܟܕ ܐܡܪܐ ܗܟܝܠ ܕܐܝܬܝܗ ܐܩܢܘܡ ܠܐܘܣܝܐ܃ ܟܠ ܗܠܝܢ ܡܫܝܚ ܐܢܐ ܐܦ ܦܓܘܪܐ܂ ܗܘ ܕܝܢ ܕܐܡܪ ܒܟܠܗ ܡܢ ܐܘܣܝܐ ܠܐܠܗܐ܃ ܡܠܟܐ ܕܐܝܬܘܬܐ ܡܫܝܚܐ܂ ܟܕ ܕܝܢ ܐܠܗܐ ܒܟܠܗ ܘܒܪܢܫܐ ܒܟܠܗ܂ ܘܗܘܐ ܒܪܐ ܟܠܐ ܚܕ ܒܗܢܐ ܢܛܪ܂ ܕܗܘ ܕܐܝܬܘܗܝ ܚܕ ܐܩܢܘܡ܃ ܡܫܝܚܐ ܐܢܐ ܦܓܘܪܐ܂ ܒܪܗ ܡܢܗ ܢܦܫܗ܃ ܠܐܠܗܐ ܐܦ ܐܘܣܝܐ ܦܪܐ ܐܢܐ܂ ܐܝܬܘܗܝ ܓܝܪ ܐܠܗܐ܃ ܘܒܟܠܗ ܡܢ ܗܠܝܢ ܕܐܝܬܝܗܝܢ ܐܝܬܘܗܝ܂ ܢܦܫܗ ܗܘܐ ܘܒܟܠܗܘܢ ܘܒܟܠܗ ܡܢ ܐܘܣܝܐ܂ ܕܡܠܟܐ ܕܝܢ ܕܐܠܗܐ܃ ܘܦܓܪܐ ܒܟܠܗ ܦܓܘܪܐ ܠܐܢܫܝܢ܂ ܡܢܐ ܐܡܪ ܐܝܟ ܠܗ ܦܓܪܐ܂ ܘܠܐ ܐܝܬ ܦܓܪܐ ܐܠܐ ܐܢ ܟܕ ܐܠܗܐ܂ ܐܢ ܓܝܪ ܕܡܠܟܐ ܗܘ ܗܘ ܕܠܐܝܬ ܘܒܟܠܗܘܢܗܘܢ ܐܝܟ ܒܗ܃ ܕܐܠܗܐ ܕܝܢ ܒܟܠܗ ܒܡܠܟܐ ܡܫܝܚܐ ܗܘ ܕܦܓܪܐ܃ ܦܓܘܪܐ ܗܘܐ ܕܙܕܩ ܗܘܐ܃ ܠܐܢܫܐ ܕܙܕܩܐ ܐܝܬܘܗܝ܂ ܒܪܐ ܕܐܒܐ ܕܗܠܝܢ ܕܙܕܩܝܢ ܒܡܠܟܐ ܢܦܪ܃ ܐܝܬܘܗܝ ܓܝܪ ܒܟܪܝܐ ܐܠܗܐ ܒܟܠܗ ܡܢ ܐܘܣܝܐ ܘܡܠܟܐ܂

ܗܠܝܢ ܐܡܪܢܢ ܒܐܬܪܗܘܢ ܐܘ ܐܬܐ ܕܐܬܝܐ܃ ܘܒܪܘܚܐ ܒܪܘܟ ܡܢ ܦܓܪܐ ܕܡܠܟ ܙܕܩܐ܂ ܠܗ ܕܦܓܪ ܠܐ ܢܒܥܐ ܢܦܫ܂ ܐܠܐ ܕܙܕܩܐ ܕܒܡܫܝܚܘܬܐ ܡܠܟܘܬܐ ܐܬܝܐܢ܂ ܘܡܬܩܪܒ ܐܢܐ ܡܢ ܦܓܪܗܘܢ ܡܢܟܠܗ܃ ܕܐܬܟܠܗܘܢ ܢܦܫܐ ܠܗܠܝܢ ܕܐܝܬ ܠܗܘܢ ܐܠܦܐܘܢ (156) ܕܐܬܐܝܢ܃ ܕܐܦ ܡܢܗ ܒܪܘܚܐ ܕܡܠܟ ܢܦܪܘܢ܂ ܘܠܐ ܟܕ ܙܒܢܐ ܢܦܫ ܗܠܝܢ ܟܠܗ ܥܠܐ ܕܡܠܟܘܢ܃ ܢܛܪ ܓܝܪ ܡܠܟܘܢ ܗܘܝܐܢܬܐ܃ ܢܐܡܪ ܒܗܐ ܟܠܐ ܐܝܟܐ ܕܒܠܘܡ܃ ܕܐܬܡܫܝܚܬܐ ܕܙܕܩ ܗܒܐ ܐܬܒܪܝܐ܂ ܘܗܘܐ ܡܪܢܫܬܐ ܕܓܝܪܐ ܕܒܪ̈ܝܬܐ ܕܐܠܗܐ ܐܬܡܠܟܢ܃ ܕܡܠܟܘܢ ܐܠܐܢ ܕܡܠܟܘܬ ܦܪܫܘܬܐ ܕܪܒܘܬܐ܃ ܒܡܫܝܚܐ ܒܒܠܘܝܬܐ ܕܠܡܫ ܐܠܘܙܐ ܐܬܡܫܚ܂ ܡܢ ܡܠܦܪܘܫ ܕܝܢ܂ ܐܬܩܢ ܒܗܘ ܕܦܠܢ ܕܢܦܫܗ܃ ܕܐܦ ܡܪܢܫܬܐ ܐܝܟܘܢ ܫܘܒܪܐ ܡܫܒܚܢܢ܂ ܐܢܐ ܕܝܢ ܒܟܠܐ ܐܢܒܝܐ܃ ܡܫܬܐ ܦܢ ܕܢܫܐ ܡܠܢܦܫ ܐܢܐ܂ ܘܟܕ ܦܓܪ ܕܐܝ ܐܢܐ ܕܐܢܫܐ܃ ܕܢܦܠܬܐ ܕܐܬܒܪܘ ܗܘܐ܂ ܠܗܘܢ ܕܝܢ ܕܒܟܠܐ ܕܡܠܟ܃ ܒܠܡܫܡܘܬܐ ܡܫܡܫܝܢ܃ ܢܦܫܗ ܠܐܘܟ ܚܫܝܫܐ ܐܦܪܐ܂ ܘܐܢ ܒܫܡܫܬܐ ܠܐܦܪܐ܃ ܘܡܫܝܚܐ ܐܬܠܐ ܒܪܐ ܡܠܟ܂ ܘܐܢ ܠܐܒܪܗ ܐܝܟ ܫܠܡܐ

voice to knowledge, and if you will search for it like silver, and glean for it like treasure, then you will know the fear of the Lord, and you will find the knowledge of God".[49]

But because a pair of the prophets are running after me, (along) with your holy writings, I should run with the pair. And first I will say to you from great Haggai, "You have sown much and [brought in][50] little".[51] For you have cast some divine seed upon earth that has a not very open heart, (namely) my mind. But cultivating this with great care, you urge on even rocky places, that you may take fruit even from (otherwise) fruitless (plants). And then I will also say the words of Hosea to you: "You are chastising and healing us: you are striking and curing us".[52]

These things are in reference to your divine letter, which teaches in truth, which finds fault in a peaceful way, which heals with grace. (*Lebon p. 157*) And I ask God that long life be given to you, and that we, the orthodox Church, may again keep the feast with your lawful presence, as (we do) now in the text for your utterance, but then adorned in the true colours of your advent, we will write these (words of the) psalms in (our) understanding, "You have had pleasure, O Lord, in your land; you have turned away the captivity of Jacob; you have forgiven the sin of your people; you have covered all their sins".[53]

The Third Letter of Sergius the Grammarian to the holy Patriarch Severus is ended.

Notes

1. *sc.* David.
2. Ps. cxl.3.
3. Sir. xxii.27.
4. Sir. xx.18.
5. cf. Ps. ix.36.
6. Prov. xv.10.
7. Prov. xv.31 according to the Vulgate and some minuscules.
8. Prov. xv.32.
9. Prov. xiii.18.
10. Sir. xiii.2.
11. cf. Jn. i.1 and 14.
12. cf. 1 Jn. i.1.
13. Lk. xxiv.39.
14. Jn. iv.24.
15. cf. Wisdom vii.22–23.
16. Jn. vi.54.
17. Jn. x.18.
18. The Syriac is [illegible]. Lebon suggests that this is an attempt to translate *ἀποκηρύσσειν*.

ܘܐܦ ܡܫܡܠܝܐ ܠܒܢܝܢܗ. ܗܢܝܢ ܠܘܬ ܕܫܠܡܐ ܕܡܢܝܐ. ܘܡܫܡܠܝܘܬܐ ܕܐܠܗܐ ܠܒܢܝ.

ܡܛܠ ܕܝܢ ܕܐܦ ܙܘܓܐ ܕܒܢ̈ܝܐ ܙܘܓܝܢ ܒܠܚܘܕ ܒܗܘܢ ܒܡܫܡܠܝܘܬܗܘܢ ܒܢܘܗܪܐ. ܘܠܐ ܒܗ ܕܒܥܗ ܕܙܘܓܐ ܐܘܪܚܐ. ܘܡܫܡܠܐ ܦܫ ܡܢ ܡܚܕܐ ܙܥܪܐ ܐܡܪ ܠܡܐܡܪ. ܘܙܟܝܗܘܢ ܡܫܪ̈ܝܬܐ ܘܣܥܪܗܘܢ ܒܢܘܗܪܐ. ܒܗܝ ܐܘܪܚܐ ܒܪܢܫ ܕܠܗ ܦܫܩ ܦܠܚ ܠܒܗ: ܢܦܠ ܕܡܟ: ܙܘܓܐ ܡܢܝܢ ܠܐܠܗܐ ܐܘܪܚܬܗ. ܒܗܝ ܕܝܢ ܒܝ ܡܠܟܝܢ ܐܢܬܘܢ ܒܡܫܬܘܕܝܘܬܐ: ܐܦ ܒܦܘܩܕܢܐ ܕܦܘܠܘܣ ܫܠܝܚܐ ܐܢܬܘܢ: ܕܐܦ ܡܢ ܕܠܐ ܦܐܪܐ ܦܐܪܐ ܠܐܦܝܟܘܢ. ܒܠܘܩܒܠ ܕܝܢ ܐܡܪ ܠܗ: ܘܩܒܠܬ ܩܠܐ ܕܗܘܐ. ܕܐܝܬ ܙܘܐ ܐܝܬ ܘܡܬܐܡܪ ܐܝܬ ܠܝ. ܡܢܐ ܐܝܬ ܘܡܫܬܚܠܦ ܐܝܬ ܠܝ.

ܗܟܢ ܒܗܝ ܐܝܟܢܐ ܠܐܠܗܐ: ܗܘ ܕܒܡܢܝܢܐ ܡܫܡܠܐ. ܗܘ ܕܡܫܡܠܝܐ ܙܒܢܐ. ܗܘ ܕܒܗ ܡܫܡܠܝܘܬܐ (157) ܡܫܬܡܠܝܐ. ܦܬܓܡܐ ܕܝܢ ܠܐܠܗܐ: ܕܒܢ̈ܝܐ ܐܘܪܚܐ ܢܫܡܠܘܢ ܠܟܠܗܘܢ. ܘܡܢ ܒܬܪ ܠܐܘܪܚܐ ܠܐܘܒ ܒܗܘܢ ܢܫܡܠܘܢܗܘܢ ܢܫܡܠܝܘܬܐ ܢܒܝܒ. ܐܝܟܢܐ ܕܗܘܐ ܦܫ ܒܬܘܕܝܬܐ ܕܒܢܐ ܡܠܐ: ܗܢܝܢ ܕܝܢ: ܒܝ ܩܠܝܠܐ ܡܢܬܐ ܕܡܬܐܡܪܝܢ ܡܫܬܟܠܝܢ: ܗܟܢ ܕܢܬܬܐ ܒܚܘܒܐ ܢܫܠܘܢ. ܙܒܢܐ ܡܢܝܐ ܠܐܘܪܚ. ܐܘܦܝܬ ܡܫܠܡܘ ܕܡܫܘܢ. ܡܫܡܠܐ ܒܘܠܐ ܕܒܫܡ ܒܫܡܐ ܡܠܗܘܢ ܣܟܘܡܗܘܢ܀

܀ܫܠܡܬ ܐܓܪܬܐ ܕܐܠܬ ܕܩܘܪܝܩܘܣ ܓܪܝܓܘܪܝܘܣ: ܟܬܒ ܡܫܡܫ ܡܠܦܢܐ ܦܛܪܝܪܟܐ܀

19. Reading ܕܢܝܐ for ܕܘܝܐ.
20. cf. Phil. ii.7.
21. Jn. xix.37.
22. Deut. x.22.
23. 1 Tim. ii.5.
24. Lebon notes: ψιλός: Id est: ad sententiam iuxta quam Christus est ψιλὸς ἄνθρωπος.
25. cf. Acts ii.22.
26. Joel iii.1.
27. For *σύνθεσις* as the Greek noun underlying ܪܘܟܒܐ, cf. p. 109.14 (Greek in Lietzmann, *op. cit.*), and p. 134.1 (Greek in Migne).
28. PG 36.325C. *Or. XXXVIII.*
29. cf. PG 36.313B and 612B. *Or. XXXVIII and XLIV.*
30. *sc.* Gregory Nazianzen.
31. cf. PG 36.113A, 328C. *Or. XXX and XXXVIII.*
32. Lebon comments here: Sensus huius sententiae neque clarus neque certus mihi videtur.
33. cf. above, p. 100.11–16.
34. p. 136, lines 18 and 19.
35. Aristotle, *Categories*, 4.1b.27.
36. cf. Heb. ii.14.
37. Plural.
38. cf. Basil, *Ep. XXXVIII, Gregorio fratri de discrimine essentiae et hypostasis*, PG 32.326 ff.
39. PG 77.241B (= ACO I, 1, 6a, p. 160.2–4). *Ep. XLVI, Ad Succ. Ep. II.*
40. Dr Lionel Wickham has pointed out to me that behind "many-footed" there may lie πολύπους, the octopus, which is well known for changing its colours.
41. cf. Sir. xxiv.32–3.
42. cf. Sir. xxiv.34.
43. cf. pp. 134–135 above.
44. *sc.* flesh.
45. cf. p. 72.10, 17–20 in Sergius' *First Letter*.
46. Ex. iii.14.
47. ܛܝܡܘܬܐ. Lebon notes: Read ܛܝܒܘܬܐ (goodness) or ܛܒܘܬܐ which suits what follows.
48. Mk. x.18.
49. cf. Prov. ii.3–5.
50. Reading ܡܫܠܬܘܢ for ܡܠܫܬܘܢ (misprint).
51. Hag. i.6.
52. Hos. vi.1.
53. Ps. lxxxiv.2–3.

Letter III of Severus

The Third Letter of the same Patriarch Severus to the Grammarian.

When I read this third letter of your Chastity, which was given me very late, I wanted to keep silent, and to let alone those things which are written by me and by you. For it is not in my authority—as you said (it was)[1]—that I should give permission that these things of yours be read, these things which are written with your authority and free will. For such a thing would be easy, and it might possibly bring me prestige and would show everyone very clearly to which sayings I had given answers. For after the second letter, it seemed superfluous to study the same things with idle talk in another way, and again to remind him who renounces reminding, and is indignant. For some wise man says, "There is reproof which is inappropriate".[2]

But because this is not appropriate for me, and it is not, as one of the prophets said, the portion of Jacob,[3] that we should prosper on the failings of brothers and derive prestige from there, (*Lebon p. 158*) but rather (it is appropriate) that we should think and say what Paul said to the Corinthians, "But we pray God that you do nothing evil, not that we may appear proven, but that you may do good even if we should appear in a poor light".[4] Because of this I have thought it right—and this while I am in this manner of flight, and secret and toilsome sojourning—with due love again to [remind][5] you in a brotherly way. For what my intention was otherwise (namely) either to maintain strict silence, or to point you out with scorn, is not only foreign to true religion but also to good manners, and is particularly hateful to God, for the sacred writing says somewhere, "He who winks his eyes with deceit gathers griefs for men, but he who reproves openly makes peace".[6]

Therefore your Chastity is reminded in every respect, that at the beginning, when you wrote to the holy Bishop Antoninus, you said about yourself that (but) lately you had gazed upon divine matters, and that you were a child in religious doctrines, and you had thought that it was in no way right that we should confess the particularity of the natures from which the one Christ was completed inexpressibly and above reason. And I, being far separated and

⁘ܐܓܪܬܐ ܕܐܬܠܗ ܕܫܠܚ ܡܢ ܕܠܗ ܕܦܛܪܝܪܟܐ ܡܪܩܘܣ ܙܒܘܪܝܘܣ ܕܒܪܛܠܡܝܘܣ⁘ ܡܢ ܦܪܝܫ ܗܘܐ ܐܓܪܬܐ ܕܐܬܠܗ ܕܒܟܬܒܬܐ ܕܡܠܟ ܕܦܘܠܘܣ ܡܩܘܕܫܐ ܐܬܩܪܝܬ ܠܝ: ܟܬܒܬ ܕܡܠܬܐ ܐܫܟܚܬ: ܘܐܫܬܥܝ ܗܠܝܢ ܕܠܝ ܘܠܟ ܡܬܝܢ. ܗܘܐ ܓܝܪ ܠܗ ܕܡܫܬܠܡ ܐܠܗܐ ܐܡܝܢܐ ܘܐܡܪܬܐ. ܗܘ ܕܐܦܣ ܕܢܬܟܬܒܢ ܗܠܝܢ ܕܠܟ: ܗܠܝܢ ܕܝܢ ܡܫܬܠܡܢ ܠܡܢܝ ܠܟ ܘܒܘܝܐ ܪܚܡܬܐ. ܕܟܠܗ ܗܘܐ ܓܝܪ ܗܘܐ ܕܐܝܟ ܗܟܢ. ܘܒܪ ܡܫܡܫܢܐ ܗܘܐ ܕܚܕܝܐ ܠܐܒܝ: ܘܐܬܐ ܠܫܠܝܚ ܠܡܪ ܦܛܪܘܣ: ܕܟܠܐ ܐܡܝܢ ܩܠܐ ܕܟܬܝܒ ܠܗ ܦܘܣ ܦܠܓܘܬܐ. ܟܕ ܓܝܪ ܐܓܪܬܐ ܕܐܩܝܡ: ܠܡܪܬܐ ܡܫܬܠܡܢܐ ܐܚܪܢܝܬܐ ܕܒܡܫܡܫܬܐ ܟܗܢ ܡܢ ܟܗܢ ܢܘܡܘܣ: ܘܐܘܟ ܢܟܘܪ ܠܟܘܢ ܕܟܠܐ ܡܬܟܬܒܐ ܦܪܝܫ ܐܦ ܡܬܟܬܒ. ܐܡܪ ܓܝܪ ܘܐܦ ܣܝܡܬܐ: ܕܐܬܐ ܡܬܩܢܢܬܐ ܗܘ ܕܠܐ ܐܠܗܐ ܦܐܝܬܐ.

ܐܠܐ ܡܛܠ ܕܗܘܐ ܠܟ ܠܐ ܦܐܝܐ: ܘܠܐ ܗܘܐ ܗܘ ܡܢܠܬܐ ܕܡܫܘܕܥ ܐܝܟ ܡܐ ܕܐܡܪ ܐܝܟ ܡܢ ܢܒܝܐ: ܗܘ ܕܒܟܘܪܐ ܘܐܒܝܐ ܢܓܠܣ: ܘܡܢ ܠܐܡ ܢܫܟ (158) ܟܢܫܘܬܐ: ܠܡܪܬܐ ܕܝܢ: ܗܘ ܕܐܡܪ ܟܠܗ ܡܫܬܠܡܐ ܦܘܠܘܣ: ܘܠܡܢܫܟ ܘܐܡܪ: ܡܪܓܠܝܢ ܕܝܢ ܟܠܗ ܠܐܠܗܐ: ܘܐܦܠܐ ܚܕܐ ܒܝܫܬܐ ܠܐܒܝܘܗܝ: ܠܗ ܕܚܝܢ ܒܩܝܡܐ ܢܠܡܚܕܐ: ܐܠܐ ܕܐܢܬܘܢ ܦܢ ܠܓܒܬܐ ܠܐܒܝܘܗܝ: ܚܝܢ ܕܝܢ ܐܝܟ ܠܐ ܒܩܝܡܐ ܢܠܡܚܕܐ: ܡܛܠ ܗܘܐ ܕܦܠܓܐ ܐܬܢܫܟܬ: ܘܗܠܝܢ ܡܢ ܟܗܢܐ ܐܫܟܚܐ ܕܒܪܘܫܐ ܐܠܗ ܐܢܐ: ܘܐܫܬܥܝܬܐ ܘܠܐ ܡܬܠܚܡܐ ܘܡܫܬܠܬܐ: ܕܒܪ ܚܘܒܐ ܕܙܕܩ: ܟܗܘܝ ܠܐܒ ܐܢܐܬܐ. ܗܘ ܓܝܪ ܕܡܢ ܐܚܪܢܝܬܐ ܐܬܐ ܟܬܪܥܝܬܐ: ܐܘ ܕܟܠ ܡܠܗ ܡܠܬܐ ܐܬܬܐ: ܐܘ ܐܪܡܝܘ ܠܟ ܒܪ ܡܫܝܚܐ: ܠܗ ܟܠܗܘܢ ܢܒܪܢܬܐ ܕܕܚܠܬ ܠܐܠܗܐ ܐܠܗܢ: ܐܠܐ ܘܕܝܠܗ ܕܚܐܪܘܬܐ. ܘܫܢܝܬܐ ܦܩܝܢ ܡܢ ܠܐܠܗܐ. ܐܡܪ ܓܝܪ ܒܝܘܡ ܘܡܠܟܐ ܡܫܝܚܐ: ܗܘ ܕܙܩܦ ܬܪܝܢܐ ܒܪ ܢܛܪܐ: ܦܪܥܢ ܠܓܒܪܐ ܒܩܠܬܐ. ܗܘ ܕܝܢ ܕܦܪܥ ܒܪ ܦܪܘܫܐ ܬܪܝܢ ܡܠܟܐ.

ܒܗܝܕܐ ܗܟܢܐ ܢܫܬܘܐ ܡܢ ܟܠ ܦܪܘܣ: ܕܒܫܘܪܝܐ ܡܢ ܟܗܢܐ ܡܫܝܚܐ ܐܠܗܘܬܐ ܐܦܝܣܩܘܦܐ ܦܠܚ ܕܘܝܕ: ܐܡܪܬܐ ܟܠ ܢܫܝܢ: ܕܗܘܐ ܐܘܡܢ ܟܗܢ ܠܐܠܗܘܬܐ. ܘܒܬܘܟܦܐ ܘܕܝܠܗ ܠܐܠܗܐ ܡܚܪܐ ܐܢܬ. ܘܦܩܕ ܗܘܝܬ ܘܠܐ ܠܓܡܪ ܙܘܓ ܕܢܗܘܐ ܕܡܠܬܐ ܕܟܝܢܐ: ܕܡܛܠܗܝܢ ܗܘ ܚܕ ܡܫܝܚܐ ܠܐ ܡܬܡܠܠܐ ܘܟܠܗ ܡܢ ܡܠܬܐ ܐܬܡܠܠ. ܘܐܦ ܡܢ ܦܪܝܫ ܗܘܐ ܒܪܘܚܐ: ܘܐܬܬܠܬ ܕܟܢܫܠ ܡܫܬܠܡ ܐܦܠܐ ܦܠܓܬܐ: ܡܢ ܟܗܢ ܩܠܐ ܕܒܢܝܢܐ ܡܩܪܒܢ ܐܡܪܬܐ: ܕܟܠ ܘܡܢ ܟܠ ܦܪܘܣ ܙܘܓ ܕܢܗܘܐ ܕܟܠܬܐ ܕܟܝܢܐ ܕܡܛܠܗܝܢ ܒܫܘܐܝܬ: ܗܘ ܕܐܝܟ ܕܒܫܘܡܠܝܐ

asked to answer your question, quoted from the words of wise Cyril, that in everything and in all respects it was right that we confess the particularities of the natures from which Emmanuel is, that is (particularities) that (lie) in natural quality, and not such that the natures should be cut off independently and separated from each other. For whoever does not confess this, arrives at the opinion of those who confuse ousiai. For (Cyril) says as follows in those things which he wrote to Diodore: CYRIL: "Therefore let us acknowledge that the body which was born at Bethlehem, even if it is not the same (*Lebon p. 159*)—I mean in natural quality—with the Word which is from the Father, yet it became his, and not of some other son beside him. But one Son and Christ and Lord is understood even when the Word was incarnate".[7] AND AGAIN AFTER OTHER THINGS: "Because we also say that in terms of particularity, flesh is in every respect of another nature from the Word which sprang from God and the Father, nevertheless, it became his by an inseverable union, so that even the Word who appeared from the ousia of God and the Father was called the seed of Abraham in the flesh, for the economy calls him this, and it does not at all injure his being that which he is. For although he is God by nature, he also truly became man, and is Son of God and the Father, not counterfeit and not of a lying name".[8] AND AGAIN AFTER A LITTLE: "But it is not the case that it is anywhere (and) in any respect unnoticed that you attempt to put to confusion those who have an orthodox doctrine, (that is) those who teach an unconfused union, and you are not ashamed as you stand in opposition, and stir everything up and down, showing the flesh (is) of another nature, (of another nature) I mean, as it were in respect to the Word from God, and if someone should confess this with you, shunning the ignorance of the confusers of natures, you at once divide the one (Christ) into two".[9]

Notice that in these things which were quoted, the Doctor clearly showed that not to confess otherness of the natures which have come together to union, and particularity, and difference as far as natural quality is concerned, does not fall outside the iniquity and foolishness of those who confuse ousiai, but comes under the rebuke which belongs to them. And as it were from the other side again, (*Lebon p. 160*) those who divide Emmanuel make this natural difference a pretext for division.

Tell me then, did I make you a confuser of ousiai when I reminded your Chastity of these things? Or have I written the charge of heresy against you, (I) who showed you the path of the Fathers, when you confessed that you were inexperienced in divine doctrines and need-

ܒܥܠܬܐ: ܘܠܗ ܒܗܘܢ ܕܡܢܗܘܢ ܘܠܗܘܢ ܢܗܘܘܢ ܦܫܝܩܝܢ ܘܢܣܝܩܝܢ ܒܢ̈ܝܐ ܡܢ ܢܒ̈ܝܐ. ܗܘ ܓܝܪ ܕܗܘܐ ܠܐ ܡܫܘܐ: ܟܠܗ ܠܡܥܒܕܢܘܬܐ ܕܝܠܗܘܢ ܕܐܦܣܩܘ ܣܓܝܐܝܢ ܐܬܐ. ܐܡܪ ܓܝܪ ܗܟܝܠ ܒܗܠܝܢ ܕܟܠܗ ܕܡܬܦܪܣ ܥܠܝ ܗܘܐ. ܀ܫܘܠܡܗ܀ ܟܕ ܗܟܝܠ ܕܓܡܪܐ ܕܐܬܐ ܒܬܪ ܐܢܫ: ܐܦ ܠܗ ܗܘ ܒ ܗܘ (159) ܐܬܠܘܗܝ ܒܥܡܘܕܝܘܬܐ ܒܣܠܬܐ ܐܡܪ ܐܢܐ: ܒܗܠܝܢ ܡܠܬܐ ܕܡܢ ܐܒܐ: ܐܠܐ ܕܡܠܬܗ ܗܘܐ ܘܠܗ ܕܐܝܟ ܐܢܫ ܒܪܐ ܫܦܝܪ ܡܢܗ. ܡܫܬܟܠܠ ܕܝܢ ܡܢ ܒܪܐ ܘܡܫܝܚܐ ܘܡܪܢܐ: ܘܟܕ ܐܬܥܒܪ ܡܠܬܐ܀ ܘܐܘܒ ܒܠܘ ܐܣܬܝܡܬܐ܀ ܡܠܟܠ ܕܐܦ ܚܕ ܐܡܪܢ ܚܕ: ܕܒܡܠܬܐ ܕܡܠܘܬܐ: ܐܣܪ ܒܗ ܐܠܗܘܬܗ ܡܢ ܡܠܦܪܘܣ ܒܣܪܐ: ܒܗܠܝܢ ܡܠܬܐ ܕܡܘܣ ܡܢ ܠܐܠܗܐ ܘܐܒܐ. ܒܪܡ ܕܡܠܬܗ ܗܘܐ: ܒܡܚܝܠܘܬܐ ܠܐ ܡܫܬܡܠܝܢܘܬܐ. ܐܝܟܢܐ ܕܐܦ ܡܠܬܐ ܗܘ ܕܡܢ ܐܘܣܝܐ ܕܐܠܗܐ ܘܐܒܐ ܐܬܝܠܕ: ܢܣܒܐ ܕܐܒܪܗܡ ܐܬܠܒܫ ܒܒܣܪ: ܕܡܢܐ ܒܗ ܒܗܘܐ ܡܒܪܢܫܐ. ܘܠܐ ܡܢܗ ܡܫܢܝܐ ܒܟܝܢܗ ܕܗܘܐ ܐܬܠܒܫ ܗܘ ܡܠܐ ܕܐܬܠܒܫ. ܒ ܐܬܠܒܫ ܓܝܪ ܐܠܗܐ ܒܒܣܪܐ: ܗܘܐ ܡܬܒܪܢܫ ܐܦ ܒܪܢܫܐ. ܘܐܬܠܒܫ ܒܪܐ ܕܐܠܗܐ ܘܐܒܐ: ܠܐ ܐܫܬܢܝ: ܘܠܐ ܕܠܡܐ ܡܫܬܢܐ܀ ܘܒܠܘ ܡܟܝܠ ܠܘܩܒܠ܀ ܐܠܐ ܠܗ ܘܠܐ ܡܬܚܝܠܐ ܐܠܗܘܬܗ ܒܝܕ ܡܢ ܡܠܦܪܘܣ. ܘܠܐܝܠܝܢ ܕܐܝܬ ܠܗܘܢ ܠܡܥܒܕܢܘܬܐ ܠܐܘܪܚܐ: ܗܠܝܢ ܕܡܠܝܢ ܚܝܘܬܐ ܠܐ ܒܡܠܬܐ: ܦܫܛ ܐܝܬ ܕܐܡܪ. ܘܟܕ ܡܫܡܠܝܘܬܐ ܥܠܡ ܐܝܬ: ܠܐ ܡܬܚܫܒ ܐܝܬ. ܘܟܠܗ ܘܡܠܐܝܬ ܡܠܦܝܢ ܚܙܝܢ ܐܝܬ: ܘܐܣܪܗ ܒ ܚܝܠܐ ܠܟܦܪܐ ܡܫܘܐ ܐܝܬ: ܐܝܟ ܕܟܠܗ ܡܠܬܐ ܕܡܢ ܐܠܗܐ ܐܡܪ ܐܢܐ. ܘܐܢ ܐܝܟ ܗܘܐ ܒܥܝܢ ܢܗܘܐ: ܒ ܡܢ ܠܐ ܡܬܒܥܝܐ ܕܒܠܝ ܢ̈ܦܫܐ ܚܙܝܢ: ܡܫܝܐ ܠܡܘܬܐ ܡܦܪܢ ܐܝܬ ܠܗܘ ܚܕ܀

ܗܐ ܓܝܪ ܒܥܠܡܐ ܕܐܬܚܙܝ ܚܘܝ ܡܫܝܚܐ: ܕܗܘ ܕܠܐ ܢܗܘܐ ܐܣܪܝܢܐ ܒܢ̈ܝܐ ܕܗܠܝܢ ܕܐܝܟܢܐ ܐܬܘ ܠܚܝܘܬܐ: ܘܡܠܘܬܐ ܘܡܫܝܚܐ: ܗܘ ܕܐܝܟ ܕܒܥܡܘܕܝܘܬܐ ܚܝܠܬܐ: ܠܐ ܢܦܠ ܠܒܪ ܡܢ ܒܘܠܐ ܘܡܫܠܡܘܬܐ: ܕܗܘܢ ܕܒܠܝܢ ܐܦܣܩܘ. ܐܠܐ ܠܐܝܬܗ ܢܦܫܐ ܕܗܠܝܢ ܐܬܐ. ܘܐܝܟ ܕܡܢ ܗܘ ܕܒܡܫܠܐ ܠܘܒ: (160) ܗܠܝܢ ܕܦܫܩܝܢ ܠܒܫܢܘܬܠܐ : ܠܡܫܝܚܐ ܗܢܐ ܒܣܝܐ: ܚܕܝܐ ܕܦܘܠܚܢܐ ܚܒܝܒ.

ܒ ܗܠܝܢ ܗܟܝܠ ܕܗܘܐ ܠܒܥܘܬܝ: ܒܐܦܝܣܩܘ ܒܒܝܬܝ ܐܡܪ ܠܟ: ܐܘ ܡܪܫܘܬܐ ܕܗܘܦܣܩܘ ܥܠܝܗ ܒܠܒܝ: ܕܢܫܠܡ ܠܟ ܚܒܠܐ ܐܒܘܬܐ: ܕܡܫܘܐ ܐܝܬ ܕܡܩܒܠܐ ܠܐܠܗܐ ܠܐ ܡܫܬܡܠܝܐ ܐܝܬ ܠܟ: ܘܫܡܥ ܐܝܬ ܒܠܐ ܗܘ ܕܡܫܘܐ ܒܗܠܝܢ ܢܬܠܘܬܐ: ܘܠܐ ܥܠ ܥܠܗ. ܡܛܠ ܓܝܪ ܗܘܐ ܒܥܠܡܐ ܘܗܘ ܐܦܣܩܘ ܕܡܠܬܐ

ing someone to direct (you) to accuracy? Not at all! For the very appearance of the discourse and the truth openly proclaim this. But when you wrote again the second letter, and rolled around the same things in it again, and say that hypostatic union is to be considered a juxtaposition[10] in accordance with the empty words of Nestorius, unless we confess that the natures were mixed, one ousia or even quality having taken place at one time, and you have made clear this opinion by means of words which you have added, I have abbreviated what you wrote, but the gist is as follows: "Therefore if the natures from which Christ is, were not mixed inconfusedly, how shall I say that those (natures) which thus have remained unmixed were united hypostatically with each other? How do I keep the definition of composition, when the natures are preserved unmixed, just as they were?" And again I was obliged to answer you kindly in accordance with my ability, and to show clearly that hypostatic union is a natural coming together in natural union, and inexpressibly and inestimably completed one hypostasis and nature of the Word incarnate, which shuns juxtaposition,[10] and similarly mingling and confusion and mixture, in (just) the same way that a man like us exists from a rational soul and from body, and from things of different sort and not consubstantial[11] with each other, there is one nature and composite hypostasis, and it is not the case that it began from composition, but after the union (*Lebon p. 161*) it ceased being composite. For you had wanted to say this, you who were affirming that from mixture unmixed, and from confusion unconfused, at one time one ousia and quality took place. Later on you added (a section) as well about holy Cyril, and said "The Father seems to say that the Word incarnate attached natures along with properties, and is one everywhere, I mean (one) nature and particularity".[12] And you said that in your own case you did not adhere to this, and you asked if I too was of this verdict.

Therefore how, when I have decreed and shown by means of many *testimonia* that it is not right for us to say that Emmanuel is of one ousia and quality and one particularity, are you again contending about these ill-sounding expressions and have set up a defence of these ill-sounding expressions, passing by all those things which were written by you in the second letter? By means of these things the whole purpose (of the argument) was directed to this, that unless we understand the natures to be mixed not even the Trinity remains a trinity, but becomes a quaternity, (that is) unless we confess that the Word incarnate has become one ousia and quality.[13] Since you wanted to establish this as well, you introduced (the term) "συμφυΐα"

ܘܡܪܢܐ. ܟܕ ܕܝܢ ܐܬܒܪܐ ܘܐܬܩܝܡ ܠܗܘܢ ܡܠܟܐ: ܘܕܢܚ ܟܕ ܕܢܚ ܠܗܘܢ ܐܒܪܗܡ ܒܗ: ܘܐܡܪ ܐܝܟ ܕܚܙܝܬܐ ܩܢܘܡܝܬܐ ܫܡܥܐ ܡܬܦܫܩܢܐ ܡܫܬܡܥܢܐ: ܐܝܟ ܒ̈ܢܝܬ ܩ̈ܠܐ ܫܪ̈ܝܟܬܐ ܕܡܬܦܪ̈ܫܢ: ܐܦ ܗܘ ܠܐ ܢܚܘܐ ܘܐܬܡܣܟܢ ܒܫܡܐ: ܟܕ ܚܕܐ ܩܢܘܡܐ ܚܕܐ ܕܝܢ ܗܘܬ ܐܘ ܐܦ ܡܫܬܘܕܥܢܘܬܐ: ܘܗܝ ܕܝܢܐ ܡܠܬܗ ܢܦܩܐ ܒܝܕ ܩ̈ܠܐ ܘܦܬ̈ܓܡܐ: ܗܟܢ ܘܟܕ ܡܠܬ ܐܝܟ ܗܘܬ ܒܪܢܫܐ: ܘܐܝܟ ܟܠܢ ܗܘܐ ܐܢܫ. ܐܦ ܗܟܢܐ ܩ̈ܠܐ ܘܫܡܥܘܗܝ ܡܫܝܚܐ: ܠܐ ܡܬܚܠܦܐ ܠܐ ܐܬܦܪܫܘ: ܐܝܟܢܐ ܠܗܠܝܢ ܕܗܟܢܐ ܗܘܘ ܠܐ ܡܬܦܪ̈ܫܢ: ܐܡܪ ܕܐܬܚܙܝܘ ܠܢܒܝ̈ܐ ܡܫܚܠܦܐܝܬ. ܐܝܟܢܐ ܕܝܢ ܠܢܘܗܪܐ ܕܙܘܗܪܐ ܐܠܗܝ: ܟܕ ܡܬܚܠܦܝܢ ܩ̈ܠܐ ܠܐ ܡܬܦܪܫ: ܐܝܟ ܕܐܝܬ ܗܘܐ ܒܗܘܢ܀ ܘܐܬܬܟܪܝܘ ܠܗܘܢ ܐܝܟ ܡܫܡܥܢܘܬܐ ܕܐܝܟ ܗܝ: ܕܒܫܡܥܬܗ ܐܦܢܐ ܠܗ ܦܬܓܡܐ. ܘܐܝܟܢܐ ܢܘܗܪܐܝܬ ܕܝܚܝܕܝܘܬܐ ܩܢܘܡܝܬܐ: ܩܢܘܡܐ ܚܕܐ ܕܚܝܕܝܘܬܐ ܚܕܐ ܐܠܗܘܬܗ. ܘܠܐ ܡܬܐܡܪܢܐܝܬ ܘܠܐ ܡܬܚܫܒܢܐܝܬ: ܫܡܥܐ ܚܕ ܩܢܘܡܐ ܘܚܝܐ ܕܡܠܬܐ ܕܡܫܬܡܥ: ܕܒܪܐ ܡܢ ܫܡܥܐ ܡܬܦܫܩܢܐ ܘܒܗ ܒܕܡܘܬܐ ܡܢ ܡܘܠܟܢܐ ܘܒܡܠܟܐ ܘܡܬܡܪܩܢ. ܐܝܟܢܐ ܕܐܦ ܒܪܢܫܐ ܕܐܝܬܘܗܝ: ܘܡܢ ܢܦܫܐ ܡܡܠܠܢܝܬܐ ܘܡܢ ܦܓܪܐ ܡܝܬܢܐ: ܘܡܢ ܫܘܡܠܝܐ ܐܣܛܘܟ̈ܣܐ ܐܪ̈ܒܥܐ ܘܠܐ ܟܠܗ ܚܝܐ ܘܢܦܫܐ: ܚܕ ܚܝܐ ܘܩܢܘܡܐ ܡܬܚܙܐ ܐܠܗܘܗܝ: ܘܟܠܗ ܡܢ ܙܘܥܐ ܦܣ ܦܪܘܩ: ܒܠܘܩ ܚܝܘܬܐ (161) ܕܝܢ ܡܢ ܗܢ ܕܗܘܐ ܐܠܗܘܗܝ ܡܬܚܙܐ ܦܣ. ܗܘܐ ܓܝܪ ܙܒܢܐ ܗܘܝܐ ܘܐܬܐܡܪ ܐܝܟ. ܕܡܢ ܡܬܦܪܫ ܠܐ ܡܬܦܪܫ: ܘܡܢ ܒܡܠܟܐ ܠܐ ܡܬܡܠܟܐ ܡܬܚܫܒ ܗܘܐ: ܕܚܕܐ ܐܝܟ ܚܕܐ ܐܠܗܐ ܘܡܫܬܘܕܥܢܘܬܐ ܗܘܬ. ܘܡܫܬܡܥ ܕܗܘܐ ܟܕ ܢܣܒ ܐܝܟ: ܘܡܬܚܙܐ ܡܢ ܚܕܐ ܡܣܬܟܠܢܘܬܐ ܘܐܡܪ ܗܘܐ. ܘܗܢܐ ܐܦܐ ܐܡܪ: ܕܒܫܢ̈ܝܐ ܚܙܝ ܕܬܟܬܒܐ ܐܦܐ. ܘܡܢ ܟܠ ܕܢܦܩ ܚܝ ܐܠܗܘܗܝ ܡܠܟܐ ܕܡܬܚܫܒ. ܘܟܕ ܐܦܐ ܐܝܟ ܘܡܠܟܐ. ܘܐܡܪ ܗܘܐ ܕܗܘܐ ܦܣ ܠܐ ܕܝܠܗ ܟܢܝܐ ܢܦܫ. ܡܬܥܠܝܐ ܕܝܢ: ܐܦ ܗܘ ܕܕܗܘܝܐ ܕܝܠܗ ܐܠܗ ܐܦ ܐܢܐ.

ܐܝܟܢܐ ܗܟܝܠ ܟܕ ܦܫܝܛܐ ܘܟܕ ܡܬܢܗܪܐ ܡܬܚܙܝܢܘܬܐ ܢܦܫܗ: ܘܠܐ ܐܦܠܐ ܢܬܡܪܚܘܢ ܠܡܬܚܘܝܘ ܕܚܕܐ ܐܠܗܐ ܘܡܫܬܘܕܥܢܘܬܐ ܘܚܕܐ ܕܡܠܬܐ: ܠܗܘܢ ܟܠ ܗܠܝܢ ܦܫܝܛ ܩ̈ܠܐ ܡܬܡܠܠܢ ܐܝܟ: ܘܡܫܡܫ ܒܪܘܚܐ ܚܙܐ ܗܠܝܢ ܦܫܝܛ ܩ̈ܠܐ ܫܡܥܐ: ܟܕ ܡܠܝܢ ܒܒܪܐ ܐܝܟܢ ܕܒܣܪܐ ܘܐܬܩܝܡ ܐܬܡܠܟܐ ܡܢܗ. ܕܒܢܝ̈ܢܫܐ ܡܠܬܗ ܙܒܢܐ ܒܗܘܐ ܡܬܚܡ ܗܘܐ. ܘܐܝܟܘ ܠܐ ܢܬܡܠܟܠ ܘܡܫܡܫܝܢ ܩ̈ܠܐ: ܐܦܠܐ ܠܡܬܚܘܝܘ ܠܡܬܚܘܝܘ ܡܬܗܘܢܐ: ܗܘܐ ܕܝܢ ܦܫܝܛܘܬܐ: ܐܦ ܗܘ ܕܠܐ ܢܬܐܡܪ ܡܠܟܐ ܘܡܬܚܫܒ: ܕܗܘܐ ܚܕܐ ܐܠܗܐ ܘܡܫܬܘܕܥܢܘܬܐ: ܗܢ ܕܐܦ ܟܕ ܙܒܢܐ ܐܝܟ ܕܐܬܩܝܡ: ܐܦ ܗܘܝܘܬܐ

(both) so that it might be of advantage to you as regards the same questions of mixture, and to demonstrate that those things from which Christ is are one ousia and quality. And again you learned from us, as we reminded you in a brotherly way, that the term "συμφυΐα" is not indicative of (just) one meaning, but when it is applied to the holy Trinity, it establishes the equality of ousia of three hypostases; but when it is applied in relation to (*Lebon p. 162*) the divine incarnation, it makes known the natural coming together of things of different ousia, and not of the same type with each other, from which was completed one nature and hypostasis, that is of the incarnate Word.[14]

Therefore you have turned these reminders into complaints in a way I do not understand, and you have made me an accuser instead of a teacher. And you have repeated words which were written to you by us in opposition to those who hold the opinion of a confusion of ousiai, and as if you were contending against a fictitious accusation, you have [made out][15] that you do not think thus as the folly of the confusers of ousiai wishes. And hence you have at once jumped up, and as you have said,[16] have anointed yourself[17] with my prayers, and it has seemed good to you that you should become an advocate of expressions which introduce the confusion of ousiai, by means of these things which you have said—(namely) that the coming together from two natures became at one time one ousia and quality. And you have done the same thing as a young man, who finds fault with a harlot, and uncovers her impudence, who is of the people[18] and a hawker, and the clamour of her beauty from ornaments, and as the Proverb says,[19] dissipation and its licentiousness, and afterwards when evening has come, he was beneath her roof and lodged with her.

But let us consider of what sort are (these words) of (your defence): how valiant and astonishing! You say that you have said "one ousia" instead of saying "one nature", and you have omitted this (word) "incarnate" in as much as it is very often confessed. But you said "one quality" as well, on the grounds that the quality of the ousia of the Word has had a share in bodily activity.[20] Now, are these things tolerable? Are these (beliefs) proper to Christians and to those who look for the judgement and the resurrection, and hear the Word of God calling (*Lebon p. 163*) out in the Gospel: "You will be justified by your words, and by your words you will be found guilty".[21] Do these things not provide the opposition with a suitable cause for laughter against us? Do we not deservedly say in lament that (song) of David the singer of holy things: "We were a reproach

ܘܐܚܝܕܐ ܡܢ̇ܬܐ ܗܘܬ ܠܡܪܕܘܬܐ: ܐܝܟ ܡܐ ܕܐܡܪ ܒܪ ܐܡܪ ܕܡܙܕܪܓܠ ܡܗܝܡܢܐ ܘܠܐܒܕܢܐ: ܘܐܬܡܢܝܬ ܠܗܠܝܢ ܕܡܢܗܘܢ ܡܗܝܡܢܐ: ܚܕܐ ܐܘܠܨܢܐ ܘܡܫܬܕܝܘܬܐ. ܘܐܘܦ ܡܢ ܗܘܬ ܡܢ ܟܕ ܐܬܚܙܝܬ ܡܕܒܪܝܢ ܗܘܘ: ܕܫܡܐ ܕܡܗܝܡܢܘܬܐ ܘܐܚܝܕܐ: ܠܗ ܡܗܝܡܢܐ ܐܠܗܘܬܗ ܕܡܢ ܡܫܝܚܐ. ܐܠܐ ܟܕ ܟܠܗ ܠܗܝܡܢܘܬܐ ܗܝ ܡܪܝܡܬܐ ܗܘܝܢ: ܠܡܫܘܐ ܐܘܣܝܐ ܡܫܡܫ ܘܠܬܠܬܐ ܩܢܘܡܝܢ. ܟܕ ܕܝܢ (162) ܡܬܟܫܦܢܘܬܐ ܠܐܠܗܘܬܐ ܥܠ ܘܡܬܐܡܪ: ܒܢܘܗܪܐ ܚܕܐ ܘܒܫܘܒܚܐ ܐܚܪܢܐ ܐܘܣܝܐ: ܘܠܐ ܩܢܐ ܐܝܟܐ ܕܢܦܪܘܫ ܡܘܕܝܢ. ܘܡܘܕܘܝ ܐܬܡܛܢ ܡܢ ܚܕܐ ܘܡܘܕܝܐ ܗܘ ܕܡܬܟܠ ܕܡܫܢܐ.

ܗܠܝܢ ܗܟܝܠ ܕܡܛܠ: ܠܐ ܢܬܘ ܐܝܟ ܐܢܫܐ ܠܥܡܐ ܕܡܘܠܕܐ ܗܒܘܗ: ܘܢܠܦ ܡܦܠܓܐ ܠܒܢܝ ܡܗܝܡܢܐ: ܘܟܠܐ ܕܡܢܟܝ ܠܗ ܡܢ ܠܥܡܠܐ ܗܠܝܢ ܕܡܬܐܡܪܝܢ ܚܣܝܪܐ ܕܐܘܣܝܐ ܐܢܫ: ܘܗܝ ܐܝܟ ܕܟܠܐ ܒܟܠܐ ܡܬܡܠܝܐ ܥܠܬܗ ܐܢܫ: ܒܪܢܫ ܒܪܘܚܐ ܕܗܘ ܗܘܐ ܡܬܐܡܪ ܐܢܫ: ܐܝܟ ܕܒܟܠܐ ܚܝܘܬܐ ܕܠܐܚܪܝܢ ܐܘܣܝܐ. ܘܡܢ ܗܘܝܐ ܡܢ ܗܠܝܢ ܗܘܢܐ: ܘܡܬܚܙܝܐ ܕܡܠܟ ܐܝܟ ܕܐܡܪܢܐ ܡܢܗܝܢ. ܘܡܛܠ ܟܠܐ ܕܩܢܘܡܐ ܚܕܐ ܘܐܘܣܝܐ ܡܦܪܫ ܠܗ ܕܠܗܘܐ ܚܠܝܦܘܬܐ: ܟܕ ܗܠܝܢ ܕܐܡܪܢܐ: ܕܒܢܘܗܪܐ ܕܡܢ ܠܐܘܟ ܩܢܘܡܐ: ܚܕܐ ܐܘܣܝܐ ܘܡܫܡܫܢܘܬܐ ܚܕܐ ܕܝܢ ܗܘܐ. ܘܗܘ ܟܕ ܗܘ ܒܚܕܐ: ܗܘ ܕܠܝܬ ܐܝܟ ܕܢܗܘܐ ܒܝܬܐ ܘܡܦܪܫܐ ܠܡܕܒܪܘ: ܗܘ ܕܒܥܠܐ ܘܡܫܡܫܢܘܬܐ ܘܗܘܝܐ ܕܡܦܪܫ ܕܡܢ ܗܟܝܠ: ܘܐܝܟ ܕܐܡܪ ܡܬܠ ܦܪܘܫܐ ܘܡܫܬܘܕܥ: ܘܡܬܐܡܪ ܒܕ ܡܟܝܠ ܙܒܢܐ: ܐܢܫ ܡܬܚܙܝܢ ܗܘܐ ܘܒܠܚܘܕ ܓܒܪܐ.

ܐܠܐ ܢܚܐ ܕܐܝܟ ܐܢܫܝܢ ܗܠܝܢ ܕܡܬܡܢܝܢ ܒܐܘܣܝܐ: ܒܥܠܐ ܙܘܥܬܐ ܘܐܩܢܘܡܐ. ܚܕܐ ܐܘܣܝܐ ܐܡܪ ܐܢܫ ܕܐܡܪܢܐ: ܢܠܦ ܕܠܐܡܪ ܡܢ ܚܕܐ. ܘܗܘ ܕܡܟܫܦܐ ܐܝܟ ܗܝ ܕܦܠܓ ܡܬܐܘܝܐ ܒܪܘܐ. ܐܡܪܢܐ ܕܝܢ ܘܚܕܐ ܡܫܡܫܢܘܬܐ: ܐܝܟ ܗܝ ܕܡܫܡܫܢܘܬܐ ܘܐܘܣܝܐ ܘܡܠܬܐ: ܠܡܥܒܕܢܘܬܐ ܓܡܝܫܢܘܬܐ ܐܠܗܘܬܗ. ܗܠܝܢ ܗܟܝܠ ܡܫܬܡܠܝܢܘܬܐ: ܗܠܝܢ ܕܝܢ ܦܠܓ ܠܒܪܢܫܝܐ ܘܡܫܡܫܝܢ ܠܒܝܬܐ ܘܡܫܠܬܐ: ܘܡܫܡܫܝܢ ܠܡܠܬܐ ܕܠܐܗܐ (163) ܕܡܢܗ ܒܐܘܣܝܐ: ܡܢ ܩܠܝܢ ܠܐܙܘܙܘܗ ܘܡܢ ܩܠܝܢ ܠܐܢܫܝܢ: ܗܠܝܢ ܕܝܢ ܠܗ ܓܘܫܡܐ ܦܐܝܐ ܗܘܝܢ ܒܠܝܢ ܠܥܘܩܒܠܐ: ܠܐ ܐܡܪܝܢ ܕܝܢ ܒܐܝܬܘܗ ܟܕ ܐܠܗܝܢ: ܗܘ ܕܗܘ ܦܪܘܦ ܒܩܢܘܡܐ ܕܝܢ: ܕܒܗܘܢ ܢܫܒܘܐ ܠܥܠܡܝܢ: ܡܘܡܐ ܘܒܘܪܟܐ ܠܐܠܗܝܢ ܕܢܬܪܢܝܢ ܠܢ:

ܐܝܟܢܐ ܓܝܪ ܕܢܚܘܐ ܢܦܫܐ ܒܓܠܗ ܘܐܠܗܝܢ ܕܠܡܫܒܚ ܠܢ: ܗܘ ܕܡܢ ܟܠܗ: ܘܡܕܡ ܢܫܡܥ: ܘܡܛܠ ܕܗܘܐ ܡܢܬܐ ܒܟܠܗ ܘܐܬܐܡܪܬ: ܟܕ ܦܫܘܛܐ ܡܢ ܩܠܐ

to our neighbours; an object of derision and a laughing stock to those round about us".[22]

For to dismiss the whole intention of those things which were written by you, which we previously set out above, and to attend to this part only which has been said, in isolation from all these words which were said before and those which were set down after, to such an extent obliges us to say, and to cut off a multitude of inadequate and useless nonsense, from which the simplicity of the truth turns away its face, (the simplicity of the truth) of those who handed on as a sacred anchor to the holy Churches, as against those who divide into two the one Christ, (namely) that it is proper for us to say "one nature incarnate of God the Word", that is of great Athanasius and wise Cyril: "Where therefore have you read in their compositions that they have called Emmanuel one ousia and quality, or one ousia incarnate of the Word?"[23] You are unable to say! For since they knew that the error of confusing the natures is contrary on the other side to those who divide the Christ, they used polished and exact terms. However, it is quite clear that one can easily find in the God-clothed Fathers—for I speak to you from my teachers, since I do not use any expression in this matter belonging to the pagan experts—the term "ousia" used instead of "one nature" and "hypostasis", in the way that holy John, who attained to the high priestly throne of Constantinople, says about the only-begotten Son of God and the Father, in the Fourth Treatise of the Commentary (*Lebon p. 164*) on the Gospel of John: (JOHN): "But this Word is a hypostatic ousia which proceeded from the Father impassibly".[24] And Basil, who is wise in these divine matters, in the First Treatise against Eunomius, says about him: (BASIL): "But since he is one in existence and one simple ousia, not composite, he names himself differently at different times, and in thoughts he makes to fit the titles which are different from each other".[25]

But none of the orthodox Doctors, I mean those who have expounded (doctrine) in the churches, ventured to call the Word one ousia or sign when it was composed with flesh of the same nature as ours, which had a rational and intelligent soul. Therefore do you alone, tell me, walk this untrodden path, and travel through the torrent and thistles? Was there a need for these truly circuitous explanations? But these things in no way bring credit to you. For even if we believed you[26] and were silent, no-one would read these things which are written by you, and say that they are such that you have written a defence. So now it is (high) time for me to say to you that thing of Homer, and very aptly, since while writing you made mention of your skill: "*ἀλλ' οὐ πείσονται Τρῶες καὶ Δαρδανίωνες*".[27]

ܡܠܘܢ ܗܠܝܢ ܕܡܕܢܚ ܐܡܪ̈ܝ ܘܦܢܝ ܕܒܠܥܘܗ ܗܢܝܢ. ܡܠܦܐ ܗܘܐ ܐܠܝܐ ܕܐܡܪ: ܘܢܦܫܗ ܡܬܚܙܝܬܐ ܕܙܘܥܐ ܕܠܐ ܡܘܦܐ ܘܠܐ ܡܫܬܪ. ܗܘ ܕܡܘܦܩܐ ܐܦܝ̈ܗ ܡܢܗ ܦܫܝܛܘܬܐ ܕܡܪܝܐ: ܕܗܠܝܢ ܕܐܠܒܫܘ ܠܒܢ̈ܬܐ ܩܕܝܫܬܐ ܐܝܟ ܐܘܪܚܐ ܕܫܘܝܘܬܐ ܠܫܡܥܠ ܗܢܘܢ ܕܦܫܝܛܝܢ ܠܡܠܘܢ ܠܒܝ ܡܫܝܚܐ: ܠܗܘ̈ܢ ܕܠܐ ܕܐܡܪ ܚܕ ܚܝܠ ܘܡܠܟܘܬܐ ܕܐܠܗܐ ܕܡܫܝܚܐ: ܙܟܐ ܠܐܝܫܘܥ ܐܠܗܘܢ: ܘܡܘܪܡܝܗ ܡܫܝܚܐ. ܐܡܠܐ ܗܒܠܐ ܡܪܝܐ ܒܥܩ̈ܒܬܗܘܢ: ܘܐܡܪܘܗܝ ܠܒܢܝܢܫܐ ܚܕܐ ܐܘܪܚܐ ܘܡܘܫܚܬܐ: ܐܘ ܚܕܐ ܐܘܪܚܐ ܕܡܠܟܬܐ ܕܫܡܝܐ. ܐܠܐ ܠܡܢܐ ܠܝ ܕܐܐܡܪ. ܟܕ ܡܕܡ ܥܠܡܐ ܕܡܫܬܡܠܝܐ ܒܗܝܢ ܠܡ ܗܢܘܢ ܕܦܫܝܛܝܢ ܠܡܫܝܚܐ: ܛܘܒܝ ܕܝܠܗܘܢ ܕܪܚܡܐ: ܩܢܐ ܩܠܐ ܕܫܠܝܛܝܢ ܘܩܪ̈ܝܢ ܐܝܬܝܗ. ܘܐܠܐ ܡܕܡܐ ܡܕܡܐ: ܕܐܝܬ ܗܘ ܕܢܦܩ ܕܠܐܠܗ ܠܗܐ ܠܫܡܥܐ ܠܐܠܗܐ ܐܒܘܬܐ: ܡܢ ܩܠܝܠܐ ܥܠܡ ܕܡܠܐ ܡܫܬܡܠܐ ܐܢܐ ܠܝ: ܟܕ ܠܐ ܟܕ ܐܢܐ ܡܠܟܬܐ ܡܕܡ ܕܩܪܝܒܐ ܕܠܐ ܒܗܘܐ: ܘܫܡܥܐ ܕܐܘܪܚܐ ܕܫܦܝܪ ܚܠܦ ܚܕ ܟܚܐ ܘܡܘܫܚܐ: ܐܦܠܐ ܕܐܡܠܐ ܕܐܡܪ ܡܕܡܐ ܗܘܝܐ ܗܘ ܕܡܬܚܙܝ ܒܥܘܕܪܢܐ ܕܝܠܗ ܒܗܝܐ ܕܡܫܬܡܠܝܢܘܬܐ: ܡܬܠ ܚܝܕܐ ܒܪܗ ܕܐܠܗܐ ܘܐܒܐ: ܒܡܐܡܪܐ ܕܐܘܪܚܐ ܕܦܘܩܕܢܐ (164) ܕܐܘܟܝܢܘܢ ܕܢܘܚ. ܢܘܚ܀ ܗܢܐ ܕܝܢ ܡܠܟܬܐ: ܐܘܪܚܐ ܡܕܡ ܐܠܗܘܗܝ ܡܫܝܚܬܐ. ܕܡܢܗ ܕܐܝܬ ܢܦܩ ܠܐ ܡܫܬܟܚܐ܀ ܘܡܫܡܠܝܢ ܕܝܢ ܗܘ ܣܢܝܩܐ ܕܗܠܝܢ ܠܟܠܗܝܢ: ܒܡܐܡܪܐ ܡܕܡܐ ܕܠܗܐ ܐܘܚܕܢܐ ܡܬܠܠ ܐܡܪ. ܀ܒܡܫܬܡܠܝܢܘܬܐ܀ ܐܠܐ ܟܕ ܚܕ ܐܠܗܘܗܝ ܒܗܘ ܕܫܡܝܐ: ܘܚܕܐ ܐܘܪܚܐ ܦܫܝܛܬܐ ܘܠܐ ܡܪܟܒܬܐ: ܒܪܝܐ ܐܚܪܝܐ ܐܚܪܝܬܐ ܡܫܡܥܘ ܢܦܫܘ: ܘܡܠܘܟܬܐ ܠܒܢ̈ܝܐ ܕܡܫܬܟܚܝܢ ܡܢ ܟܢܘܫܐ ܡܠܟܝܢ܀

ܠܐ ܐܝܟ ܕܝܢ ܡܢܗܘܢ ܕܩܠܝܠܐ ܠܐܘܪܚ ܗܘܝܐ: ܗܢܘܢ ܕܦܫܘ ܩܕܡܝܬ ܐܡܪ ܐܢܐ: ܐܡܪܢ ܕܐܡܪ ܚܕܐ ܐܘܪܚܐ ܐܘ ܡܫܘܕܥܐ ܠܡܠܟܬܐ ܟܕ ܐܬܘܪܒ ܠܗܐ ܒܗܪܐ ܒܪ ܟܝܢ: ܕܐܝܬ ܠܗ ܢܦܫܐ ܡܠܟܠܟܬܐ ܘܡܕܘܒܪܢܘܬܐ. ܒܠܚܘܕܝܗ ܗܘܠܐܡܪ ܠܝ: ܗܘܐ ܐܘܪܚܐ ܠܐ ܕܪܝܫܬܐ ܡܬܟܠܝ ܐܢܐ: ܘܒܪܢܫܘܬܐ ܘܕܘܪ̈ܫܐ ܥܠܝܗ ܐܢܐ: ܘܐܬܠܬܝܗ ܟܠ ܦܘܩ̈ܕܢܐ ܗܠܝܢ ܩܕܝܫܐ ܒܘܪܟܐ: ܐܠܐ ܗܠܝܢ ܘܠܐ ܟܠ ܡܠܘ ܡܟܝܠ ܠܝ ܠܡܘܫܚܬܐ. ܐܦ ܥܠܡ ܘܚܝ ܢܘܡܘܣܝ: ܘܢܛܠ: ܠܡܢܐ ܐܝܟ ܕܦܐܪܐ ܗܠܝܢ ܕܠܡܥܢ ܡܢܗ: ܘܐܡܪ ܕܗܠܝܢ ܗܘܝܐ ܐܠܗܝܢ: ܐܝܟ ܡܐ ܕܟܕ ܢܦܩ ܐܢܐ ܒܪܘܚܐ ܡܬܠܠ. ܘܒܝܐ ܗܘ ܠܗ ܡܫܡܠܐ: ܕܦܠܛ ܠܡܫܬܡܠܐ ܗܘ ܕܗܘܡܪܘܗ ܐܡܪ ܠܝ: ܡܛܠ ܕܟܕ ܦܠܚ ܐܢܐ ܒܗܘܦܐ ܒܪܝܐ ܕܐܘܡܢܘܬܝ. ܐܠܐ ܠܐ ܡܬܛܫܝܢ ܠܣ̈ܘܪܘܗ ܘܙܕܝܩܘ.

Because of this, with a loving intention, we exhort your Love, that you bid farewell to crafty words like these, and that you reverence simplicity of faith, and do not rush easily to speech about doctrines, but reckon that it is right to cleave to the Fathers in everything, if at any time you should fall into the necessity of writing or speaking like this. For it is not a slight thing that (*Lebon p. 165*) we should stumble in these matters, or say something which is not properly threshed out, or that we should not everywhere guard ourselves beforehand as far as is understood from marauders and the grasps of the opposition. For if we are going to search for those things which are not said warily, it is time for us to say that the holy Trinity also is one hypostasis, because we find Eustathius of blessed memory, who was Bishop of Antioch, in the Commentary on the ninety-second psalm, said in these words (that) the Father and the Son are one hypostasis: (EUSTATHIUS): "The two do wonderful things at the same time invisibly, but the divine Scriptures very often attribute the majesty of their work to one, since they introduce a duality from unity, but teach a unity from duality, in which there is one hypostasis of divinity".[28]

But who does not know that *οὐσία* is derived from *εἶναι* but *φύσις* from *πεφυκέναι* and again *ὑπόστασις* from *ὑφεστηκέναι* and *ὕπαρξις* is derived from *ὑπάρχειν*? And in this meaning these terms are not at all different from each other. For thus the Luminary of the Church, Athanasius himself, made known, when he wrote to the Bishops in Africa: (ATHANASIUS): "From these things, it is right, brothers, that we should notice that those who were at Nicea breathe (the words) of the scriptures, since God himself says in Exodus ''*Εγώ εἰμι ὁ ὤν*'[29] and by means of Jeremiah, 'Who stood [in his hypostasis][30] and saw his Word?'[31], and after a few things, 'And if they had stood in my hypostasis, and if they had heard my words'.[32] But if[33] hypostasis is ousia, and has no other meaning than that which is, (*Lebon p. 166*) which Jeremiah calls '*ὕπαρξις*' saying, 'Neither have they heard the voice of his being'.[34] For *ὕπαρξις* is *ὑπόστασις* and *οὐσία*: for it is[35] and exists.[36] For since Paul too understood this, he wrote to the Hebrews, 'He is the radiance of (his) glory, and the likeness of (his) hypostasis'.[37] But since these men, who seem to know the scriptures, and call themselves wise, are unwilling to say 'hypostasis' in relation to God—for they wrote this at Ariminum and in their own other assemblies—how was their deposition not just, since they say, even they, like the fool in (his) heart, 'There is no God'?[38]"[39]

Therefore (just) as we learn from the quotation of the Doctor that

ܡܛܠ ܗܘܐ ܒܠܘܩܒܠܐ ܕܣܘܟܠܐ ܠܣܘܟܗ ܡܠܟܝܢ ܡܢܗ: ܕܒܪ̈ܝܬܐ ܕܐܝܟ ܗܟܝܢ ܬܐܡܪ ܡܠܦܢ. ܘܒܟܝܢܘܬܐ ܕܗܝܡܢܘܬܐ ܬܐܡܪ: ܘܠܐ ܬܘܪܥ ܕܒܥܠܬܗ ܒܟ̈ܠܐ ܡܛܠ ܦ̈ܠܚܐ. ܐܠܐ ܬܬܝܣܒ ܕܗܠܐ ܘܠܐܟܝܢܐ ܒܒܠܟܝܢ ܬܐܡܪ: ܐܝܟܘ ܕܒܪܟ ܒܐܝܬܐ ܬܦܠܠ ܕܡܕܡ ܕܐܝܟ ܗܟܢܐ ܬܬܠܘܒ ܐܘ ܬܐܡܪ. ܠܐ ܓܝܪ ܝܚܘܕܝܐ (165) ܕܒܗܠܝܢ ܢܥܒܕ ܐܘ ܡܕܡ ܕܠܐ ܦܩܝܕ ܡܢܘܗ ܢܐܡܪ: ܐܘ ܕܠܐ ܡܢ ܟܠ ܕܐܝܟ ܡܢ ܡܩ̈ܒܠܐ ܘܒܟ̈ܬܒܐ ܕܫܘ̈ܒܚܐ ܐܝܟ ܕܡܠܦܢܘܬܐ ܢܥܒܕ ܢܛܪ ܢܥܡ. ܐܦ ܓܝܪ ܒܠܥܕ ܡܢܗ ܘܗܟܝܢ ܕܕܒܠܥܕ ܠܐܢܫ ܐܡ̈ܝܪܢ ܒܟܠ: ܘܡܫܠܡܢܘܬܐ ܢܦܩܢ ܒܗܟܝܢ ܕܐܡ̈ܝܪܢ ܠܐ ܝܘܡܢܐܝܬ. ܒܟܠܐ ܗܘ ܠܝ: ܕܐܦ ܒܠܒܠܘܬܐ ܡܥܝܩܬܐ: ܕܐܝܟ ܡܪܝܡܐ ܢܐܡܪ. ܡܛܠ ܕܡܬܒܥܝܢ ܠܗܘ ܕܒܗܘܢܐ ܬܘܒܠܐ ܐܘܣܛܘܟܣܐ: ܗܘ ܕܗܘܐ ܐܣܟܡܐ ܕܐܝܩܢܐ: ܕܒܟܝܢܐ ܕܡܫܘܚܬܐ ܕܐܝܟ ܢܚܬܝܢ: ܠܐܒܐ ܘܠܒܪܐ ܕܐܝܟ ܡܪܝܡܐ ܐܠܗܘܬܗ ܒܟ̈ܠܐ ܗܟܝܢ ܐܡܪ. ܘܐܘܣܛܘܟܣܐ ܕܐܬܢܝܗܝ ܡܢ ܒܪ ܒܗ ܒܪ ܒܗ ܡܕܡ ܐܦܣܘܬܐ ܠܐ ܡܬܚܫܚܐ. ܗܘ ܕܝܢ ܪܘܚܐ ܒܕܝܐ ܕܗܟܝܢ. ܒܚܕ ܕܝܢ ܐܦ̈ܝܢ ܡܚܢ̈ܬܐ ܡܫܡܫ ܩ̈ܠܒܐ ܠܟ̈ܬܒܐ ܕܐܘܪܚܬܐ ܕܝܢ ܡܢ ܒܥܘܗܕܢܐ ܡܫܟܚ. ܒܥܘܗܕܢܐ ܕܝܢ ܡܢ ܬܘܪܥܬܐ ܡܫܟܢ. ܒܗܘ ܕܐܝܟ ܡܢܘܗܝ ܐܠܗܘܬܗ ܕܐܟܘܬܐ܀

ܘܐܠܐ ܡܕܡ ܠܐ ܢܒܥܐ: ܕܐܘܣܝܐ ܦܝ: ܡܢ ܗܘ ܕܐܠܗܘܬܗ ܡܫܬܡܫܐ: ܒܝܬ ܕܝܢ ܡܢ ܗܘ ܘܡܢܢ: ܘܐܘܒ ܡܢܘܗܝ: ܡܢ ܗܘ ܕܡܫܝܚ. ܘܒܬ ܡܢ ܗܘ ܕܐܠܗܘܬܗ ܡܫܬܡܫܐ. ܘܒܗܘܢܐ ܒܡܘܕܥܐ: ܠܐ ܡܕܡ ܡܢ ܚܕܪܐ ܡܫܬܟܚ ܗܟܝܢ ܒܩ̈ܢܘܡܐ. ܗܟܢܐ ܓܝܪ ܘܐܘܣܝܐ ܕܒܪܐ ܐܬܝܠܝܕ: ܒܪ ܒܗ ܐܩ̈ܢܘܡܐ ܕܒܦ̈ܪܨܘܦܐ ܡܬܚ̈ܙܝܢ ܐܘܕܥ. ܘܐܬܝܠܝܕ܀ ܡܢ ܗܟܝܢ ܕܝܢ ܡܬܦܫܩ ܕܐܠܗܐ ܐܢܫܐ: ܕܗܟܝܢ ܦܝ ܕܒܪܝܫܐ: ܗܟܝܢ ܕܩ̈ܠܒܐ ܡܫܡܫ: ܒܪ ܕܘ ܠܐܠܗܐ ܐܡܪ: ܒܡܫܡܫܢܐ ܦܝ: ܕܐܢܐ ܐܠܗܐ ܗܘ ܕܐܠܗܘܬܗ: ܒܪ ܐܘܣܝܐ ܕܝܢ: ܦܝ ܡܢ ܒܡܫܡܫܘ ܘܒܪܐ ܡܫܠܡܘ. ܘܒܠܦ ܝܚܘܕܝܐ. ܘܠܗ ܡܫܘ ܒܡܫܡܫ. ܘܠܗ ܡܫܡܫܘ ܩ̈ܠܒܐ. ܐܦ ܕܝܢ ܡܢܘܗܝ ܐܘܣܝܐ ܐܠܗܘܬܗ: ܘܒܠܦ ܒܗ ܡܕܡ ܐܚܪܝܢ ܕܡܬܝܕܥ: ܐܠܐ ܗܘ ܗܘ (166) ܕܐܠܗܘܬܗ: ܗܘ ܕܐܘܣܝܐ ܠܗܠ ܡܫܡܫܘ ܒܪ ܐܡܪ: ܘܠܐ ܡܫܡܫ ܒܪܐ ܦܠܠ ܕܠܗ: ܡܢܘܗܝ ܓܝܪ ܘܐܘܣܝܐ ܠܗܠ ܐܠܗܘܬܗ. ܐܠܗܘܬܗ ܓܝܪ ܘܡܫܝܚܐ. ܗܘܐ ܓܝܪ ܘܒܪ ܡܫܬܡܠܝܐ ܦܝܠܦܘܣ ܡܠܦ ܒܒܪ̈ܢܫܐ. ܗܘ ܕܐܠܗܘܬܗ ܙܒܢܐ ܕܐܬܒܘܣܡܬ ܡܘܡܝܐ ܘܡܘܡܐ. ܗܟܝܢ ܕܝܢ ܕܡܫܬܠܒܪ ܕܝܕܝܢ ܩ̈ܠܒܐ: ܘܡܫܡܫܝܢ ܢܦܫܗܘܢ ܕܐܠܗܘܬܗ ܡܫܝ̈ܚܐ: ܒܪ ܠܐ ܒܪܝܢ ܕܢܐܡܪܘܢ ܡܢܘܗܝ ܒܗܠ ܠܐܠܗܐ: ܗܘܐ ܓܝܪ ܦܠܒܘ ܒܐܘܣܝܘܬܗ ܘܒܩ̈ܢܘܡܐ ܐܚ̈ܪܢܐ ܕܠܗܘܢ. ܐܡܝܢ ܠܗ

there is interchange of these terms of εἶναι and ὑφεστηκέναι, in the same way we are instructed by those (Doctors) to recognise the difference of ousia and hypostasis, and we hear holy Basil writing to Amphilochius and saying as follows: (BASIL): "Ousia and hypostasis have this difference, which the common has in comparison with the particular".[40] And because of this, when the Fathers deal with theology, and explain a term concerning the inhomination, they use these terms which are rightly distinguished, so that there might be not even one thing not uncovered in these considerations when they are set out. Thus when wise Cyril writes in the Second Volume against the blasphemies of Nestorius, he says: (CYRIL): "For one nature is now understood after the union, that which is incarnate, belonging to the Word".[41] And when he writes the Third Letter to the same man, he says: (CYRIL): "Therefore it is right that we attribute all the words in the Gospel to one person, and to one hypostasis, that (hypostasis) of the Word incarnate".[42] For he knew that the term "nature" is also frequently applied for the signification of kind, as when (*Lebon p. 167*) Basil said in the Treatise on Faith: (BASIL): "There the Father and the Son and the Holy Spirit, one nature uncreated".[43] And Gregory the Theologian, in the Treatise on Pentecost: (GREGORY): "O Sirs, confess the Trinity of one divinity, (or) if you wish, of one nature".[44] And holy Cyril too, in the Fourth Volume against the blasphemies of Nestorius said: (CYRIL): "For one nature is understood of the divinity in the holy and consubstantial[45] Trinity".[46]

But you, setting aside the teachings of these men, produce Aristotle, as if from somewhere impenetrable, praising him, and saying, "Aristotle, who is called ὁ νοῦς",[47] and you think (him) worth your announcing (him) for us with thunder from hides, as somewhere Salmoneus[48] is said to have done in the fable. For know, know clearly, that Gregory the Theologian, who was accurately instructed in the opinions of the philosophers, and was able to become an expositor of them, and does not, like us, say such and such from hearsay, passes sentence of condemnation on the opinion of Aristotle which introduces the soul of man (as) mortal—even if those who play at being Aristotelians and stretch out a great beard, and while they praise (him) with words, attempt with a proud mind to conceal his iniquitous opinion, interpreting in what way they like the term "ἐντελέχεια", for this is what he calls the soul of man. For that Doctor of true religion, whom we have mentioned, wrote in this way in the Treatise against the Eunomians, [GREGORY]:[49] ("Attack ....) Aristotle's petty Providence, and (his) system, and discourses about

ܕܐܬܐܬ ܗܘܬ ܡܬܪܣܝܣ ܕܝܠܗܘܢ: ܘܐܡܪܝܢ ܗܘܘ ܐܝܟ ܡܫܠܐ ܟܠܗܘܢ. ܕܐܝܬ ܠܠܗܘܬ܀

ܐܡܪܐ ܗܟܝܠ ܕܗܘܐ ܡܠܟܝܢ ܡܢ ܒܪܐ ܟܠܐ ܕܡܟܠܝܐ: ܕܡܬܐܦܬܐ ܐܝܬ ܕܗܠܝܢ ܡܫܡܫܐ: ܕܢܦܫ ܕܐܬܠܗܘܢ ܘܡܫܡܫܝܢ: ܟܕ ܟܪܝܐ ܡܬܪܘܝܢ ܐܢܘܢ: ܕܟܕ ܚܘܫܒܐ ܕܐܘܟܝܐ ܘܫܘܝܐ. ܘܡܫܟܝܢ ܚܕ ܠܟܝܢܐ ܒܫܡܠܝܘܬܗ ܕܦܠܚ ܠܘܬ ܐܡܬܟܘܢܘܗ ܘܐܡܪ ܗܟܝܠ. ܀ܒܫܡܠܝܘܬܗ܀ ܐܘܟܝܐ ܘܫܘܝܐ ܗܝ ܗܘܣܟܐ ܐܝܬ ܠܗܘܢ: ܗܘ ܘܐܝܬ ܠܟܝܢܐ ܠܘܬ ܡܠܝܢ܀ ܘܡܛܠ ܗܝ ܕܝ ܠܐܘܠܨܢܐ ܟܕܝܢ ܐܟܘܬܐ: ܘܡܟܠܬܐ ܕܡܛܠ ܡܬܪܢܝܢܘܬܐ ܢܦܫܝ: ܒܡܩܘܡܐ ܗܟܝܢ ܕܬܠܬܐ ܡܦܪܫܝܢ ܡܬܚܝܝܢ. ܐܡܪܐ ܕܐܦܠܐ ܚܕܐ ܠܐ ܠܟܝܢܘܬܐ ܠܗܘܐ ܠܩܢܘܡܐ ܗܟܝܢ ܕܫܡܫܝܢ. ܗܟܝܠ ܟܕ ܡܠܟ ܡܫܝܚܐ ܩܘܪܝܠܘܣ ܠܦܘܡܐ ܕܐܪܝܢ ܕܠܘܬܗ ܠܢܘܦܘܗܝ ܕܢܣܛܘܪܝܘܣ ܐܡܪ. ܀ܩܘܪܝܠܘܣ܀ ܚܕ ܟܪܝܐ ܘܡܢ ܟܕܘ ܡܫܬܟܚܐ ܚܕܐ ܡܢ ܠܬܪ ܚܕܝܘܬܐ: ܗܘ ܕܠܗ ܕܡܟܠܬܐ ܕܡܟܫܪ܀ ܘܟܕ ܐܠܗܐ ܕܐܬܠܝܬ ܠܘܬܗ ܟܕ ܠܘܬܗ ܡܩܪܒ ܐܡܪ. ܀ܩܘܪܝܠܘܣ܀ ܟܕ ܟܝܢ ܠܚܕ ܦܪܘܨܐ: ܡܠܟܝܢ ܩܢܘܡ ܩܠܐ ܗܟܝܢ ܕܐܬܦܠܓܘܬ ܙܘܓ ܕܫܡܫ. ܘܠܫܘܝܐ ܚܕ ܕܡܟܠܬܐ ܕܡܟܫܪ܀ ܢܝܚ ܗܘܐ ܟܪ ܕܫܡܐ ܕܚܝܐ: ܐܦ ܟܠ ܗܘܢܓܐ ܕܟܝܢܐ ܡܬܝܠܕ ܕܩܢܡ ܫܪܝܢܐ. ܐܝܟ ܐܡܪܐ (167) ܕܐܡܪ ܒܫܡܠܝܘܬܗ ܒܡܬܐܡܪܐ ܕܡܛܠ ܗܡܝܢܘܬܐ. ܀ܒܫܡܠܝܘܬܗ܀ ܠܐܡ ܐܠܐ ܘܟܪܐ ܘܪܘܚܐ ܕܡܪܝܐ: ܚܕ ܟܝܢܐ ܠܐ ܟܪܝܐ܀ ܘܟܪܝܣܛܝܢܘܣ ܡܟܠܝܠ ܠܟܝܢܬܐ: ܒܡܬܐܡܪܐ ܕܟܠ ܦܠܓܘܬܗ. ܀ܟܪܝܣܛܝܢܘܣ܀ ܕܚܕܐ ܠܟܝܢܘܬܐ ܐܘ ܗܟܝܢ ܠܡܠܟܝܘܬܐ ܐܘܪܗ. ܐܢ ܕܝܢ ܙܟܝܢ ܐܢܬܘܢ ܕܚܕ ܟܝܢܐ܀ ܐܦ ܗܘ ܕܝܢ ܩܕܝܫܐ ܩܘܪܝܠܘܣ ܠܦܘܩܕܢܐ ܕܐܪܟܢܐ ܕܠܘܟܠ ܠܢܘܦܘܗܝ ܕܢܣܛܘܪܝܘܣ ܐܡܪ. ܀ܩܘܪܝܠܘܣ܀ ܚܕ ܟܪܝܐ ܡܫܬܟܚܐ ܟܝܢܐ ܕܐܠܗܘܬܐ ܠܡܠܟܝܘܬܐ ܩܕܡܝܬܐ ܘܩܘܡ ܟܝܢܐ܀

ܐܝܬ ܕܝܢ ܟܕ ܠܡܦܠܚܢܐ ܕܗܟܝܢ ܡܟܢܫ. ܠܐܘܣܛܛܝܘܣ ܐܝܟ ܕܡܢ ܕܗܘܪܐܬܐ ܕܠܐ ܡܬܡܠܟ ܡܠܬܐ ܐܝܬ ܠܡܕܒܪܬܐ. ܟܕ ܦܬܚܘ ܐܝܬ ܠܗ ܘܐܡܪ ܐܝܬ: ܗܘ ܕܡܬܐܡܪ ܗܘܐ ܐܘܣܛܛܝܘܣ. ܘܐܬܛܟܒ ܠܝ ܡܟܘܐ ܐܝܬ ܟܪܝܡܐ ܕܡܢ ܟܪܝܐ: ܐܟܪܐ ܕܟܗܢ ܗܟܝܢܘܣ ܕܡܒܝ ܗܘܐ ܡܬܐܡܪ ܒܡܠܐ. ܕܝܢ ܟܪܝܐ ܕܝܢ ܟܢܝܫܘܬ: ܕܟܪܝܣܛܝܢܘܣ ܡܟܠܝܠ ܠܟܝܢܬܐ: ܗܘ ܕܟܠܡܫܝܚܐ ܕܦܠܓܘܬܐ ܚܠܬܐܝܬ ܙܘܓ ܗܘܐ: ܘܡܫܡܫ ܗܘܐ ܕܝܗܘܐ ܡܫܡܫܢܐ ܕܗܟܝܢ: ܘܟܠ ܐܦܘܗܝ ܡܢ ܡܫܟܢܐ ܕܦܠܓ ܐܡܪ:

the mortal[50] soul, and the humanism of (his) opinions".[51] (*Lebon p. 168*)

But yet it is not our business that we should investigate this, how Aristotle thinks about the soul. "For what concern is it of mine, that I should judge also those outside?",[52] says holy Paul. For I know this clearly, that none of those who consider that the human soul is rational and intelligent and not mortal says this, that it is one ousia and quality along with a mortal and sensible body, or (with) the man who is composed from these. And we say this particularly strenuously in the case of Emmanuel—that no-one of intelligence says that the nature of God the Word and flesh endowed with a soul and with a mind, which was united hypostatically to him, has become of one ousia and quality.

And I am unable to see this either, (namely) how you distinguish qualities from natures, and (then) say that the quality of the Word has shared with the quality of the body.[53] For whom have you seen of the Father Theologians, who ever burst[54] (out with) this particularly foolish statement in the Church? For all of them hold to a union of natures, in which—beyond doubt—those naturally fitted signs are seen inseparably. For because of this, when you ask "What then? The moment we say Emmanuel is from two natures, are we obliged to confess as well (that he is) two proprieties?", I have given sentence in saying that this is superfluous, and by means of many and uncontentious discourses I have demonstrated that which has been said. And you have again called a reminder like this "an accusation", saying: "A fourth expression has become a risk to me, as I am called to judgement on the charge that I have set aside ousiai, and interweave composition out of signs".[55] For when you repeat the same things, and (then) again deny that you are saying (them), (*Lebon p. 169*) as far as I can see, nothing can be found to be said as a cure. For on the one hand you are ashamed of and renounce those reasonings, by means of those (things) which have already been written and proved to be in the wrong and exposed, but on the other hand you fasten onto the terms, and just like your tragedian,[56] you say, "ἡ γλῶσσ' ὀμώμοχ' ἡ δὲ φρὴν ἀνώμοτος".[57]

But because you have written, "Let us be indulgent to the accurate (findings) of the philosophers, even if they are not of our fold, (and) particularly to (their) interpretations of terms",[58] know that you have written this outside of the law of the Church. For none of the Doctors of true religion said, "We make pagan philosophy a [leader][59] in our studies of terms and of words", but they say they accept it subsequently, as a handmaid, in so far as it agrees with the

ܦܩܕ ܚܘܒܐ ܗܠܝܢ ܠܡܥܘܠܗܘ ܕܐܪܣܛܛܠܝܣ: ܕܠܢܦܫܐ ܕܒܪ̈ܢܫܐ ܡܥܘܢܬܐ ܡܠܠܐ. ܐܦ ܦܘܪܘܠܝܢ ܕܐܪܣܛܛܠܝܣܐ ܚܒܝܒ: ܘܦܝܠܐ ܚܟܝܡܐ ܝܕܝܥ: ܘܟܠ ܠܐܘܪܚܬܐ ܙܥܘܪܬܐ ܙܥܘܪܬܐ ܕܝܢ ܡܚܝܚܝܢ ܚܝ̈ܠܐ: ܠܡܥܘܠܗܘ ܡܫܬܠܝܢܬܐ ܗܟܢ ܕܒܗܘܢ: ܗܟܐ ܕܐܬܚܟܡܐ. ܘܚܝܠܐ ܓܝܪ ܡܫܡܠܐ ܗܘ ܠܢܦܫܐ ܕܒܪ̈ܢܫܐ: ܟܠܗ ܗܘ ܕܦܐܪܐ ܠܗܘܢ ܡܫܡܫܝܢ. ܥܒܕ ܓܝܪ ܗܘ ܡܫܠܡܐ ܕܝܕܥܬܐ ܐܠܗܝܬܐ ܘܕܐܬܚܘܝܝ: ܒܡܐܡܪܐ ܕܟܠܗ ܐܘܢܩܝܡܘ ܗܘܐ ܙܝܐ. ܐܪܣܛܛܠܝܣ܀ ܡܢܗܘܬܐ ܙܥܘܪܬܐ ܡܟܠܬܐ ܘܐܘܡܢܝܬܐ: ܘܟܠܐ ܕܡܛܠ ܢܦܫܐ ܡܥܘܢܬܐ. ܘܐܢܫܘܬܐ ܕܡܟܠܬܐ.

(168) ܒܪܡ ܕܗܘܐ ܢܓܪܐ: ܕܐܡܝܢܐ ܐܪܣܛܛܠܝܣ ܡܫܡܫ ܡܛܠ ܢܦܫܐ: ܠܗ ܕܡܢ ܐܡܝܢ. ܥܠ ܠܟ ܓܝܪ ܕܐܦ ܠܗܘܠܝܢ ܕܠܒܪ ܐܘܕܝ: ܐܡܪ ܩܕܡܝܐ ܦܘܠܘܣ. ܗܘܐ ܕܝܢ ܚܕܐ ܐܢܐ ܒܟܠܗܝܢ: ܘܠܐ ܐܝܟ ܡܢ ܗܠܝܢ ܕܡܫܠܡܬܐ ܘܡܕܘܟܝܬܐ ܘܠܐ ܡܥܘܢܬܐ ܡܫܡܫ ܕܐܠܗܝ ܢܦܫܐ ܐܢܫܝܬܐ: ܐܡܪ ܠܗܘܢ: ܕܟܠ ܦܓܪܐ ܡܥܘܢܬܐ ܘܡܬܕܪܟܐ: ܕܡܢܐ ܐܘܣܝܐ ܐܠܗܝ ܘܡܫܡܫܘܬܐ: ܐܘ ܠܒܪ ܐܢܫܐ ܕܡܬܕܒܪ ܡܢ ܗܠܝܢ. ܘܦܝܫ ܡܬܪܐܝܬ ܗܘܐ ܟܠܗ ܒܡܥܘܢܬܐ ܚܠܠܝܬܐ ܐܡܪܝܢ. ܘܠܐ ܐܝܟ ܕܐܝܬ ܠܗ ܗܘܝܐ ܐܡܪ ܠܚܝܐ ܕܡܠܟܐ ܐܠܗܐ ܘܠܒܣܪܐ ܡܫܝܚܐ ܘܡܗܘܝܐ ܗܘ ܕܐܬܚܝܒ ܠܗ ܦܘܡܐܠܝܬ: ܕܗܘܐ ܕܡܢܐ ܐܘܣܝܐ ܘܡܫܡܫܘܬܐ.

ܐܦܠܐ ܗܘ ܐܡܪ ܠܝ ܕܐܝܬܐ: ܕܐܝܟ ܡܦܪܫ ܐܝܬ ܡܫܡܫܘܬܐ ܡܢ ܒܝ̈ܬܐ: ܘܐܡܪ ܐܝܬ ܡܫܡܫܘܬܐ ܘܡܠܟܐ ܕܐܬܚܙܝ ܠܡܫܡܫܘܬܐ ܕܦܓܪܐ. ܡܛܠ ܓܝܪ ܚܕܘܬܐ ܡܢ ܐܒܗ̈ܬܐ ܡܩܒܠܝܢ ܠܐܠܗܝܬܐ: ܘܦܠܓ ܡܫܠܡܘܢ ܒܒܝܬܐ: ܗܘܐ ܡܠܟܐ ܕܦܝܫ ܡܫܡܠܐ. ܟܠܗܘܢ ܓܝܪ ܚܕܘܬܐ ܕܒܢ̈ܝܐ ܡܫܡܫܝܢ. ܕܒܗܘܢ ܡܬܚܙܐ ܡܢ ܟܠܦܪܘܣ ܠܐ ܡܦܪܫܐܝܬ ܡܩܘܕܫܐ ܗܠܝܢ ܕܡܫܝܢ. ܡܬܚܘܐ ܓܝܪ ܕܝ ܡܫܠܡܢܘܬܐ ܕܐܝܕܐ ܡܫܘܚ: ܒܗܢ ܗܘ ܕܢܐܡܪ ܡܢ ܠܐܘܝܢ ܚܢܝܢ ܠܡܫܡܫܘܬܐ: ܘܗܘ ܕܗܘܐ ܐܦ ܠܐܘܪܚ ܕܬܟܠܬܐ: ܦܩܕ ܕܝ ܐܡܪ ܐܢܐ: ܕܡܬܪܐܬܐ ܗܘ ܗܘܐ. ܘܟܕ ܟܠܐ ܗܓܝܢܬܐ ܘܠܐ ܡܬܚܝܠܐ: ܗܘ ܕܐܬܐܡܪܬ ܚܘܝܐ. ܘܐܘܟ ܠܟܘܗܢܐ ܕܐܝܟ ܗܘܐ: ܡܘܬܪܢܐ ܫܡܥܘܢ ܕܝ ܐܡܪ ܐܢܐ. ܘܡܠܟܐ ܕܐܬܚܙܝ ܡܫܡܫ ܠܟ ܒܡܫܝܚܘܬܗ. ܕܝ ܡܬܐܡܪܐ ܐܢܐ ܠܒܝܬܐ ܘܒܪܢܫܐ ܐܘܣܝܣ. ܘܡܢ ܡܩܘܕܫܐ ܡܬܢܨܚܢܐ ܙܘܥܐ: ܕܝ ܓܝܪ ܕܝܢܝ ܕܝ ܕܝܢܝ ܐܡܪ ܐܢܐ: ܘܐܠܐ ܦܦܪ ܐܢܐ ܘܠܐ ܐܡܪ ܐܢܐ: ܐܢܐ (169) ܡܠܟܐ ܠܐܡܪܐ ܠܐܠܗܘܬܐ: ܠܐ ܡܕܝܢܐ ܕܢܡܫܚ ܐܝܟ ܕܠܟ ܡܬܚܙܝܐ. ܒܗܝܢ ܦܝܪ ܓܝܪ ܒܫܡܫܘܬܐ: ܒܝ ܗܢܝ ܕܡܢ ܒܗ ܐܬܚܙܝ ܘܐܬܦܫܩ ܘܐܬܦܪܫ: ܡܬܚܙܝ ܐܢܐ ܘܦܦܪ ܐܢܐ. ܒܟܠܐ ܕܝܢ ܐܝܟ

teachings and considerations of truth. And at once, therefore, Amphilochius of reverend memory, when he sent a letter with verses in metre to Seleucus, wrote somewhere in this way: "Like a judge introducing a sentence in agreement with the law, command the study of words which is found among the pagans to serve, as is proper to the freedom of true studies, and to the all-wise study of the scriptures. For it is right that the wisdom of the Spirit which is from above and comes from God should be mistress of the instruction which is below as of a handmaid who is not puffed up in vain, but is wont to serve modestly. For it is right that that which is below should be subject to that which is from God."[60]

But great Basil, on evil Eunomius' making mention of "possession" and "privation",[61] before he rebuked his artifice, made this very thing alone the great pretext of complaint, (namely) that from contemptible philosophy (he) should introduce (*Lebon p. 170*) new terms into the discourse of true religion. For he wrote as follows in the First Treatise of those against (that) adversary: (BASIL): "But it is not difficult to show that he gabbles these things from the wisdom of the world, from which he has lifted up his neck,[62] and in this way has set down innovations in terms. For they belong to Aristotle, as those who have read his work *The Categories* would be able to say—discussions about possessions and privations, saying that privations are secondary to possessions. But it was sufficient for us, to show he was speaking not from the teachings of the Spirit, but from the wisdom of the princes of this world,[63] to quote against him these (words) of the psalm, 'The transgressors of the law have related babble to me, but not as your law, O Lord'.[64] And as we learn that these things which are said are not from the teachings of our Lord Jesus Christ, his voice will be remembered: 'When he lies, he speaks according to his own nature',[65] and in this way we should cut short the greater part of his words, since henceforward we make known to everyone that there is no partnership between us and them: 'For what is the unanimity between Christ and Beliar, or what portion has the believer with the unbeliever?'[66]"[67] For in the Letter to the young men, the Doctor says that first it is right that we should grasp the doctrine of truth in concepts and in terms, but as something extra and subsequently (we should) also use profane philosophy, which completes the ornament and grace of the leaves which bend towards the fruit. And he wrote as follows: (BASIL): "Now if there is some affinity between the (bodies of) teachings, a knowledge of them would be necessary for us; but if not, at all events, (by) placing them side by side, we will learn the difference (between them), (which

ܐܝܟ: ܘܐܠܐ ܒܠܚܘܕ ܕܐܝܟ ܦܘܐܬܐ ܕܡܢܟ ܠܟܠܢܐ ܐܡܪ ܐܝܟ ܕܟܡܠܐ ܐܡܠܐ: ܠܐܘܚܕܢܐ ܕܝܢ
ܘܠܐ ܡܬܡܨܝܢܐ.

ܡܛܠ ܕܝܢ ܕܐܬܒܥܝܬ: ܕܒܗܠܝܢ ܫܘܚܠܦܐ ܕܦܬܓܡܐ: ܐܦ ܠܐ ܐܬܚܙܝܘ، ܡܢ ܕܘܟܬܐ
ܕܡܢ: ܦܝܫ ܒܦܫܝܛܘܬܐ ܕܟܠܐ ܡܬܡܨܝܢ: ܕܐܢ ܢܫܟܚ: ܕܠܒܪ ܡܢ ܢܡܘܣܐ ܕܟܝܢܐ
ܡܬܒܥܐ ܗܘܐ. ܠܐ ܓܝܪ ܐܝܟ ܡܢ ܡܠܦܢܐ ܕܝܠܟ ܠܐܠܗܐ. ܐܡܪ: ܕܦܫܝܛܘܬܐ
ܕܠܒܪ: ܕܫܐ ܒܟܠܗܝܢ ܣܝܡ ܒܡܠܦܢܐ ܕܡܢ: ܕܡܬܒܥܝܐ ܘܟܠܐ. ܐܠܐ ܢܬܒܥܐ ܐܝܟ
ܐܟܡܐ ܐܡܪܢ ܕܡܢܗܝܢ ܠܗܘܐ: ܐܫܝܐ ܕܒܗ ܡܠܦܢܐ ܘܦܬܓܡܐ ܕܒܪܐ ܕܝܠܗ. ܘܡܫܝܚܐ
ܗܘܝܘ : ܐܦܣܩܘܦܘܣ ܗܘ ܕܒܗܘܢܐ ܕܝܠܗ ܠܐܠܗܐ: ܟܕ ܒܢܝܫ ܒܗܐ ܡܬܘܣܦ
ܠܒܪܐ ܗܘ ܕܡܫܘܚܕܐ ܕܡܫܝܚܐ: ܗܟܢܐ ܒܪܘܚ ܩܘܕܫܐ. ܘܒܡܠܦܢܐ ܕܟܠܐ ܕܒܗ
ܚܝܠܐ ܐܝܟ ܕܢܝܐ ܕܦܫܝܛܐ ܢܡܘܣܐ ܡܫܝܚܐ ܘܢܩܫܘܫ ܠܦܫ: ܐܝܟ ܕܦܐܐ ܠܒܪܝܬܐ
ܘܡܠܦܢܐ ܒܝܬܪܐ: ܘܒܬܐܘܪܝܐ ܫܡܥܬ ܒܟܠ ܕܟܠܒ. ܟܐܢܐ ܓܝܪ ܕܫܡܥܬܐ
ܕܪܘܚܐ ܕܡܢ ܒܒܠܐܝܬܘ ܘܡܢ ܠܐܠܗܐ ܐܢܬ: ܡܪܝܐ ܠܗܘܐ ܕܡܪܕܘܬܐ ܕܒܪܝܬ. ܐܝܟ
ܕܐܡܪܬ ܕܒܗ ܡܪܢܐܝܬ ܡܬܢܚܐ: ܕܐܬܚܡ ܕܝܢ ܢܦܩܬ ܡܢܝܐ. ܒܗܘ ܓܝܪ
ܕܠܐܠܗܐ: ܗܘ ܕܒܪܝܬ ܕܝܢ ܕܐܬܒܥܝ܀

ܒܫܠܡܗ ܕܝܢ ܕܥܐ: ܟܕ ܐܘܢܩܘܣ ܒܥܠܐ ܐܬܒܥܝ ܒܡܘܬܐ ܘܓܠܝܘܬܐ ܡܢ ܩܕܡ
ܕܢܚܫ ܢܬܒܥܐ: ܕܝܢ ܗܘܐ ܒܠܚܘܕ ܒܒܪܝܬܐ ܕܥܠܡܐ ܕܡܬܛܟܣܐ ܒܒܪ: ܗܘ ܕܡܢ
ܦܫܛܘܬܐ ܡܛܠܬܐ ܢܫܠ ܒܫܠܟܬܐ ܕܒܝܬ ܠܐܠܗܐ: ܒܪܐ (170) ܥܠܐ ܚܕܬܐ
ܕܡܫܟܚܐ. ܥܠܟ ܓܝܪ ܒܥܬܐܡܪܐ ܩܕܡܝܐ ܕܗܘܐ، ܕܒܬܪܗ ܕܒܒܒܪܒܐ ܗܘܝܐ.
܀ܒܫܠܡܗ܀ ܘܗܠܝܢ ܕܝܢ ܕܡܢ ܫܡܥܬܐ ܕܒܟܠܐ ܦܫܝܛ: ܕܡܢܗ ܐܘܪܚ ܩܕܡܘ:
ܘܡܬܒܪܬܐ ܦܫܝܛܐ ܕܟܠܐ ܕܐܝܟ ܗܟܢ ܫܦܝܪ: ܠܐ ܡܫܝܐ ܕܐܝܬܝܐ. ܘܐܘܫܛܛܢܫ ܓܝܪ
ܐܬܚܙܝ. ܐܝܟ ܡܐ ܕܐܦ ܐܡܠܢ ܕܡܪܗ ܒܗܠܝܢ ܡܛܟܣܘܬܐ ܕܢܫܝܡ ܕܡܠܗ: ܐܝܟ
ܕܢܐܡܪܘܢ ܟܠܐ ܡܛܠ ܩܝܡܬܐ ܘܓܢܝܒܘܬܐ. ܕܐܘܪܚܬܐ ܕܩܝܡܬܐ ܐܡܪ ܕܐܬܚܙܝ
ܓܢܝܒܘܬܐ. ܠܟ ܕܝܢ ܫܦܝܪܐ ܗܘܐ ܕܒ ܢܚܘܗܝ ܕܠܗ ܡܢ ܡܠܦܢܐ ܕܪܘܚܐ: ܐܠܐ ܡܢ
ܫܡܥܬܐ ܕܐܘܪܚܐ ܕܒܟܠܐ ܗܘܐ ܡܫܟܠܠ: ܗܠܝܢ ܕܡܬܡܟܪܐ ܢܐܡܪ ܒܗܘܢ. ܘܐܬܒܥܝ
ܠܟ ܒܒܪܗ ܢܡܘܣܐ ܦܫܝܛܐ. ܐܠܐ ܠܐ ܐܝܟ ܢܡܘܣܐ ܡܢܐ. ܘܟܕ ܡܠܦܢ ܕܠܗ ܡܢ
ܡܠܦܢܐ ܕܡܢܝ، ܢܡܘܣ ܡܫܝܚܐ ܐܬܚܙܝ ܗܠܝܢ ܕܡܬܐܡܪܢ: ܢܛܪ ܒܪܐ ܥܠܐ
ܕܠܗ. ܘܐܬܚܙܝ ܕܡܫܟܠܠ ܕܓܢܒܐ: ܡܢ ܗܠܝܢ ܕܠܗ ܡܫܟܠܠ. ܘܒܗܘܢ ܙܢܐ
ܡܘܓܝܐ ܕܡܠܦܢܘܗܝ ܢܦܫܗ ܠܟ. ܟܕ ܡܢ ܗܘܕܐ: ܠܒܠܝܢ ܒܒܢܝܢ ܚܝܠܬܐ: ܕܠܐ ܚܕܐ

is of advantage) not least for the establishment of that which is better. But yet, to what (true) comparison (*Lebon p. 171*) can you hit upon, as you compare each one of the disciplines? But (perhaps), just as it is the peculiar virtue of a plant to sprout fair fruit, but the leaves which hang upon the branches also bring some decoration: so too the first fruit of the mind is truth, yet it does not lack grace,[68] or that it should be decked in profane wisdom, as the leaves provide some sort of covering and a not unpleasant appearance for the fruit".[69]

Therefore even holy Cyril makes use of this example, when he wrote in the Second Letter to Succensus: (CYRIL): "For it is not the case that 'one' is predicated truly only of simples in nature, but (it is predicated) also of those which have come together in composition".[70] But in the Treatise of question and answer, *That Christ is One*, as if adding (it) as something extra he said this: (CYRIL): "For so it seems good even to the pagan experts".[71]

Therefore why, when I have reminded your Chastity with humble intention of these things, and of things like these, are you indignant at the lines?[72] For did you not say that you are not expert in the doctrines of true religion, and, "I am a young child in these (matters)"?[73] For we shall again bring to your remembrance these sayings of yours. But in (your) letter you falsely call me an Ecumenical Doctor. For I am become a fool because you compel me.[74] But is it an insult that the schoolmaster should draw lines over inaccurate words? So then will the youth also be indignant when the professional scribe denounces letters which are not well written?

But now you say that you have been left as a spark in the East, and (are) the voice of the Church:[75] (*Lebon p. 172*) (something) which even if someone else should say of him, a man would blush. But we did not know that this was the case for you as regards yourself, and we wrote letters as to a student, and one needing to be led. And because of this, we wrote confidently, knowing your untried nature in these matters, which excused you and (your) questions seemed to be from a desire for instruction and not from contentiousness. But now, since you struggle on behalf of words said in an unlearned way, you have made inexperience and ignorance a premeditated sin. Because of this, and since I have pity on your soul—I say this with God as my witness—I have proceeded to this third piece of advice, and I advise you to keep distant from words of this sort.

For if we grant, according to your word, that I have the rank of the sun, though I am ashamed as I say this openly, while you again are a spark, it ensures that a spark, which from all respects is an issue

ܡܫܐܠܬܐ ܐܝܬ ܠܢ ܠܘܬܟܘܢ. ܐܝܟܢܐ ܓܝܪ ܡܫܬܘܕܐ ܠܡܫܝܚܐ ܠܟܠ ܟܠܢܫ: ܐܘ ܐܝܟܢܐ ܡܢܝܢܐ ܠܡܫܘܡܫܢܐ ܥܡ ܠܐ ܡܫܘܡܫܢܐ܀ ܥܠܬܐ ܓܝܪ ܕܟܠܗ ܠܥ̈ܠܡܐ ܐܡܪ ܗܘ ܡܫܒܚܐ. ܠܡܢܐ ܗܘ ܩܠܐ ܕܐܝܠܝܢ ܡܫܒܚܝܢ ܕܥܢܝܢ: ܒܩܕ̈ܝܫܐ ܘܒܩܕ̈ܝܫܬܐ: ܡܢ ܬܠܬܐ ܓܝܪ ܘܡܫܬܐܠܝܢ: ܐܦ ܒܡܫܡܫܢܘܬܐ ܕܠܒܪ ܠܡܫܝܚ: ܘܡܫܡܫܢܐ ܠܗܠܝܢ ܘܬܫܒܘܚܬܐ ܕܬܫ̈ܒܚܬܐ ܕܢܫܡܥ ܠܟܠ ܦܘܪܫ. ܡܟܐ ܕܝܢ ܗܟܝܠ. ܀ܒܩܕܝܫܘܬ܀ ܐܢ ܗܟܝܠܐܝܬ ܒܡܠܘܬܐ ܡܕܡ ܠܩܒܠܐ ܟܠܗ ܢܚܘܐ. ܐܟܙܢܐ ܕܗܘܐ ܠܢ ܡܟܠܗܘܢ: ܐܢ ܕܝܢ ܠܐ: ܐܠܐ ܗܘ ܕܟܠ ܟܠܗ ܢܚܘܐ ܡܫܡܫܝܢ ܢܟܠܦ ܡܫܠܡܐ: ܠܐ ܥܒܕܐ ܠܡܫܡܠܝܘܬܐ ܕܗܘ ܘܡܫܬܪܐ. ܠܟܢ ܗܟܝܠ ܒܝܕ ܡܕܡܐ (171) ܐܝܬ ܟܠ ܚܕܐ ܡܢ ܡܬܪܥܝܢܘܬܐ ܙܒܢܐ ܢܫܡܫ ܠܢ. ܐܠܐ ܐܟܝܢܐ ܗܘ ܕܐܝܬܘܗܝ ܡܫܡܠܝܘܬܐ ܒܡܠܘܬܐ ܕܒܝܠܬܐ: ܗܘ ܕܐܝܬ ܗܘܬ ܡܫܝܚܐ ܒܦܬܪܐ ܦܬܐ: ܡܫܡܥ ܕܝܢ ܙܒܢܐ ܡܕܡ ܘܬܫ̈ܒܚܬܐ ܕܐܝܟ ܒܩܘܫܬܐ: ܗܟܝܠ ܐܦ ܕܫܡܝܐ. ܦܬܪܐ ܗܘ ܦܘܕܢܐ ܡܕܪܐ. ܒܡܠܬܗ ܕܝܢ ܕܠܐ ܢܫܒܘܩ: ܘܠܐ ܗܘ ܕܒܫܡܫܬܐ ܒܪܢܫܐ ܗܘܬ ܡܫܒܚܐ. ܐܝܟ ܬܫ̈ܒܚܬܐ ܡܕܡ ܕܐܟܣܢܝܐ: ܕܒܦܬܪܐ ܚܙܬܐ ܠܗ ܘܠܐ ܦܐܝܐ ܡܘܒܠ܀

ܒܗܝ ܗܟܝܠ ܬܘܦܣܐ: ܒܝܕ ܘܡܕܡܐ ܡܫܬܡܠܝܘ ܡܫܡܫܝܢ: ܥܠܬܐ ܕܐܬܐܡܪ ܕܟܠܗ ܫܘܡܠܝܘܬ ܡܟܐ. ܀ܫܘܡܠܝܘܬ܀ ܠܗ ܓܝܪ ܟܠܗ ܦܪ̈ܨܘܦܐ ܒܚܝܠܐ ܒܠܫܢܗ ܡܫܬܐܡܪ ܚܕ ܚܕܪܐܝܬ. ܐܠܐ ܐܦ ܟܠ ܗܠܝܢ ܕܒܪܘܚܐ ܡܫܒܚܝܢ܀ ܒܡܐܡܪܐ ܕܝܢ ܕܫܘܠܐ ܘܦܘܫ ܦܠܓܘܬܐ ܗܘ ܕܚܕ ܗܘ ܡܫܡܫܢܐ: ܗܘ ܗܘܐ ܐܡܪ: ܐܝܟ ܕܡܢ ܬܠܬܐ ܐܘܫܦ. ܀ܫܘܡܠܝܘܬ܀ ܗܟܝܠ ܓܝܪ ܦܦܪ ܐܦ ܠܡܫܝ̈ܚܐ ܕܟܠܗ܀

ܠܡܢܐ ܗܟܝܠ ܒܝܕ ܐܝܢܐ: ܗܠܝܢ ܘܐܝܟ ܗܠܝܢ ܥܡ ܬܘܕܝܬܐ ܡܫܡܫܢܘܬܐ ܠܒܪܫܘܬܐ ܒܗܕܐ: ܡܫܡܫܢ ܐܝܬ ܟܠ ܫܘܟܠܐ. ܐܘ ܓܝܪ ܠܐ ܐܡܪܬ ܘܠܐ ܡܫܡܫܢܐ ܐܝܬ. ܕܫ̈ܒܚܐ ܕܕܝܠܗ ܠܟܘܠܐ: ܘܡܢ ܐܝܟ ܒܗܠܝܢ. ܐܘܦ ܓܝܪ ܗܠܝܢ ܕܠܝܬ ܢܚܘܕܝܢ. ܕܡܫܬܐܠܢ ܕܝܢ ܡܫܒܚܐ ܕܐܫܬܠܡ ܠܗ ܥܠܬܐ ܕܟܠ ܐܝܬ. ܗܘܐ ܓܝܪ ܫܟܠܐ ܡܫܬܟܠ ܕܐܝܬ ܠܐܠܗ ܐܝܬ ܠܗ. ܙܒܢܐ ܗܘ ܕܝܢ ܗܘ ܕܡܫܒܚܐ ܫܘܬܦܐ ܢܫܪܘܐ ܟܠ ܩܢܐ ܩܠܐ ܗܠܝܢ ܠܐ ܒܫܪܝܪܐ. ܡܕܡ ܐܦ ܠܝܬ ܢܠܒܫ: ܒܝܕ ܫܦܝܪܐ ܫܘܬܦܐ ܗܠܝܢ ܘܠܐ ܫܡܝܪ ܡܠܟܝܢ ܒܪܐ.

ܐܠܐ ܗܟܝܠ ܐܡܪ ܐܢܬ: ܕܐܝܟ ܒܟܘܪܗܢܐ ܐܫܬܟܚܬ ܒܡܕܝܢܬܐ: ܘܒܪܬ ܩܠܐ ܐܢܬ ܕܒܝܬܐ. (172) ܗܘ ܕܐܦ ܐܚܪܢܐ ܢܐܡܪ ܡܫܬܡܠܝܢ: ܡܬܚܫܒ ܐܢܬ. ܐܠܐ ܠܐ ܡܕܡ ܗܘܝܢ ܕܗܘܝܐ ܐܝܬ ܗܘܐ ܠܢ ܡܫܬܟܠ ܢܫܡܥ. ܐܝܟ ܕܙܒܢ ܐܢܫ ܡܠܘܦܐ: ܘܡܫܡܫ ܕܢܗܘܐ ܒܥܕܢ

of the sun, should shine out with (beams) which are like the sparkling of the sun. Therefore show (me) when, in the six years I spoke in the Church of the Antiochenes and wrote many letters, at any time I once said Emmanuel is one ousia, and of one signification and of one particularity.

But why do you say that you were wounded by us, and you wish to be healed, as if we were striking (you)? For (all we are doing is) remind you, making use of the teachings of the Fathers, in which there is every doctrine for healing and recovery and ordinance and strength. But you do not realise that you wound yourself, and thrust away the healing voices of the Fathers. Thus, when I said in the second letter that God is above ousia, but we use the term "ousia", using (*Lebon p. 173*) at the same time the poverty which is with us, and I brought to this (point) the evidence of Gregory the Theologian and of holy Cyril,[76] I was again believed to have made an attack upon what is said, and (it seemed right to you) to introduce and say, as something unusual, what is well-trodden[77] for all God-fearers, (namely), "I call God ousia, because I have learned from him who said, 'He who is, sent me'",[78] as if the term "above ousia" introduces that which is without being, and (as if) the Fathers had not heard wise Paul saying: "It is right for him who applies himself to God to believe that he exists".[79] For that which is above ousia in all respects is, in that it is. Therefore it ill became you, plotting undue things, to oppose the words of the Doctors with empty attacks.

But again when I said that no-one ever applies "propriety" with any precision to God, as (he would) to things which are subject to definitions, and I introduced the chapter of Evagrius[80] who wrote: (EVAGRIUS): "If either genus or species or difference or property or accident is affirmed for every enquiry, yet none of the above mentioned can be found (to apply) in the case of the holy Trinity. Let us worship in silence what is inexpressible",[81] you have tried to trip up the saying which we would state scripturally, and have written: "But you have defined, and very clearly, that the propriety of God (is) grace:[82] 'Why do you call me good? No-one is good, except one, God'.[83] For if a propriety is that thing which belongs to someone and to him alone—(and) now according to the quotation above it belongs to God alone to be good—(then) clearly (*Lebon p. 174*) something of this sort is a definition of a propriety".[84] Therefore what are you saying, (my) fine man? Is goodness thus the (official) propriety of God, just as laughter (is supposed to be) of man, and neighing of horse? Well then, state first what God is in ousia, and thus we may recognise what precisely his propriety (is). For it is clear

ܗܘܘ ܠܒܪ̈ܝܬܐ. ܘܡܬܗܠܠ ܗܘܐ: ܐܦ ܟܕ ܡܬܟܠܝܢ ܗܘܘ ܟܠܗܘܢ ܗܘܘ. ܘܚܙܝܢ ܗܘܘ ܘܐܝܬ ܗܘܐ ܠܗ ܠܐ ܡܫܝܚܘܬܐ ܗܝ ܕܒܗܘܢ ܕܥܡܐ ܣܓܝܐܐ ܙܘܥܐ. ܘܦܘܪܫܢܗ ܘܡܠܟܐ ܘܟܠܗ ܕܡܢܝܢܐ ܕܥܡܗ ܗܘܘ ܘܐܝܬܝܗܘܢ ܒܥܠܠܐ. ܗܟܢ ܕܝܢ ܟܕ ܡܬܬܠܬܠ ܐܢܐ ܣܦܩ ܥܢܝܬ ܩ̈ܠܐ ܕܐܡܪ̈ܬܝ ܠܐ ܡܬܟܠܝܢ: ܒܟܕܪܘ ܟܠܐ ܡܫܝܚܘܬܐ ܘܟܠܐ ܚܕܘܬܐ: ܣܗܒܬܐ ܕܡܢ ܡܫܚܘܬܐ. ܡܬܗܠܠ ܗܘܐ ܘܟܕ ܚܙܐ ܐܢܐ ܟܠܗ ܢܩܡܝ ܟܕ ܠܐܠܗܐ ܗܦܩܝ ܐܡܪ ܐܢܐ ܘܟܠܐ ܡܬܟܠܐ ܗܘܐ ܕܐܬܟܠܬ ܢܦܫܗ. ܘܦܠܚܝ ܐܢܐ ܠܟܝ: ܕܐܬܪܚܩ ܡܢ ܥܢܝܗ ܩ̈ܠܐ ܕܐܝܟ ܗܟܢܐ.

ܐܘ ܒܪܝ ܡܬܠܒܫ ܡܟܝܟܘܬܐ ܕܝܠܟ: ܘܐܢܐ ܦܘ ܠܦܘܬ ܐܝܬ ܠܟ ܕܩܡܠܐ: ܟܡܢܝܬܐ ܕܝܢ ܟܕ ܗܘܐ ܐܡܪ ܐܢܐ ܡܬܚܝܒ ܐܢܐ: ܐܝܟ ܕܝܢ ܠܐܘܦ ܒܟܘܪܝܬܐ: ܕܢܩܐ ܐܬܝܗ̇: ܘܒܟܘܪܝܬܐ ܡܢ ܡܟܦܪܘܗ ܕܪܘܚܐ ܡܗܝܡܢܐ ܐܬܝܗ̇: ܕܗܘܟܢ ܕܕܡܢ ܠܡܬܥܪ̈ܝܢܘܬܐ ܗܟܢ ܕܡܫܡܠܐ ܠܗܘܐ ܡܫܘܐ. ܚܙܐ ܗܘܫܠ ܕܟܕ ܙܕܩܐ ܕܠܗ ܩܢܝܢ ܡܬܟܠܠ ܐܢܐ ܒܕܢܐ ܘܐܬܦܘܫܒܬ: ܘܐܬܪ̈ܘܬܐ ܡܫܬܐ ܠܟ: ܘܐܡܪܢܐ ܠܡܫܘܐܡܠܟܘܬܗ ܕܒܗ: ܕܚܕܐ ܐܦ ܚܕܐ ܐܘܣܦܐ ܐܬܠܗܘܢ: ܘܚܕ ܩܘܫܬܐ ܘܚܕܐ ܘܡܟܠܬܐ.

ܠܡܫܐ ܕܝܢ ܐܡܪ ܐܢܐ ܕܡܢ ܒܟܠܗ: ܘܐܝܟ ܗܘ ܕܡܫܬܚܠ ܠܐܬܐܩܠ ܩܕܡ ܐܢܐ. ܡܢ ܒܪܝ ܒܗܘܢܝ ܟܕ ܐܬܡܣܝܢ ܒܦ̈ܠܚܬܐ ܘܐܟ̈ܪܙܬܐ: ܘܟܠܗ ܡܟܠܬܐ ܘܐܩܫܘܬܐ ܘܡܫܘܠܡܬܐ ܐܝܬ ܒܗܘܢ ܘܠܒܫܐ ܘܫܠܝܐ. ܘܐܝܬ ܕܝܢ ܡܫܝܐ ܐܝܟ ܠܟܫܡܝ: ܠܐ ܚܙܝܬ ܐܝܟ. ܘܟܠܩܝܟ ܩ̈ܠܐ ܡܬܐܫܢ̈ܝܬܐ ܘܐܟ̈ܪܙܬܐ ܕܫܦܝ ܐܝܟ. ܗܟܢܐ ܕܟܕ ܐܡܪܢܐ ܐܢܐ ܠܒܪ̈ܝܬܐ ܘܐܘܦܝ: ܘܟܠܗܘܢ ܡܢ ܐܘܣܝܐ ܐܬܠܗܘܢ ܠܐܠܗܐ: ܡܬܚܫܚܝܢ ܕܝܢ ܒܟܫܠܐ ܘܐܘܣܝܐ: ܟܕ (173) ܐܟܚܕܐ ܒܡܫܡܫܢܘܬܐ ܕܟܠܗ̇ ܡܬܚܫܚܝܢ ܚܝ: ܘܐܬܠܬ ܠܗܘܐ ܡܫܘܕܥܘܬܐ ܕܒܪ̈ܢܫܘܬܗ ܡܫܡܠܠ ܠܐܠܗܘܬܐ: ܘܡܫܘܡܠܝܘܬܗ ܚܝܬܐ: ܠܐܘܦ ܐܫܬܠܟܢܐ ܘܡܟܠܟ ܚܫܦܐ ܟܠܠ ܗܝ ܘܐܡܢܐ: ܘܐܝܟ ܐܡܫܝܚܬܐ ܡܟܝܟ ܗܝ ܕܟܠܗܘܢ ܕܫܪܟ ܠܐܠܗܐ ܕܫܠܐ: ܠܟܪܝܬܐ ܠܐܬܐ ܘܐܡܪ: ܘܐܘܫܝܐ ܦܪܐ ܐܢܐ ܠܐܠܗܐ: ܡܬܗܠܠ ܘܡܟܠܟ ܡܫܗ ܘܐܡܪ: ܘܗܘ ܕܐܬܠܗܘܢ ܚܒܝܒ. ܐܝܟ ܡܠܐ ܕܡܟܠܬܐ ܕܟܠܗܘܢ ܡܢ ܐܘܣܝܐ: ܗܝ ܘܠܐ ܐܬܠ ܡܟܠܐ. ܘܠܐ ܠܟܘܠܗܘܢ ܡܫܡܠܐ ܘܐܡܪ: ܟܕ ܡܫܡܗ ܐܟ̈ܪܙܬܐ: ܘܗܠܐ ܠܟܘܢ ܘܡܬܐܡܪܢ ܠܐܠܗܐ ܕܢܗܝܡܢ ܘܐܬܠܗܘܢ. ܗܘ ܒܪܐ ܘܟܠܗܘܢ ܡܢ ܐܘܣܝܐ: ܡܢ ܡܟܦܪܘܗ ܒܗܝ ܘܐܬܠܗܘܢ ܐܬܠܗܘܢ. ܠܐ ܦܠܐ ܗܘܐ ܡܬܗܠܠ ܕܟܕ ܡܬܚܫܒ ܐܢܐ ܠܡܬܪ̈ܐ: ܒܟܡܢܐ ܡܬܡܠܐ ܘܟܠܠ ܩ̈ܠܐ ܕܡܟܠܬܐ ܠܡܫܘ.

from the start that an ousia is something other than a propriety, for a propriety appears in relation to ousiai. But it is necessary that you attribute accident as well (to God), and those other things from which definitions are brought together, and (thus) you bring God under the limitation of definitions.

But because you thought that the scriptural testimony which says, "No-one is good, except one, God", confirms this ill thought-out statement for you, take note of the scripture which said, "To the only wise God".[85] Therefore, because a propriety properly is that which belongs to one man, according to your words wisdom is also found clearly to follow the principle of a propriety. Therefore by means of these witless and illogical (exercises) two proprieties have appeared for us (in God). But yet, having relied in this way on cool audacity, you have knocked upon the stern of the boat, as it is said, and you have made peace with us at the end, and have honoured those things which are not your own, and have said, "But yet, it is necessary that we should honour these great matters in silence, for God is above ousia and propriety".[86]

But yet, note that wise Basil, in the Letter to Terentius takes goodness not (as) a property but (as) ousia, writing as follows: (BASIL): ". . . . the term 'οὐσία' is generic, like goodness or divinity or anything else which is thought of".[87] (*Lebon p. 175*) And in the Third Treatise against Eunomius he said: (BASIL): "But if we affirm that the ousia of God (is) light, or life or the good, the totality of his existence is life, and all light and all good. But the life has joined to it τὸ ἀγγένητον. How can that which is simple in ousia not be incomposite?"[88] Because of this the Doctor said not fixedly but hesitantly, that the ousia of God is either divinity or goodness, or light or life, because in truth we do not know what God is in ousia. But to the term "ousia" are referred those things which in this way in common and in equality of honour apply to the three hypostases which are distinct in their own characteristics, of whom the Father is not begotten and is from no-one, the Son is begotten, and the Holy Spirit (is) by procession.

And you were indignant at the lines! But while you rage at the voices of the Fathers, again speaking scripturally, I will not be indignant, but will endure humbly the hopping about of your mind. And *do not imagine* that you are arguing with someone of your own profession, or one who raises his eyebrows from his robes. And do not imagine it a mighty achievement to become an advocate of words which (as) I have very often said, are unpracticed and full of mistakes, lest the prophetic word be thought to refer to us as well, as

ܠܘܬ ܕܝܢ ܡܢ ܐܡܪܢܐ ܐܢܐ ܕܟܠܗ ܐܠܗܐ ܡܫܬܐܠܬ ܕܡܠܬܐ ܐܦ ܠܐ ܐܝܬ ܡܕܡ ܐܡܪ: ܐܝܟ ܕܗܘܐ ܫܘܟܢܐ ܕܡܟܠܝܢ ܒܠܫܢܐ: ܘܐܠܐ ܡܫܠܬܗ ܕܐܘܪܓܢܣ ܕܡܠܟ: ܀ܐܘܪܓܢܣ ܕܐܢ ܒܟܠ ܡܘܬܐ: ܐܘ ܒܣܝܡܐ ܐܝܬ ܠܗ ܕܡܬܡܠܟ: ܐܘ ܐܘܟܝܐ ܐܘ ܡܘܣܟܢܐ: ܐܘ ܕܡܠܬܐ ܐܘ ܒܣܝܡܐ: ܘܠܐ ܡܕܡ ܕܝܢ ܡܢ ܗܠܝܢ ܕܐܬܐܡܪ ܐܝܬ ܠܡܣܡܟܘ ܠܗܘܐ ܠܐܠܗܘܬܐ ܡܫܝܚܬܐ: ܒܡܠܬܐ ܢܣܒܝܢ ܗܘ ܕܠܐ ܡܬܐܡܪ܀ ܘܐܘܣܝܐ ܕܒܟܠܐ ܒܡܟܠܬܐ ܕܡܬܒܠܬ ܠܐܡܪ ܢܣܝܒ ܘܫܠܡܬ: ܕܡܠܬܐ ܕܝܢ ܕܐܠܗܐ ܘܦܫܝܛ ܒܠܫܢܗ ܠܡܬܒܠܬ ܠܐܝܣܡܬ. ܒܡܠܐ ܦܪܐ ܐܝܬ ܠܗ ܠܡܠܐ. ܘܠܐ ܐܝܬ ܠܡܠܐ ܐܠܐ ܐܢ ܚܕ ܐܠܗܐ. ܐܢ ܓܝܪ ܕܡܠܬܐ ܗܘ ܕܠܗ ܠܐܝܬ ܘܠܡܫܘܕܥܘ ܐܝܬܘܗܝ: ܕܐܠܗܐ ܕܝܢ ܘܠܡܫܘܕܥܘ ܒܡܠܬܐ ܡܫܝܚܬܐ ܠܡܠܐ: ܒܠܫܢܗ (174) ܗܘܐ ܕܐܝܟ ܗܕܐ: ܐܣܘܦܐ ܐܝܬܘܗܝ ܕܕܡܠܬܐ܀ ܡܢܐ ܗܟܢܐ ܐܡܪ ܐܢܬ ܐܘ ܐܢܫܐ. ܗܟܢܐ ܐܝܬܘܗܝ ܠܡܠܐ ܕܡܠܬܐ ܕܐܠܗܐ: ܐܝܟ ܡܢܐ ܕܕܒܪ ܐܢܫܐ ܒܫܘܒܚܐ: ܘܒܫܘܬܦܐ ܕܡܠܬܐ: ܡܕܡ ܐܡܪ ܡܫܝܚܐ: ܡܢܐ ܒܐܘܣܝܐ ܐܝܬܘܗܝ ܐܠܗܐ. ܘܗܟܢܐ ܡܫܬܘܕܥܝܢ ܕܡܢܐ ܗܘ ܡܬܢܣܒܐ ܕܡܠܬܐ ܕܠܗ. ܡܫܝܚܐ ܓܝܪ ܚܝܠܐ ܕܡܢ ܐܒܘܗܝ ܐܝܬܘܗܝ ܐܘܣܝܐ ܒܟܪ ܡܢ ܕܡܠܬܐ. ܕܡܠܬܐ ܓܝܪ ܒܠܐܘܣܝܐ ܡܬܝܕܥܐ. ܐܝܟܢܐ ܕܝܢ ܕܐܦ ܒܣܝܡܐ ܠܐܬܐ: ܘܗܠܝܢ ܐܢܫܝܢ ܕܡܢ ܡܬܒܣܡܝܢ ܠܐܢܫܐ. ܘܐܝܟ ܡܣܡܟܢܘܬܐ ܕܐܢܫܐ ܠܝܬ ܠܐܝܬ ܠܐܠܗܐ.

ܡܛܠ ܕܝܢ ܕܐܦ ܡܫܘܕܥܘܬܐ ܕܡܠܬܐ ܗܘ ܕܐܡܪܐ: ܘܠܐ ܐܝܬ ܠܡܠܐ ܐܠܐ ܐܢ ܚܕ ܐܠܗܐ: ܐܡܪܢܐ ܕܡܫܪܪܐ ܠܟ ܡܠܬܐ ܗܘܐ ܘܠܐ ܡܣܝܡܬܐ: ܕܗܐ ܠܗ ܒܡܠܬܐ ܕܐܡܪ: ܠܡܫܘܕܥܘܬܗ ܣܡܝܟܐ ܠܐܠܗܐ. ܡܛܠ ܗܟܝܠ ܕܕܡܠܬܐ ܡܬܢܣܒܐ ܐܝܬܘܗܝ ܗܘ ܕܚܝܝܢ ܐܝܬ ܐܝܬܘܗܝ: ܡܫܬܟܚܐ ܐܝܟ ܣܡܝܟܬܐ ܐܝܟ ܩܠܐ ܕܡܢ ܒܠܫܢܗ: ܕܡܠܬܐ ܕܕܡܠܬܐ ܐܝܬ ܠܗ. ܠܐܘܪܚ ܗܟܝܠ ܕܬܠܬܐ: ܒܡܢ ܗܠܝܢ ܡܫܘܕܥܘܬܐ ܘܠܐ ܡܠܬܐ ܐܬܝܗܒ ܠܢ. ܘܒܬܪ ܡܢ ܟܠ ܡܬܚܘܝܢܘܬܐ ܕܐܝܟ ܗܟܢܐ ܐܬܐܡܠܟ: ܢܣܒܬ ܒܝܕܥܬܗ ܕܐܠܗܐ ܐܝܟ ܗܘ ܕܡܬܐܡܪܐ: ܘܒܟܝܢܐ ܡܢܐ ܒܟܝܢ ܒܝܕܥܬܐ. ܘܡܥܒܕ ܗܠܝܢ ܘܠܐ ܕܡܢ ܘܐܡܪܢܐ. ܒܬܪ ܐܠܗܐ ܕܗܠܝܢ ܕܪܘܚܢ ܒܡܠܬܐ ܢܣܒ. ܐܝܬܘܗܝ ܓܝܪ ܐܠܗܐ: ܠܒܠܠ ܡܢ ܐܘܣܝܐ ܘܕܡܠܬܐ.

ܘܒܬܪ ܕܗܐ ܕܢܣܝܡܐ ܒܡܫܝܚܘܬܗ ܒܛܝܒܘܬܐ ܕܒܗܝ ܠܡܪܢܝܬܗ ܠܡܠܘܬܐ ܠܗ ܠܕܡܠܬܐ ܡܦܠܓ: ܐܠܐ ܠܐܘܣܝܐ. ܡܢ ܩܕܡ ܗܟܝܠ. ܒܡܫܝܚܘܬܗ܀ ܡܠܬܐ ܦܬ ܘܐܘܣܝܐ ܕܓܘܐ. ܕܐܝܟ ܐܡܪ. ܠܡܘܬܐ. ܐܘ ܠܐܠܗܘܬܐ. ܐܘ (175) ܐܢ ܡܕܡ ܐܚܪܝܢ

about someone from those who were before, (namely) "He loved shame (more) than his glory".[89] For better is humility, which our Lord approved for us, saying, "He who humbles himself will be exalted".[90]

But if you persist in these things, which I pray will not be the case, with words of this type of which I suppose you are become an advocate, in accordance with the Gospel, I shall shake off (my) garments and the dust of my feet,[91] and say to them what (*Lebon p. 176*) has been said by the wise man who has been quoted many times above: "There is a word which is clothed about with death: may it never be found in the inheritance of Jacob!"[92] But I urge you that you run on your own, and that you write under (your own) authority not only these things which have already been written by you, but also all others which you wish (to write), but let me alone. You would be an advocate of my ignorance before the judgement seat without dissimulation. For since I know these things which are written by you, and they go beyond what is right, if I were to be silent, on all accounts I would pay the punishment for silence, and for many I would be a source of harm, as one who was silent in those matters where it was particularly inappropriate that I should be silent. But on the other hand, it is right that I be reckoned with those who have already died, (I) who strive not to be seen,[93] and am now more than ever put to flight by enemies in (my) tracks, as I hear, and I am unable without fear to publish discourses in opposition, for those who wish to be involved in them. For as God hears, I say that in love for you, I sent both those things which were written before, and now these, while at the same time I prayed and took pains to procure irreproachability for you on all hands. For it is right that we should not only have a mind giving praise but a tongue giving praise as well. For it is not our striving in any old way that is crowned, but our striving lawfully, and not our emulating in some way or other, but our doing so with knowledge. For it belongs to wisdom that we learn with a humble and balanced and unquarrelsome mind. For the same wise man says again, "The wisdom of a poor man will lift up his head, and make him sit in the midst of the great".[94] And the instruction of (the Book) of Proverbs gives command saying, (*Lebon p. 177*) "If you will invoke wisdom, and will give your voice to knowledge, and if you will search for it like silver, and glean for it like treasure, then you will know the fear of the Lord, and you will find the knowledge of God. For the Lord gives wisdom and from his countenance wisdom and knowledge, and he lays down treasures for those who do rightly (for) redemption".[95]

ܡܠܘܝܐ܀ ܘܡܬܐܡܪܐ ܕܝܢ ܕܐܬܩܢ ܕܟܠܗ ܐܘܢܩܘܣ ܐܡܪ. ܀ܒܡܫܠܡܘܬܗ܀ ܐܦ ܕܝܢ ܐܘܣܝܐ ܗܝ ܕܐܠܗܐ ܢܗܘܪܐ ܡܫܡܫܝܢ: ܐܘ ܚ̈ܝܠܐ: ܐܘ ܛܒܬܐ: ܘܟܠܗ ܗܘ ܗܝ ܕܐܠܗܘܬܗ. ܚ̈ܝܠܐ ܐܠܗܝܐ ܘܟܠܗ ܢܗܘܪܐ ܘܟܠܗ ܛܒܬܐ: ܕܢܦܩܐ ܕܝܢ ܒܚ̈ܝܠܐ ܐܝܬ ܒܗܘܢ ܠܐ ܐܝܬܝܘܬܐ: ܐܝܢܐ ܕܗ ܠܐ ܡܬܒܥܝܐ ܗܘ ܕܒܐܘܣܝܐ ܦܫܝܛܐ܀ ܡܛܠ ܗܘܐ ܒܗ ܡܫܬܠܡܐ ܐܡܪ ܡܬܒܥܝܐ: ܐܠܐ ܡܫܬܡܠܝܐ. ܕܐܘܣܝܐ ܐܠܗܝܐ ܕܐܠܗܐ: ܐܘ ܐܠܗܘܬܐ: ܐܘ ܛܒܘܬܐ: ܐܘ ܢܗܘܪܐ ܐܘ ܚ̈ܝܠܐ: ܡܛܠ ܕܒܡܪܐ: ܠܐ ܡܬܚܫܒ ܚܕ ܕܡܢܐ ܐܠܗܘܬܐ ܒܐܘܣܝܐ ܠܐܠܗܐ. ܐܠܐ ܒܬܒܥܬܐ ܕܐܘܣܝܐ ܡܫܬܡܠܝܐ ܗܘܝܢ ܘܐܝܟ ܗܘܝܐ ܟܝܢܐܝܬ. ܘܒܡܫܡܫܘ ܐܡܪܐ ܠܡܠܐܟܐ ܩ̈ܘܡܝܢ ܕܡܩܪܒܝܢ ܒܬܘܕܝܬܐ ܕܬܫܒܘܚܬܐ ܠܒܪ̈ܝܬܐ. ܕܒܗܘܢ ܐܦܠܐ ܗܝ ܠܐ ܐܝܬܝܗ̇ ܐܠܗܘܬܐ: ܘܟܠܗ ܡܢ ܐܒܐ. ܒܪܐ ܕܝܢ ܝܠܝܕܐܝܬ. ܪܘܚܐ ܕܝܢ ܡܦܩܢܐ ܢܦܘܩܐܝܬ.

ܘܐܝܬ ܗܝ ܐܠܗܘܬܐ ܒܡܫܘܚܬܐ. ܐܝܬ ܕܝܢ ܟܕ ܦܦܪ ܐܝܬ ܟܠܗ ܟܝܢܐ ܟܠܐ ܘܐܟܘܬܐ: ܠܐܒ ܘܡܬܒܥܬܐ ܐܡܪ ܠܐ ܡܬܒܥܐ ܐܢܐ. ܡܫܡܫ ܐܢܐ ܕܝܢ ܡܫܡܫܢܘܬܐ ܕܪ̈ܐܙܐ ܕܐܘܪܫܠܡ. ܘܠܐ ܠܐܒ ܕܟܠܗ ܐܝܟ ܡܢ ܟܝܢ ܐܘܣܝܘܬܗ: ܘܒܪܝܟܐ ܪܝܫܐ ܡܢ ܐܣܛܠܐ ܡܢܗܘܢ: ܬܘܒ ܟܠ ܩܠܐ. ܘܠܐ ܡܬܡܠܠܢܘܬܐ ܠܐܒ: ܟܕ ܗܘ ܕܠܗܘܐ ܡܫܠܡܢܐ ܒܟܝܢܗ ܩܠܐ ܠܐ ܡܬܦܫܩܐ: ܗܘ ܕܩ̈ܝܢܝ ܡܫ̈ܡܫܢܝ ܐܡܪ̈ܐ: ܘܩܝܡܝܢ ܡܘܡܐ ܡܫܡܠܐ. ܐܡܬܝ ܘܠܐ ܐܦ ܡܛܠܒܢܝ ܠܐܒܐ: ܘܐܡܪܐ ܡܟܠܬܐ ܢܟܝܬܐ: ܐܝܟ ܡܠܐ ܕܡܛܠܐܝܬ ܡܢ ܗܠܝܢ ܡܩܕܫܐ: ܗܘ ܕܐܝܟ ܙܒܢܐ ܡܢ ܡܘܒܕܘܬܗ. ܛܒܐ ܓܝܪ ܡܫܡܫܢܘܬܐ ܗܘ ܘܡܢܝ ܐܫܠܡܬ ܠܟ ܟܕ ܐܡܪ. ܕܗܘ ܕܡܫܡܫ ܢܫܡܐ ܠܐܘܡܢܝ.

ܐܦ ܕܝܢ ܒܗܘܢ ܠܗܘܐ: ܗܘ ܕܡܬܠܐ ܐܢܐ ܘܠܐ ܠܗܘܐ: ܟܠ ܟܝܢܐ ܟܠܐ ܡܢ ܕܐܝܟ ܗܘܝܐ: ܗܠܝܢ ܕܐܡܪܢܐ ܕܗܘܐ ܐܝܬ ܫܘܠܛܢܐ: ܐܘܫܠܐܝܬ ܡܫܩܠ ܐܢܐ ܩܠܐ ܘܡܠܐ ܕܩܛܠܐ. ܘܐܡܪ ܐܢܐ ܒܗܘܢ: ܗܘ (176) ܕܐܡܪܐ ܒܡܫܡܫܐ ܕܒܫܠܡܘܬܗ ܕܩܝܡܝܢ ܡܫܡܫܢ̈ܝ. ܘܐܝܬ ܡܟܠܬܐ ܕܫܘܡܠܝܘܬ ܡܫܡܠܐ ܡܘܠܐ. ܠܐ ܠܡܠܟܢ ܒܪܢܫܐ ܕܡܫܡܫ. ܡܫܡܫ ܐܢܐ ܠܟ ܕܝܢ ܕܡܢܝ ܘܠܟ ܠܐܘܪܐ: ܘܠܐ ܒܠܒܘܫ ܗܠܝܢ ܕܡܢ ܒܪܗ ܐܠܗܐ ܡܢܝ: ܐܠܐ ܘܐܦܪܝܫܘܬܐ ܡܟܠܗܘܢ ܐܟܡܐ ܕܙܟܐ ܐܝܟ ܡܠܘܐ ܒܡܘܟܟܐ: ܘܡܫܡܫܢܘ ܠܗ: ܘܠܐ ܡܬܟܠܐ ܠܗܘܐ ܐܝܬ ܠܗ ܫܘܠܛܢܐ: ܡܢ ܕܡܢ ܘܠܐ ܡܫܡܫ ܒܠܘܩܒܠ. ܟܕ ܢܦܩ ܐܢܐ ܓܝܪ ܗܠܝܢ ܕܡܬܚܫܒܢ ܡܢܝ: ܘܡܟܝܠ ܡܢ ܦܠܚܐ ܐܢܬ: ܐܦ ܐܡܠܘܟ: ܡܢ ܡܠܦܢܘܬ ܠܐܒܐ ܗܘܐ ܐܢܐ ܕܗܠܐ. ܘܠܡܫܡܠܐ ܗܘܐ ܐܢܐ ܡܬܡܚܝܐ ܕܡܫܡܫܢܐ: ܐܝܟ ܗܝ ܕܦܠܚܬ ܒܗܠܝܢ ܕܦܩܝܕ ܠܐ ܩܠܐ ܗܘܐ. ܐܠܗܘܬ. ܟܕ ܕܝܢ ܘܐܦܪܝܫܘܬܗ

But as for those who want to introduce the Henoticon—wnicn contains a confession of the orthodox faith—at a time when the wickedness at Chalcedon and the Tome of Leo, which blasphemes more than anything, remains dominant, and do not, as is lawful, explicitly anathematise (these things), in the manner which prevailed in the days of Macedonius and Flavian of ill-repute, and by this contrive to lead astray those who are more simple, I have said and I have written everything rightly and wisely. To which (simple ones), the practice, which Dioscorus of reverend memory—the Archbishop of Alexandria, who was our co-worker—established, brings great benefit, when he showed before everyone the purity of the Church, both in doctrine, and in the absence of the joining of communion with heretics, and drew many from those who were separated, and joined (them) (as) limbs to the body.

The Third Letter to Sergius the Grammarian has ended.

Notes

1. cf. pp. 155–156 in the text above.
2. Sir. xx.1.
3. Jer. x.16.
4. 2 Cor. xiii.7.
5. Reading [Syriac] for [Syriac].
6. Prov. x.10.
7. Cyril, *Contra Diodorum Tars. Episc.*, (Pusey edn., Vol. 5), p. 499.17–500.4.
8. Place not found.
9. Cyril, *Contra Diodorum Tars. Episc.*, (Pusey edn., Vol. 5), p. 502.10–17.
10. The Syriac is [Syriac]. cf. p. 140, line 29 above, where the Greek underlying [Syriac] is κατὰ παράθεσιν.
11. [Syriac].
12. cf. above, p. 102.8 ff., and p. 121.2 ff.
13. cf. p. 99 above.
14. cf. pp. 125 and 126 above.
15. The Syriac is [Syriac] which is very obscure. Possibly the underlying Greek is from κατασκευάζω: cf. Lampe, *Patristic Greek Lexicon*, (Oxford, 1961) under κατασκευάζω, §7.
16. cf. p. 150 above.
17. Note in margin: Anointed: as an athlete.
18. Note in margin: Who is of the people, because she is a whore before everyone.
19. cf. Prov. vii.11.
20. cf. p. 152 above, lines 3 and 4. Here Severus reads [Syriac] (activity) where Sergius had [Syriac] (signification, denotation). One might notice that on p. 135.15 above, Severus read [Syriac] (activities) where Harvard Syriac 22 reads [Syriac] (signs; marks; indications).
21. Mt. xii.37.
22. cf. Ps. xliii.14.
23. This is a difficult passage to translate, and what is offered is only one attempt. Here the passage in inverted commas ("Where therefore ....") follows from "obliges us to say," ....

ܐܝܟܢܐ ܕܐܬܐ ܕܒܗ ܗܘܝܢ ܘܡܢܗ ܡܢ ܟܕܘ ܐܬܝܠܕ. ܗܘ ܕܙܕܩ ܐܢܐ ܗܘ ܕܠܐ ܐܬܝܠܕ. ܘܗܘܐ ܠܡܪܐܝܬ ܡܢ ܩܢܘܡܐ ܒܢܩܒܘܬܐ ܡܬܦܪܩ ܐܢܐ ܐܝܟ ܕܡܦܪܫ ܐܢܐ. ܘܠܐ ܕܝܢ ܡܚܫܒ ܐܢܐ ܕܡܬܡܠܠܐ ܐܝܟ ܩ̈ܠܐ ܕܠܐ ܕܡܠܐ: ܠܗܘܢ ܕܢܝܚ ܕܒܗܘܢ ܢܚܙܘܢ. ܟܕ ܡܦܢܐ ܓܝܪ ܠܠܗܐ ܐܡܪ ܐܢܐ: ܕܚܘܒܐ ܕܟܠܢ ܗܘܝܢ ܡܩܒܠܬܐ: ܘܗܘܝܢ ܕܗܘܐ ܐܬܬܠܒ ܦܚܝܬܐ. ܘܟܕ ܐܝܬ ܠܟ ܕܚܠܬܐ ܐܚܝܕܐ ܘܡܫܬܠܛܢܐ: ܕܡܢ ܡܟܝܠ ܐܙܠ ܠܟ ܗܘ ܕܠܐ ܒܕܝܠܐ. ܙܕܩ ܠܟ ܓܝܪ: ܕܠܗ ܒܠܚܘܕ ܗܘܐ ܢܗܘܐ ܐܝܬ ܠܟ ܡܡܚܝܢܐ: ܐܠܐ ܘܠܗܢܐ ܡܠܝ ܡܡܚܝܢܐ. ܠܗ ܓܝܪ ܗܘ ܕܐܝܬܘܗܝ ܐܝܟ ܕܗܘ: ܐܠܐ ܘܗܘ ܕܡܬܚܙܐ ܐܝܬܘܗܝ ܡܫܬܡܠܝܐ. ܘܠܐ ܗܘ ܕܐܝܬ ܐܝܟ ܕܗܘ. ܐܠܐ ܗܘ ܕܒܗ ܐܝܕܝܐ: ܘܡܟܝܠܬܐ ܓܝܪ ܐܝܟܢܐ: ܟܕ ܡܬܚܙܝܐ ܡܡܫܡܫܢܝܬܐ ܘܠܐ ܡܬܢܝܐ ܠܟܘܢ. ܐܡܪ ܓܝܪ ܠܘܬ ܗܘ ܟܕ ܗܘ ܒܥܒܪܐ ܡܫܝܚܐ ܕܡܫܝܚܘܬܐ ܘܡܫܡܫܢܐ ܠܐܘܪܚܐ ܕܡܘܬܐ. ܘܟܕ ܗܘܐ ܬܘܕܝܬܐ ܠܐܒܘܗܝ. ܘܡܪܢܘܬܐ ܕܡܠܟܐ ܦܫܝܐ ܟܕ (177) ܐܡܪܐ. ܕܐܦ ܗܘ ܕܒܡܫܝܚܘܬܐ ܠܐܡܪܐ: ܘܟܕ ܥܒܕܐ ܠܐܠܗܐ ܒܪܐ ܡܠܟ: ܘܐܒܘܗܝ ܕܐܝܟܢܐ ܐܝܟ ܟܗܢܐ: ܘܐܝܟܢܐ ܐܝܟ ܫܡܫܐ: ܗܝܕܝܢ ܠܐܦ ܕܡܫܝܚܐ ܕܒܪܐ ܘܡܫܡܫܢܐ ܕܠܠܗܐ ܠܐܒܘܗܝ. ܘܒܪܐ ܗܘܐ ܡܫܝܚܐ: ܘܡܢ ܦܪܨܘܦܗ ܡܫܡܫܢܐ ܘܟܗܢܐ. ܘܫܡܫܐ ܡܫܡܫܢܐ ܠܗܘܢ ܕܡܬܦܪܩܝܢ ܦܘܪܩܢܐ.

ܠܟܠ ܗܠܝܢ ܕܝܢ ܕܗܘܝܬܘܢ: ܕܐܝܟܢܐ ܐܝܬ ܠܗ ܕܗܢܝܘܬܐ ܠܐܘܪܚܐ ܒܟܠܢ ܕܒܟܘܢ: ܟܕ ܡܐܪܝܢܐ ܦܫܝܐ ܒܗܠܝܢ ܕܒܠܒܝܘܬܐ: ܘܡܬܚܙܝܐ ܡܠܐ ܡܢ ܟܠ ܛܘܒܐ ܘܠܐܦ: ܘܠܐ ܢܦܩܢ ܒܟܠܗ ܟܕ ܡܢܗܠ ܐܝܟ ܕܐܝܟܢܐ ܢܗܘܘܢܝܬܐ. ܐܝܟ ܐܡܫܝܚܐ ܘܐܝܟ ܒܢܩܒܘܬܐ ܕܒܢܝܐ ܡܢܗܠ ܡܗܕܝܢ ܘܦܠܚܝܢ: ܘܗܘܘ ܠܗܘܢ ܕܠܗܝܢ ܦܩܘܕܝܢ ܡܢ ܛܒܝܢ ܕܒܥܘܢ: ܐܬܪܝܐܢ ܘܡܫܡܫܢܝܬܗ ܠܡܬܒܝܢ ܘܐܡܪܐ ܘܠܗܠܟ. ܠܐܝܟܢ ܘܡܠܐ ܠܗܘܢܝܐ ܡܫܡܠܝܐ: ܘܦܪܥܘܢ ܕܡܢܗ ܗܘ ܕܠܗܘܢܝܐ ܡܫܝܐ: ܕܡܫܬܪܪܘܢ ܙܒܢܐ ܘܐܦܝܣܩܘܦܐ ܕܐܠܟܣܢܕܪܝܐ. ܗܘ ܕܗܘܐ ܒܪ ܠܥܩܒܗ. ܟܕ ܠܒܝܫܐ ܕܒܢܝܐ ܘܡܬܪܥܝܢܐ ܘܛܠܐ ܡܠܟܬܐ ܕܡܐܦܠܐ ܕܟܠܗ ܗܘܬܡܐ ܡܢ ܟܠܗ ܡܢܗ. ܘܡܬܢܝܐ ܡܢ ܗܠܝܢ ܕܦܪܝܫܝܢ ܠܝ. ܘܐܡܪ ܗܘܝܐ ܠܝܘܡܬܐ.

✤ ܫܠܡܬ ܐܓܪܬܐ ܕܬܠܬ ܕܠܘܬ ܣܪܓܝܣ ܓܪܡܛܝܩܘܣ ✤

24. PG 59.47C.
25. PG 29.525A.
26. Note in margin: Believed you: ratified you (as) true.
27. *Iliad*, 8.154.
28. Eustathius: *Fragmentum Commentarii in Psalmum Nonagesimum Secundum*, pp. 212–3 in J. B. Pitra, *Analecta Sacra* (Paris, 1883), Vol. 4. Also see M. Spanneut, *Recherches sur les écrits d'Eustathe d'Antioche, avec une éd. nouv. des fragments dogmatiques et exégétiques* (Lille, 1948), pp. 32–33; and No. 38, p. 107 (Latin only).
29. Ex. iii.14.
30. The Syriac reads ܒܩܝܡܗ. Lebon notes: Read ܒܩܘܡܗ. The Greek is ἐν ὑποστήματι.
31. Jer. xxiii.18.
32. Jer. xxiii.22.
33. Lebon notes that the Syriac translator read "εἰ δέ" in place of "ἡ δέ".
34. Jer. ix.9.
35. ἔστι.
36. ὑπάρχει.
37. Heb. i.3.
38. Ps. xiii.1.
39. PG 26.1036A–C.
40. PG 32.884A. *Ep. CCXXXVI.*
41. PG 76.60D (= Pusey edn. Vol. 6, p. 94.10–11).
42. PG 77.116C (= Pusey edn. Vol. 6, p. 28.21–23).
43. PG 31.465C.
44. PG 36.440B.
45. ܫܘܬܦ ܟܝܢܐ = ὁμοουσίῳ (H. syr. 22 = ܒܪ ܟܝܢܐ).
46. PG 76.180D (= Pusey edn. Vol. 6, p. 187.17–18).
47. cf. p. 151 above.
48. Apollodorus, I.9.7. cf. S. P. Brock, *The Syriac Version of the Pseudo-Nonnos Mythological Scholia* (Cambridge, 1971), Scholia to Invective ii.2, pp. 132–133.
49. The text reads: ܐܪܝܣܛܘܛܠܝܣ. Lebon notes: This word belongs to the quotation: emend ܕܐܪܝܣܛܘܛܠܝܣ [ܠܦܝܠܣܘܦܘܬܗ].
50. Migne reads: τοὺς θνητοὺς περὶ ψυχῆς λόγους. Severus, or the translator, might seem to have read "θνητοῦ".
51. PG 36.24B–C.
52. 1 Cor. v.12.
53. cf. above, pp. 152.3 (Sergius) and 162.25 (Severus). One should note how Severus has re-phrased Sergius on both occasions.
54. Note in margin: It is "expounded" [ܡܦܫܩ] in another manuscript.
55. cf. above, pp. 86.8; 101.24; 135.14; 155.4 ff.
56. Note in margin: (The word) ܐܝܠܐ (is derived) from ܐܝܠܐ.
57. Euripides, *Hippol.* 612.
58. cf. p. 151, above.
59. Reading ܪܓܐ for ܕܓܐ (misprint).
60. PG 37.1592–1593: lines 240–250.
61. ἕξις and στέρησις. See below, and Aristotle, *Categories*, ch. 10.
62. So the Syriac translator has rendered the Greek ὑφ' ἧς ἐκτραχηλισθείς: "by which he has been overthrown". PG 29.532A.
63. cf. 1 Cor. ii.6.
64. Ps. cxviii.85.
65. Jn. viii.44.
66. 2 Cor. vi.15.
67. PG 29.532A–B.
68. Note in the margin: He calls beauty "grace".
69. PG 31.568B.
70. PG 77.241B (= ACO, I, 1, 6a, p. 160.2–3).

71. cf. PG 75.1285C (= Pusey edn. Vol. 7, p. 360.12).
72. Note in margin: He calls the heretical marks "lines".
73. cf. the foot of p. 72 above.
74. cf. 2 Cor. xii.11.
75. cf. p. 156 above.
76. cf. above, p. 138.6 ff, and 12 ff.
77. Note in margin: Trodden: ploughed.
78. cf. above p. 155.13 ff.
79. Heb. xi. 6.
80. cf. above, p. 137.26–138.2.
81. cf. Socrates, *H.E. III*, 7 (PG 67.396B).
82. Note in margin: He seems to call Christ "grace". But Lebon suggests that it should be read ܛܝܒܘܬܐ: "goodness". cf. above, p. 155.16 ff.
83. Mk. x.18.
84. cf. above, p. 155.16 ff.
85. Rom. xvi.27.
86. cf. above, p. 155.22 ff.
87. PG 32.789B.
88. PG 29.640B.
89. cf. Hos. iv.18.
90. Lk. xiv.11.
91. cf. Mt. x.14.
92. Sir. xxiii.12.
93. i.e. by the authorities.
94. Sir. xi.1.
95. Prov. ii.3–7.

The Apology of Sergius

Of the same Sergius to the Patriarch Severus.

To my master in Christ, (and) to the Fathers (who are) philosophers. Sergius, humble Grammarian. Treatise of apology.

Shem and Japheth (are thought) commendable sons in (their) race, because when (their) father lay naked, they did not endure even the sight, but with noble shame, covered (him) with a garment.[1] But Ham is like a runaway slave: for he laughs, and made sport of the drunkenness of him who begot (him). (*Lebon p. 178*) We, immoderate men, foolishly act worse than this, and are scornful in the unrestrained manner of enemies. For as the Father establishes us in the fair raiment of virtue, and drank all the cluster of discretion, and is watchful in himself, we falsely attribute nakedness and the worst drunkenness to him, still craving for the earthly Israel—(that Israel) which when Moses in an outstanding way managed the governorship, very much reviled that just man. We have emulated that Absalom, who even cast eyes on the kingdom of (his) father. Even the Book of the Law has not held in check the shamelessness of our words, which decrees death on sons who even justly speak against those who begot (them).

But some, doubtless, will reject me as a demagogue, and will tell me that integrity was given up, but later I put on an act in some way for the sake of appeasing (your) person. But calling to witness him who tests the hearts and the kidneys, and the judgement throne, taking up my tract, I will make my apology anew, making integrity first in honour. May I be found guilty in the midst of ten thousand ministering angels, if anything was done in this matter for the sake of the appeasing of (mortal) man: but may I fall short of the hope to come, if I intentionally sin against the truth.

But I think this struggle which I am undertaking is arduous, since two sorts of opponents are rising up against me. For as some of the opponents of the Father misrepresent (his) words to their own confusion, expecting the song to be inharmonious, we will say in opposition to them (borrowing) from our harp, "May the deceitful lips be silent, which speak wickedness against the just man".[2] But in the same way, doubtless some of our own side have gone astray because

܀ܕܝܠܗ ܬܘܒ ܕܝܠܗ ܕܣܪܓܝܣ: ܠܘܬܗ ܕܦܛܪܝܪܟܐ ܣܐܘܝܪܐ܀
ܠܡܪܝ ܩܕܝܫܐ: ܠܐܒܘܐ ܦܝܠܣܘܦܐ: ܣܪܓܝܣ ܥܒܕܐ ܓܪܡܛܝܩܘܣ: ܡܐܡܪܐ ܕܡܘܡ ܒܪܘܚܐ. ܡܩܠܣ ܓܝܣܐ ܩ̈ܢܝܐ ܩܕܡ ܘܩܕܡ: ܕܟܕ ܐܬܦܪܣ ܐܚܐ: ܐܦܠܐ ܠܚܝܐ ܗܟܢܐ. ܐܠܐ ܥܡ ܠܐܝܟܢܐ ܡܠܘܐܐ: ܥܡܠܐ ܥܡܗ. ܚܕ ܕܝܢ ܥܒܕܐ ܐܢܐ ܘܒܪܘܟܐ ܐܠܗܘܗܝ ܒܝܬܐ: ܓܢܒ ܓܒܪ. ܘܪܘܡܢܐ ܕܗܘ (178) ܕܠܟܝ. ܪܡܐ: ܕܥܠܝܡ ܡܢ ܗܠܝܢ ܡܫܬܠܝܢ ܣܓܝ ܒܢ̈ܝܐ. ܘܒܝܬܐ ܥܪܝܐ ܕܒܢ̈ܝܢܒܝܐ ܫܠܛܝܢ. ܟܕ ܓܒܪ ܐܝܟ ܒܐܣܟܝܡܐ ܫܦܝܪܐ ܕܡܬܘܪܬܐ ܦܫܝܛܐ ܠܝ: ܘܡܫܟܚܐ ܥܠܘܗܝ ܕܢܩܘܬܐ ܐܬܠܝ: ܘܡܢ ܒܩܡܘ: ܒܪܛܝܢܬܐ ܘܪܘܡܢܐ ܘܫܠܝܬܐ ܠܟܠܗܘܢ ܡܫܬܠܝܢ: ܟܕ ܥܠܐ ܐܫܬܪܝܬ ܒܥܪܝܐ ܕܒܪܘܠ ܦܬܓܡܝܢ. ܗܢܘܢ ܕܟܕ ܡܢܗܐ ܘܫܠܝܬܐ ܦܬܓܡ ܘܫܠܝܬܐ: ܡܕܝܢ ܗܘܐ ܠܥܠܬܐ ܦܓܥ. ܒܐܣܟܡܐ ܗܘ ܛܒ. ܗܘ ܕܐܦ ܥܠ ܡܫܬܘܬܐ ܕܐܒܐ ܚܝܐ ܐܘܪܚ. ܘܠܐ ܡܠܬܐ ܢܗܘܘܢ: ܥܠܐ ܡܬܚܫܒܢܘܬܐ ܕܩ̈ܠܝܢ ܡܦܩ. ܕܗܘܐ ܡܬܚܡ ܥܠ ܩ̈ܢܝܐ ܐܝܠܝܢ ܕܐܦ ܒܐܝܬܝܗ ܐܡܪܝܢ ܠܗܝܡܢܘܬ ܗܢܘܢ ܕܐܝܬܝܗ.
ܐܠܐ ܠܝ ܐܝܟ ܥܒܪ ܐܝܟ ܡܫܝܚܐ ܢܗܘܘܢ ܘܢܬܚܪܘܢ. ܕܒܐܝܬܘܬܐ ܦܫ ܕܢܦܫܐ ܐܬܠܝܠܗ. ܠܡܘܬ ܕܝܢ ܠܚܝܐ ܕܦܪܘܩܐ ܩܕܡ ܢܗܘܐ ܒܐ̈ܦܐ. ܐܢܐ ܕܝܢ ܟܕ ܠܗܘ ܕܥܒܪ ܠܒܩ̈ܬܐ ܘܩܕ̈ܝܫܬܐ ܢܦܩ ܐܢܐ ܗܘܝܬ: ܘܠܫܘܪܝܐ ܗܘ ܕܢܦܠ: ܟܕ ܠܡܠܟܐ ܦܛܠܐܐ ܡܬܕܪܟ ܐܝܟ ܒܪܘܚܐ: ܟܕ ܠܗ ܠܒܐܝܬܘܬܐ ܩܕܡ ܐܢܐ ܡܩܒܠ ܐܢܐ: ܒܡܕܝܢܬܐ ܕܩܘܠ ܦܠܓܐ ܕܩ̈ܠܝܬܐ ܬܐܘܪܐ ܡܫܝܚܐ: ܠܝ ܩܕܡ ܠܥܐ ܚܝܐ ܕܓܒܪܐ ܒܗܘܐ ܡܫܠܐ ܐܬܕܟܪܐ. ܐܦ ܕܝܢ ܘܡܢ ܗܒܪܐ ܕܠܟܝ. ܐܝܟܘ ܕܒܓܢܝ ܐܟܘܠ ܒܡܪܘܐ.
ܓܘܢܐ ܕܝܢ ܪܒܐ ܗܢܐ ܡܫܟܚ ܐܢܐ ܕܒܥܝܢ ܐܢܐ: ܟܕ ܩܠܝܠ ܕܪܐ ܒܩ̈ܪܒܐ ܡܫܟܚ ܠܝ. ܐܬܦܝ ܓܒܪ ܡܢ ܒܢ̈ܝܢܒܝܐ ܕܐܒܐ ܟܕ ܡܢܪܡܝܢ ܠܠܒܗ ܩܠܐ: ܠܥܠܐ ܡܬܘܪܬܐ ܕܠܥܘܢ. ܐܠܐ ܟܕ ܡܫܬܡܝܢ ܘܠܐ ܡܠܬܐ ܡܫܠܐ: ܡܢ ܡܠܬܐ ܕܠܝ ܫܘܬܦܘܬܗ ܢܐܡܪ ܠܗܘܢ. ܘܠܐ ܡܬܩܠܠܢܝܬܐ ܢܩܘܡ ܫܩ̈ܠܐ ܢܩܠܝܢܝܬܐ: ܐܝܟܢ ܕܩܥܠܝܢ ܥܠ ܕܝܢܐ ܪܘܡܐ. ܟܕ ܕܝܢ ܟܕܡܘܬܐ: ܐܬܦܝ ܥܒܪ ܡܢ ܗܠܝܢ ܕܠܟ: ܒܡܘܢܐ ܫܡܐ ܕܕܝܢܘܬܐ ܛܒܘ. (179) ܘܡܢ ܦܘܡܐ ܠܐܚܐ ܡܕܝܢ. ܠܐܝܟܢ ܕܥܡ ܡܠܐܠܐ ܢܚܝܐ ܢܦܫܗ: ܫܡܥܘ ܩ̈ܢܝܐ ܡܪܕܘܬܐ ܕܐܒܐ. ܘܣܘܪܕ ܕܐܬܒܗܝ ܫܘܬܦܐ܀ ܟܕ ܓܒܪ ܡܬܚܡܢ

of the ambiguity (of the term) "propriety", (*Lebon p. 179*) and revile the Father because of uncertainty. We will instruct these with the wise proverb, "Hear, O sons, the instruction of (your) father", and "Give heed that you may know the meaning".[3] For when the meaning of the ambiguity is sought out, it lays open the contentious way. And I plead that we give heed to those things which are said, setting aside every contentious ambition.

Even the wise pagans confess that God is cause, but they also teach second and third gods. The sons of the Hebrews worship one God, but they make him barren, and separate the Rational from the Rational,[4] and are jealous of the Holy Spirit. Therefore how have we learnt about these matters? God indeed (is) cause, but he is the first and the middle and the last: "Before me there was not, and after me there will not be another".[5] Again, we confess one God, but we know the oneness of the Trinity in mystical theology. The Manichaeans profess the Trinity, and this after some mighty work, which they change beforehand. Sabellius also professes the Trinity, but he does not acknowledge the hypostases of it. But Arius who was mad set his Trinity in heathen ideas, enumerating together and imagining all these ousiai belonging to it. But we, children of the mystery of true instruction, confess the Trinity in the pattern of those things which were said before, but at the first both in distinct hypostases and pointing towards one ousia. Mani and Apollinaris and Eutyches profess one nature of God the Word after the birth from the Virgin; but the first supposed the inhomination to be imaginary, while the second stumbled to imperfect opinions,[6] but mad Eutyches introduces not only a shadow, but a complete change, outside the mystery. But as for us, how do we (judge) concerning the one nature which was composed from divinity and perfect manhood? It is clear that the flesh did not exist before (the union), but comes (into existence for the purpose of) that mystical union. Therefore notice (*Lebon p. 180*) how on the one hand the terms (are) common, but on the other hand these doctrines define what is set down.

Thus even Nestorius, and all those who are fellow-drinkers of Nestorius, profess properties, but not (properties) of the incarnate Word, but of those natures which they understand in Christ, even after the false union which (is accepted) among them. But then Nestorius, finding fault with Father Cyril, writes from exile to Theodoret: (NESTORIUS): "Herein in a secret way, he confuses the properties of the natures".[7] But Theodoret said in a statement of opposition to the Third Anathema: THEODORET: "Therefore how does he ascribe wickedness to those who divide the properties of

ܣܘܟܠܐ ܕܣܘܡܐ ܥܡܐ: ܟܕܐ ܚܙܝܐ ܦܪܐ. ܘܚܘܪ ܒܗܠܝܢ ܕܡܬܐܡܪܢ ܡܥܩܒ ܐܢܐ. ܟܕ ܡܪܢܫܝܢ ܡܢ ܟܠܗ ܚܝܐ ܚܙܝܐ.

ܠܐܠܗܐ ܒܟܠܐ ܡܘܕܝܢ ܚܫܒܢܐ ܘܫܘܒܩܐ ܐܠܐ ܘܠܟܬܒܐ ܠܐܘܪܚܐ ܘܠܟܬܒܐ ܡܟܫܢ. ܚܕ ܠܐܠܗܐ ܩܢܝܐ ܕܒܬ̈ܝܐ ܡܫܡܪܝܢ. ܐܠܐ ܒܟܪܐ ܒܟܝܢ ܒܗ. ܘܡܢ ܡܛܠܠ ܡܟܠܠ ܦܫܩܝܢ. ܘܒܪܘܚܐ ܩܕܝܫܐ ܡܫܬܡܗ ܒܗ. ܐܡܝܢܐ ܗܟܢܐ ܚܕ ܡܬܚܙܐ ܗܟܢ ܡܠܟܝܢ: ܒܟܠܗ ܦܢ ܠܐܠܗܐ. ܐܠܐ ܒܗ ܩܕܡܝܐ ܘܡܨܝܐ ܘܐܚܪܝܐ. ܩܕܡ ܠܐ ܗܘܐ. ܘܒܬܪ ܐܚܪܝܐ ܠܐ ܢܗܘܐ. ܚܕ ܓܝܪ ܠܐܠܗܐ ܡܘܕܝܢ. ܐܠܐ ܠܡܫܘܕܥܘ ܠܐܠܗܘܬܐ ܢܟܪܝܢ ܚܝܢ. ܒܡܫܡܠܝܘܬܐ ܠܐܠܗܘܬܐ ܘܐܝܬܝܗ. ܠܐܠܗܘܬܐ ܐܡܪܝܢ ܩܢ̈ܘܡܐ. ܗܢܘ ܓܝܪ ܒܠܚܘܕ ܚܝܠܐ ܡܕܡ ܘܡܬܩܢ ܡܫܠܡܢ. ܠܐܠܗܘܬܐ ܐܡܪ ܐܦ ܡܫܡܠܝܘܬܐ. ܐܠܐ ܩܢܘܡܐ ܕܗܘܐ ܠܐ ܢܩܒܠ. ܐܘܣܝܐ ܕܝܢ ܕܚܕܐ: ܠܐܠܗܘܬܗ ܒܬܠܝܬܝܘܬܐ ܩܢܘܡ̈ܐ ܐܘܕܝ. ܟܕ ܦܫܝܛܐ ܐܚܝܕܐ ܘܡܠܟܝܢ ܗܟܢ ܐܘܣܝܣ ܕܡܠܬܗ ܡܠܬܗܘܢ. ܚܕ ܕܝܢ ܩܢܘܡ ܕܐܝܬܐ ܕܩܕܝܫܐ ܩܕܝܫܐ: ܠܐܠܗܘܬܐ ܦܢ. ܒܗ ܒܝܕܥܬܐ ܕܗܟܢ ܕܦܪܩ ܐܬܐܡܪ ܡܘܕܝܢ. ܐܠܐ ܦܪܫܘܬܐ ܘܒܩܢܘܡܐ ܡܩܛܥܐ: ܘܙܘܥܐ ܟܠܐ ܚܕܐ ܐܘܣܝܐ. ܚܕ ܒܝܬܐ ܕܡܠܟܘܬܐ ܠܐܠܗܐ ܟܠܗ ܟܒܪ ܕܡܢ ܒܠܗܘܬܐ ܐܡܪܝܢ: ܡܠܟܐ ܘܐܦܘܠܝܢܪܝܘܣ ܘܐܘܢܘܡܝܐ. ܐܠܐ ܗܝܐ ܦܢ ܐܠܗܘ̈ܬܐ ܡܠܟܢܫܝܢܘܬܐ. ܗܟܐ ܕܝܢ ܟܠܗ ܡܫܬܘܕܥܐ ܠܐ ܡܫܬܡܠܝܐ ܟܢܫ. ܦܠܛܐ ܕܝܢ ܐܘܢܘܡܝܐ: ܒܗ ܠܡܫܠܡܐ ܒܟܢܘܫ: ܐܠܐ ܡܣܬܟܠܐ ܡܠܬܗ ܡܟܠܠ ܠܟܪ ܡܢ ܙܘܓܐ. ܚܝܢ ܕܝܢ ܐܡܝܢܐ ܐܝܟ ܟܢ ܡܬܚܙܐ ܚܕ ܟܝܢܐ ܕܡܢ ܠܐܠܗܘܬܐ ܘܐܝܬܘܬܐ ܡܫܬܡܫܢܝܬܐ ܐܬܐܡܪܬ: ܚܝܬܐ ܕܟܕ ܠܐ ܦܪܩ ܐܬܐܡܪ ܒܒܣܪܐ. ܐܠܐ ܒܟܠܗ ܗܝ ܕܚܝܘܬܐ ܘܐܝܬܘܬܐ ܐܚܝܕܐ ܘܗܘܐ. ܚܝܘ
ܗܟܢܐܐܝܬ ܡܫܬܘܐ ܦܢ ܕܟܠܗ: ܗܢܝܢ ܕܝܢ ܕܐܬܟܢܫܬܐ ܡܠܟܝܢ ܒܟܢܫܐ. (180)

ܗܟܢܐ ܘܬܒܝܠܬܐ: ܣܛܘܪܢܝܢܘܣ ܘܟܠܗܘܢ ܗܟܢ ܕܐܠܗܘܗܝ ܦܣܝܩܬܐ ܕܣܛܘܪܢܝܢܘܣ ܐܡܪܝܢ. ܐܠܐ ܒܗ ܕܡܠܟܬܐ ܕܡܠܟܢ. ܐܠܐ ܕܟܬܒܐ. ܐܡܟܝܢ ܕܐܦ ܟܠܗ ܚܝܘܬܐ ܕܒܟܠܗܘܬܐ ܕܟܠܗܘܢ ܡܫܬܠܡܝܢ ܒܡܫܝܚܐ. ܣܛܘܪܢܝܢܘܣ ܕܝܢ ܗܟܢܐ ܟܕ ܦܪܐ ܡܢ ܐܦܣܘܪܐ ܠܐܬܐ ܡܘܪܟܘܣ ܡܠܟ ܟܠܐ ܠܐܒܘܪܛܝܘܣ. ܣܛܘܪܢܝܢܘܣ܀ ܗܘܝܐ ܡܬܛܦܠܢ ܕܬܟܠܐ ܕܒ̈ܢܝܐ ܡܟܠܟܠܢ܀ ܠܐܒܘܪܛܝܘܣ ܕܝܢ ܒܟܠܟܠܐ ܕܟܣܘܠܐ ܕܚܙܝܐ ܕܠܐܟܠܐ ܐܡܪ. ܠܐܒܘܪܛܝܘܣ܀ ܐܡܝܢܐ ܗܟܢܐ ܒܘܠܐ ܡܟܠܟ ܒܠܐܡܢ ܕܕܬܟܠܐ ܕܒ̈ܢܝܐ ܡܫܝܚܝܢ: ܕܠܐܠܗܐ ܕܡܢ ܩܕܡ ܟܠܟܠܐ: ܘܒܪ ܐܢܫܐ ܕܐܬܝܠܕ ܒܚܪܬܐ ܕܩܫܬܐ܀ ܘܒܘܟܐ ܕܐܝܬܝܗ܀ ܡܕܡ ܟܕ ܕܬܟܠܐ ܕܟܠܝܢ ܡܢ ܒ̈ܢܝܐ ܐܡܪܝܢ ܚܝܢ: ܠܟܫܪ ܡܫܝܚܐ ܡܬܩܒܠ܀ ܘܟܒܫܬܐ܀ ܢܫܐ ܕܬܟܝܢܐ ܐܢܘܢ ܕܡܫܚܐ. ܠܐ ܡܫܘܬܐ ܟܕ ܐܢ

the natures of God who was before the ages and of the man who was assumed at the end of days?"[8] AND IN THAT ON THE EIGHTH: "Well then, professing the properties of each one of the natures, we worship our Lord Christ".[9] AND IN THAT ON THE TENTH:[10] "Passions are proper to the passible, for the impassible is higher than passions. Therefore the form of the servant suffered, it being recognised that the form of God is along with it; therefore it was not God who suffered, but the man from us assumed by God".[11] But Leo says with all fury: LEO: "The particularity of each one of the natures is kept. For each one of the natures keeps without loss its own particularity".[12] AND AGAIN: "For each form effects in companionship with the other the particularity which belonged to it: the Word effecting this which is of the Word, but the body completing this which is of the body. For the former of them is radiant with marvels, but the latter fell under insult".[13] But the many-headed wickedness of Chalcedon says: FROM THE SYNOD OF CHALCEDON: (*Lebon p. 181*) "One Lord Jesus Christ is known in two natures, and the difference of the natures is not suppressed anywhere because of the union, but rather the particularity of each one of the natures is kept".[14]

Therefore what did the Father of the Church[15] say as a result of these unholy (statements)? Did he, like those who were quoted before, set up two natures, understanding these in Christ after the union, and attributing (an individuating) particularity to each one of them? Not at all, but speaking in agreement with the Fathers, he attributes these (properties) of our flesh to the Word who was incarnate. Therefore those men say that the Temple of the Word was seen, hungered, thirsted, suffered, rose; but the Father along with Cyril proclaims Emmanuel, or rather along with Isaiah, Emmanuel who the Word was born from a woman, and along with John cries out in a loud voice that (the Word) was seen and touched,[16] and clearly establishes that he hungered and thirsted, and that he was fastened to the cross, and having endured death for three days, he proclaims that he bestows life on men.

But I ask whence do these things (come) to the Word, that he should be seen and touched, that he should suffer in a human way? Surely because he was incarnate? For the particularity of the Word (is) invisibility, untouchableness, being high above every passion; but of an ensouled body, to hunger and to thirst and to suffer. Therefore (even) as he remained the Word—thus preserving to himself the properties of divinity—yet preserving the integrity of the flesh, (so) too he receives these (properties) of our flesh. Therefore

ܡܢ ܫܢܝܐ: ܝܬܝܪ ܐܝܬܘܗܝ ܪܒܐ. ܣܓܝ ܗܘܝܠ ܕܡܘܬܐ ܕܚܒܪܐ. ܡܛܠ ܕܟܕ ܐܝܬܝܗ̇
ܒܡܢܗ̇ ܕܡܘܬܐ ܕܐܠܗܐ. ܡܕܝܢ ܠܗ ܐܠܗܐ ܗܘ ܕܚܝ. ܐܠܐ ܒܪܢܫܐ ܗܘ ܕܡܝܬ ܕܡܢ ܐܠܗܐ
ܐܬܝܠܕ܀ ܠܐܘ ܕܝܢ ܒܗ ܡܠܬܗ ܒܒܪܢܫܘܬܐ ܐܡܪ. ܀ܠܐܘ܀ ܟܕ ܢܛܪܐ ܕܡܠܟܬܐ ܘܡܠܟܝܢ
ܡܢ ܫܡܝܐ. ܢܛܪ ܓܝܪ ܡܠܟܝܢ ܫܡܝܐ ܠܐ ܒܪܝܫܐܝܬ ܕܡܠܟܘܬܗ܀ ܀ܘܠܘܩܒ܀ ܫܪܒܐ ܓܝܪ
ܟܠ ܕܡܘܬܐ ܒܗ ܡܬܦܣܬܐ ܕܗܘ ܐܡܪܬܐ: ܕܡܠܟܬܐ ܕܗܘ ܕܗܘܐ ܠܗ. ܟܕ ܡܠܟܬܐ
ܦܢ ܫܦܪ ܗܘܐ: ܗܘ ܕܐܝܬܝܗ ܕܡܠܟܬܐ. ܓܘܫܡܐ ܕܝܢ ܡܫܡܫܐ ܗܘܐ: ܗܘ ܕܐܝܬܝܗ
ܕܓܘܫܡܐ. ܘܗܘܝܐ ܦܢ ܓܝܪ ܡܫܘܘܢ ܡܛܠܝ ܒܬܘܡܪ̈ܬܐ. ܗܝܐ ܕܝܢ ܒܪܒܪܐ ܢܦܠ܀
ܒܡܘܬܐ ܕܝܢ ܗܘܝܠܬܐ ܩܝܡܐ ܘܕܡܠܟܘܬܐ ܐܡܪܐ. ܀ܡܢ ܗܘ̈ܝܘܗܝ (181)
ܘܕܡܠܟܘܬܐ܀ ܚܕ ܡܕܡܐ ܡܫܘܫ ܡܫܝܚܐ: ܕܠܐܦܝ ܟܢ̈ܫܝܢ ܡܠܟܘܬܗ. ܘܠܐ ܒܝܘܡ
ܡܘܣܟܦܐ ܕܫܢܝܐ ܡܕܝܢ ܡܬܠܝܠ ܚܕܘܬܐ. ܢܛܪܐ ܕܝܢ ܡܠܟܘܬܗ: ܕܡܠܟܬܐ ܕܟܠ ܚܕ
ܡܢ ܫܢܝܐ܀

ܡܟܝܠ ܗܘܝܠ ܡܢ ܗܝܕܝܢ ܠܐ ܡܫܟܚܐ ܐܡܪ ܐܢܐ ܕܚܒܪܐ. ܐܦܐ ܠܐܦܝ ܫܢܝܐ ܗܟܢ ܐܝܟ
ܗܢܘܢ ܕܡܬܡܢ ܐܬܐܡܪܘ: ܐܝܟ ܦܢ ܕܗܝܕܝܢ ܒܠܘ ܚܕܘܬܐ ܡܫܬܟܚܐ ܒܡܫܝܚܐ:
ܘܠܟܠ ܚܕ ܡܢܗܘܢ ܢܦܩ ܕܡܠܟܘܬܐ: ܘܠܐ ܠܓܡܪ. ܐܠܐ ܟܕ ܗܝܕܝܢ ܕܩܕܡܝܢ ܠܐܒܗ̈ܬܐ
ܐܡܪ: ܠܡܠܟܬܐ ܕܐܬܐܡܪ ܢܦܩ ܘܗܝܕܝܢ ܕܫܪܐ ܕܡܢ. ܗܢܘܢ ܗܘܝܠܐܡܪܝܢ: ܕܐܬܚܙܝ
ܗܘܝܠܐ ܕܡܠܟܬܐ. ܒܗ ܙܒܢ. ܣܓܝ ܡܢ. ܐܦܐ ܕܝܢ ܒܗ ܡܬܟܠܡܐ ܠܡܫܬܘܐܠܘ:
ܡܟܠܝ ܕܝܢ ܒܗ ܐܡܪܝܢ: ܠܡܫܬܘܐܠܘ ܕܐܬܚܙܝ ܡܢ ܐܝܬܝܐ ܡܠܟܬܐ ܡܬܚܙܐ. ܘܒܗ
ܡܘܚܝ: ܕܐܬܚܙܝ ܘܐܬܬܟܝܢ ܒܒܪܐ ܠܐ ܪܒܬܐ ܦܪܐ. ܘܗܘܝܐ ܒܗ ܘܙܕܩ ܡܥܒܕܐ
ܢܟܝܬܐ. ܘܗܘܝܐ ܒܪܚܡܬܐ ܐܬܐܡܪ. ܘܟܕ ܫܡܥ ܡܘܬܐ ܕܐܟܠܬܐ ܢܦܫܝ: ܕܦܢ
ܠܬܫܒܚܬܐ ܫܪܝܐ ܐܒܪܐ.

ܐܠܐ ܡܢ ܐܡܬܝ ܗܘܝܠ ܠܡܠܟܬܐ ܡܫܡܫ ܐܝܟ: ܗܘ ܕܝܠܝܕܐ ܘܐܬܟܫܦ: ܗܘ ܕܚܝܐ
ܐܝܬܝܗ. ܠܗ ܡܛܠ ܕܐܬܐܡܪ: ܕܡܠܟܬܐ ܓܝܪ ܕܡܠܟܬܐ: ܠܐ ܡܬܐܚܝܕܘܬܐ. ܠܐ
ܡܬܟܢܫܘܬܐ. ܗܘ ܕܪܡ ܡܢ ܟܠ ܚܝܐ. ܕܟܣܝܐ ܕܝܢ ܡܫܬܡܠܝܐ: ܗܘ ܕܢܬܒܥ ܘܢܗܘܐ
ܘܚܝܐ. ܐܟܘܬ ܗܘܝܠ ܕܗܘ ܡܠܟܬܐ ܟܕ ܡܬܬܪ ܠܒܪܢܫܐ: ܗܘܝܐ ܟܕ ܢܛܪ ܠܫܡܗ
ܕܬܡܠܟܬܐ ܗܘܝܠ ܕܐܠܗܘܬܐ: ܘܗܘܝܠ ܕܒܪܢܫܐ ܕܡܢ ܟܠܗܘܢ. ܠܗ ܟܕ ܠܗ ܗܘܝܠ
ܠܡܠܟܬܐ ܐܠܗܐ ܐܡܪܝܢ ܡܢ: ܡܬܐܚܝܕܐ ܘܠܐ ܡܬܐܚܝܕܐ. ܟܕ ܡܬܐܚܕܐ ܓܝܪ ܡܢ
ܦܫܝܛܐ: ܠܐ ܡܬܐܚܕܢܝܬ ܐܝܬܘܗܝ ܗܘܐ ܒܗ ܐܦܐ. ܠܗ ܟܕ ܠܗ ܕܐܬܐܡܪ ܡܢ ܐܝܟ
ܠܐܠܗܐ: ܘܡܢ ܐܦܐ ܒܬܘܟܠܬܐ. ܐܠܗܐ ܗܘܐ ܦܢ ܡܢ ܡܕܡ ܡܠܘܗܝ ܠܒܢܝܐ (182)

we profess the same God the Word, visible and invisible, for when he was seen by men, he was invisibly with the Father; the same who was born from the Father Almighty, and (was born) God from the virgin mother; in the former case incorporeally from before all ages, (*Lebon p. 182*) (in the latter case) corporeally within the last times; the same impassible and passible: impassible in the ousia of the Father, but passible in human flesh. You see how the definition has preserved for him immutability, (holding) him at the same time God and body. Of him who displays the particularity of a body in a godly manner, we do not say that the natures exist and each one (of) them is seen out of its own properties and activities, but we hold that the Word himself became flesh, and displayed these (properties) of the flesh.

And let no-one think the definition is foolish, introducing particularity and nature (existing) independently: for the principle of things which are composed joins[17] some two or more, but completes one nature of the living creature: it allows the particularity of each one of them to appear, but yet not divided but recognisable together, as we are able to find out in the case of the nature of man. To be cut is a property of a body, but to perceive a blow is of an animated body: but it does not receive cutting in some (one) nature, but show perception in another, but there appears in one and the same composite nature both cutting of the body and perception of the soul. A (man) rejoices, and by means of a laugh makes known the cheerfulness of the soul: and he is grieved, and a tear has announced distress. Thus also in the case of the one composite nature of Christ, we will see the Word is born, but from a virgin mother: it is not the case that in one nature it happened to him that he should be born, but in another he effected what is strange, as Leo raved, saying, "The Word performs that which is of the Word, but the body completes that which is of the body",[18] but (there is) one nature which is born, and in a miracle effected being born; hungered, thirsted, not compelled, but willingly; walked, but the sea was able to be walked on by (his) feet; (*Lebon p. 183*) and at the end he died, not that he had awaited the necessity of death, but when it was right, he dissolved death, for "I have the power to lay down my life and to take it up again",[19] and he taught the truth of (these) words by means of the resurrection.

You see how some natures receive their [properties][20] and activities not cut apart or separately recognised, but the divinity and the humanity of the Word who was incarnate appear together. Let them show me what was done after the incarnation (which) was merely human. And I will not say a tear, for that came divinely, for he was immediately summoning Lazarus whom he pitied, and though he

ܠܐ ܓܘܫܡܢܐܝܬ. ܗܘܐ ܕܝܢ ܓܒܗ ܕܒܢ̈ܝ ܐܢ̈ܫܐ ܓܘܫܡܢܐܝܬ. ܠܗ ܟܕ ܠܗ ܠܐ ܚܫܘܫܐ ܘܚܫܘܫܐ. ܠܐ ܚܫܘܫܐ ܡܢ ܒܐܘܣܝܐ ܕܐܒܐ. ܒܒܣܪܐ ܕܝܢ ܐܢܫܝܐ ܚܫܘܫܐ. ܚܙܐ ܐܝܟ ܐܢܫܐ ܡܠܬܐ ܢܗܘܐ ܠܗ ܠܐ ܡܬܚܫܢܘܬܐ: ܘܡܛܠܗܕܐ ܐܟܚܕܐ ܘܓܘܫܡܢܐ ܒܗܕܐ: ܕܗܘ ܕܐܦ ܕܡܠܬܐ ܕܓܘܫܡܐ ܦܓܪܐ ܠܐܠܗܘܬܗ ܡܚܘܐ: ܠܐ ܐܡܪܝܢ ܕܟܝ̈ܢܐ ܡܫܡܫܝܢ: ܘܗܠܝܢ ܡܚܕ ܡܢ ܕܡ̈ܠܐ ܘܡܥܒܕܢܘܬܐ ܕܝܠܗ ܡܫܝܚܐ. ܐܠܐ ܠܗ ܠܡܠܬܐ ܡܫܡܫܝܢ ܚܕ ܕܗܘܐ ܒܣܪܐ: ܘܗܠܝܢ ܕܒܣܪܐ ܗܢܘܢ.

ܘܠܐ ܐܝܟ ܢܣܛܘܪ ܕܡܫܡܫܐ ܡܠܬܐ: ܘܐܠܗܘܬܐ ܘܚܝܠܐ ܡܢܗ ܘܠܗ ܡܠܐ. ܡܠܬܐ ܓܝܪ ܕܡܬܩܪܝܐ: ܠܘܬ ܡܕܡ ܡܫܡܫܐ ܐܘ ܡܠܐܟܐ. ܚܕ ܕܝܢ ܟܝܢܐ ܡܫܡܫܢܐ ܕܚܝܘܬܐ: ܕܡܠܬܐ ܕܡܚܕ ܡܢܗܘܢ, ܡܘܬܐ ܘܬܐܣܪܐ. ܒܪܡ ܠܗ ܕܡܫܥܒܕܐ. ܐܠܐ ܕܐܟܚܕܐ ܡܬܝܕܥܐ. ܐܡܪܐ ܕܒܗ ܟܝܢܐ ܕܒܪܢܫܐ ܐܝܟ ܕܝܪܘܗ. ܗܘ ܕܡܫܬܟܚ ܡܢ ܕܡܠܬܐ ܗܘ ܕܦܓܪܐ. ܐܠܐ ܗܘ ܕܒܓܘܫܡܗ ܒܫܡܫܘܬܐ ܕܦܓܪܐ ܡܫܡܫܐ ܐܠܗܐ. ܐܠܐ ܠܗ ܒܟܝܢܐ ܡܢ ܡܕܡ ܦܫܝܛܐ ܡܟܠ: ܒܐܡܪܢܐ ܕܝܢ ܡܬܓܫܡܢܘܬܐ ܗܢܘܢ. ܐܠܐ ܒܚܕ ܘܗܘ ܟܕ ܗܘ ܟܝܢܐ ܡܪܟܒܐ ܡܫܝܚܐ. ܘܗܘ ܕܦܫܝܛܐ ܕܦܓܪܐ: ܘܗܘ ܕܒܡܬܓܫܡܢܘܬܐ ܕܢܦܫܐ. ܚܙܐ ܘܒܚܕ ܓܘܫܡܐ ܡܘܕܥ ܦܪܝܫܘܬܐ ܕܢܦܫܐ. ܘܡܬܝܠܦ. ܘܕܡܠܬܐ ܒܡܠܬܐ ܡܣܬܒܪܐ. ܗܟܢܐ ܘܟܠܐ ܚܕ ܟܝܢܐ ܡܪܟܒܐ ܕܡܫܝܚܐ: ܠܡܠܬܐ ܚܕܐ. ܘܡܬܐܡܪ ܡܢ ܐܠܐ ܡܢ ܐܒܐ ܒܬܘܠܬܐ. ܠܗ ܟܕ ܟܝܢܐ ܡܬܓܫܡ ܗܘ ܕܡܬܝܠܕ: ܒܐܡܪܢܐ ܕܝܢ ܗܘ ܐܩܢܘܡܬܐ ܡܣܒܪ ܐܚܝ ܕܚܒܐ ܠܘܬܟ. ܕܡܠܬܐ ܡܢ ܐܡܪ ܡܒܪ ܗܘ ܘܐܠܗܐ ܕܡܠܬܐ: ܦܓܪܐ ܕܝܢ ܡܫܡܠܝܐ ܗܘ ܘܐܠܗܐ ܕܦܓܪܐ܀ ܐܠܐ ܚܕ ܟܝܢܐ ܗܘ ܕܡܬܐܡܪ ܘܒܡܬܝܕܥܘܬܐ ܠܒܪ ܡܝܘܬܐ. ܟܫܦ. ܙܗܘ. ܠܗ ܟܕ ܡܬܐܡܪ ܐܠܐ ܒܪܘܚܐ. ܘܟܠܗ. ܐܠܐ ܡܛܠ: ܟܝ̈ܢܐ ܡܬܝܕܥܝܢ ܗܘܐ. (183) ܘܒܚܪܬܐ ܡܫܡܫ. ܟܕ ܠܗ ܠܐܢܫܐ ܕܡܘܬܐ ܡܝܬ: ܐܠܐ ܐܝܟܢܐ ܘܩܛܠܬܐ ܗܘܐ: ܕܗܘ ܓܪܐ ܠܡܘܬܐ. ܡܬܘܒܠܐ ܠܗܘܢ ܓܝܪ ܐܝܟ ܟܕ ܕܐܡܝܢ ܢܦܫܗ ܘܠܘܬ ܐܒܘܗ. ܘܡܛܠ ܗܕܐ ܕܫܒܩܐ ܒܚܕ ܡܫܝܚܐ.

ܚܙܐ ܐܝܟ ܐܡܝܪ ܠܐ ܦܫܝܛܝܢ ܟܝ̈ܢܐ ܡܕܡ: ܐܘ ܟܕ ܡܢܗܘܢ, ܘܠܗܘܢ, ܡܬܐܡܪܝܢ: ܡܫܡܫܝܢ ܕܡܠܬܐ ܕܝܠܗܘܢ, ܘܡܥܒܕܢܘܬܐ: ܐܠܐ ܐܟܚܕܐ ܡܫܝܚܐ ܠܐܠܗܘܬܐ ܘܐܢܫܘܬܐ ܕܡܠܬܐ ܕܐܬܒܣܪ: ܗܢܘܢ, ܠܘ ܡܢܝܐ ܐܢܫܝܐ ܒܠܚܘܕ ܐܬܒܣܪ ܒܠܘ ܡܬܒܣܪܢܘܬܐ. ܘܠܐ ܗܘ ܕܡܠܬܐ ܐܡܪ. ܠܐܠܗܘܬܗ ܓܝܪ ܗܘܬ. ܩܪܐ ܗܘܐ ܓܝܪ ܡܚܘܐ ܠܠܒܪ ܗܘ ܕܪܫܡ ܟܠܗܘܢ. ܘܟܕ ܡܫܝܚܐ ܡܠܬܐ ܚܝܐ ܗܘܐ: ܘܟܠܐ ܙܘܥܐ ܡܫܬܥܒܕ ܗܘܐ. ܕܡܠܬܐ ܐܡܪܝܢ ܕܐܓܘܢܐ ܕܗܘܐ ܚܝܐ. ܐܠܐ ܘܗܠܝܢ ܠܡ̈ܠܐ ܘܕܬܫܡܫܬܐ ܕܡܢ

was putrifying, the dead man became alive and made haste to run. They speak of sweat and perplexity in relation to the Passion? But these things also (happened) divinely, and surpass our reasonings, so that by means of human passions he might lead men [to][21] impassibility. But what will they say about (his) death? Will he await this utterly human thing, which takes possession of the body? We are persuaded: thus God is he who preserved even the properties of divinity, and suffered humanly. For because of this he also became a complete man that he might bear our weakness, and giving (his) back on our behalf to scourging, he conferred honour upon the wound which the ancient [serpent][22] set against our soul.

I have these things, which I learned from the Father. But it is right that we should demonstrate (this) in the very words (of the Father), and should make the confirmation of the definition more firm. For he says as follows in the First Letter: FROM THE PATRIARCH SEVERUS: "Because we say as well that a man like us is a living creature, rational, mortal, and capable of reason and knowledge: and because there is one nature and hypostasis from two, the whole living creature is said to be (*Lebon p. 184*) mortal, and the whole (living creature) is called rational, and we do not say that we do not know in what it is rational, or in what it is mortal—but our knowing this does not divide the composition from which the one living creature is composed. (It is) the same as well in the case of the study of Emmanuel".[23] AND AGAIN: "Therefore if someone should wrongfully divide Emmanuel with a duality of nature after the union, there also occurs a division at the same time, along with the difference of the natures, and the properties are divided in every respect aptly for the natures".[24] AND AGAIN: "But we shun dividing the one Christ into a duality of natures after the union. For when he is divided, the properties of each one of the natures are divided at the same time".[25] AND AGAIN: "And the properties of the humanity will become (the) properties of the divinity of the Word, and again the properties of the Word will be acknowledged (as) the properties of the flesh".[26] AND AGAIN: "Therefore the properties of the Word became (those) of manhood, and again those of manhood, properties of the Word".[27] AND AGAIN: "But we anathematise speaking of 'Two natures after the union', (where) (those natures) will consequently attract their own activities and properties".[28] AND AGAIN: "The natures are not implied independently and in individual existence, for to say this belongs to (the position of) those who mutilate (Christ) with a duality after the inexpressible union, and not to us, who profess him to be one from two".[29] AND

ܒܒ̈ܢܝ. ܕܟܕ ܣܓ̈ܝܐ ܐܢ̈ܫܐ. ܢܟܪ ܠܠܒܗ ܐܢܫܐ ܠܐ ܚܫܘܫܐܝܬ. ܡܛܠ ܕܝܢ ܗܕܐ ܘܟܠ ܡܘܬܐ ܢܬܡܪܘܢ: ܟܘܠܗ ܡܢ ܟܠ ܦܪ̈ܘܫ ܐܢܫܐ. ܢܩܘܐ ܟܕ ܐܚܝܕ ܠܦܓܪܐ. ܡܬܚܫܚܝܢ ܣܝܡ. ܠܟܠܐ ܗܟܝܠ ܐܝܬܗܘܢ. ܗܘ ܕܐܦ ܕܫ̈ܡܝܐ ܘܕܐܪ̈ܥܬܐ ܢܛܪ: ܘܣܟ ܐܢܫܝܬܐ. ܡܛܠ ܗܘܐ ܓܝܪ ܐܦ ܒܪܢܫܐ ܡܫܡܫܢܐ ܗܘܐ ܕܡܣܒܪܢܘܬܐ ܢܛܪ. ܘܟܕ ܚܙܐ ܣܟܠܝܢ ܠܦܓܪܐ ܗܘܐ: ܢܦܪܘ ܠܚܫܘܫܐ: ܗܘ ܕܣܘܐ ܒܠܚܘܕ ܠܡܦܠܛ ܢܦܫ ܫܦܝ.

ܗܟܝܠ ܟܕ ܡܢ ܐܝܟ ܢܦܫܐ ܐܝܬ ܠܗ. ܫܦܝܪܐ ܕܝܢ ܕܟܘܠ ܒܟܠܐ ܚܙܐ: ܘܐܡܪ ܡܫܡܠܝܬܐ ܢܚܟ ܗܘܙܪܐ ܕܡܟܠܬܐ. ܐܦܢ ܓܝܪ ܠܦܓܪܐ ܡܢܫܡܬܐ ܗܘܬ. ܀ܘܡܢ ܕܦܓܪܢܐ ܫܠܘܛܐ܀ ܡܛܠ ܕܐܦ ܒܪܢܫܐ ܕܐܘܠܝ ܐܡܪܝܢ ܘܐܝܬܘܗܝ. ܚܫܘܬܐ ܡܟܝܠܬܐ ܡܫܬܐܬܐ: ܡܡܟܟܝܢܬܐ ܕܗܘܝܐ ܘܡܕܝܟܬܐ. ܘܡܛܠ ܕܡܢ ܬܪܝܢ ܚܕ ܟܝܢܐ ܘܩܢܘܡܐ ܐܝܬܘܗܝ: ܟܠܗ ܚܫܬܐ ܡܬܐܡܪܐ (184) ܡܫܬܐܬܐ: ܘܟܠܗ ܡܫܬܡܫܐ ܡܟܝܠܬܐ. ܘܠܐ ܐܡܪܝܢ ܕܠܐ ܢܟܝܢ ܟܝܢܐ ܚܕ ܡܟܠܠ: ܟܝܢܐ ܕܝܢ ܡܫܬܐ. ܐܠܐ ܟܠܗ ܗܘ ܕܢܟܝ ܗܘܐ ܠܪܘܚܐ ܡܫܟܚܐ: ܕܡܢܗ ܡܪܘܚܐ ܚܕܐ ܚܫܬܐ. ܗܟܝܠ ܘܟܠܗ ܠܐܘܪܚܐ ܕܡܫܘܬܐܘܬܐ܀ ܀ܘܠܘܬ܀ ܐܢ ܗܟܝܠ ܠܡܫܘܬܐܘܬܐ ܢܦܩܝܢ ܐܝܟ ܒܠܥܕ ܠܡܪܘܚܬܐ ܕܒ̈ܢܝܐ ܟܠܗ ܣܝܡܬܐ: ܟܕ ܡܘܣܟܐ ܕܒ̈ܢܝܐ: ܡܢ ܡܟܦܪܘܢ ܐܚܝܕܐ ܙܘܥ ܐܦ ܦܘܠܚܢܐ. ܘܡܘܟܠܬܗ ܡܬܦܠܚܝܢ ܕܐܟܠܬܐ ܠܣܥܬܗ ܠܒ̈ܢܝܐ܀ ܀ܘܠܘܬ܀ ܡܢ ܗܘ ܕܝܢ ܕܢܦܩܝܢ ܠܡܪܘܚܬܐ ܕܒ̈ܢܝܐ: ܗܘ ܕܟܠܗ ܣܝܡܬܐ ܠܟܕ ܡܫܡܫܐ ܒܪܘܫܝ. ܟܕ ܡܬܦܠܚܝܢ ܓܝܪ: ܐܚܝܕܐ ܡܬܦܠܚܝܢ ܘܐܟܠܬܐ ܕܟܠ ܚܕ ܡܢ ܒ̈ܢܝܐ܀ ܀ܘܠܘܬ܀ ܘܐܟܠܬܐ ܕܐܢܫܘܬܐ: ܕܐܟܠܬܐ ܕܫܬܝܐ ܢܗܘܐ ܕܡܟܠܬܐ. ܘܐܟܠܬܐ ܠܘܬ ܕܡܟܠܬܐ: ܕܐܟܠܬܐ ܕܒܣܪܐ ܠܡܦܠܚܝܢ܀ ܀ܘܠܘܬ܀ ܩܘܡ ܗܟܝܠ ܕܐܟܠܬܐ ܦܘܡ ܕܡܟܠܬܐ: ܗܟܝܢ ܕܐܢܫܘܬܐ. ܘܐܟܠܬܐ ܕܝܢ ܠܘܬ ܕܐܢܫܘܬܐ ܗܟܝܢ ܕܟܠܗ ܕܡܟܠܬܐ܀ ܀ܘܠܘܬ܀ ܐܠܐ ܗܘ ܕܢܐܡܪ ܠܟܠܗ ܣܝܡܬܐ ܠܘܬ ܒ̈ܢܝܢ: ܘܡܦܩܬܗ ܢܗܘܘܢ ܢܛܪܝܢ ܠܡܫܬܪܝܘܬܗܘܢ ܘܐܟܠܬܗܘܢ ܡܫܪܝܢ܀ ܀ܘܠܘܬ܀ ܠܗ ܕܡܢܗܘܢ ܘܠܗܘܢ ܘܡܫܘܬܐ ܘܕܟܝܐ ܡܫܬܡܫܝܢ ܒ̈ܢܝܐ. ܗܘܐ ܓܝܪ ܕܗܘܢ ܕܦܫܡܝܢ ܠܗ ܠܡܪܘܚܬܐ ܠܟܠ ܣܝܡܬܐ ܠܐ ܡܫܬܡܠܝܢܬܐ ܐܬܡܗ ܕܢܬܡܪܘܢ: ܘܠܗ ܕܟܠܡ ܐܢܫܝܢ ܕܚܕ ܡܢ ܬܪܝܢ ܡܫܘܚܝܢ ܠܗ܀ ܀ܘܠܘܬ܀ ܡܢܝܢ ܗܘ ܕܡܦܩܝܢ ܠܗ ܠܡܫܘܬܐܘܬܐ: ܘܠܬܪܝܢ ܒ̈ܢܝܢ ܡܬܝܚܝܢ ܠܗ ܠܟܠ ܣܝܡܬܐ ܠܐ ܡܫܬܡܠܝܢܬܐ: ܡܦܩܝܢ ܗܘ ܒ̈ܢܝܐ ܘܡܫܬܪܝܘܬܐ ܘܐܟܠܬܐ. ܘܕܬܪܝܢ ܒ̈ܢܝܢ ܕܡܫܬܪܝܢ ܫܠܡ ܘܠܐ ܒܪܝܫܝܬܐ ܣܝܡ ܗܟܝܢ ܕܠܗܘܢ܀

AGAIN: "Therefore he who divides Emmanuel, and defines him in two natures after the inexpressible union, along with the natures divides the activities and properties as well, and establishes two natures which act and without diminishment undergo what is their own".[30] AND AGAIN: "Therefore he who divides Emmanuel to a duality of natures after the inexpressible union, divides with him, as (*Lebon p. 185*) we have often said, the activities and properties as well".[31] AND AGAIN: "For because there is one who acts, his activity is also one and the active motion".[32] AND AGAIN: "But when they divide (Emmanuel) by speaking of two natures after the union, they divide at the same time also those things which each nature attracts naturally as properties".[33] AND AGAIN: "Those things which we would say the flesh suffers, are sufferings of the incarnate Word, although his divinity is not defective, in that he is impassible; for to whom we say the flesh belongs, we hold the sufferings peculiar to the flesh in all respects also belong to him".[34] AND AGAIN: "We will reckon (it is) iniquitous to divide (Christ) into a duality of natures after the union, and consequently the activities and properties, for everything is cut with a duality and is reduced to a split diversity and divided in everything, whether you speak of activities or properties".[35] But in the same way, and from the Second Letter: FROM HIM: "But the principle of the union, because of the economy, allows those things which in nature are properties of the flesh to be called properties of the Word. In the same way, it made those things which in ousia are properties of the Word to be called properties of the flesh".[36] AND AGAIN: "But even if they are in nature properties of humanity, they became, because of the economy also properties of God the Word, and he is said to have hungered and thirsted, and been tired from a journey".[37]

What words more God-fearing than these, or what teaching more in agreement with the Fathers, says that the properties of the body became in all respects (those) of the Word? But those who confess before that (the Word) lacks the properties of the flesh, in every respect renounce even the incarnation. From where do we learn that he was truly incarnate? (*Lebon p. 186*) Surely from the fact that he voluntarily displayed all that belongs to the flesh? Surely it did not belong to the Word before the incarnation that he should hunger and thirst? Surely since these things belong to our nature, they became God's by means of the supreme union of the body? Thus they are no longer made the properties of natures as it were existent in their own principle, but of the only-begotten Son of God, who was composed impassibly to (be one with) a body.

ܠܐ ܚܝܘܬܐ ܒܬܪ ܒܢ̈ܝܐ ܠܬܘܪܓܡܐ ܠܡܫܘܐܠܘ ܘܡܫܠܝܢ ܗܘܢ ܗܘ ܀ܒܘܠܘ܀
ܡܬܡܫܠܚܢܘܬܐ: ܡܫܠܝܢ ܒܗܘܢ ܐܝܟ ܡܐ ܕܪ̈ܓܝܢ (185) ܡܣܒܪ̈ܢܐ ܐܡܪܝ ܚܝܢ:
ܘܡܬܚ̈ܒܝܢܘܬܐ ܘܬܟܠܬܐ܀ ܀ܒܘܠܘ܀ ܡܛܠ ܟܝ ܕܝܢ ܗܘ ܗܘ ܕܡܢܟ: ܚܝܐ ܗܘ
ܐܦ ܡܬܚܒܝܢܘܬܗ ܘܪܘܚܐ ܗܘ ܡܬܚܒܝܢܐ܀ ܀ܒܘܠܘ܀ ܟܕ ܡܫܠܝܢ ܕܝܢ ܒܗܘܢ ܕܐܡܪܝܢ
ܬܘܒ ܟܢ̈ܫܝܢ ܒܬܪ ܚܝܘܬܐ: ܡܫܠܝܢ ܐܚܪܢܐ ܘܗܠܝܢ ܐܝܟܢ ܕܐܝܟ ܕܬܟܠܬܐ ܟܝܠܬܗ
ܥܠ ܟܝܠܐ ܝܕܥ܀ ܀ܒܘܠܘ܀ ܐܝܟܢ ܕܢܐܡܪ ܕܝܠܗ ܒܟܬܒܐ: ܗܠܝܢ ܚܝ̈ܠܐ ܕܡܠܬܐ
ܘܐܬܟܬܒ ܐܬܚܙܝ. ܟܕ ܠܗܘܢ ܗܘ ܠܐ ܡܟܬܒ. ܗܘ ܕܝܢ ܕܐܠܐ ܚܝܠܐ ܗܘ. ܕܗܘ ܟܝܢ ܘܐܡܪܝܢ
ܚܝܢ ܕܕܝܠܗ ܗܘ ܒܟܬܒܐ: ܕܝܠܗ ܕܗܘܐ ܡܢ ܡܠܦܢܘܬܐ ܢܣܒܝܢ ܚܝܢ: ܘܚܝ̈ܠܐ ܕܬܟܠܬܐ
ܕܟܬܒܐ܀ ܀ܒܘܠܘ܀ ܘܟܕ ܠܐ ܚܫܒܘܢ: ܠܗܘܢ ܕܡܫܠܝܢ ܠܬܘܪܓܡܐ ܕܒܢ̈ܝܐ ܕܒܬܪ
ܚܝܘܬܐ: ܘܡܫܬܠܡ ܒܡܬܚ̈ܒܝܢܘܬܐ ܘܬܟܠܬܐ. ܡܠܟܝܢ ܟܝܢ ܒܗܢ ܬܘܪܓܡܐ
ܡܬܦܫܩ: ܘܠܐܣܒܪܬܐ ܡܫܠܝܬܐ: ܘܒܡܬܚܫܒܢ ܡܫܠܝܬܐ ܦܪܝܫ. ܘܠܝ
ܡܬܚܒܝܢܘܬܐ ܐܬܐܡܪ ܘܠܝ ܕܬܟܠܬܐ܀ ܟܕ ܒܝܕܘܬܐ ܕܝܢ ܘܡܢ ܐܝܟܢܐ ܕܐܬܝܢ. ܀ܕܝܠܗ܀
ܡܠܬܐ ܕܝܢ ܕܚܝܘܬܐ: ܗܠܝܢ ܕܟܝܠܐ ܕܬܟܠܬܐ ܕܟܬܒܐ: ܡܛܠ ܡܒܪܢܘܬܐ ܕܬܟܠܬܐ
ܕܡܠܬܐ ܗܘܐ ܕܐܬܐܡܪܝ. ܟܕ ܒܝܕܘܬܐ ܗܠܝܢ ܕܐܬܘܣܦܐ ܕܬܟܠܬܐ ܕܡܠܬܐ:
ܕܬܟܠܬܐ ܕܟܬܒܐ ܒܟܝܢܐ ܕܐܬܡܪܝܢ܀ ܀ܒܘܠܘ܀ ܐܠܐ ܐܦ ܒܟܝܠܐ ܕܬܟܠܬܐ ܕܐܬܘܣܦܬܐ
ܐܬܚܫܒ: ܐܦ ܕܡܠܬܐ ܠܟܠܗ ܬܘܗܝ ܕܬܟܠܬܐ ܕܐܬܘܣܦܬܐ ܡܛܠ ܡܒܪܢܘܬܐ. ܘܗܘ
ܡܬܐܡܪ. ܘܒܟܢ ܘܡܢܗܘܢ ܘܠܐ ܡܢ ܐܘܪܚܐ܀

ܐܝܟ ܟܕ ܩܠܐ ܕܐܬܡܪ ܡܢ ܗܠܝܢ ܕܬܟܠ ܡܢ ܟܠܗܘܢ: ܐܘ ܐܚܪܐ ܐܚܪܐ ܡܬܦܫܩܐ:
ܕܐܬܡܪܬ ܟܕ ܒܗܢ ܐܒܗ̈ܬܐ ܩܕܡܝ: ܕܡܠܬܐ ܦܫ ܐܡܪܐ ܕܩܕܡ ܡܢ ܡܠܦܢܘܬܐ ܕܬܟܠܬܐ
ܕܦܓܪܐ. ܐܝܟܢ ܕܝܢ ܕܡܬܚܫܒ ܡܬܚܒܝܢ ܕܝܠܗ ܠܗ ܕܬܟܠܬܐ ܕܗܟܢܐ: ܒܦܪܝܢ ܡܢ
ܟܠ ܦܪܘܫ ܐܦ ܒܡܬܒܣܪܢܘܬܐ. ܡܢ ܐܝܟܐ ܡܬܩܫܝܢ ܚܝܢ ܕܐܬܐܡܪ (186) ܒܡܪܘܬܐ.
ܠܗ ܡܢ ܗܘ ܕܟܠܗܘܢ ܗܠܝܢ ܕܟܬܒܐ ܕܚܝܠܗ ܚܘܝ: ܕܟܠܐ ܕܒܥܝܢ ܘܪܘܚܐ ܐܝܟ
ܗܘܐ ܠܡܠܬܐ ܡܢ ܩܕܡ ܡܬܒܪܢܝܘܬܐ: ܠܗ ܟܕ ܐܬܡܪܝܢ ܗܠܝܢ ܕܟܝܠܐ ܕܡܠܟ:
ܬܘܗ ܕܠܬܘܪܐ ܒܝܕ ܚܝܘܬܐ ܘܡܫܠܝܬܐ ܕܦܓܪܐ: ܡܕܝܢ ܠܐ ܡܫܠܝܢ ܕܬܟܠܬܐ ܕܟܝܠܐ ܐܦ
ܒܡܠܬܐ ܕܠܗܘܢ: ܐܝܟ ܡܐ ܕܡܫܡܫܝܢ ܦܬܓܡ̈ܐ. ܐܠܐ ܕܡܣܬܒܪܐ ܒܗܘ ܕܠܬܘܪܐ: ܗܘ
ܕܟܠܐ ܦܓܪܐ ܐܬܪܟܒ ܠܐ ܡܫܬܡܠܝܐ.

ܟܕ ܠܡܬܦܫܩܘ ܗܠܝܢ ܐܒܗ̈ܬܐ ܡܠܟܝܢ ܒܡܫܠܬܐ: ܠܐ ܢܚܘܐ ܠܪܘܚܐ ܕܠܬܘܪܐ: ܟܕ
ܡܬܚܫܒܝܢ ܚܝܢ ܠܡܫܠܡܘ ܡܪܘܐ. ܚܝܐ ܕܐܬܡܪ ܡܢ ܟܠ ܕܗܘܐ ܢܣܒ ܚܝܢ: ܕܟܕ

When we write these laws of the Fathers in (our) minds, we will not provoke to anger the Spirit of God, by acting deceitfully against the truth. Will we suffer a sorrow more miserable than all, because while admitting that we err on behalf of the fear of God, we still put up such a fight in the sight of everyone?—When we will have sacrificed beforehand our captain, will we go to the barbarians, that now we may appear easily caught, being widowed[38] of order, from lack of leadership? For justly one after another,[39] the sees of the interior region declare this (man) our leader, among whom he was the first in the east (as) Patriarch to drive out the folly of Chalcedon—and at a time when our affairs had become grievously ill: for first Paul, and then Diodore, is the defiler of the eastern congregations, (and) with these also Theodore; and Nestorius too was from here, and fell sick in Byzantium, and Ibas and Theodoret and Andrew are not from somewhere else either. From us too Cyrus and John sprang up, and Persia, the evil twig, planted similar evil opinions.

Well then, it is right that we should honour him who turned away all the sickness of the whole place. But let us not turn our sword against ourselves. Therefore let us honour the Father with truth, for the Law punishes abusive sons, for "He who speaks evilly to (his) father or (*Lebon p. 187*) mother will surely die".[40] But the Wise Man of the Church accepts sober sons, for "A wise son gives joy to his father".[41]

The Apology of Sergius the Grammarian is finished.

Folio 1ª reads:

This is the book of Michael bar Qt", which he bequeathed to the monastery of the Syrians which is in the desert of Skete of Egypt. May God make his soul to rest in the dwelling places of the righteous and just and write his name in the Book of Life, and make ⟨his deeds⟩[42] a good remembrance, through the prayer of the one who gave birth to God and of all the saints. Amen.

Notes

1. cf. Gen. ix.22–23.
2. Ps. xxx.19.
3. cf. Prov. i.8 and iv.1.
4. H. syr. 22 = ܡܒܘܥܐ (spring, fount).
5. cf. Is. xliii.10.
6. ܡܕ̈ܥܐ could possibly mean "intellects".
7. Loofs, *Nestoriana, op. cit.*, p. 198 (*Fragment of a Letter to Theodoret*).
8. PG 76.404.C–D (= Pusey edn. Vol. 6, p. 410.27–29). *Apol. contra Theod.*

ܐܡܪܝܢ ܕܚܠܦ ܕܚܫܗ ܐܠܗܐ ܛܥܝܢ܆ ܘܟܠܗ ܗܘܐ ܡܪܐ ܠܟܝܢ ܟܠܝܢ ܚܘܝܢ܆ ܟܕ ܠܢܘܢ ܚܠܐ ܕܡܢ ܡܕܡܝܢ ܕܟܝܢܢ܆ ܠܗܐ ܒܬܟܪܐ ܐܬܟܝܢ܆ ܐܡܝܐ ܕܦܩܝܩܢ ܠܡܬܬܐܡܪܘ ܡܫܡܠܐ ܢܛܪܐ܆ ܟܕ ܡܢ ܛܘܒܐ ܡܛܠ ܠܐ ܙܡܢܘܬܐ ܡܙܕܟܝܢ. ܠܗܘܐ ܚܢܢ ܒܐܝܬܝܗ ܟܠܗ ܒܥܘܩܣܬܐ ܕܚܠܠܐ ܢܡܐ ܕܡܢ ܡܫܘܡ. ܡܢ ܗܟܝܢ ܕܡܕܡܐ ܦܛܪܝܪܟܐ ܠܟܕܝܫܐ ܠܐܣܘܛܐܐ ܕܟܠܡܕܘܐ ܛܪܘ. ܘܟܕ ܡܫܬܐܠ ܟܬܒܘܗܝ ܗܘܘ ܗܟܝܢ ܕܡܢ܆ ܟܬܘܒܐ ܚܢܢ ܩܕܝܫܐ ܡܕܡܐ ܦܢ ܦܘܠܐ܆ ܠܡܐܪܘܡ ܕܝܢ ܕܡܪܘܙܘܣ ܐܠܗܘܗܝ ܡܫܒܚܬܐ܆ ܟܡ ܗܟܝܢ܆ ܘܐܬܐܘܪܘܣ. ܘܣܛܘܪܝܣ. ܡܢ ܗܘܟܐ܆ ܟܪܘܣܛܘܣ ܐܬܪܗ. ܗܡܟܐ ܕܝܢ ܘܐܬܐܘܪܘܛܐ ܘܐܝܕܪܐ܆ ܠܗ ܡܢ ܕܗܘ ܐܝܬܝܗ ܐܠܗܘܬܗ. ܡܛܠ ܕܝܢ܆ ܘܡܘܪܐ ܘܡܘܚܝܢ ܚܘܫܘ܆ ܘܡܫܡܠܝܐ ܟܝܢܝܐ ܦܪܨ܆ ܚܘܩܝܢ ܟܬܒܐ ܕܕܝܠܗ ܢܟܝܠ. ܡܕܝܢ ܠܗܘ ܕܟܠܗ ܟܘܪܗܢܐ ܕܟܠܗ ܐܬܪܐ ܗܟܘ܆ ܟܐܢܐ ܕܢܦܪ ܚܝ. ܐܠܐ ܠܐ ܫܦܠܐ ܕܡܢ ܢܗܦܘܟ ܠܗܘܦܟܠ ܢܩܡ. ܢܦܪ ܗܟܢܠ ܠܐܒܐ ܟܡ ܡܪܘܐ܆ ܢܡܘܫܐ ܚܢܢ ܡܟܢܫ ܠܟܬܒܐ ܡܪܝܚܐ. ܗܘ ܠܟܡ ܚܢܢ ܕܐܡܪ ܟܡܐܬܐ ܠܐܒܐ ܐܘ (187) ܠܐܡܐ܆ ܡܘܬܐ ܢܦܘܬܐ. ܠܟܬܒܐ ܕܝܢ ܢܩܦܐ܆ ܚܟܝܡܐ ܕܟܝܬܐ ܡܫܡܠܐ. ܟܪܐ ܠܟܡ ܚܢܢ ܚܟܝܡܐ ܡܚܝܐ ܠܐܒܘܗܝ.

܀ܫܠܡ ܡܫܡ ܟܪܘܚܐ܆ ܕܦܪܝܫ ܒܪܛܠܡܘܣ܀

ܐܠܗܘܗܝ ܡܠܟܐ ܗܘܐ ܕܡܫܬܐܠ ܒܪ ܩܛܠܐ܆ ܕܡܟܝܢ ܠܒܪܐ ܕܫܘܪܝܐ ܕܟܡܕܒܪܐ ܘܐܦܫܛܐ ܕܡܪܘܡ܀ ܕܐܠܗܐ ܢܚܝܢ ܢܦܫܗ ܒܐܘܪܐ ܕܩܐܪܐ ܘܙܕܝܩܐ. ܘܢܛܪܘܟ ܡܫܪܗ ܟܫܦܪܐ ܕܚܝܐ. ܘܟܠ...ܗܘܢ ܢܟܝܢ ܕܘܟܪܢܐ ܛܒܐ. ܟܕ ܨܠܘܬܗ ܕܟܢܝܐ ܐܠܗܐ ܘܕܟܠܗܘܢ ܩܕ̈ܝܫܐ. ܐܡܝܢ.

9. PG 76.429A (= Pusey edn. Vol. 6, p. 454.11–12). *Apol. contra Theod.*

10. Lebon notes: Read "TWELFTH".

11. cf. PG 76.449B. Sergius omits some of the Greek which is in Migne (= Pusey edn. Vol. 6, p. 490.18–23). *Apol. contra Theod.*

12. PL 54.765A and cf. 763A. *Ep. XXVIII, ad Flavianum* ("*The Tome*").

13. PL 54.767A–B.

14. cf. T. H. Bindley and F. W. Green: *The Oecumenical Documents of the Faith* (London, 1950), p. 193.118–121; ACO II, 1, 2a, p. 129.30–33.

15. *sc.* Severus.

16. cf. I Jn. i.1.

17. The Syriac is ܡܫܡܫܢܐ from ܫܡܫ, not from ܫܠܡ.

18. PL 54.767B.

19. cf. Jn. x.18.

20. Reading ܕܠܝܠܘܬܐ for ܕܠܘܠܘܬܐ.

21. Reading ܟܠܐ for ܠܐ.

22. Reading ܚܘܫܐ for ܚܘܫܝ.

23. cf. above, p. 76.

24. cf. above, pp. 77–78.

25. cf. above, p. 79.

26. cf. above, p. 79.

27. cf. above, p. 80.

28. cf. above, p. 80.

29. cf. above, pp. 80–81.

30. cf. above, pp. 85–86.

31. cf. above, p. 87.

32. cf. above, p. 87.

33. cf. above, p. 88.

34. cf. above, pp. 89–90.

35. cf. above, pp. 93–94.

36. cf. above, p. 121.

37. cf. above, p. 139.

38. i.e. being left without a Bishop.

39. Reading ܡܛܠ ܡܛܠ for ܡܛܠ.

40. Ex. xxi.16.

41. Prov. x.1.

42. Reading ܠܡܥܡܪܘܬܗܝ for ܗܝ ⟨...⟩ܠܡ.

BIBLIOGRAPHY OF WORKS CITED

PRIMARY SOURCES

Orationes ad Nephalium, ed. and tr. by Joseph Lebon, *CSCO* 119, 120 (Syr 64, 65), Louvain 1949.

Le Philalèthe, ed. et trad. par Robert Hespel, *CSCO* 133, 134 (Syr 68, 69), Louvain 1952.

Youssef, Youhanna Nessim, 'Arabic Manuscripts of the *Philalethes* of Severus of Antioch', *Proche-Orient Chretien*, 2001, 51, issue 3, p 261-266.

Eiusdem ac Sergii Grammatici: Epistulae Mutuae, ed. and tr. by Joseph Lebon, *CSCO* 119, 120 (Syr 64, 65), Louvain 1949.

A Collection of Letters from Numerous Syriac Manuscripts, ed. and tr. by Ernest W. Brooks, *PO* 12, 14 (Paris 1919-20), 163-342; 1-310.

The Sixth Book of the Select Letters of Severus, Patriarch of Antioch, in the Syriac Version of Athanasius of Nisibis, ed. and tr. by Ernest W. Brooks, 4 vols, London 1902-4).

Youssef, Youhanna Nessim, 'Letter of Severus of Antioch to Anastasia the Deaconess', *Bulletin de la Société d'Archéologie* 40, 2001, 126-136.

Severos' letter to John the soldier, ed. with introd. and transl. by Sebastian Brock, *GöF Syriaca* 17 (Wiesbaden 1978) 53-75.

Les HOMILIAE CATHEDRALES de Sévère d'Antioche (in the Syriac translation of Jacob of Edessa) ed. and tr. in *PO* (Turnhout, Belgium, and Paris, 1922-77).

Homilies 1-17, ed. and tr. by M.Brière and Francois Graffin, PO 38.2 (Turnhout, Belgium, 1976-7) 254-455.

Homilies 18-25, ed. and tr. by M.Brière and Francois Graffin, *PO* 37.1 (Turnhout, Belgium, 1975) 6-167.

Homilies 26-31, ed. and tr. by M.Brière, Francois Gaffin and Christopher J.A.Lash, *PO* 36.4 (Turnhout, Belgium, 1971-4) 540-665.

Homilies 32-9, ed. and tr. by M.Brière, Francois Graffin and Christopher J.A.Lash, *PO* 36.3 (Turnhout, Belgium, 1972) 396-528.

Homilies 40-5, ed. and tr. by M.Brière and Francois Graffin, *PO* 36.1 (Turnhout, Belgium, 1971), 8-137.

Homilies 46-51, ed. and tr. by M.Brière and Francois Graffin, *PO* 35 (Turnhout, Belgium, 1969), 288-379.

Homilies 52-7, ed. and tr. by R.Duval, *PO* 4 (Paris, n.d.), 1-94.

Homilies 58-69, ed. and tr. by M.Brière, *PO* 8 (Paris, n.d.), 209-396.

Homilies 70-76, ed. and tr. by M.Brière, *PO* 12 (Paris, n.d.), 1-163.

Homily 77, Greek and Syriac texts ed. and tr. by M.-A.Kugener and E.Triffaux, *PO* 16 (Paris, 1922), 761-863.

Homilies 78-83, ed. and tr. by M.Brière, *PO* 20 (Paris, 1928), 273-434.

Homilies 84-90, ed. and tr. by M.Brière, *PO* 23 (Paris, 1932), 1-176.

Homilies 91-98, ed. and tr. by M.Brière, *PO* 25 (Paris, 1935), 1-174.

Homilies 99-103, ed. and tr. by I.Guidi, *PO* 22 (Paris, 1929), 207-312.

Homilies 104-112, ed. and tr. by M.Brière, *PO* 25 (Paris, 1943), 625-815.

Homilies 113-9, ed. and tr. by M.Brière, *PO* 26 (Paris, 1947), 265-450.

Homilies 120-5, ed. and tr. by M.Brière, *PO* 29 (Paris, 1960), 74-262.

La Première Homélie cathedrale de Sévère d'Antioche, tr. by E.Porcher, Revue de l'orient chrétien 19 (1914), 69-78, 135-42.

Homily 90 (First Catechetical Homily on the Holy Trinity), tr. by Iain R. Torrance, *Orthodoxia: The Journal of the Ecumenical Patriarchate* [ISSN 1106-4889], Thessaloniki, Vol 2.1, 1997, pp 60-86.

Homilies 18 and 41 (on the 40 Martyrs), tr. by Iain R. Torrance, in *Malphono w-Rabo d-Malphone* (Studies in Honor of Sebastian P. Brock), ed. by George A. Kiraz, Piscataway, NJ: Gorgias Press, 2008, pp 717-734.

The Hymns of Severus and Others in the Syriac Version of Paul of Edessa, as revised by James of Edessa, ed. and tr. by Ernest W. Brooks, PO 6, 7 (Paris, 1911), 1-179, 593-802.

Liber contra impium Grammaticum, ed. and tr. by Joseph Lebon, *CSCO*, 93, 94, 101, 102, 111, 112 (Syr 45, 46; 50, 51; 58, 59), Paris and Louvain 1929-38.

La Polémique antijulianiste, ed. and tr. by Robert Hespel, *CSCO* 244, 245 (Syr 104, 105), Louvain 1964.

SECONDARY SOURCES

Ancient sources

Athanasius of Antioch, *The Conflict of Severus*, ed. and tr. from Ethiopic by E.J.Goodspeed, *PO* 4 (Turnhout, 1971), 575-717.

Youssef, Youhanna Nessim and Allen, Pauline, tr. and preface, *The Arabic life of Severus of Antioch attributed to Athanasius of Antioch*. Turnhout, Belgium: Brepols, 2004. *Patrologia Orientalis*, t. 49, fasc. 4, no. 220. (the Arabic version of the previous source)

John of Beth Aphthonia, *Vie d'Sévère*, ed. and tr. by M.-A.Kugener, *PO* 2 (Paris, 1907), 207-264.
George, Bishop of the Arabs, *A homily on Blessed Mar Severus, Patriarch of Antioch*, ed. and tr. by Kathleen E. McVey, Louvain, Peeters, 1993.
Zacharias the Scholastic, *Vie d' Sévère*, ed. and tr. by M.-A.Kugener, *PO* 2 (Turnhout, 1971), 1-115.
Zacharias the Scholastic, *The Syriac Chronicle known as that of Zachariah of Mitylene*, tr. by Frederick J. Hamilton and Ernest W. Brooks, London 1899.

Modern material

Anton Baumstark, 'Das Kirchenjahr in Antiocheia zwischen 512 und 518', *RQ* 11 (1897) 31-66.
M.Brière, 'Introduction générale aux homélies de Sévère d'Antioche', *PO* 29 (1960) 7-72.
Sebastian Brock, 'Some New Letters of the Patriarch Severos', *StPatr* 12 (TuU 115, 1975) 17-24.
Robert P.Casey, 'Julian of Halicarnassus', *HThR* 19 (1926) 206-13.
Roberta C. Chesnut, *Three Monophysite Christologies: Severus of Antioch, Philoxenus of Mabbug and Jacob of Edessa*, Oxford 1976.
W.E.Crum, 'Sévère d'Antioche en Egypte', *ROC* 3 (1922-3) 92-104.
René Draguet, *Julien d'Halicarnasse et sa controversie avec Sévère d'Antioche sur l'incorruptibilité du corps du Christ*, Louvain 1924.
William H.C.Frend, *The Rise of the Monophysite Movement*, Cambridge 1972.
Gérard Garitte, 'Textes hagiographiques orientaux relatifs à saint Léonce de Tripoli. II L'homélie copte de Sévère d'Antioche', *Muséon* 79 (1966) 335-386.
Francois Graffin, 'La catéchèse de Sévère d'Antioche', *OrSyr* 5 (1960) 47-54.
Francois Graffin, 'La vie à Antioche d'après les homélies de Sévère. Invectives contre les courses de chevaux, le théatre et les jeux olympiques', *GöF Syriaca* 17 (1978) 115-30.
Patrick T.R.Gray, *The Defence of Chalcedon in the East*, Leiden 1979.
Aloys Grillmeier with Theresia Hainthaler, *Jesus der Christus im Glauben der Kirche*, Band 2/2, Freiburg 1989 = *Christ in Christian Tradition*, Vol 2/2, London and Louisville 1995.
A de Halleux, 'Le "synode néochalcédonien" d'Alexandrette et l' "apologie pour Chalcédoine" de Jean le Grammairien', *RHE* 72 (1977) 593-600.
Robert Hespel, *Le Florilège Cyrillien réfuté par Sévère d'Antioche: Étude et édition critique*, *BMus* 37 (1955) 1-255.
H.-J.Höhn, 'The Preacher', Chapter 2 in Aloys Grillmeier, *Christ in Christian Tradition* 2/2 (1995) 129-147.

E. Honigmann, *Évêques et évêchés monophysites d' Asie antérieure au VI siècle* (CSCO 127, Subsidia 2), Louvain 1951.

Christopher J.A.Lash, 'The Scriptural Citations in the Homiliae Cathedrales of Severus of Antioch and the Textual Criticism of the Greek Old Testament', *StPatr* 12 (TU Band 115, Berlin 1975) 321-7.

Joseph Lebon, *Le Monophysisme sévérien*, Louvain 1909.

Joseph Lebon, 'Le pseudo-Denys l'Aréopagite et Sévère d'Antioche', *RHE* 26 (1930) 880-915.

Joseph Lebon, 'La Christologie du monophysisme syrien', in *Das Konzil von Chalkedon: Geschichte und Gegenwart*, ed A.Grillmeier and H.Bacht, Würtzburg 1951, Bd I 425-580.

J.Mateos, 'Théologie du baptême dans le formulaire du Sévère d' Antioche', *OrChrA* 197 (1974) 135-61.

C.Moeller, 'Nephalius d'Alexandrie: un représentant de la Christologie néochalcédonienne au début du sixième siècle en orient', *RHE* 40 (1944) 73-140.

V.C.Samuel, 'The Christology of Severus of Antioch', *Abba Salama* 4 (1973) 126-90.

V.C.Samuel, 'One Nature of God the Word', *GOTR* 10/2 (1964) 37-51.

V.C.Samuel, 'Further Studies in the Christology of Severus of Antioch', *Ekklesiastikos Pharos* 58/3-4 (1976) 270-301.

J.-M.Sauget, 'Une découverte inespérée: L'homélie 2 de Sévère d'Antioche sur l'Annonciation de la Theotokos', in R.H.Fischer (ed) *A Tribute to Arthur Vööbus. Studies in Early Christian Literature*, Chicago 1977, 55-62.

Iain R. Torrance, *Christology after Chalcedon: Severus of Antioch and Sergius the Grammarian*, Norwich 1988, Oregan 1998.

Iain R. Torrance, 'Paradigm Change in Sixth-Century Christology: The Contribution of Gregory the Theologian to the Christology of Severos of Antioch', *GOTR* 36/3-4 (1991) 277-85.

Wilhelm de Vries, 'Sakramententheologie bei den syrischen Monophysiten', *OrChrA* 125, Rome 1940.

Wilhelm de Vries, 'Die Eschatologie des Severus von Antiochien', *OrChrP* 23 (1957) 354-80.

Arthur Vööbus, 'Découverte d'un memra de Giwargi évêque des arabes, sur Sévère d'Antioche', *Muséon* 84 (1971) 433-6.

Lionel R.Wickham, 'Severus of Antioch on the Trinity', *StPatr* 24 (1993) 360-72.

William A.Wigram, The Separation of the Monophysites, London 1923.

N.Zambolotsky, 'The Christology of Severus of Antioch', *Ekklesiastikos Pharos* 58/3-4 (1976) 357-386.

Recent material

Allen, Pauline, 'A bishop's spirituality: the case of Severus of Antioch', in P. Allen, R. Canning, L. Cross (eds) with B.J. Caiger, *Prayer and Spirituality in the Early Church*, 1998, vol. 1, Brisbane: Centre for Early Christian Studies, 169-80.

Allen, Pauline, 'Severus of Antioch as pastoral carer', *Studia Patristica* XXXV, Ascetica, gnostica, liturgica, orientalia, 2001, p 353-68.

Allen, Pauline, 'Severus of Antioch as a source for lay piety in late antiquity', in M. Maritano (ed.), *Historiam Perscrutari. Miscellanea di studi offerti al prof. Ottorino Pasquato*, Rome, 2002, LAS, 711-21.

Allen, Pauline and Hayward, C.T.R., *Severus of Antioch*. London, New York: Routledge, 2004.

Alpi, Frédéric, *La Route Royale: Sévère d'Antioche et les Églises d'Orient (512-518)*. Beirut: Presses de l'Ifpo, 2010, 2 volumes, 540 p.

Ambjorn, Lena, translated with an introduction, *Zacharias, Bishop of Mytilene: The life of Severus*. Piscataway, New Jersey, Gorgias Press, 2008.

Andrade, Nathanael J., 'The Syriac life of John of Tella and the frontier politeia', *Hugoye* 12 no 2 Summer 2009. http://syrcom.cua.edu/Hugoye/

Aubineau, Michel; Séd, Nicolas, 'Une citation retrouvée de Jean Chrysostome, Catachesis de iuramento, chez Sévère d'Antioche, Contra additiones Juliani', *Vigiliae christianae* 39 no 4 D 1985, p 340-352.

Beatrice, Pier Franco, 'Pagan Wisdom and Christian Theology According to the Tübingen Theosophy', *Journal of Early Christian Studies* 3 no 4, Winter 1995, p 403-418.

Brakmann, Heinzgerd, 'Severos unter den Alexandrinern: Zum liturgischen Diptychon in Boston', *Jahrbuch für Antike und Christentum* 26, 1983, p 54-58.

Burris, Catherine; Rompay, Lucas van, 'Some further notes on Thecla in Syriac Christianity', *Hugoye* 6 no 2, 2003. http://syrcom.cua.edu/Hugoye/

Élisée, Hieromoine, 'Une controverse sur le pêche d'origine en Orient au VIe siecle' (A 6th Century Controversy over Original Sin in the East), *Proche-Orient Chretien* 55, 2005, issue 1, p 6-23.

Erickson, John H., 'Reception of the non-Orthodox into the Orthodox Church', *Diakonia* 19, no 1-3, 1984-1985, p 68-86.

Gelston, Anthony, 'Notes on a Citation of Chrysostom by Severus', *Journal of Theological Studies* ns 50, no 1, April 1999, p 162-163.

Gray, Patrick T R., 'An anonymous Severian Monophysite of the mid-sixth century', *Patristic and Byzantine Review* 1, no 2, 1982, p 117-126.

Halleux, André de, 'Die Genealogie des Nestorianismus nach der frühmonophysitischen Theologie', *Oriens Christianus* 66, 1982, p 1-14.

Kofsky, Aryeh, 'Severus of Antioch and Christological Politics in the Early Sixth Century', *Proche-Orient Chretien* 57, 2007, Issue 1-2, p 43-57.

Lamoreaux, John C., 'The Provenance of Ecumenius' Commentary on the Apocalypse', *Vigiliae christianae* 52, no 1, 1998, p 88-108.

Lucchesi, Enzo, 'L'homélie XXIV de Sévère d'Antioche dans un papyrus copte de Vienne', *Journal of Theological Studies* ns 33, no 1 April 1982, p 182-183.

Malaty, Tadros Y., 'Christology in the Coptic Church: the nature of God the word incarnate', *Coptic Church Review* 7, no 1, Spring 1986, p 4-14.

Menze, Volker L., 'Priests, laity and the sacrament of the Eucharist in sixth century Syria', *Hugoye* 7, no 2, 2004. http://syrcom.cua.edu/Hugoye/

Menze, Volker L., *Justinian and the Making of the Syrian Orthodox Church*. Oxford: Oxford University Press, 2008, 336 p.

Parmentier, Martien F. G., 'A Syriac Commentary on Gregory of Nyssa's Contra Eunomium', *Bijdragen* 1988, 49, Issue 1, p 2-17.

Perrone, Lorenzo, 'Il Dialogo contro gli aftartodoceti di Leonzio di Bisanzio e Severo di Antiochia', *Cristianesimo nella storia* 1980, 1, issue 2, p 411-442.

Roux, René, 'L'exégèse biblique dans les Homélies cathédrales de Sévère d'Antioche', *Studia ephemeridis Augustinianum* 84, 2002.

Roux, Rodolfo, 'The concept of orthodoxy in the Cathedral homilies of Severus of Antioch', *Studia Patristica* XXXV, Ascetica, gnostica, liturgica, orientalia, 2001, p 488.

Weaver, David, 'Exegesis of Romans 5:12 among the Greek fathers and its implications for the doctrine of original sin: 5th-12th centuries', *St Vladimir's Theological Quarterly* 29, no 3, 1985, p 231-257.

Youssef, Youhanna Nessim, 'Arabic Manuscripts of the *Philalethes* of Severus of Antioch', *Proche-Orient Chretien* 2001, 51, issue 3, p 261-266.

Youssef, Youhanna Nessim, 'Notes on the cult of Severus of Antioch in Egypt', *Ephemerides Liturgicae* 115, 2001. p 101-107.

Youssef, Youhanna Nessim, 'An Arabic text attributed to Severus of Antioch on the Robber', *Bulletin de la Société d'Archéologie* 41, 2002, p 53-69.

Youssef, Youhanna Nessim, 'The Homily on St Philotheus ascribed to Severus of Antioch', *Coptica* 1, 2002, p 169-221.

Youssef, Youhanna Nessim, 'Coptic monastic sites in the seventh and eighth centuries according to a homily ascribed to Severus of Antioch', *Coptic Church Review* 23, no 4, Winter 2002, p 103-106.

Youssef, Youhanna Nessim, 'Recommendations to the priests: Severus of Antioch or Severus of el-Ashmunein', *Journal of Coptic Studies* 4, 2002, p 187-196.

Youssef, Youhanna Nessim, 'The quotations of Severus of Antioch in the book of the Confessions of the Fathers', *Ancient Near Eastern Studies* 40, 2003, p 173-224.

Youssef, Youhanna Nessim, 'Some patristic quotations of Severus of Antioch in Coptic and Arabic texts', *Ancient Near Eastern Studies* 40, 2003, p 235-244.

Youssef, Youhanna Nessim, 'Severus of Antioch as seen by modern Coptic historians', *Coptic Church Review* 24, no 4, Winter 2003, p 98-107.

Youssef, Youhanna Nessim, 'Coptic fragment of a letter of Severus of Antioch', *Oriens Christianus* 87, 2003, p 116-122.

Youssef, Youhanna Nessim, 'An Arabic text attributed to Severus of Antioch on the Robber', *Bulletin de la Société d'Archéologie* 42, 2003, p 119-125.

Youssef, Youhanna Nessim, 'The homily on the Archangel Michael attributed to Severus of Antioch – revisited', *Bulletin de la Société d'Archéologie* 42, 2003 p 103-117.

Youssef, Youhanna Nessim, 'Severus of Antioch in the History of the Patriarchs of the Coptic Church', *Parole de l'Orient* 28, 2003, p 435-458.

Youssef, Youhanna Nessim, 'A new fragment of a life of Severus of Antioch?' *Oriens Christianus* 88, 2004, p 111-116.

Youssef, Youhanna Nessim, 'The Coptic catena on the four gospels according to Severus of Antioch: I. The Gospel of Matthew', *Bulletin de la Société d'Archéologie Copte* 43, 2004, p 95-120.

Youssef, Youhanna Nessim, 'A Coptic version of the Homily 28 of Severus of Antioch', *Bulletin de la Société d'Archéologie Copte* 43, 2004, p 121-126.

Youssef, Youhanna Nessim, 'The Coptic Marian homilies of Severus of Antioch', *Bulletin de la Société d'Archéologie Copte* 43, 2004, p 127-140.

Youssef, Youhanna Nessim, 'Fragments of the Coptic version of the Sixtieth homily of Severus of Antioch', *Bulletin de la Société d'Archéologie Copte* 43, 2004, p 141-144.

Youssef, Youhanna Nessim, 'Notes on the traditions concerning the Trisagion', *Parole de l'Orient* 29, 2004, p 147-159.

Youssef, Youhanna Nessim, 'Severus of Antioch in the Coptic Liturgical books', *Journal of Coptic Studies* 6, 2004, p 141-150.

Youssef, Youhanna Nessim, edited and translated, 'A homily on Severus of Antioch by a bishop of Assiut (XV century)', Turnhout, Belgium: Brepols, 2006. *Patrologia Orientalis*; t. 50, fasc. 1, no 222.

Youssef, Youhanna Nessim, 'Severus of Antioch in Scetis', *Ancient Near Eastern Studies* 43, 2006, p 142-163.

Youssef, Youhanna Nessim, 'The pseudo Severii', *Bulletin de la Société d'Archéologie Copte* 45, 2006, p 147-151.

Youssef, Youhanna Nessim, 'The role of Severus of Antioch in the dialogue between Greek, Coptic and Syriac cultures', *Parole de l'Orient* 31 (2006) p 163-184.

www.ingramcontent.com/pod-product-compliance
Lightning Source LLC
Chambersburg PA
CBHW061444300426
44114CB00014B/1832

* 9 7 8 1 5 9 3 3 3 9 7 1 5 *